Immediation I

Immediations

Series Editor: SenseLab

> "Philosophy begins in wonder. And, at the end, when philosophic thought has done its best, the wonder remains"
> – A.N. Whitehead

The aim of the Immediations book series is to prolong the wonder sustaining philosophic thought into transdisciplinary encounters. Its premise is that concepts are for the enacting: they must be experienced. Thought is lived, else it expires. It is most intensely lived at the crossroads of practices, and in the in-between of individuals and their singular endeavors: enlivened in the weave of a relational fabric. Co-composition.

> "The smile spreads over the face, as the face fits itself onto the smile"
> – A. N. Whitehead

Which practices enter into co-composition will be left an open question, to be answered by the Series authors. Art practice, aesthetic theory, political theory, movement practice, media theory, maker culture, science studies, architecture, philosophy ... the range is free. We invite you to roam it.

Immediation I

Edited by Erin Manning, Anna Munster, Bodil Marie Stavning Thomsen

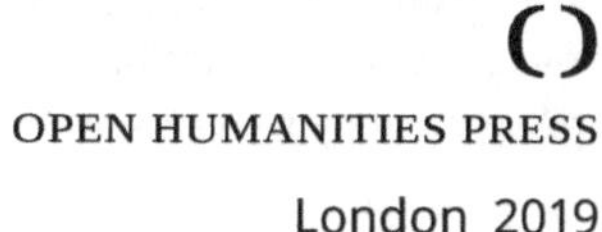

OPEN HUMANITIES PRESS
London 2019

First edition published by Open Humanities Press 2019

Cover Design by Leslie Plumb

Typeset in Open Sans, an open font.

Print ISBN 978-1-78542-084-9
Vol I Print ISBN 978-1-78542-061-0
Vol I PDF ISBN 978-1-78542-062-7
Vol II Print ISBN 978-1-78542-024-5
Vol II PDF ISBN 978-1-78542-025-2

Freely available online at:
http://openhumanitiespress.org/books/titles/immediation

OPEN HUMANITIES PRESS

Open Humanities Press is an international, scholar-led open access publishing collective whose mission is to make leading works of contemporary critical thought freely available worldwide. More at http://openhumanitiespress.org

Contents

List of Diagrams and Figures

First Movement

The World Immediating

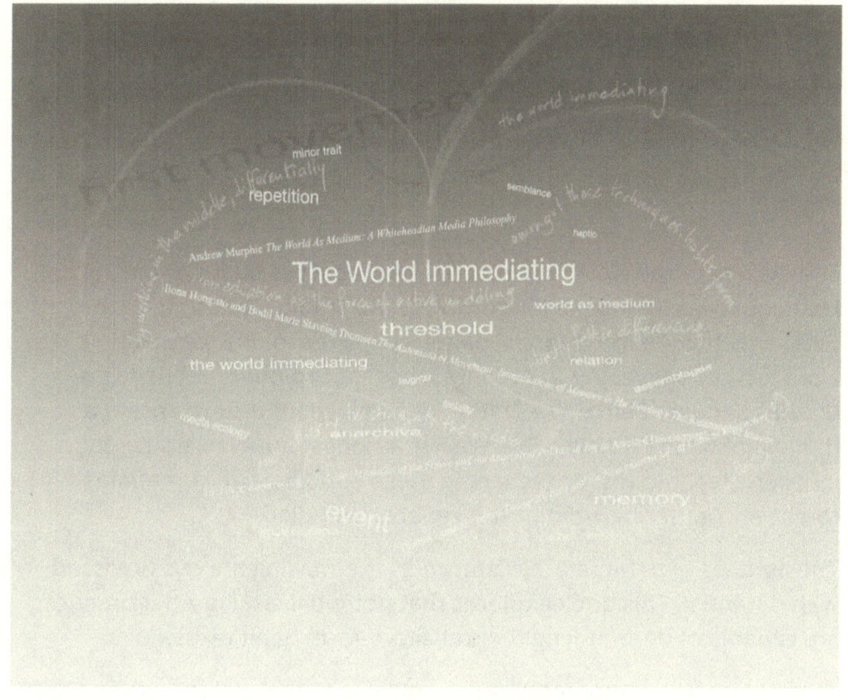

Erin Manning, Anna Munster, Bodil Marie Stavning Thomsen

Twisting Into the Middle 1

> Our realities pass into each other by twisting into the middle
> *Mattie Sempert*

> Every image, everywhere, is more than what we see.
> *Nathaniel Stern*

The making of the world is a practice. A practice is built on techniques—a technique for getting to the studio, or getting to the desk, a technique for ending a paragraph, a technique for quieting a process, or enlivening it. Amongst those techniques, habits form. Charles Sanders Peirce's definition of an object or a substance is a "bundle of habits" (2009, 279). We live amongst bundles, endlessly inventing techniques for reshaping these bundles, and sometimes, rarely, encountering what hasn't yet been bundled.

The bundles of habituated existence-in-the-making are criss-crossed with potential. This book explores that potential, asking what practices are capable of de-bundling the transitory form habit takes.

That habits feel de-potentialized is only due to their taking a form that feels pre-visited. The feeling of pre-visiting has a time-signature. It replays according to a timing felt as known. But what of other times scurrilously weaving through what we have come to know as habit? Immediation provides a lexicon for beginning to conceive of this scurrilousness. Even more, it proposes a felt account of the wiggly lines themselves. For immediation cuts right through, into the middle, and from there, it explores what exceeds the mediation of a form pre-visited.

Immediation is a relational technique. It exceeds mediation, troubling the very idea that an event requires the external force of mediation.

In doing so, it cuts through even those bundles we most connect to mediatory processes. Immediation activates the uneasy timings that exceed all takings-form.

With immediation as a starting point, the bundle reveals itself as a momentary middling in an existence too untimely to measure from an external reference point. Even habits become strangely creative, their tendencies more acutely visible—tendencies not only for confirmation (the habituated path from house to bus stop) but also for deviation (the smell of the blooming tree slowing down the walk).

This is a book about these tendencies, engaging with the push and pull of what conforms and how it deviates. What stands out in this process are practices and techniques more than objects of study: what immediation does is trouble the very notion of an object's capacity to stand-in for experience. Immediation activates the what-else of the habitual bundling, orienting us toward what an object can do in an ecology of practices, an object shape-shifting in its relation to forces troubling its perceived consistency.

To trouble consistency requires a beginning-in-the-middle. This book is an experiment in the creation of techniques for middling. There are myriad ways and modalities of middling: art, in its most radical and affective moments, plunges into and from the middle of events; political constellations and social assemblages, far from providing fixed or stable formations, are in the middle of imperceptible movements re- and decomposing. Art that *works* immediates the art "work," the "artwork" having become institutionally very much a bundle of habits in the artist-art form-art gallery constellation of the contemporary art market.

Becoming aware of the effects of imperceptible movements and modulations taking place in the middling means to connect to the forever changing forces of immediation. Think immediation as the force of active middling through which events come to expression. Immediation not as an experience of, but a withness of experience that orients, in the living, what living can be. Think immediation as the middling technique through which an awareness is felt that what moves events is not an exterior force, not a human exterior to the act, but an acting ecology. This acting ecology is always more-than human, an ecology of practices. Living-in-the-act moves the event, and it is in the immediacy of this moving that the event moves into its potential. This book explores the potentials that come alive in this middling.

The immediating middling is unsettling. It is unnerving to find ourselves in the midst rather than at the willful beginning of a process. We are so accustomed to seeing the world as the unfolding of our personal volition! And so we resist. We opt for mediation instead, setting the world apart from the things that occur in it, setting the things that occur in the world apart from ourselves.

And a highly mediated world increasingly folds 'ends' back to meet this volitional beginning—a world of milestones accomplished, outcomes aligned with aims, forms severed from the processuality of their initial movements of unfolding. Both personal volition and neoliberal predictive sociality ride hand-in-hand with assemblages of mediation.

That immediation composes with mediation is always important to attend to lest we veer, by habit, back to the safety of mediatory practices. The operative question is: what can immediation do that mediation cannot? What does mediation obscure that immediation foregrounds?

Attending to and tending immediation means acknowledging that the process doesn't begin and end with intermediaries. It means challenging the thought that the perspective on experience is, first and foremost, ours, a human perspective. It means acknowledging the radically empirical quality of all comings-together, radically empirical in the sense that what moves *is the middling*, the terms of the relation continuously altered by that movement.

A shift from a human-centered, subject-oriented perspective is a hard thing to qualify in a language that seeks to order experience according to subjects and objects. In Andrew Murphie's words: "Th[e] making of the world is serially immediate. Data and its being drawn into events therefore rely on an ongoing process of instances of immediation. What we call 'mediation' is just a linked series of these events of immediation" (Immediation 1, 18).

Techniques are required for making immediation felt. Techniques for immediation do not simply generate new things or objects. Instead they find and enact different ways to live in and with the world, different ways *to world.*

Anna Munster

Prelude

What if we were to throw away all our formations of "medium" yet media continued ... variably? Discard all channels, black boxes, symbolic meanings, projections, senders, decodings and messages. Media that no longer bring us the story, build infrastructure, poll, opine, comment, like, store, remediate. Media no longer hiding behind techniques of insinuation, claims to representation. What, then, still forms in middling variability? What assembles technically; materializes imagistically, sonically, linguistically; gathers socialities; ekes out communicabilities; signals politically? Expresses more-than-humanly and collectively?

The world. The world immediating. A chattering, lively and inquisitive worlding. A worlding that does without mediation and reportage because it *does*—sometimes too speedily or otherwise at snail's pace. Doings reaching tentacle-like and jumping off to other temporalities, "bifurcations, divergences, incompossibilities, and discord belong to the same motley world ... It is a world of captures instead of closures," Deleuze notes (1993, 8).

The world is eventful, "something doing" (Massumi, 2015a: 152). But it has a style—a singular mode of immediating. Andrew Murphie proposes that the world makes and is made as series: "What we call 'mediation' is just a linked series of these events of immediation" (Immediation 1, 18).

The immediate and the represented no longer divide sequentially or cardinally. Instead, they meet in the middle, in the doing, in the world's singular processuality. But if the world's immediating is singular it is also multiplicitous, always working differentially with scales, speeds, durations. The world immediates differentially developing its own serial techniques.

Immediating never draws from a passive reservoir but rather actualizes the world's potential vigorously, actively. Among its many actualizations: art, media. Such events assemble singular modes of doing, engaging and activating conjunctions of humans, organic and inorganic entities. Such events are creative, generating media. Media do not inform "us" about the world; media are in-formed by the world's lively communicability. *Immedia*.

Immediation is a not a technique or practice that returns to a primacy of sensation. What it can offer instead is a radically empirical feeling of the *nonsensuous*: "… an experience of immediation, of a sort of nonsense or nonsensuous orientation that cannot be parsed from the physical orientations alone" as Thomas Lamarre writes, grasping the immediation of artist Xu Bing's installations and drawings (Immediation 1, 88). What is at stake here is less the question of form and more the inevitable *deformations* that in-form the becoming of mattering. Matter's lively immediating.

Immediation, while directly felt, lies in *differencing* movements of the felt. While in no way wishing to privilege the position (already too formed), of the artist, we do propose that tending to the "aesthetico-," to how expressivity singularizes, allows us to start in the middle and elsewhere than the mediated, represented, already formed. Immediation is a challenge to sequential and cardinal arrangements of temporality, as Toni Pape draws to our attention: "A concept of immediation challenges us to think these relational complications of the present by pastness and potential and to consider how such immaterial yet felt aspects like memory and affect can be composed for and how they factor into the actual experience of [amongst everything else] media" (Immediation 1, 67).

By working in the middle, differentially, the texts in this anthology trouble distinctions that have formed by assuming that time unfolds chronologically to divide and separately position the world and then media; matter and then representation; perception and then its memories. The texts here do not place memory as a formation that *follows* a present and "immediate" perception. Rather immediation works speciously to thicken and complicate the present. Perception and memory form concurrently and synchronously yet differentially.

Perception is conceived as *in-forming*, not as an action carried out by a subject—human or other, or given. Ilona Hongisto and Bodil Marie

Stavning Thomsen illustrate this in their essay which proposes to actively conceive of anarchiving as an immediating procedure. Here memory doesn't form through the work of archiving, which would incur secondary, memorializing activities. Moving with Hu Jieming's installation, *The Remnants of Images* (2013), they propose instead that immediation can be affectively experienced through anarchival techniques that can "foreground what is still emergent in past moments" (Immediation 1, 48).

Immediation, directly felt in differencing. A differencing in which passing-into can create past-presents, present-presents, future-pasts in ordinary events and in para-ordinary ethico-aesthetic experience. Immediating—a practice for developing techniques to stay with duration, with the world, with events and to pass away with them all, in their continuous variation.

Andrew Murphie

The World as Medium: A Whiteheadian Media Philosophy

> ...the world can be conceived as a medium for the transmission of influences...
> *Whitehead (1978: 286)*

Optogenetics, Travelling Worms and the Creation of Virtual Environments

Recently[1] scientists developed a way to "non-invasively" monitor the neural activity of worms as they moved (Faumont et. al 2011). This solved a longstanding problem involving experimental work with animals—how do you monitor such a tiny thing as a neuron in a free moving animal?[2] The new method involves what can best be described as an elaborate media assemblage, although it's not the kind that would usually be studied in media departments.

The first elements of this assemblage are the moving, and one assumes thinking, feeling worms. These worms are literally "premediated," as Richard Grusin puts it (Grusin 2010). Their neurons have been tampered with by optogenetics. The second element of this assemblage is this optogenetics, a true "biomedia" (Thacker 2004). Far from being just "non-invasive," however, the use of optogenetics in the experiment involves an inventive and very troubling mix of the "non-invasive" and the highly invasive. Optogenetics in this case involves the use of genetics to sensitize the worms' neurons to light. The experiment can then allow two things. Light can be used to control the worms' neurons (and therefore worm experience, feeling and movement). The neurons can also be made to respond to light in a way that makes them more trackable and/or recordable. The third aspect of this assemblage is a kind of idiosyncratic virtual reality system. The system can respond very quickly and precisely as it tracks its inhabitants (in this case worms with optogenetically adjusted neurons). It can then stimulate particular neurons at particular points in space, even as the worms move. It tracks the worms, "by linking optogenetic photostimulation of sensory neurons to the x-y position of the tracking target with great precision" (Faumont et. al 2011). This allows the system to create constantly adjusting virtual environmental effects; a kind of responsive, 3D world. Virtual environmental effects induced include "chemical or thermal gradients...food patches...[and] virtually textured environments," created "in ways that transcend" the usual low level of the "ability to manipulate physical properties of the environment on the scale of microns and milliseconds." As one blogger puts it, "If you know your worm neurons, you can stimulate one [to] make it think it has suddenly touched something with its nose or that the environment is suddenly very salty" (The Cellular Scale 2012).

The induced 3D effects involved are obviously not quite the same as those found in a 3D VR world *inside a headset* such as Oculus Rift. One very significant difference is that the experiment involves a direct technical intervention within the wider world—one in which neuronal s(t)imulation intersects with the worms' movement through the physical environment. In this, such an experiment is also a technical intervention at the point at which micro (neurons) meets macro (worm perception, worm thought, worm and world). If the result is a little like a low level worm "cyberspace," this is a cyberspace blended through the regular physical reality of worms.[3] Using this media assemblage the scientists were able to make images of particular neurons at high levels of magnification as the worms moved through their physically-technically affected and systematized environment.

This experiment is just one example of the increasingly flexible series of media-world assemblages with which we now live. Such assemblages have become more common as we move into relations with media that quite literally move us/the world and with which we can move the world.

In order to approach this situation, I will shortly discuss Alfred North Whitehead's media theory—that is, his own media theory as much as the way his philosophy might contribute to other media theories. This will be based on his concept of the "world as a medium." First, however, I will begin discussing these media-world assemblages by suggesting three things about how the data involved can be thought as the basis for contemporary media-world assemblages of all kinds.

First, data is not only, in any simple way at least, what it is too often still thought to be. Data is not, in any simple way at least, a question of information representing events, relayed clearly and faithfully from elsewhere, via mediation.[4] Rather, as with the worms, data is always in the middle of things, contagious and highly vulnerable to contagion. This means data is messy. One better way to think data in this messiness or shifting complexity is in Whitehead's terms—data as "potentials for feeling" (88). In his terms data is not really a simple record of previous events. It is rather like a moment in a compressed and heavily modulated series of recordings and re-recordings. Each recording is in some ways faithful and in others completely not. "Information" in these terms becomes a matter of carrying some aspects of the *intensity* of past events through the series. Of course, any data carries its own intensive relations with, and of, other data. However, in a Whiteheadian approach to media, data can only carry intensities in so far as these intensities have been able to constantly replenish and re-activate themselves through a series of immanent presents, at all moments in the processes involved. Data then is the bringing of these intensities as potentials for feeling directly into events (the VR modified experience of worms). Yet of course the events themselves can also be considered data in Whitehead's terms. They come to carry their own potentials for feeling, in the present, and into the future (neurons meet worm mobility meets optogenetic stimulation, meet scientists, with each their different potentials for feeling, moving into the future).

In all this data is powerful precisely because data is the potential for feeling that, actualized, makes the world. Working with data is this actualization of world in process, in and through feeling, and in and through the repotentializing of feeling. And data here means all data, not just digital data, which is only one way of moving the potential for feeling. This making of the world is serially immediate. Data and its being drawn into events therefore rely on an ongoing process involving instances of what we can call immediation (as Alanna Thain, Christoph Brunner, Massumi, Manning and others have called it).[5] What we call "mediation" is just a linked series of these events of immediation. At every point of the transit involved in what Whitehead calls actual events or actual occasions, something is lost and something gained. Thus the ongoing need for redundancy, and, for example, technical processes such as convolution in signal processing (Murphie 2013). The trace of past events that each data event carries is therefore complex and always somewhat "corrupted." The overall result is something like a variable shimmer of patterned intensities involving moves between potentials of feeling and activated feeling (the earlier direct optogenetic alteration of neurons enables the present direct stimulation of the perception of/movement through the world of the worms, all by altering potentials for feeling). The traces of these series, in the current moment, are what we call history, though this is "history in the present" (Foucault in Massumi 2015a: 207-208). Any re-activating of the traces of past intensities in this process (creating "saltiness" for worms) is work that must take place within the event. It is work done by all the elements of world involved, and work that has its own momentum as changing world. This work gathers and holds together feelings. This gathering and holding includes the re-activating of "history". As above though, history here involves a changing semi-coherence of data, along with a particular— these days more obviously changing—media-world assemblage. It is history as "the fraction of a second that is the order of magnitude of what Foucault calls 'effective history'" (Massumi 2015a: 207).

The momentum of this work carries through a series of events passing varying data to other times and places. The question of powers[6] from this perspective involves thinking in terms of participation in something like a pulsing or phasing between events of emergence and perishing (Massumi 2015b:154-155). This is again something basic to the technology of signal and signal processing, which is in turn basic to media and communications. Yet along with such basic technical powers of what we usually consider signal, there are other powers, also "signaletic" in a broader sense. In short, the powers found in any event are multiple (powers of worms, neurons, experimenters, light, genetics, "saltiness," gravity, the earth, etc). They might sometimes even include, if in diminished form, aspects of that which we sometimes still call the "human."

The second point about data—now considered as potential for feeling—is related to this. The politics of data-based media is not only a question of what is being recorded and how events are being represented and put to use in distant, broader networks—that is, of data travelling *outwards* from events and being used for a kind of representation of general populations and individual movements, elsewhere (in some security silo or corporate bunker). Such a politics is also a question of what data events—as potentials for feeling—are travelling *into* other events, taking their more immanent and immediate part in events. This applies to every occasion of immediation along the way (thus allowing a rethinking of, for example, social media, political communication and so on).

The third point about data as potential for feeling is that data as any kind of ordering is only so relationally (although this also means differentially, with "relation" as contrast or intensity). Order—intrinsic order within an event and social order between events—is made and remade in events themselves. Order is formed (and unformed) when data meets data and intensities are distributed, whether this involves a series of signal events of patterned changes in voltage in a computer, or sunlight meeting the eye/skin/nervous system—or perhaps all of these together, as mimicked and modulated in the experiment with worms. Thus data as ordered is only ever fully ordered immanently (in fact, this immanent ordering of feeling is the event). Further, as above with data, any kind of ordering is always accompanied by a novelty within and disruption to existing order, although this destruction is not of course total. In short, as events form and dissolve, "information" is not preserved and neither the "message" nor world involved remain the same. In coming together with other events of feeling in media-world events, data itself is transformed—simply put, its order is constantly corrupted.

Such ongoing events of potential feeling meeting feeling, with no going back, are at the heart of all media events. However, this forward-moving process, with no return, is not exactly a question of media-worlds being subject to the work of "time's arrow."[7] Rather they are in themselves the ongoing work of a multiplicity of arrows. Their collective process is what we take for time, and for the immediating world as time.

Media and World

The worm-optogenetics-VR assemblage is an emblematic contemporary media assemblage. It has a degree of "self-awareness" about the power of the potential for feeling in making the world. Unhappily though, in this the worm-optogenics-VR assemblage provides a perfect technical diagram for contemporary control. It is a big step up from Bentham's (Foucault's) Panopticon toward a more effective society of control, or perhaps a step up again from that. It is at the same time "non-invasive" and invasive in the extreme. It partners a very effective form of surveillance with control at the very root of movement/perception/ thought. It creates fabulations that nevertheless become material aspects of the world, additives to the world as it would otherwise have been. These are fictive but no less real, responsive aspects of world. They systematize worlds and adapt and change in real time with these worlds. Such systems allow a highly fluid trapping and immanent control of any creatures—including but not restricted to humans— that both move and think at the same time. Approaches to media and communications need to be able to analyze such situations. Yet what is mediating what in such set ups?

In general, contemporary media and world are often finding what seem to be strange continuities and overlaps. Direct, exploitable and constantly inventive continuities between media and world are now the rule, not the exception. Indeed, the overlap sometimes seems almost total. Yet I will suggest that what looks strange in such assemblages has always been the case. As Whitehead points out, the continuities are there because the entire world has always been a medium. At the same time, it is true that there are significant differences in the way that contemporary media capitalize on this. First, they possess more technical power to work within the entire world as medium. Second, they are premised on a kind of self-awareness of this media-world overlap. They increasingly diagram media/world relations in *acceptance* of world as medium and media as world.

Whitehead's simple idea—*the world as medium*— is the concern of the rest of this chapter. The idea of the world as medium gives a different, in many ways more effective way of grasping the situation that produces such dystopian events and of the politics that this involves. Luckily, however, it is an idea that is not restricted to dystopian instances such as the worms with which I have begun. There are many more positive examples of the contemporary realignment of media with the world as medium. There are, for example, new idiosyncratic and elaborate media assemblages such as the blockchain database technologies and cryptocurrencies that potentially disrupt established financial systems and much more (Lotti 2015). These have the potential for direct and dramatic intervention in social organization in favour of increased (or, it has to be admitted, perhaps decreased) social equality. There is the immediation of crises by new media tools directed more obviously towards participation in the world as medium, such as Ushahidi (which involves crowdsourced crisis mapping).[8] There are new and exciting forms of social organization (such as p2p and maker culture) that are premised on the maintenance and distribution of intensity throughout the social while defying given political models and syntaxes (see Gilbert 2013).[9] A final example is the hugely extended web of multiple events of immediation found between climate change and climate science—in the ongoing exchanges between weather and climate as expression of the world as medium and the complex network of sensors and other media tools and techniques (such as computer modeling and visualization) the make up the science, as another expression of the world as medium (Edwards 2013). It is the world as medium that allows the literal sensing (feeling, immanently and continuously) of the differential intensities that make up the reality of climate change, both in geographical terms and over time. It allows us to feel these intensities with a much finer sensitivity. The media-world assemblage involved then is subtly attuned to all kinds of variation. Without this, climate change would be more or less imperceptible. Or rather we would feel it differently—vaguely for the most part, roughly in events of weather or climate chaos. In all such cases, thinking media in terms of the world as medium involves thinking media as the moving immanence of feeling—and of the power of feeling—over time.

In fact, media and communications assemblages that attend to the powers of immediation of events and worlds, and that do not conform to our usual roping off of "media"—whether by theory, academic department or industry—now confront us everywhere. They are increasingly our world. As has been suggested already, they raise questions about both "world" and "media and communications."

Towards a Whiteheadian Theory of Media and Communications

This chapter seeks to address such questions by rethinking media and communications in the light of Whitehead's thinking. It does this via one of Whitehead's less explicitly discussed ideas, that "the world can be conceived as a medium for the transmission of influences" (1978: 286). This idea is arguably central to Whitehead's process "philosophy of organism" (1978: 18).[10] Taking the world as medium seriously would radicalize, and is radicalizing, both thinking and working with media and communications. It provides a different and powerful way to understand all world/media relations—past, present and future. Mediation and communication come to be understood as a general condition of the world, although neither world nor media remain the objects/processes with which we are familiar. Much is therefore at stake, as those defined objects/processes not only underpin current media industries and established academic disciplines. They also underpin any number of other "ecologies of practice" (Stengers 2002: 262) that depend on models and practices drawn from media and communications industries and disciplines, from education to management to psychology to much of contemporary science. Indeed, Christopher Vitale suggests that the concept of the world as a medium is "the starting place which perhaps can serve as the foundation for a new paradigm within the realm of contemporary thought" (2009).

There are three main concerns when it comes to thinking media and communications with Whitehead. First, there is of course attending to Whitehead's little remarked upon concept of the world as medium. Second, in the light of this we can suggest that Whitehead himself provides a comprehensive "media theory," one that resituates media and communications as part of the world, indeed *as* world. Media and communications are no longer viewed as one slice of world somehow different from the larger, supposedly non-media, non-communicating part of it. Third, there is little doubt that Whitehead's ideas have extensively influenced thinking about, and practices in, media and communications, in often unacknowledged yet very fundamental ways over the past hundred years.[11] Moreover, his thought is currently seeing a revival in thinking about media and communications, as it has elsewhere.[12] Some of the details of this third point are dealt with in two extended footnotes.

Shortly I will take up Whitehead's "media theory" to explore the way in which Whitehead's thinking gives a philosophical groundless ground for understanding contemporary media events as participants in a broader world—a world that is itself a series of events of mediation and communication. There will only be the space to sketch elements of Whitehead's philosophy, seen from the perspective of the world as medium. This will lead to a consideration of signal, so basic to media and communications, and to Whitehead's own version of signal. In Whitehead's thinking, signals would take their place as the vectors for the transmission of feeling (e.g. 1978: 163 & 315) that are so important to his world as medium.

In some ways this chapter follows recent thinkers at the junction of ecology and media (Parikka 2013 and 2014, Robbert 2013a & 2013b, Herzogenrath 2008). Indeed Bernd Herzogenrath suggests something very close to the idea of the world as medium while describing the work of Deleuze and Guattari in relation to the environment:

> The world is media, in a manner of sensation and contracting ... it is possible to continue from [Deleuze and Guattari's] philosophy of cosmic vibrations towards directions of a natural philosophy of media where the term starts to encompass the recording of time in rocks, the capacities of transmission in plants and animals, the weird sensations for example in insects that perceive not only through eyes and ears, but through chemicals as well. (2008: 20)

Adam Robbert's summary of the core of this "natural philosophy of media" is incisive[13]:

> Earth is a kind of medium, and we are inside of it. We are not just dependent upon Earth for its resources to produce media technologies, Earth is itself a medium involved in terrestrial evolution. (2013b).

If so, perhaps it is time, without completely abandoning everything we know about and do with media, to let go of many of our framings and disciplinary field limits, along with foundational concepts of processes and objects. In so far as we continue to inhabit dominant conceptions of media and communications, we might need, once again, to rethink "media and mediation as *conceptual objects* in their own right ... whether or not there is even such a thing as a media object" (Galloway, Thacker and Wark 2013: 1-6). When discussing the affective intensity that is also central to Whitehead's "critique of pure feeling" (Whitehead 1978: 113),[14] Massumi even suggests that we might not even "need a concept of mediation," even if affective intensity "includes very elaborated functions like language" (Massumi in Massumi and Zournazi 2002: 214-215). One way of responding to such provocations is indeed to accept all the world as medium, yet this requires us to develop new concepts of media and communication that do not separate them from a world that also mediates.[15] This might require a more complex but also humble understanding of "our" media and communications in relation to the rest of what is happening in the world—a true "media ecology." The entire world becomes a medium for the "vector transmission" of feeling. This is also a world that is constantly recreated as novelty is added with each coming together of what Whitehead calls "actual entities" or "actual occasions," the "final real things of which the world is made up" (1978: 18).

The World as Medium—and Media as World(s)

For Whitehead, the world as medium is indeed one of the vector transmission of feeling. In its process of becoming, one emerging actual entity or actual occasion feels a number of immediately previous entities. It "prehends" them—feels them from the perspective of that occasion's gathering of prehensions into its own becoming. This can only be serial. That is, an occasion can only prehend another occasion as a kind of past or futurity (or potential).[16] The other actual occasions prehended by an occasion, however, might also feel or prehend each other separately (though again, somewhat serially). Thus what an actual occasion "A" feels at any given time is a combination of both direct and relayed feelings or prehensions[17] (from B, C, D, etc.) (Whitehead 1978: 226).[18] Over time in this complex relay of feeling any "former entity"[19] becomes "data for the latter" (that is, in a feeling or prehension). As discussed earlier in this chapter, what Whitehead means by "Data" "are the potentials for feeling" (88). Whitehead also calls these potentials for feeling "objects." Of course, "the initial data of a complex feeling, as mere data, are many" (230). However, this is "felt [as though] they are one in the objective unity of a pattern" (231)[20]. As the becoming of an actual occasions proceeds, there is eventually what Whitehead describes as a "fully clothed feeling whereby the datum is absorbed into the subjective satisfaction—'clothed' with the various elements of its 'subjective form' " (52).

Composed of such becomings, Whitehead's world is one of worlds, plural, and of course every occasion is its own world. As Whitehead puts it: "each actual entity arises out of its own peculiar actual world," with "each actual world as a medium" (1978: 284). Any of these worlds is a medium for the transmission of vectors of feeling and the ongoing transmissions and gatherings of transmissions of all worlds make up the "world" as a whole.

In this, any event or "actual" occasion is both extremely private and public. Even though entities form in a way that is, as Whitehead puts it, governed by an ideal of privacy and giving rise to what he calls "private emotion," the "vector form is not lost, but is submerged ..." (1978: 212). In fact, this "private" emotion can never be closed off to the more "public" vectors of feeling of the world as medium (and at that this emotion arises in entities that are not in any sense always or even often what we would call "human").[21] Here:

> ... the reason why the origins are not lost in the private emotion is that there is no element in the universe capable of pure privacy ... the notion of pure privacy [is] self-contradictory. Emotional feeling is still subject to the third metaphysical principle, that to be "something" is "to have the potentiality for acquiring real unity with other entities." Hence, "to be a real component of an actual entity" is in some way to "realize this potentiality." Thus "emotion" is "emotional feeling" and "what is felt" is the presupposed vector situation ... the notion of "passing on" is more fundamental than that of a private individual fact. (212)

Within this "passing on," there are, as Michael Halewood points out, many forms of communication. These include but exceed human language:

> ... although human language is clearly, in itself, communicatory, both Whitehead and Deleuze insist that there are other forms of communication that are integral to existence ... Therefore language is one form of communication among many. (Halewood 2005b: 72)

Halewood also suggests that language itself "is not to be distrusted, but is itself to be seen as diverse." That is, "there will be different languages for different entities or assemblages of entities." (72)

How then is communication to attain some kind of clarity? It does so in terms of the immanent specificity of the way that prehensions are gathered together in a unique actual occasion. As Halewood puts it: "all information ... can only be fully understood if the manner in which it presents itself is taken into account. In this sense, the qualitative aspect of all information is an integral aspect of all information so that the world becomes 'objectively qualitative' " (2005a: 79).

Arising from and moving through the specific instances of unique actual occasions, in the transmission of vectors of feeling, is a different aspect of the world as medium. This is shifting potentiality. Whitehead calls this the "extensive continuum" (1978: 66).[22] This is like Deleuze's "virtual."[23] It "expresses the solidarity of all *possible* standpoints throughout the whole process of the world" (Whitehead 1978: 66, my emphasis). It is "*the reality of what is potential*, in its character of a real component of what is actual" (66; my emphasis). More simply, the extensive continuum is the abstract "potentiality for division" (67). Like Deleuze's virtual it is actualised, here by further actual occasions that again and again "atomize the extensive continuum" as they gather prehensions, or vector transmissions of feeling, in their own unique way.

In sum, in Whitehead's process philosophy, data, that is, the objectification of previous actual occasions as potentials for feeling in the shifting extensive continuum as a whole, are felt and drawn into what Whitehead calls a concrescence of becoming[24]—that is they are prehended (grasped and gathered). This concrescence finds satisfaction in an ongoing series of new, fully achieved actual entities or actual occasions. Actual occasions are therefore complex gatherings of real/potential world(s), moving as world in and of vectors of transmission of feeling. "Satisfaction," however, will mean the end of any particular actual occasion, although aspects of it will be taken up (differentially) in prehensions for other actual occasions.

This flow of actual occasions is also the flow of experience. The gathering of concrescence is the "togetherness of experience ... of its own kind, explicable by reference to nothing else" (Whitehead 1978: 189). This is not just a question of human experience but of any subject-"superject." All the world is therefore capable of experience (see Shaviro 2014), with "any actual entity at once the subject experiencing and the superject of its experiences" (Whitehead 1978: 29). At the same time, the subject here is not the subject as we usually think of it, something perhaps somewhat separate from the world at large. It is rather something like the world itself as it begins to head towards an actual occasion, begins to take on the particular form (the "subjective form") of an actual occasion. What then is an object? As Whitehead puts it "the word 'object' thus means an entity which is a potentiality for being a component in feeling; and the word 'subject' means the entity constituted by the process of feeling, and including this process" (88). What he calls the "superject" is the end result of an actual occasion—its satisfaction. The superject is therefore something that "emerges from the world" (88). Whitehead opposes it to the Kantian subject, from which the world supposedly emerges.

Through all this the world as medium is fundamental in that "the vector character of prehension is fundamental" (317). This lies at the heart of Whitehead's philosophy of organism and what he calls his critique of pure feeling. Indeed, Whitehead simply states that "All things are vectors" (1978: 309, my emphasis). This means the "displacement of static stuff by the notion of fluent energy." It means ongoing productive relations between different aspects of this fluent energy. It also means that everything involves vector transmission—fluent and relational. Everything is a kind of immanent process of (im)mediation or, in a very basic sense, communication.

Yet Whitehead has a somewhat broader concept of the vector than that of basic mathematics, by which I mean that of a mono-directional line with a particular force. For Whitehead, vector simply "means definite transmission from elsewhere" (116). Whitehead also mentions "vector transference" (xxv), "vector transition" (164), and "vector feeling" (163)[25].

As Steven Shaviro puts it:

> Feeling, as such, is the primordial form of all relation and all communication ... feeling can be conceived as vector transmission, as reference, and as repetition. These three determinations are closely intertwined. Every feeling involves a reference to another feeling. But reference moves along the line of the vector. Feeling as reference is a transmission through space, a direction of movement ... every new process of becoming "involves *repetition* transformed into *novel immediacy*" (Whitehead, 1978:137). (Shaviro, 2009: 63)

This is immediation precisely described without being named. Finally, in Whitehead's media theory there is no grounding difference in nature between different types of vector transmission ("technical" or "natural", human or nonhuman, for example).

I will now suggest that this vector transmission can also be understood as signal. Thus Whitehead's philosophy is one in which the complexity of signal at the level of the world is paramount.

New Paradigms, No Paradigms

Our usual models of media and communications, with their tight and unforgiving syntaxes,[26] can perhaps now be seen for the rigid models they are. Their orderings order the world rather too much into hierarchies of mediation and communication. Whitehead's media theory questions much of this. Following Whitehead, we can open up the ordering, the syntax of feeling. Doing so, we open up the world to itself, or more correctly open up the possibilities of participating differently in the dynamic ecologies of the world. Recent science gives us many provocations in this respect. Here I will only mention two. First, there is an example of a questioning of syntax in the nervous system. Using something like a Shannon-Weaver model of communication in the context of neural activity, it had until recently been thought that the axons that extend out from dendrites in the brain only transmitted signal away from the dendrites to which they were attached. However, it has recently been suggested that they are bi-directional. They can also signal inwards, towards their own dendrite. In fact, they can also "talk" to each other and "compute" separate from the dendrite (Northwestern University 2011). Second, there is an example of a questioning of hierarchies concerning sites of sensation and thinking. Again involving the way that something like a central processing media model comes into the understanding of the nervous system, the skin has long been thought as a receptor for information that would later be "processed" in the central brain. However, recently it has been suggested that calculation can occur at the skin itself, in fingertips (Umeå University 2014). In both these examples sites of something like mediation are rethought in terms of a world (im)mediating itself in many more diverse sites and in different patterns of relation than are usually assumed by key models for our thinking and culture (including models of the way that media and communication function). Both these examples suggest a multi-directional and multi-situational intensification of vectors of feeling, of signal that is open to ongoing variation. The experiment with the worms with which this chapter began capitalises on this, as do so many contemporary assemblages involving media. Anywhere where the sites and syntaxes of the vector transmission of feeling can be reworked expands the communicational capacity (we might say instead, the relational intensity or affective capacity) of the "necessarily communicating world" (Deleuze and Guattari 1987: 280).[27] The sites and syntaxes of feeling might be reworked by what we used to think of as either nature or culture, or both in adventurous combination.

Indeed, in this complexity of signal at the level of world, there is no "bifurcation in nature." The so-called bifurcation of nature was something Whitehead diagnosed as at the root of many problems (Whitehead 2007: 26). Only one aspect of this bifurcation was the working assumption that human perception was of one kind of nature, and the world beyond it another. For Whitehead, however, perception is a part of the world, and not of a different nature. More generally, he insisted that there are not two separate parts of nature, usually taken to be nature apprehending—thought or perception—on the one hand, and nature apprehended—a supposedly less active "material" world—on the other. In a different context Whitehead refers to this as the difference between "nature alive" and "nature lifeless." Here the more specific versions of this bifurcation would be nature mediating and nature mediated, or nature communicating and nature communicated. Yet if the world is medium then so are media and communications world. There is not a world that is then mediated by something other than world, or some subset of world. Everything is nature alive. We must therefore be able to account for an ongoing mix of signal events of all types (matter, thinking, perceiving, feeling, modeling, movements, electronics, the weather) in intermixed ontogenetic terms.

However, much of media and communications—disciplines, practices or industries—is still based on concepts and practices fueled by a "bifurcation of nature." Understanding all the world as medium might then suggest the end of media and communications studies, and perhaps of media and communications, *as we have too often thought them up to now.*

We have to expand the notion of medium while in some ways undoing it (again, we can no longer conceive of mediation as occurring between other aspects of the world that are not mediated). Concepts of "media" and "communications." "interaction," even "relations" based on exchanges of information between already formed, personal or even human individuals—suddenly seem far less relevant, perhaps fundamentally misshapen (Massumi 2011: 39-86). The same applies to much related to media and communications: signal, signs, transmission, culture, society, affect, objects, subjects. This is not just a question of philosophy but of the kinds of practices, even media institutions, communities and industries, we envisage and create. With Whitehead (and others of course), we can rethink a world that consists of something like ongoing (im)mediation. Thinking in terms of the world as medium also recasts what has been perhaps the twentieth century's quite understandable central problematic, a globalised world over-run by "the media" (understood in its usual restricted sense). In this problematic, contra everything suggested in this chapter, the world has only recently become a technology-imposed world as medium, something it was not before. The result is a "contaminated" world, over-run with media and communications, with media technologies, networks, techniques of spin and media cycles taking over politics, and so on. There is of course a troubling reality to this. Even though this is a model of communication at odds with the understanding in this chapter, it has to be acknowledged that a "false" model or concept can be as powerful in practice as a more "correct" one, if widely disseminated and put to use, especially in the building of socio-technical systems. Indeed, Massumi has described the current moment of exactly this as a "becoming-environmental of power" (Massumi 2009: 153; Dieter 2011). Thinking in terms of the world as medium might provide a way of matching this becoming-environmental of power while undermining it through more genuinely ecological concepts of world and medium.

I have suggested earlier in this chapter and elsewhere that impulses towards an acceptance of something like Whitehead's concept of the world as a medium are in fact found in some of the dynamics of contemporary media (Murphie 2004; 2014). As I began writing this chapter, the Occupy movement in Hong Kong was using meshwork technology (specifically the FireChat App) to reorder communications, away from the established and controllable internet, in order to hold together a series of actual occasions within a world, intending to bend that world away from its current formations. You can also see this in philosophy, which has made a return to "ecology" in many ways. We are beginning to see this accepted, very reluctantly, but nevertheless insistently, in a politics that is for example besieged by climate change, and can no longer refuse the world as a medium in which we are immersed (although I would define politics now as precisely this tension between two different ideas of the world as medium—something like Whitehead's world as medium versus the "becoming-environmental of power").

In order to understand how the real dynamics of the world as medium play out in all the above areas and others, the question of signal is crucial.

Intensity, Difference and Signal

> Any two forces, being unequal, constitute a body as soon as they enter into a relationship.
>
> *Deleuze (2006: 37)*

Some significant shifts are needed in order to go with the world as medium (and not just philosophically but in what Massumi calls a "speculative pragmatism" [2011: 29]). The main shift involves being better able to remain with signal as feeling. To put this slightly differently, it involves being able to remain with signal as differential intensity, without immediately retreating to an impoverished concept of information (and usually of signal, which is reduced to mere carrier). This is something perhaps understood by any mathematician, electrical engineer, jazz musician, activist or even perhaps cyberneticist. I will tease this out.

First up, intensity here *is* difference—or better, intensity is differences coming together and differences differentiating. As Deleuze puts it, to say difference and intensity is to say the same thing: "The expression 'difference of intensity' is a tautology ... Every intensity is differential, by itself a difference" (1994a: 222).

Intensity always involves a differential of energies or forces. (As we shall see, Whitehead terms this a "contrast" [1978: 228]). Forces and energies as a kind of moving flow of difference are intensities. This flow creates specificities through time, like whirlpools—gatherings together of intensities (feelings, prehensions) into events or actual occasions. Think of a glance across a crowded room. Or think of the gathering and movement of voltage within power lines or computing, and, in conjunction with this, of electromagetic waves in wifi, or light within the fibreoptic cable, that enable networks. Think of a body moving through, with and as moving world—as worlding. Think of the weather. Think of a thought: poised at the junction of the flow/capture of intensities or prehensions moving between general vectors of feeling as world, our body's own movement through this, and the ongoing drift of electro-chemical signal complexity in the brain. All of these are themselves made up of further actual occasions. For example, the brain involves billions of actual occasions—instances of the world as medium—at any given moment. The practical reality of the brain is that there is a constant redistribution, within the brain itself, of *proprioceptive feeling*—neuronal gatherings of intensities or prehensions. These lead, for example, to the constant changing of relative strength of connection in neurons (Kandel 2007), just as larger scale proprioception leads to changing relations between muscles and so on in the body. Thinking is literally feeling. Thinking involves—though it is not reduced to—a basic and literal flow of proprioceptive intensities of the brain—the brain as world as medium feeling itself differentiating.

Or, think of the well-known Occupy Wall Street poster of a female dancer beautifully balanced on top of the sculpture of a bull found at Wall Street, one of the heart(s) of the constitution of contemporary world. Or, think of all of these events as both separate and together. This is the richness of feeling as world, and world as feeling. As Erin Manning puts it:

> Think feeling here in the Whiteheadian sense, as propulsor to experience, always in the realm of the impersonal. This is not human feeling or emotion. It is affective tonality. It is the generative force [we might say the gathering of intensities], singular to this event, that moves the event toward its resolution. Each event has a tone, a singular expressivity, an enjoyment, as Whitehead would say. (2013: 20-21)

Deleuze and Guattari give a full explanation of the relation between differential intensities, signal and sign[28] within these generative forces and singular events.

For Deleuze, I have already suggested, intensities are difference differing. Affect is the power to immerse within this—for one gathering of differential intensities to be affected by, and affect other intensities without totally falling apart.[29] This affective power is the onto-genetic power that holds the ongoing creation of world—or something like Whitehead's "organism"—together. Another word for this shifting intensity, thought in tandem with affective power, might be *signal*.

It is here that we can turn to Bodil Marie Stavning Thomsen's perceptive work on signaletic materials in media arts. She draws on Deleuze's *Cinema 2* to suggest some crucial steps to broaden an understanding of signal. Starting with the idea that today "the signal is the message" (2012), Thomsen notes a number of ways in which the traditional matter—what *matters* as well as the actual *materials*—of media and communications has been transformed with electronic and digital media. For one thing:

> ... the "image as sign" has ... increasingly been replaced by "the signaletic material" that became present on the surface of the video-screen as electronic lines and dots, leading neither to a representation of time nor space but to a becoming of time itself in the live signal and further to time as the dominant vector of digital variation, even within the production of images ... (2012)

Even more dramatically perhaps:

> ... in a new media framing the "haptic" surfaces have scattered all over, surpassing the inscription of the materiality of the grid in the tradition of avant-garde minimalism or abstract aesthetics.

The "signaletic image" has indeed exceeded the grid in a way that was only dreamt of by Deleuze but that—on the other hand—was well under way in the video technology. (2012)

Here Thomsen turns to Lazzarato's remark that it is "no longer quite simply about an image that is going to be seen but about an image in which you interfere. ..." (Lazzarato 2002: 79).[30] It is not too far from this to the optogenetically activated worms having their neural signals monitored as they participate in the creation of virtual environments—in which case it is not only an image in which other aspects of the world as medium can interfere, but a kind of "image" that you become, among other images (as Bergson thought it). The contemporary signaletic image increasingly aligns itself with the world as medium, which is to say a mesh of signals or interwoven vector transmissions of feeling. This suggests something of an impersonal matrix of forces driving media and communications, notably but not only within media arts, to catch up with the full potential of signal and world, with "each actual world," "as a medium for the transmission of influences" (Whitehead 1978: 284).

Again, at the heart of this is signal—the world as signal. Here, however, signal is not the carrier of message, but rather what Deleuze called a *different/ciator* (Deleuze 1994: 207). It is, at the same time, a bringing together of intensities in transit. This of course means that signals are not channels within a non-signal world, or channels between pre-existing worlds, but world itself. All the world—in fact worlds in plural—are transmission-worlds, an assemblage of signal intensities, in constant collision, cooperation and chaotic overlap with each other.

In this context media and communications, not only as carriers of signal intensities but as assemblages of signal intensities themselves, head towards what I call elsewhere "differential media," and "differential life" (Murphie 2014; 2005). Differential media is a term that understands media as ontogenetic, and only secondarily if at all as a series of discrete media forms. It is media moving with the possibilities of variability and intensity. It is media considered as amodal, the ambivalently modal, or the precariously complex modal, rather than simply the "multi-modal." It is individual media instances accommodating themselves to being no more than temporary gatherings within the broader dynamics of the world as a medium. Differential media are differential first because they are involved in media events that are active participants in the self-creation of the world. Their force is not in their newness per se, but in their powers of ongoing differentiation. This gives them a great flexibility—one that resonates within the broader world (as itself medium). And this resonance gives media as we usually think of them their ability to participate in the rest of the world's ongoing differentiation.

To return to Whitehead, the basic elements of this gathering and movement of differential intensities are in the region of what Whitehead called simply "contrasts" (1978: 228). Contrasts are what unify sense data into actual occasions. They form patterns by which "the sensa are experienced emotionally, and constitute the specific feelings whose intensities sum up into the unity of satisfaction" which is the aim and end of the occasion (1978: 115).

Whitehead's contrasts are like Deleuze's differential intensities. They involve a kind of asymmetrical relation that is based on active contrast. Or, they involve a kind of *non*-relation in which active difference is the key. Blue is not white is not yellow is not green is not red and there is no easy communication or resolution between them. There is indeed a differential intensity within such contrasts. A contrast is not, however, an "opposition," or "dialectic." It does not have to be resolved. Whitehead points to the "contrast between blue and red" (1978: 228) [think of a Rothko painting with blue and red—No. 14 for example]. Although a contrast is not always a matter of a simple pair—contrasts can be multiple (229).

So far so good. Yet this is not a minor concern. Much, if not all, of what we experience, we could say of what makes the world itself, is contrast.[31] Contrasts are, at the least, a major part of the "individual definiteness" (228) of an "actual occasion" (and for Whitehead, remember, everything is an actual occasion—chairs, mountains, skipping, a thought, a painting, a brush stroke, worms and optogenetics and virtual environments coming together in a particular instance).

Let's take this a little further. We are used to the idea, whether or not we agree with it, that things are not the solid entities or objects we take them for. They are really a coming together of relations. Our concept of "things" is misplaced, involving what Whitehead calls "misplaced concreteness" (1967b: 72). Whitehead goes further than this however. Relations are often taken to be smooth in some sense (for example smooth relations, often taken to be more "authentic," are the aim of much of communications studies and industry). Yet relations are not smooth. As suggested earlier, they are not even relations. When we think relations we are still being too abstract. For Whitehead, "what are ordinarily termed 'relations' are abstractions from contrasts" (Whitehead 1978: 228).

In the light of this understanding of relation as contrast, what might seem Whitehead's actual occasions' "relationality" has to be qualified. What is really meant by "relations" is a gathering together, maintenance and creation of new contrasts—differential intensities. We can begin to understand why the world as medium is not a world of "ideas" per se, or even things or objects and subjects, at least not first up. It is instead a world of feeling, of intensity, of the differential. In this world, signal is feeling (intensity of contrast, whether found in the differentials that produce voltage and its variations or a cold wind on the skin). Indeed, we can define signal as feeling *in movement*, which is to say the world in movement, which is to say the world communicating/contrasting itself as it creates itself. All this is made absolutely clear by our poor optogenetically activated worms.

Differential Series/Difference and Repetition

This is going on all the time, throughout the shifting web of Whitehead's actual events or occasions, as differences differ, as "changing changes" (Massumi 2002: 10), as signals signal, as prehensions or feelings are gathered, split, and so on. The whole world *changes with each gathering*.

For Deleuze such changes—micro or macro and in-between—form what he calls "heterogeneous series." These are series of intensities, as experienced at the macro level in a series of weather events for example, as in the "weather lately has been dreadful" or, simply, in what we call "climate," or in a series of events in stock trading—a bull or bear market.

Deleuze describes signal as that which emerges when two or more of these heterogeneous series communicate (understood here as forming a new intensity or contrast): lightning as intensity between the series of the heavens and of the earth; voltage in a power line as electrical potential difference; weather and fossil fuel consumption (and other series) in climate change; tax and politics; or my body, events on the cinema screen, the bodies of others and popcorn in the cinema.

How do these heterogeneous series come together? They communicate, but not as we usually think communication. They literally come together via feeling, which is also to say signal. An example is the dark precursor, the channel that forms in the air that precedes and makes the path for a flash of lightning. Both dark precursor and lightning are a feeling out of events in ground and sky by each other. Both involve gatherings of prehensions that lead to a series of actual occasions. Communication as we usually think it—messages or even information—is a side effect, at best a perspective on the formation of channels of feeling in actual occasions. Indeed, Sean Watson has suggested that communication is primarily "a matter of structural modulation of the body and nervous system" (1998:38). Whitehead and Deleuze suggest something similar, but with regard to the "nervous system" of the broader world. Signal is a structural modulation of the world's own self-feeling or perception, via an ongoing communication between heterogeneous series.
Signal is thus found everywhere, and at all scales, down to the level of the ongoing genesis of channels in the "dark precursors" by which the world gathers the elements of its own microperception. Within this, Whitehead understands the "human body" as a kind of signal transducer or modulator for world, "...as a complex 'amplifier'—to use the language of the technology of electromagnetism" (1978: 119). To summarise all this, signal is contrast in motion. All a sign is is an instant of gathering/tension within signal. It is a perspective on signal. Any sign is thus an actual occasion or gathering of actual occasions.

One of the hard lessons here is that, as Guattari puts it, "Language is everywhere, but it does not have any domain of its own. There is no language in itself" (2010:27). It arises from forces and events in which it participates, and which in fact it is.

Moreover in this, as I began to suggest earlier, any syntax or reliable ordering is fluid or transient at best. This is difficult for most theories of perception, cognition, or aesthetics, let alone media and communications theorists and practitioners (think of the syntax of Kant's sublime for example, with the triumph of reason over imagination as a kind of punctuating full stop, or of the often challenged syntax of Shannon and Weaver's mathematical model of communication, or think of the forced syntaxes of models of learning with their objectives and outcomes, or of political process and decision making). There is no universal or permanent syntax, either to language or experience. As syntax is indeed an attempt to order language, expression and power, this is a powerful realisation. As Guattari puts it:

Content and expression are not attached to one another by virtue of the Holy Spirit. In the "beginning" of assemblages of enunciation, we find neither verb, nor subject, system, nor syntax ... Thus, content does not crystallise a universal world but a worldliness marked by contingent fields of force ... (2010: 45-46)

Both the existence and stable ordering of signs as we usually think of them are hollowed out. They are haunted by process. They become actual occasions like anything else, transitory events of signal.[32] Yet, if this means the dissolution of the sign as a foundation concept, can we say we have reached any kind of foundation in the signaletic?

If we have, this foundation is a groundless ground. Signals are slippery, changelings by nature. They are (topological) border zones (of differential contrast and tension), "fields of transduction" (Brunner and Fritsch 2011). Signal is always "signal processing," rather than anything like symbolic computation (or, symbolic processing is really just a form of signal processing). Signals constantly change the signaletic fields through which they move, and on which they depend, a variation from within which they are (Murphie 2002). In this respect, in their intensive contrasts, signals might be a matter of "co-emergence in differentiation" (see Bertelsen 2004 on Bracha Ettinger). Nothing is neatly sent, travels and arrives, or certainly not in any neat order. Or, a signal is more often travelling than sent or arrived. Or, more accurately it is always sent, arriving and travelling at the same time—immediated and immediating.

What We're Up Against

So there it is—a sketch of the world or worlds as medium for the vector transmission of feeling. In some ways this suggests the end of media studies, perhaps in the manner that Foucault suggested the "end of man," in favour of the world as formed by the movements of sea and sand.

This may be what we have to deal with, beyond, before and perhaps after what are still important issues of representation, rights and so on. We are confronted by, in fact we are, an extremely complex web, not even syntactically certain, of vectors of the transmission of feeling, shifting contrasts, of differential life in the world as medium. If it appears that this suggests some wild, "Deleuzean" celebration of difference, this is the case, although the situation is complex. Taking the "world as medium" seriously means accepting that difference and wildness are unavoidable and should be embraced, if with sobriety. This is also just as much a question, given the complex political situation of the world, of realising "what we're up against." What we're up against is not the world, but our own differential passaging with it.

Notes

1. I am grateful to Erin Manning, Greg Seigworth and Brian Massumi for very useful editorial comments on this chapter. Many thanks also to the Canadian Social Science and Humanities Research Council for the Partnership program that funded the Immediations grant that made it possible to write this.
2. This does not solve the ethical problem.
3. There is a startling resonance here with Jakob von Uexküll's 1934 account of a much earlier experiment with the perception and movement of a poor snail. In this the snail was placed on a rubber ball in water, with its shell clamped in place. It could "move" without getting anywhere. The snail was then encouraged to crawl onto a stick, sometimes while being beaten with it. The experiment demonstrated that the snail had a very different sense of time—"if the blows are repeated four or more times a second [fewer times than this and it moves away], the snail begins to crawl onto the stick. In the snail's environment, a stick that moves back and forth four or more times a second must be at rest" (von Uexküll 2010: 72). Between von Uexküll's snail and the VR-induced worms there is of course the historical development of cybernetics, interfaces based on embodied cognition and the like of game and other design based on operant conditioning (see Schüll 2012: 107). Our

own entrained media miseries and freedoms are intertwined with such developments and to an extent re-activate them, if with more variations than ever before.

4. Something like "representation" is part of this. However, in immediation this is better understood as the appropriation of data—here taken to be felt aspects of the events themselves rather than representations of events—by other events or occasions. This is what Whitehead calls "prehension" (1978: 18).
5. On immediation see Thain 2005, Massumi 2011: 72, and Brunner 2012.
6. Power will be taken here as the coming together of values and intensities, or values as intensities and vice versa (Jones 1998: 145).
7. See footnote 12 for a discussion of the idea, based in part on Whitehead's philosophy, of media providing a forward-movement in events, especially in the work of Parisi and Goodman 2009, Parisi 2013 and Hansen 2015.
8. http://www.ushahidi.com/.
9. See the P2P Foundation at http://p2pfoundation.net/Main_Page and the work of Michel Bauwens.
10. The concept of the world as medium is explained late in Whitehead's *Process and Reality* (1978: 284). However, Whitehead notes at this point (286) that he has explained it in a key earlier section of the book on data, the senses and perception in the modes of "causal efficacy" and "presentational immediacy" (115-128), although here the concept is not named as such.
11. Bertrand Russell and Whitehead's *Principia Mathematica* influenced Claude Shannon (of Shannon and Weaver and the communications "model of the century" or "mother of all models" [Hollnagel and Woods 2005: 11] fame), Norbert Wiener (who founded cybernetics and is often regarded as another founder of modern communications), John Von Neumann (who among other things conceived of the current architecture of computing) (Gardner 1987: 17), and Warren McCullough and Walter Pitts (two of the key founders of contemporary neuroscience, especially the idea that the brain could carry out logical, procedural calculations). Jeremy Rifkin has also suggested that Wiener's cybernetics is a "mechanical analogue of process philosophy" (2005: 219). Alan Turing also read *Principia Mathematica*. Herbert Simon and Allen Newall's initial foray into (symbolic) artificial intelligence in 1956 was also inspired by it, and this led to much of the next three decades of AI research (Seising and Sanz 2011: 14). Gregory Bateson's work has multiple variations on Whitehead's work (his use of Russell and Whitehead's work on logical types for his concept of hierarchies of communication, his focus on process, and what seem obvious parallels between concepts such as the world as a medium and Bateson's ecology of mind, despite Bateson's occasional denials). Then there is Susanne Langer, Whitehead's PhD student and friend, an early "media ecologist," and one of the great thinkers of affect, way before the supposed "affective turn." She dedicated the final decades of her life to explaining the human mind, conceived via feeling, via

process philosophy. Lewis Mumford was also inspired by Whitehead's idea of process (see also Wright 2006: 142). Marshall McLuhan read Whitehead extensively (see Coupland 2010: 45, 59), although he only actually quotes Whitehead on very general matters, notably, at the beginning of *The Medium is the Message*, that the "major advances in civilization are processes that all but wreck the societies in which they occur." In fact, Whitehead pre-empts the very basis of McLuhan's thought—the medium is the message. Whitehead writes, "These extensive relations do not make determinate what is transmitted; but they do determine conditions to which all transmission must conform" (1978: 288–see also Shaviro 2009: 52). In a similar but again perhaps more comprehensive manner than McLuhan, Whitehead further understands the "the human body" as a kind of signal transducer or modulator, "...as a complex 'amplifier'—to use the language of the technology of electromagnetism" (1978: 119). Even more than this, he preempts McLuhan's prescription that each medium changes the ratio of the senses involved in engagement with the world and that this is its prime effect. Whitehead writes, "the predominant basis of perception is perception of the various bodily organs, as passing on their experiences by channels of transmission and of enhancement" (119). Whitehead also writes, in a manner that is again strikingly prescient of the basics of McLuhan's thinking (here concerning the ration of the senses in different epochs):

In the phraseology of physics, this primitive experience is "vector feeling," that is to say, feeling from a beyond which is determinate and pointing to a beyond which is to be determined. But the feeling is subjectively rooted in the immediacy of the present occasion: it is what the occasion feels for itself, as derived from the past and as merging into the future. In this vector transmission of primitive feeling the primitive provision of width for contrast is secured by pulses of emotion, which in the coordinate division of occasions appear as wave-lengths and vibrations. In any particular cosmic epoch, the order of nature has secured the necessary differentiation of function, so as to avoid incompatibilities, by shepherding the sensa characteristic of that epoch each into association with a definite pulse. Thus the transmission of each sensum is associated with its own wavelength. (1978: 163)

Of course, beyond this, Whitehead writes of "transmission," "vectors," "data," and "medium."

The irony here is that, despite his enormous influence on common conceptions of media and communications, Whitehead in the end suggests that we have too limited a concept of mediation. Ironically, the idea that there's too much mediation (a world over-run by media which would otherwise run smoothly) leads media theory and practice astray. *We have too small a concept of mediation.*

Gertrude Stein and Whitehead were friends (see Lorange 2014). Friedrich Hayek quotes Whitehead on habit, "extending the number of important operations which we can perform without thinking about them" (Whitehead in Hayek 1945: 527), and extends the "profound significance of this" in terms of external rules and processes into his discussion of the price system. This is something of a presentiment of the work of Parisi, Goodman, myself, Hansen and others (although I'm not suggesting anyone is drawing explicitly on Hayek here). Raymond Ruyer, the French philosopher who among other things presented a sophisticated information theory, also wrote on Whitehead. There are also connections between Whitehead and Gilbert Simondon. Gilles Deleuze and Félix Guattari took up Whitehead in their work (on Guattari's reading of Whitehead see Alliez and Goffey 2011: 14). A key term in Guattari's *Schizoanalytic Cartographies* (2012), "grasping," is an attempt to take Whitehead's central concept of "prehension," and from there perhaps "concrescence," in new directions.

12. I plan another piece of writing to discuss the past and present of Whitehead's take up in thinking about media. The beginning of an indicative list would be as follows (with no claim to total coverage): thinking about the nonhuman and media (Haraway 1997: 146, Parikka 2010: 61 & 78), affect, the virtual and media (Massumi 2002, 2011), media ecologies (Fuller 2005), the more-than-human (Manning 2013), contemporary media and film ecology (Ivakhiv 2013), ecological philosophy and media ecology (Robbert 2013a; 2013b), abstract experience, media and the social (Goffey 2008, Toscano 2008) information, language and social theory (Halewood 2005a, 2005b and 2012), computing and digital, networked media (Murphie 2005, 2012, 2014, Parisi 2009a, 2009b and 2013, Goodman 2010, Parisi and Goodman 2009, Parisi and Portanova 2011, Portanova 2013, Barker 2012, Sha 2013, Hansen 2012 and 2015, Shaviro 2009 and 2014) and more. Of these, Parikka extends mediation as world to questions involving insects and geology. Parisi, Goodman, Portanova, myself and Hansen think Whitehead's extensive continuum in terms of computing, sound, dance and contemporary media, although all in quite different ways. For them, our ongoing engagement with the environment is supplemented by technical engagements. Our perception and thinking are affected by this, but we are not always aware of all of it. Much of the tenor of these kinds of approach is summed up by Parisi and Goodman as follows:

    "We argue that the need for a user to actively intervene to synthesize continuity, is predicated on a metaphysic of continuity over discontinuity whereby lived experience is added via subjective temporalities to the digital pre-programmed space in order to explain novelty. Instead, we sidestep the problem of ontologizing either the continuous or the discontinuous, the analog or the digital, hinting at, via Alfred N. Whitehead's notion of the 'extensive continuum,' a kind of rhythmic anarchitecture of cyclic discontinuity, or as Leibniz might say, an ecology of nonconscious counting, in which flow is continuously split, cut and broken, while simultaneously the atomic virtually congeals. Such a conception allows room for abstract potentialities, such as computational entities, to produce real affectivities in the form of contagious algorithms perceived nonsensuously" (2009: unpaginated).

    Matthew Fuller qualifies such arguments a little earlier, writing on Fuller's own inversion of Whitehead's misplaced concreteness and objectification as built into technical systems.

    "Objectification, in Whitehead's use of the term, is built into technical devices. A sensor used to register the presence in the air of a particular chemical exists solely in order to recognize the only things it can recognize. It has a molecularly precise perspectivalism. The information it is able to deliver means nothing, however, unless it is mobilized by the kind of associational operations that Haraway points to. Bodies are not homogenized absorptions of the forces they are in relation with; otherness is not dissolved. And it is in asking how to explore the potential associationality of a system—the paradoxical, recursive self it composes by the interrelation of these multiple forces—that works such as these produce themselves as further questions" (2005: 105).

Parisi (2013) also draws brilliantly on Whitehead to find infinite worlds in algorithmic computation (substantially rewriting our thinking about computing and world). To my knowledge few if any of these have discussed Whitehead's "world as a medium" directly (aside from Vitale, who I discuss elsewhere in this chapter, and, briefly, Fuller and Goffey). Of course, the concept is often implied just by taking up Whitehead's work. My concern here is to extend the use of Whitehead's concept beyond media and communications as they are often conceived, even as "new media," to world, in order to reconceive the fields involved.

13. See also Robbert on Earth Aesthetics (2013a) and Jussi Parikka (2013) on what Robbert calls "Geocentric Media Ecology" (2013b). In the course of discussing Parikka's work, Herzogenrath notes that: "Parikka attempts to think through some of the consequences of what a more environmental, ecological and biophilosophical understanding of 'media' could entail. In this context, media is considered somewhat parallel to a Deleuzian understanding of a body: it is a force field, a potentiality, an intersection point where forces of the cosmos contract to form certain potentials for affects and percepts" (2008: 19). For a broader and more Heidegger influenced understanding of media in ecological terms, see Peters 2015.

14. Of course, this makes aesthetic considerations more important than all others (see Shaviro 2012).

15. In "immediation" but also perhaps in newer, richer concepts of mediation such as that of Sarah Kember and Joanna Zylinska (2014).

16. Whitehead has a "doctrine of contemporary independence" of occasions. Put simply this emphasizes the fact that contemporary occasions are necessarily independent of each other. Massumi points out that what this really means is that not only contemporary, but all "occasions of experience cannot be said to actually connect to each other" (2011: 21). Their relation is one of non-relation, one could say of contrasts that produce differential intensities. As Massumi puts it, occasions "may only 'come together' in the sense of being mutually enveloped in a more encompassing event of change-taking-place that expresses their differential in the dynamic form of its own extra-being". Of course, as both Massumi and Judith Jones (1998) argue in their different ways, intensity is what makes occasions, and as Whitehead points out, occasions are all there is. So intensity is the groundless ground for Whitehead's philosophy without a substance. Contrast and the differential become crucial throughout.

17. In fact, prehensions are a little more complex that this. There are "physical prehensions" of other actual entities or occasions and "conceptual prehensions" of eternal objects (values or colours for example). There are also "positive prehensions" or "feelings" and "negative prehensions" that "eliminate from feeling" (Whitehead 1978: 23).

18. Matthew Fuller and Andrew Goffey mention the "world as a medium" in an endnote in *Evil Media*. Noting that media "in the very broad sense ... are irreducible elements in the composition and configuration of affect" (2012: 4), they comment that "Given two entities A and D, for example, [Whitehead] says, 'The medium between A and D consists of all those actual entities which lie in the actual world of A and D'" (2012: 174; Whitehead 1978: 226). Christopher Vitale (2009) gives one of the fuller accounts of the concept when discussing the world's ongoing creation within/by a self-differing substance. Vitale points out that "such a usage requires that we rethink precisely what we mean by a medium—medium for whom? Does a medium require a subject which is thereby mediated?"

19. Simply put, actual occasions *become* "former," even at very small time scales, as they are felt. This is part of the process in "process philosophy."

20. This is very close to Bateson's understanding of pattern as communication.

21. Whitehead's understanding of private and public also allows us to rethink the public/private division so important to media theory and practice.

22. The "extensive continuum" and related ideas from Whitehead are taken up by a number of thinkers with regard to media. See footnote 12.

23. Halewood (2005b) also points this out. At the same time, the exact relation between the extensive continuum, the virtual and potential is complex. In fact, if one were to take the virtual as the fullness of relational potential, the extensive continuum shades somewhere between this and the specificity of the actualities through which it is modulated and for which it provides the potentials. Massumi writes: "The extensive continuum, or extensive plenum, is the 'general scheme' (not to be confused with the sensorimotor schema) of potential space-time relationships, as it is integrally produced and differentially modulated from the singular 'standpoint' (standing-out) of a particular experiential event" (2015a: 134). Manning suggests that "The extensive continuum is more vague. It is the withness of the vastness of durational plenitude. Singular movement develops out of this extensive continuum, emergent in relation to all of the micropotentialities of pastness and futurity that make up an event. 'This extensive continuum is one relational complex in which all potential objectifications find their niche. It underlies the whole world, past, present and future' (Whitehead, 1978: 66)" (2009). Whitehead himself differentiates between what he calls "(a) the 'general' potentiality, which is the bundle of possibilities, mutually consistent or alternative, provided by the multiplicity of eternal objects"—something like the virtual—and "(b) the 'real' potentiality, which is conditioned by the data provided by the actual world. General potentiality is absolute, and real potentiality is relative to some actual entity, taken as the standpoint whereby the actual world is

defined"—which is the extensive continuum (Whitehead 1978: 65). In sum, the extensive continuum is perhaps easiest understood as a proto-extensivity-temporality that is less virtual than the full virtual but potential rather than yet actual. Of course, all three of these are found together.

24. For a valuable and complex take on such issues with regard to contemporary media and Whitehead see Hansen 2015. At the same time, this is one that self-acknowledges a fairly provocative, interesting, yet in the end for me unnecessary, "inversion" of Whitehead as usually understood (Hansen 2015: 13). My many points of disagreement concerning his interpretation of other thinkers—including Whitehead—are not of great interest here. What can one say then? It's perhaps a question of fit. For me the fuller question of the world as a medium begins to open up far more in the work of many of the thinkers with which Hansen disagrees, notably Massumi, Manning, Parisi, Debaise and Shaviro (and even some with whom he seems in accord, such as Judith Jones—see her disagreement with Jorge Luis Nobo on a key point for Hansen, specifically that "there appears to be no need for a 'mediating' function of creativity" [Jones 1998:63]). Hansen's framework does allow him to make a great many very useful points on the contemporary specificity of digital media and the human.

25. For at least two decades the most comprehensive and useful theory of the vector in media and political terms has been that of McKenzie Wark (e.g. 1994, 2004). Wark takes the idea of the vector from Virilio and Deleuze and does not, as far as I know, draw on Whitehead. Wark has always considered technology, including media, in the terms of the world, notably and recently in terms of the anthropocene (2015) but also earlier in terms of "first", "second" and "third" nature (2004). The political take on this is best summed up as "to the vector the spoils" (Wark 2006).

26. In this respect Donna Haraway has spoken of "a world whose grammar we may be inside of but where we may, and can, both embody and exceed its representations and blast its syntax" (Haraway and Goodeve, 2013: 122). As correct as this is, however, sometimes it seems that media and communications are themselves blasting their own syntax, and we are playing catch up. Indeed, the world often seems to blast its own syntax. Guattari writes that "Content and Expression are not attached to one another by virtue of the Holy Spirit. In the 'beginning' of assemblages of enunciation we find neither verb, nor subject, system, nor syntax ..." (2010: 45). Yet as soon as we form a discipline, model or even habit, we emphasise some syntaxes as acceptable and some as not. This is now under challenge from all sides.

27. Some recent examples: the possible development of brain-to-brain interfaces (Yong 2013); the use of sound "to selectively activate brain, heart, muscle and other cells using ultrasonic waves"—"sonogenetics" instead of optogenetics (Anon. 2015); the development of new interfaces not only in entertainment but in the military, such as helmets that are so integrated with key aircraft systems that to look can also be quite literally to aim and perhaps to fire (Golson 2015); VR projection systems that project directly onto the retina (Stevens 2013); the bicycle in Moving Image Research

Laboratory/Alanna Thain's Cinema-Out-of-the Box system in Montréal which not only transports the portable cinema to any location in the city, but powers it when there (cinema goers ride the bike in a stationary position and this charges the projector and so forth), thus transforming the conditions of cinema (see http://mirl.lab.mcgill.ca/?page_id=814). Regarding the latter, I recently watched a documentary about the rewilding of a city vacant lot, on that very vacant lot. It is hard to think of a clearer example of the acceptance of the world as medium in the design of media experience in what is a true reworking of the "cinematic apparatus."

28. I have detailed Deleuze and Guattari's account of signal and sign elsewhere (Murphie 2010) including Guattari's use of Whitehead's "grasping" (287).
29. This is not just a matter of a wild, Deleuzean intensity-driven life. Or, to put this more precisely, in such a life, everything here applies just as much to the most banal events of daily life. It is more a question of the conditions by which the world always works.
30. Thomsen's translation.
31. Whitehead differentiates between different levels at which organisms can work with contrast. Lower "organisms" do not have the same ability to work with contrast as higher "organisms". Thus they do not have the same intensity. This is also to do with different degrees of freedom between the physical and mental. I am grateful to Erin Manning for this point. What Whitehead calls "eternal objects" are carriers of potential for contrast.
32. To say that events are transitory is not to say that they have no endurance (even lightning endures, in itself, and in how it is prehended, for example a split tree or fire). Indeed, there is a kind of multi-scalar endurance of events in Whitehead's philosophy, "eternal objects", and even "enduring objects". Although these are topics for another time, Whitehead develops a concept of "societies" of actual occasions and it is societies that have a kind of complex duration (anything that has duration is a "society" for Whitehead). There is also the question of the sign and feeling in relation to what Whitehead calls conceptual prehension.

Ilona Hongisto and Bodil Marie Stavning Thomsen

The Automata of Movement: Immediations of Memory in Hu Jieming's *The Remnants of Images* (2013)

In his mixed media installation *The Remnants of Images* (2013) exhibited at the White Rabbit Gallery in Sydney, Australia (August 27, 2014 – February 1, 2015), Chinese media artist Hu Jieming (b. 1957) displays digitally remediated and re-mastered photographs from his childhood in Maoist China. In the images, a body suddenly draws from the mass, performs a dance movement or touches the face of someone in the crowd. Others perform repetitive gestures that differ from the public façade of the Maoist regime of the 1950s, '60s and '70s. A kissing couple, children playing, the flight of a bird, or an airplane looming as if suspended forever in the sky are some of the instances the gallery guest might remember from Jieming's installation. For the artist, the installation is part of an ongoing exploration of personal and collective memories and their elusive nature:

> Nations cannot survive without a history, Hu Jieming says, and people cannot live without memory. China is notorious for 'editing' the past, but personal recollections too are unreliable. Ask a group of people to recall an event they all witnessed and each one will have a different story. Looking at private photos or historical records, we learn that things we remember didn't happen as we imagine, or never took place at all.... "The past is alive," says the artist, "But it is impossible to remember it perfectly." (Anonymous 2014: 22)

In *The Remnants of Images*, Jieming approaches the past with partially animated photographs from family albums, news archives and the Internet. The images are displayed on glass screens of various sizes and stored in aged metallic filing cabinets and lockers that speak of the

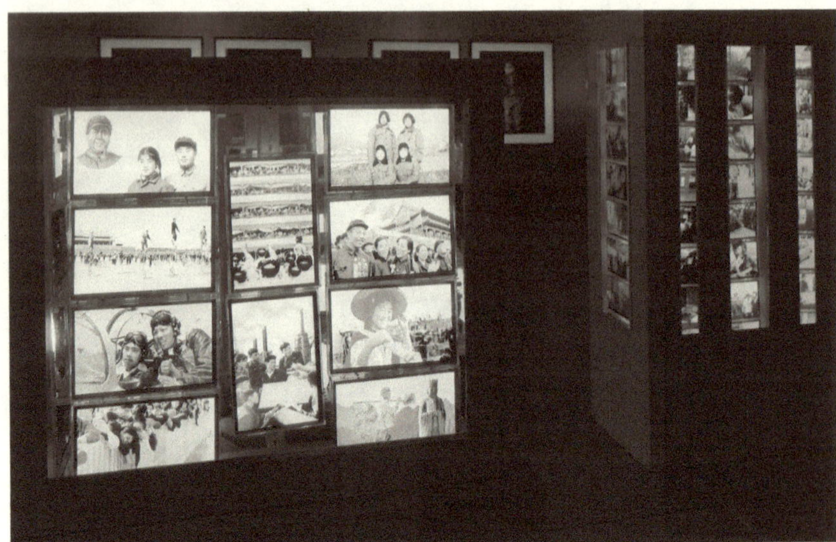

Figure 1. Hu Jieming, detail from *The Remnants of Images*. Image courtesy of the artist and the White Rabbit Gallery.

institutional facet of memory production. As the motorized drawers of the cabinets open and close and the animations mobilize the seemingly still photographs, the installation invites the visitor into a space where the past that evades accurate representations gives itself up for "immediations of memory." Here, we argue, the installation invites the viewer to engage with the liveliness of a past that we may or may not be familiar with.

In our approach, immediations of memory spell out the creative potential in the archival pieces that move beyond the determinate power of a referential past. Thus, immediation is neither a representational practice attempting to establish a more immediate experience of reality (i.e. "immediacy," see Bolter & Grusin 1999) nor a procedure to undo the bounds of archival images in order to approach reality "unmediated." In our understanding of the term, immediations of memory unlock representational stratifications—such as those construed by ideologies, perceptual habits or everyday regulations—with the purpose of reactivating the potentials of a past that has been laden with explanations and interpretations. Bypassing the call for accurate recollections, immediations of memory foreground what is still emergent in past moments that we can no longer access or come to know as such.[1]

In *The Remnants of Images*, immediation entangles with the simple artistic gesture of adding movement. The motorized archival setup and the flickering animations extract the past depicted in the images from official and personal narratives of Chinese history and stir the gallery visitor's established take on the past. The spills of unruly memories impinge on the gallery visitor in a way that calls for reconsiderations of both archival practices and the immediacy of their experience.

The Archive and the Common

At the White Rabbit Gallery, Jieming's piece was part of a group exhibition titled *Commune* that focused on the quotidian aspects of life in China, the trials and tribulations of ordinary people and their communities. The photographs in the installation portray people in collective situations and public environments: schools, factories, public transportation and meeting places. In gathering images from private and public domains and storing them in metal cabinets in the installation space, Jieming's piece raises questions about the purpose of archiving at this moment in time. The explicit repository nature of the installation setup invites the viewer to consider the intermingling of the iconic and the everyday in the images, and moreover, to wonder how these images determine our perceptions of Maoist China.

However, this is just the initial introduction to the archival dynamics of *The Remnants of Images*. As one moves around and in between the cabinets in the exhibition space, the display begins to act in a different register. What stands out is not so much the recognizable content of the images, but their spatial arrangement. As a drawer closes automatically before one has had the time to take in and reflect on the images, one is vividly reminded of the control involved in establishing and accessing archives. The mechanic noise of the motorized cabinets enhances the sentiment of a control mechanism out of one's reach.

Another thing bound to strike the gallery visitor is that the modulations of movement do not fuse into each other seamlessly. The random mechanical movement of the cabinet drawers and the flickering digital animations of the photographs create jittery patterns that escape traceable storylines. Although one eagerly spends a long time in front of each cabinet to examine the movement patterns and to follow the variations within the photograph's own motif, Hu Jieming's archive presents itself as a shimmering collection of fleeting images.

Yet, the installation refuses to postulate its ephemeral screens of memory in terms of restrictions or limitations. Instead, it points to ways in which archival images and hence the image archive in itself can be opened up and activated anew. Here, the arrangement of images into series is of importance. As the photographs, derived from different sources and representing various individuals, places and situations, are arranged into horizontal and vertical series they draw attention to the connections and disconnections between them. The uneven columns of glass screens in vertical cabinets and the shuffled horizontal rows of images in the metal drawers do not offer a linear cinematic narrative one could follow and decipher; instead, each image is given as a possible starting point for a new story. Thus, instead of offering an array of archival images that represent a past time for which the dimensions have already been settled or instead of proposing an alternative to an already established vision of the past, the installation proposes to begin again. To view each image as a possible opening to a past that cannot be redeemed as such.

Jieming's approach to the archival reminds us of another project that addresses archival politics and the question of the commune under communism. The Polish artist Marysia Lewandowska and her British collaborator Neil Cummings spent years researching the remnants of amateur film clubs in Poland. Established during the communist period and in conjunction to industrial locales, the film clubs existed outside official cultural production and professionally mediated film circles. With hundreds of film clubs in existence in the late 1960s, the network disappeared and most clubs disbanded once the regime change in 1989 closed down factories. Lewandowska and Cummings traced down club members and the amateur films produced in the early 2000s and restored a selection of films in collaboration with the amateur filmmakers under the title *Enthusiasts*. The project includes films from the 1950s to the 1980s under three thematic headings—*Love, Labour, Longing*.

Enthusiasts was first exhibited to the public at the Centre for Contemporary Art in Warsaw, Poland, in June 2004. Curated by Lukasz Ronduda in collaboration with Lewandowska and Cummings, the exhibition hosted the screenings in specially made cinemas within the galleries. In addition, the exhibition included a reconstruction of a clubroom and an archival lounge, where visitors could watch film club productions not included in the screenings at will. The collection of amateur films expresses the underbelly of cultural production in communist Poland and brings forth the rich variety of cinematic desires and practices at that time. However, the artists note that they felt a display of alternative cinema was not enough. They note that one of the fundamental issues that stuck with them from the exhibition was the need to turn archives from repositories and economies of display to collaborative spaces: "The archive designates a territory and not a particular narrative, but perhaps the archive, too, may be constituted as a creative space for engagement" (Cummings & Lewandowska 2007: 149).

Taking the idea of the archive as a communal creative space seriously, Lewandowska and Cummings set out to expand on the archival lounge and make the amateur films free online under a Creative Commons license. Their goal is to enable the downloading, re-making and re-mixing of the amateur films, and thus emphasize collaborative negotiation over the "making" of the work of art (Cummings and Lewandowska 2007: 150).

There are two things in *Enthusiasts* that are particularly useful in relation to our engagement with Hu Jieming's installation. The first has to do with intervening in the structures of ownership that determine the archived, and the second deals with the shared communal spaces created around and with archives. In a talk, Lewandowska (2015) outlined these points in relation to *Enthusiasts*. For her, the project required that the artists bend the notion of authorship from a proprietary role toward responsibility. Hence, their archival gestures—collecting, restoring and displaying Polish amateur films—were never geared towards establishing an alternative archive they would be the "owners" of. Rather, in working with amateur films, authorship began to signal responsibility for what happens to the collected films. For Lewandowska and Cummings, this translated into the necessity to pass the archived films on to future audiences, to facilitate their circulation.

Second, and what is perhaps most interesting for the present purposes, Cummings and Lewandowska speak of artworks as "nodes in networks of social exchange" (Cummings & Lewandowska 2007: 134). For them, these exchanges align with gift economies that are the underbelly of economies based on ownership. In *Enthusiasts*, restoring and screening film club productions is an act of returning a gift. This is a response to the gift the artists were given in the form of the films. Receiving and returning gifts produces a relationality of belonging in a social network. A commune, if you will.

Both *Enthusiasts* and *The Remnants of Images* raise questions about what it means to collect films and images and to display them in public institutions. Both projects move on the edges of public and private archives and reflect on what the political function of such collections can be. Equally, the institutional critique in both projects intermingles with a desire to turn archival images into common property. In *Enthusiasts*, this takes place through an engagement with copyright law and distribution strategies, whereas *The Remnants of Images* addresses the idea of the common by way of immediation. Instead of working toward truthful representations of the past, the installation seeks to activate the liveliness of a past that evades representation. The digital animations and mechanically moving archival cabinets align with a future-oriented worldview that asks how the emergent liveliness of an unruly past affects the creation of memories in the present. Thus, the ethico-political implications of Jieming's aesthetics resonate with what Félix Guattari calls "the responsibility of the creative instance with regard to the thing created" (1995: 107).

Blandness and Movement

At first sight, the visual themes of the images in Hu Jieming's installation do not seem particularly praiseworthy. Recognizable motifs from The People's Republic are displayed side by side with images of bicycles and television sets, to name just a few. However, it is precisely the bland demeanor of the images that proves significant in Hu Jieming's installation. The ordinary and insignificant motifs connect *The Remnants of Images* to a wider tradition of Chinese thought and aesthetics, where plainness is actually a desirable quality. An illustrative example might be Ai Wei Wei's sculptural installation of millions of sunflower seeds at the Turbine Hall of Tate Modern in October 2010 - May 2011. The vast amount of insignificant seeds had to be measured against the information that each sunflower was made of porcelain and was handcrafted by a huge amount of artisans. In his noteworthy essay *In Praise of Blandness* (2004), François Jullien examines *dan*—rendered *fadeur* in French, blandness in English—as a key tenet within the value system of Chinese art and even as an aesthetic ideal, such as during the Song dynasty (960-1126). For the present purposes, it is perhaps most interesting that according to Jullien, blandness does not refer to the absence of qualities, but actually articulates the possession of all attributes equally.

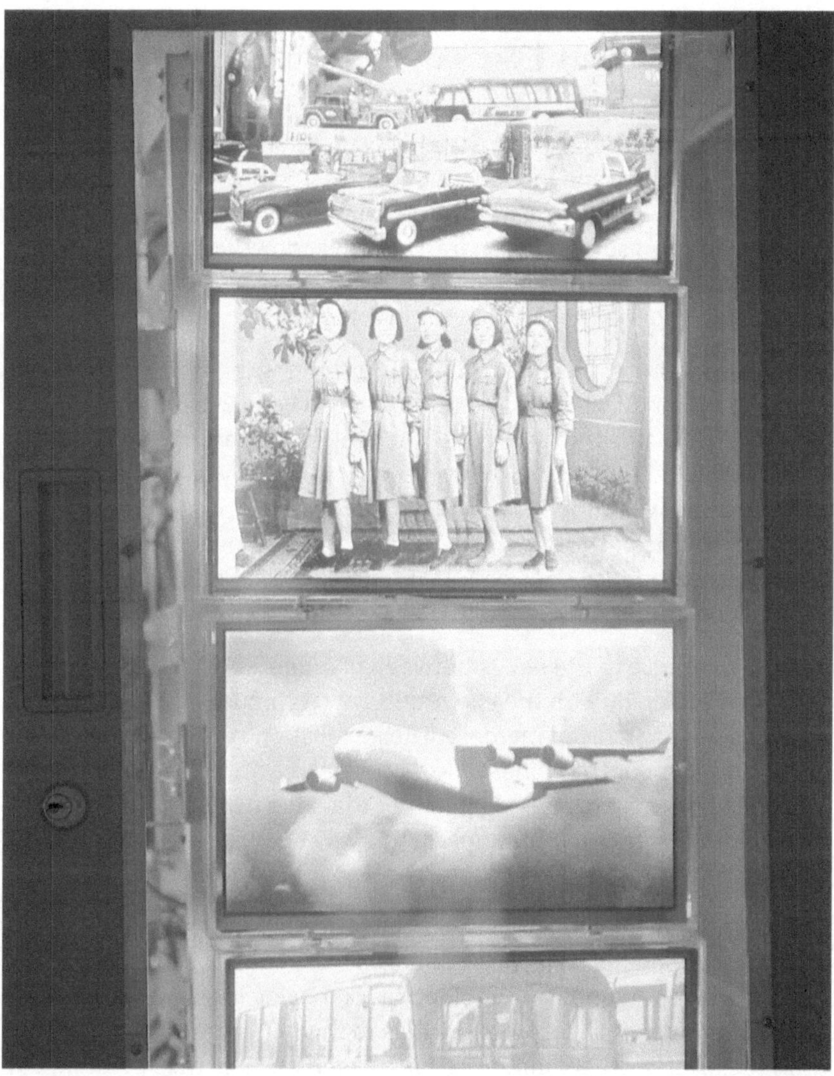

Figure 2. Hu Jieming, detail from The Remnants of Images (2013). Image courtesy of the artist and the White Rabbit Gallery.

The starting point to Jullien's exploration is Roland Barthes' struggle to describe the cultural "elsewhere" of China in relation to Western thought. To him, China—in contrast to Japan—lacked readable signs, making it an immense and ancient country "and yet very new, where meaning is so discreet as to become a rarity" (Jullien 2004: 28). Barthes activates the term blandness in describing his impressions, and Jullien re-activates it to account for a realm of perception where "meaning can never again be conceived as closed and fixed but remains open and accessible" (Jullien 2004: 33).

The openness of meaning ties in with an aesthetic sensibility where "[t]he unique and extraordinary can only be achieved through the common and plain, and blandness of expression presumes originality" (Jullien 2004: 133). Jullien's use of "the common" in relation to blandness is different from "something shared" in Lewandowska's sense. Jullien often returns to the limpidity of water to explicate how the common enables the experience of all flavors in art:

> It constitutes a transformation—a conversion—the "beyond" of which is already contained within, leading consciousness to the *root* of the real, to the *center* from which the process of things flows. It is the way of deepening (toward the simple, the natural, the essential) of detachment (from the particular, the individual, the contingent). This transcendence does not open onto another world, but is lived as immanence itself. (Jullien 2004: 143–144)

Jullien's reference to the nexus between blandness and the common resonates strikingly with the exploration of "commune" in Hu Jieming's re-activation of archived memory. The installation addresses the common fragments of Chinese past—collected from private albums and online news archives—in a manner that intertwines the bland still motifs with flicker and mutations. In this way the installation expresses the past as a common field of reference, acting in the present.

The mechanical movement of the archival display and the jerky animations open the collection of images to a series of potential interpretations. In one filing cabinet, black moving irises sweep across the photographs, as if looking for clues to their interpretation. As the drawer closes, the viewfinder-like forms keep moving, thus pointing out the impossibility of arriving at any definitive conclusions. The images remain in the realm of potential.

In a vertical cabinet showing ten screens on one side, the figure of a woman worker keeps flashing whereas the background of the image stays still, intact. On the screen just above, a group of smiling party members is forever preserved in the past tense of the photograph, yet four state flags behind them keep moving. In a third photograph that depicts aviators in the cockpit of a plane, the background is animated with a flock of birds flying through. Whether it is the background, the front, or a small detail that is animated, the experience of watching these images soon takes leave of meticulous readings of Chinese history and instead opens up to an array of flickers and jolts.

Here, the well-known themes of official parades and smiling people come to life, with a difference. The conventional photographic portrayal of a people crowding in groups or participating in official ceremonies is supplemented with animated gestures and fragments of movement patterns with which the installation opens up the sphere of the portrayed bodies and their environment. Importantly, *The Remnants of Images* does not replace the collective with the individual—as a counter-image to a state-imposed Maoist identity—but keeps the sphere of engaging with the past open by way of movement. The re-mastering of photographs and their archival display is not designed to represent an alternative private history to the official one edited by the Chinese government. In this way, the installation deviates from the tradition of visual representation that focuses on facial expressions and individual features—well known for Western audiences from the Christian tradition of painting that extends also to photography and film as described by Gilles Deleuze and Félix Guattari as the white wall, black holes "faciality" (Deleuze & Guattari 1987: 185). In *The Remnants of Images*, the supplemented movements are machine-like, autonomous, and attached to the archived photographs as "automata of movement" which are described by Deleuze in his discussion of electronic and computerized images (Deleuze 1989: 264). The tiny iterative quiverings that infuse the photographs with autonomous movements thus have a potential to work diagrammatically in the archival material put forth by Hu Jieming. As the automatic movement mutates the form of photographic posture it also accentuates a possible reversibility and re-organization of a memory or an imagination of the past. The automatic, odd movements and gestures and the combinations of pictures from vast reservoirs of private, public and internet collections make the exhibited images escape their signifying function of combining bodies to fit a specific space and time in history.

Put differently, these purely automatic movements thus enable a diagrammatic working across time, bound to affect the gallery guest. Deleuze's notion of "the signaletic material" that underlines how the "non-language-material" of the visible images of film escapes clear signification could be activated here (Deleuze 1989: 29; Thomsen 2012). The "signaletic material" is to Deleuze neither "enunciation" nor "utterances" but only "an *utterable*" (Deleuze 1989, 29; Deleuze's emphasis). The awareness of this signaletic material might be raised by stressing the cut between images (as in the films of Jean-Luc Godard). Deleuze also brings out how directors like Fritz Lang, Carl Th. Dreyer and Akira Kurosawa have activated "the spiritual automata" by way of robots, dummies, idiots and androids to stress how the "automatic movement" of film can potentially communicate a "shock which arouses the thinker in you" (Deleuze 1989: 156). The surplus *utterable* of visible images can thus hold a direct affective impact that to Deleuze is a requirement for thinking. Deleuze uses Spinoza's term "the spiritual automata" to transversally connect the sensation of the automatic movement of film with the ability to actually think in acknowledging that new thoughts are produced by way of sensing affect (Deleuze 1989: 156; Thomsen 2001).

In his attribution of automatic gestures to the motifs of the archival images, Hu Jieming's artwork also potentially de-territorializes the historical signs denoting Mao's China to the gallery guest. New thoughts can be activated, if the gallery guest moves with the blandness of the ordinary bodies and things displayed. Once they have escaped their historical framings, these motifs can be seen anew as inhabiting the shared space (with the gallery guest) of the *utterable*. The repetitions, mechanical movements and animated bodies of *The Remnants of Images*, in other words, places an emphasis on the *remnants* as what can be *immediated*. For, even though the significations of Mao's China are explicitly there in the frozen motifs of the photographs, the event has definitely "perished" in Brian Massumi's words (Massumi 2015b: 154). The added "automata of movement" that activates the "spiritual automata" enhances that the image remnants are "ready for reactivation" (Massumi 2015b: 154). It is thus important to stress Massumi's point—that immediation contains both "the emergence and the perishing, the conformal persistence and rearising, the cut of the new and the continuity, the physical and the mental, together, as mutually imbricated modes of process" (Massumi 2015b: 155).

It is on this level that Hu Jieming's installation inaugurates a commune —not by sharing a memory archive, but by a shared sensation of *utterables* initiated by the "motor automata" of the images. In this way, the installation offers a transitory experience from stratified archived memories to immediations of the remnant potentials of the images. This again reactivates François Jullien's explanation of blandness as "a transitory stage constantly threatened with obliteration":

> Transitory between two poles: on the one side, a too-tangible, sterile, and limited manifestation; on the other, an overly volatile evanescence, where everything disappears and is forgotten. Caught between the dangers of signifying too much and of ceasing to function as a sign at all, the bland sign is just barely one. It consists not of the absence of signs but of a sign that is in the process of emptying itself of its signifying function, on the verge of becoming absent: as marks of an invisible harmony, or scattered traces. (Jullien 2004: 93)

The digitally applied motor animations foreground simple movements of arms, legs, clothing, wheels and the like next to an immobile background or foreground. The gallery guest encounters small, reiterated patterns of movement, performed by hitherto motionless bodies that belong to another historical time and ideological space. Hu Jieming's artwork transversally creates an interpellation as if from the "motor automata" of how individuals are formed according to ideology—in dialogue with Althusser's definition of ideology as "the imaginary relationship of individuals to their real conditions of existence" (Althusser 1972: 162). According to Althusser, this imaginary bond becomes palpable when an individual reacts by turning around when hearing a policeman's public interpellation "Hey, you there!" By this very move the individual becomes a social subject that can indeed be subjugated to the law (Althusser 1972: 174). Hu Jieming's interpellation by way of the "hey, you there!" of the "motor automata" might, on the other hand, allow the gallery guest a line of flight away from the workings of ideology. The gesture of immediation in Hu Jieming's artwork holds the possibility of interpellating the "spiritual automata" that might enable a search for the blandness or the interconnectedness of thought, body, activity and event—then and now. And even though the gallery guest might not be Chinese nor even know anything about China then or now, an invitation to embark on a memory path of re-activated remnants is established. As an interpellated "you" invoked from the past by this person's or thing's "automatic movement," "you" instantly want to know more about the atmosphere of the then ordinary situation of what was utterable or not utterable within this specific ideology.[2]

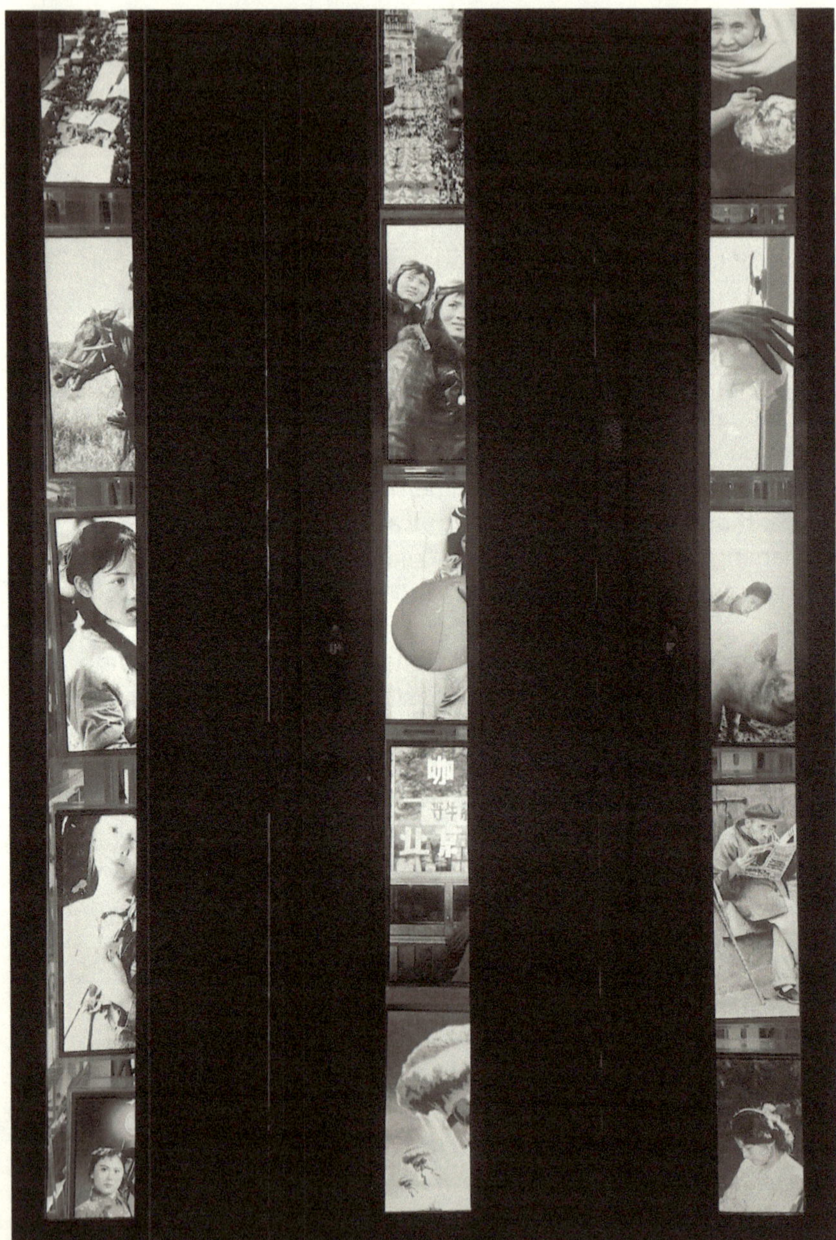

Figure 3. Detail from The Remnants of Images (2013). Image courtesy of the artist and the White Rabbit Gallery.

Life and Laughter

The Remnants of Images presents itself as an archival installation where the power of the past is literally evoked by giving the photographic momentum a new "filmic" dimension. This dimension, however, does not entail a narrative counter-history to official recollections edited by the Chinese government, but comes with playful excess that makes habitual ways of remembering stumble. In the installation, the captured moments from personal and public archives are transformed into flows toward futurity the way a metaphor can dissolve into metonymy or pure expression.

Hu Jieming's "post-cinematic" interventions in official histories and personal stories transpose archived memories to flickers and fluctuations. Here, cultural narratives and personal stories give way to archival excess freed from the photographs stored in the battered filing cabinets. With the different animations, the images on display become expressive of dimensions that are not coded in them. To reiterate, they become signaletic material for memories to come.

Here we would like to turn to Deleuze's short text on stuttering in *Essays Critical and Clinical*. Deleuze remarks that stuttering is "an affect of language and not an affectation of speech" (1997: 110). He mentions among other authors Beckett, who makes his texts move and roll by entering depicted action in the middle, where "the characters speak like they walk or stumble" (1997: 111). The animated excess of the archived images in Hu Jieming's piece makes archived memories—both public and private ones—stutter. The animations open up and let loose the stutter of archived memory, its stumbling underbelly, if you like:

> Everyone can talk about his memories, invent stories, state opinions in his language; sometimes he even acquires a beautiful style, which gives him adequate means and makes him an appreciated writer. But when it is a matter of digging under the stories, cracking open the opinions, and reaching regions without memories, when the self must be destroyed, it is certainly not enough to be a "great" writer, and the means must remain forever inadequate. Style becomes nonstyle, and one's language lets an unknown foreign language escape from it, so that one can reach the limits of language itself and become something other than a writer, conquering fragmented visions that pass through the

> words of a poet, the colors of a painter, or the sounds of a musician. (Deleuze 1997: 113)

While acknowledging and addressing the stratified and controlled nature of archived memory, *The Remnants of Images* activates regions that are "without memories." Facing a past that evades thorough and accurate representations, the installation works with the "remnants" of mediated images—archival excess—and turns it into signaletic material for memorywork in the gallery space. The archival excess that gets activated and expressed in the installation does not belong to public histories or private recollections; instead, the animated images in the automated filing cabinets produce a transversal cut to both domains and call out for less stratified visions of Mao's China.

The gallery guest might experience the stuttering animations as utterables or immediations that can neither be formed as enunciations nor utterances. Rather, they are *utterables* that will eventually be taken up in language and molded into utterances, but, until then, it is replete with potential (Deleuze 1989: 29). The archival excess in Jieming's installation can precisely be sensed as an utterable; signaletic yet a-signifying matter. An endlessly jumping animated male figure and a solitary hand waving in the crowd do not belong to individual or official memories; they signal memories of Maoist China that have not yet taken the form of cultural memories nor personal recollections. A flickering female figure in the midst of agricultural work or a group of unicyclists, who are forever suspended between the position captured in the photograph and its animation, present the gallery visitor with a charge of lively potential that escapes rigid archival structures and the memories they produce.

However, what is perhaps most striking in Hu Jieming's immediations of memory is their comic aspect. Indeed, the archival excess released in the installation setup and the animated images come with a soft humorous touch. The automatic movements of the people in the images as well as the motorized movements of the battered filing cabinets offer a retrospective position of gentle comic critique of the ways in which life in Mao's China was controlled. This is in line with Henri Bergson's definition of the comic as the combination of "the illusion of life and the distinct impression of a mechanical arrangement" (Bergson 2009: 54–55). The repetitive gestures added onto the photographs and the random mechanical movement of the archival cabinets punctuate conventional approaches to images of the past as well as their storage and display. Interventions in the images break established ways of thinking about the past and thus open the field of archival memory to new approaches.

The Remnants of Images, however, is not satisfied with retrospective critique. Hu Jieming's work addresses the past in an immanent relation to the present, and hence any critique of the past intertwines with what takes place in the present. This resonates with Marysia Lewandowska's postulation of the archive as an open field: "I think artists often use archives in order to connect not necessarily with the past, but really to point to how certain processes in the present are connected to precedents in the past" (Lewandowska 2015: 51:50).

The automata of movement in *The Remnants of Images*, then, does not address only what took place in Mao's China, but concerns also contemporary ways of engaging with images and archives. The commune thus proposed is not one forever sealed in the past, but it is actively fashioned in the present. One way of thinking about the commune proposed by *The Remnants of Images* is to continue with Bergson's formula of the comic as "something mechanical in something living" (2009: 60).

Whereas Bergson argues that laughter ripples up when flows of life are punctuated with awkward, mechanical missteps—such as Charlie Chaplin's aberrant walk—it is equally possible to think about laughter and joy swelling up when life is freed from stratified mechanisms. In *The Remnants of Images*, this happens when the animations crack open both official narratives and personal recollections. The archival excess that spills out is charged with liveliness that impinges on the gallery visitor as a sensation of overwhelming joy. Here, the resulting laughter no longer belongs to retrospective criticism but resonates in the gallery space as a shared sensation of *utterables*, activated by the stuttering sounds and movements of the installation's "motor automata." Activated by the signaletic material or the bland sign devoid of clear signifying functions, the shared event-space of joint sensations offers immediate access to the potentials of a commune. This space can be shared in the same way as jests, jokes or puns are shared amongst a group. As Bergson underlines, the shared immediation of laughter is social(izing) and creates momentary and relational recognitions of mental space.

Like in Marysia Lewandowska's descriptions of the experiments with an-archiving the remnants of films in the Polish film-archive from the 1960s, the proposed commune of the barely utterable is an open field. Its consistency is neither fixed nor secure, but held together on a molecular level within the social gesture of laughter (Bergson 2009: 20). Thus, *The Remnants of Images* inaugurates an ephemeral commune of gallery visitors who are offered the chance to remember with archival excess; the liveliness of a past that cannot be redeemed as such.

Notes

1. The analysis of immediations of memory in Hu Jieming's piece was first presented as a paper by Bodil Marie Stavning Thomsen at the NECS conference, summer 2015. Our collaborate reworking of this paper also echoes Ilona Hongisto's discussion of documentary imagination in terms of the *more-than-referential* of photographs and archival images. Hongisto argues that documentary films capture and express what is still emergent in still images by framing them, a cinematic act that endows the documentary with a capacity to imagine. (Hongisto 2015: 25–63; 2013)
2. In his *The Machinic Unconscious. Essays in Schizoanalysis*, Félix Guattari reaches a similar line of flight in discussing how "machinic rhizomes" can form an "unmediated relation between systems of coding and material flows" (Guattari 2011: 102).

Toni Pape

Resurrecting Television: Memories of the Future and the Anarchival Politics of Joy in *Arrested Development*

Remembering Feeling

Think of a film or television series that marked you as a teenager. Remember it for a moment.

What is it that returns as a memory? Is it the story, a character, or a particular audiovisual style? Or is it, more vaguely and more intuitively, the feeling of that film or program? If you had to describe that feeling, that sensation, how would you articulate it? How exactly did that film, that television series *move* you?

This feeling—the affective tone that moving images can sustain for hours, months or, in the case of some television programs, even years—is something that the disciplines within the wider field of media studies rarely speak of. Wilfully or not, they often ignore that which is the most memorable about a film or TV series or novel, that which probably moved most of us to study and practice one or the other of these media in the first place: a singular aesthetic experience. This feeling is one of the ways in which artworks act in the world; it is also where their ethical and political projects partially play out. Were you moved to tears or laughter? Did you move in fear or fury? You name your felt singularity if you can. A radically empirical theory of immediation that starts from experience can help articulate the felt relations through which art is lived as well as their ethico-political potential.[1] The radical empirical impetus of this chapter consists in including the often-excluded *memory* of *affect*.

This is what the practice of reviving cancelled TV shows requires us to think as it draws on remembered feelings to reactivate a seemingly defunct past. A considerable number of fictional TV series that were cancelled years ago now return to the screen in various ways. Consider the TV series *Veronica Mars* that ran on the network The CW (formerly UPN) from 2004 to 2007. Released to theaters in March 2014, the *Veronica Mars* movie revisits the heroine and former teenage private eye, now a lawyer in New York City. In May 2014, the channel Fox ran a ninth "limited event season" of *24*, which had gone off the air four years earlier. The HBO show *The Comeback* originally aired its first season in 2005, after which it was cancelled. Nine years later, in November 2014, the series had a comeback, with HBO airing a full second season. In the fall of 2015, NBC aired *Heroes: Reborn*, a miniseries that revisits the universe of the TV show *Heroes* (2006-2010). Fox has scheduled a revival of *The X-Files* (1993-2002) for January 2016 and the cable network Showtime announced in October 2014 that a new season of *Twin Peaks* (ABC, 1990-1991) would be coming to the network.[2] Clearly, there is a market for the recycling of television's past, a trend that is enabled by a number of conditions which will be discussed below in due course. Beyond these conditioning factors, however, the trend towards resurrecting television series also speaks to a changed experience of the medium and its past. There is no market without desire. An engagement with the singular comedic project of *Arrested Development* (Fox 2003-2006, Netflix 2013) will show that resurrected programs can modulate the ways in which one encounters television and participates in its attention economy. This is not least because programs that return from the past challenge conventional notions of televisual time.

Televisual Time and Memories of the Future

The time of television has often been conceived as an ephemeral, yet persistent present. As early as 1962, Umberto Eco wrote that "the aspect of television that would seem most interesting and fruitful to our research is also *its most characteristic, unique to the medium*: namely, live broadcasts" (1989: 107, emphasis added). Liveness constitutes "the very particular 'time' of television, so often identifiable with real time" (106). According to Raymond Williams, the "defining characteristic" of broadcast television consists in the organization of programming into "a continuous flow" that supplants programs, commercials and announcements to keep viewers in its thrall (2003: 86, 95).[3] Here too, there is an understanding that the medium harnesses the now of experience to generate its unrelenting, blurry presence.

Mary Ann Doane holds that the "major category of television is time," and more precisely "an insistent 'present-ness' ... a celebration of the instantaneous" (1990: 222).

Though the importance of live broadcasting, flow, and instantaneity has been questioned and re-evaluated on many occasions,[4] these accounts point to a key aspect of the medium in previous decades. The experience of television is characterized by collective amnesia, which also leaves its mark on the field of television studies, for instance in teaching. If students in 2016 only vaguely know of programs like *Twin Peaks* or *Sex and the City*, this is not because they are ill-bred philistines, but because the very notion of a *canon* does not operate in television studies in the same way it does in, say, film studies. And, from my perspective, that is not a bad thing. There is a legitimacy and felt necessity to revisiting the history of film—going by regions, periods, currents, genres, *auteurs*—that the medium of television does not seem to foster in the same way.[5] The experience of individual programs comes and goes like little habits we pick up and drop. If we believe Umberto Eco, we are in fact giving in to the infantile pleasure of repetition that leads us to delight in "always and ever the same story" when we watch a serial on TV: every week, series like *Columbo* or even *Dallas* habitually contract into a repetition of the same narrative schema (1994: 86-87). In this sense, one might argue, the experience of television is more concerned with a continuous re-inscription of the present than a revisitation of the past.

But *habit* is perhaps more productive than this account gives it credit for. Habit may well ground experience in the present, but it describes a temporal movement that exceeds the undifferentiated recurrence of a past. We might think of habit as a pulse, contracting and releasing, that composes a "living present" (Deleuze 1994: 73). That the present is alive means that it *passes*, that it enfolds the past and unfolds into the future. In other words, the force of habitual repetition neither suspends us in an instantaneous present nor shackles us to the past; it forcefully pulls us into the future. Brian Massumi emphasizes this aspect when he states that habit understood as "repetition is a recollection of what has not yet come—a memory of the future" (2015b: 64). On the one hand, then, habit must be understood as both self-reinforcing and as carrying a charge of futurity. As a medium of repetition, television certainly crafts habits that pull us into their next contraction. These habits include not only various modes of viewing from weekly airing schedules to binge-watching. (The "just one more" of binge-watching is also the "again" of repetition.) The habitual movement of television also sweeps up production schedules, distribution models, and narrative structures. In this sense, habit is indeed the pre-forming of an indeterminate future. On the other hand, the workings of a memory of the future are not confined to the re-inscription of a regular (or regulated) present. In fact, it can persist without contracting and hold itself in reserve over long durations. Following David Lapoujade, a memory of the future can be described as "something which has been present, that has been sensed, but *that has not been acted*" (Lapoujade 2013: 22). This unacted past retains an "explosive force" that is held in abeyance to be released in a creative act (89; see also 8-9). This is the case of many a cancelled TV show whose aesthetic, political or ethical project was cut short for pragmatic (mainly economic) reasons. Something that remains to be acted in images and sound emerges from the past and appeals to the present. Resurrected television series introduce this sense of a distant past and its lasting potential for future creation into the media ecology of television.[6] In this, revivals must be distinguished from other televisual repetitions in the forms of reruns, remakes or reboots. Instead of airing the same material again or completely re-imagining and re-casting a preexisting program, the purpose of reviving a series is to give new life to the original incarnation, to continue the story of *this* particular character or group of characters, to reactivate an experience of pastness.

In previous decades, the cancellation of a show would indicate the definite end of a program in that specific setup. As James Poniewozik notes in *Time* magazine:

> Once upon a time, that would have been it, case closed. *Veronica Mars* was just one in a long line of series loved too hard by too few: *My So-Called Life*, *Freaks and Geeks*, name your passion.... Today, TV shows die the way characters do on *24* (coming back in May!): unless you cut off the head and burn the body, they can always rise again. (Poniewozik 2014: 56)

The increasing frequency at which what Poniewozik also calls "zombie shows" rise from the dead is enabled by a number of conditions. First of all, television programs no longer disappear as quickly as they used to. While this has been the case ever since the advent of the VCR, the availability of TV fiction has considerably increased through new modes of distribution such as DVD, video-on-demand (VOD) services and illegal file sharing or streaming. On the one hand, these innovations have allowed the industry to extend chains of distribution and fund productions through additional sources of income (besides advertisement or subscriptions).[7] On the other hand, they have created the possibility for wider audiences and fan communities to develop *after* the original airing of a program. For instance, the viewer data for *Arrested Development*, thoroughly mined by VOD service Netflix, indicated that "whereas most canceled cult shows maintain a small, diehard fan base, *Arrested Development*'s was getting bigger" (Poniewozik 2013). Thus, data mining must also be understood as a contributing factor as it makes the long-term development of fan cultures more transparent. Finally, a variety of new funding models allow for programs to return outside the more conventional production channels: besides the new content providers such as Netflix and Amazon Studios, these models include crowdfunding and selling shows between networks and their different audiences.[8] These factors do not 'cause' the resurrection of TV shows in a straightforward way. Rather, they must be thought of as enabling conditions in a shifted media ecology that makes it possible for a memory of the future to be activated and propelled towards a resurgence in the present.

While the recent development activates individual memories of the future, it certainly does not invent them. Past experience always holds lasting intensities and creative potentials. Media pasts are no exception in this. Who knows how many desired revivals do not find the right conditions, how many unproduced scripts are lying in a desk drawer? Even so, that past is not dead and gone, but still animates the contemporary, waiting to make ingress in a present that cannot shake it off. What television discovers through revivals is that novelty is not a thing of the future, to be revealed once we overcome remaining obstacles; it can be launched from the past once the conditions for such an emergence are in place. A concept of immediation challenges us to think these relational complications of the present by pastness and potential and to consider how such immaterial yet felt aspects like memory and affect can be composed and how they factor into the actual experience of media.

The Comedic Topologies of *Arrested Development*

Mitchell Hurwitz's *Arrested Development* has drawn on a nonlinear notion of time since its very beginning. As a short introduction, it may suffice to say that the show tells "the story of a wealthy family who lost everything, and the one son who had no choice but to keep them all together" ("Top Banana," Season 1, Episode 2). Indeed, nothing much changes about this situation during the first three seasons of the show (Fox, 2003-2006). "It's arrested development," after all. Despite Michael Bluth's best efforts at keeping his dysfunctional family together, his selfish parents—George who's been arrested for defrauding investors of the Bluth Company; the fabulously cruel matriarch Lucille; as well as his spoilt siblings, magician Gob, socialite Lindsay, and grad student Buster— continuously manage to upset the family fates. Until the end of the third season, nothing much has changed for the Bluths. The same goes for character development: besides the growing attraction between the children of the family, cousins George Michael and Maeby, and Buster's loss of his left hand to a loose seal (read: Lucille), none of the characters undergo any growth to speak of. If anything, they become more set in their ways. What, then, is it, in the midst of so much apparent stasis that moves the series?

Arrested Development works as a growing archive of family trivia, as a web of cross-references that becomes denser with every episode. The show's unconventional comedy relies partly on the ways in which the obnoxious relatives play each other and play off of each other. Thus, as the plot forever treads on the spot, eternally stuck at square one of developmental arrest, the viewer gradually accumulates an abundance of the Bluth's quirks and oddities, their individual challenges and recurring failures. Indeed, much of the joy that the show creates arises from the flashes of recognition one experiences as one of the relatives rubs another's shoulder (a family habit that expresses both compassion and contempt), as Lindsay's husband and "nevernude" Tobias unintentionally conveys his suppressed homosexuality again, or as George Michael proves his inability to catch anything yet another time. In this way, the aesthetic experience of watching *Arrested Development* relies heavily on the creation and reactivation of a network of memories. Yet, unlike other TV genres that heavily rely on repetition, such as the traditional sitcom with its catchphrases and running jokes, *Arrested Development* tweaks repetition and habit in such a way as to allow for the unexpected. This has to do with two contrasting rhythms of the series: the speed of the narration and the slowness with which individual comic references return. In terms of plot development and dialogue, *Arrested Development* moves extremely fast, rarely allowing the viewer enough time to trace all the ramifications of a character's actions or consider the elusive references of a repartee. The editors of an online wiki for the series write: "Each episode crams enough jokes, flashbacks, cut-aways, call-backs, call-forwards, and subtle background jokes in 22 minutes that each viewing reveals more jokes."[9] Every encounter with the image repotentializes it. In terms of individual call-backs, however, the show can be extremely slow and take episodes or even seasons to make reference again to a most insignificant plot element. Here is a small but noteworthy example: In the episode "Justice is Blind" (season 1, episode 18), Lindsay breaks her heel on a statue of the Ten Commandments in front of the courthouse and protests for it to be removed (to insist on the separation between church and state). Twenty-two episodes later, in "Righteous Brothers" (s. 2, ep. 18), we see the statue again during one of the family's numerous visits to/escapes from the courthouse; this time the statue is—more safely—placed on the courthouse lawn. Lindsay's activist work has borne its meagre fruit.[10] On this second occurrence, no further reference is made to the statue; it is very easy to miss. And yet, there it is, carefully placed for the attentive viewer to spot. It is the *smallest joke*, one that probably does not land with the majority of the audience, let alone on a first viewing. It is a *minor* trait of the image—much less noteworthy than the episode's plotline or the characters' relations—that activates a past and pulls it into the present. All of a sudden, these two moments, separated in linear time by more than a season, move into experiential proximity. In the moment of recognition, the present episode is comically charged with layers of past. Moreover, the trait, if noticed, retroactively reconfigures the past, pulling out a thread of thought that was weaving itself through the series all along. Was the statue of the Ten Commandments more important than initially thought, perhaps as a sort of standard to measure the crooked morals of the Bluth family? Does it occur in more episodes other than the two mentioned above? These questions bring out the third aspect of the minor jokes in *Arrested Development*: they destabilize the conventional relation between foreground and background.[11] Here, the set is not merely a container for the protagonists' banter as in many traditional sitcoms (the living room, the kitchen, the café/bar). The Bluths inhabit a *milieu* through which the series' ethico-aesthetic project comes to expression. In short, because of this humour in the visually, temporally, and narratively minor mode, it is never quite certain where comedy happens or exactly when it is going to strike in *Arrested Development*. This is because the comedy of this show isn't topical; that is, pertaining only to the episode at hand: this joke right here, right now. Instead, the comedy of *Arrested*

Development is topological: the series is a dynamic spacetime that folds back and forth on itself in a continuous form-taking, creating new points of contact between its various elements. In so doing, *Arrested Development* continuously remixes characters, locations, props and past events.

Unlike conventional catchphrases or running gags, this remix of jokes does not feed off the regular re-performance of the same line by the same character. Catchphrases produce a little smile of recognition. The hilarity of *Arrested Development*'s persistent jokes, by contrast, results from the show's ability to come to a recurrence differently each time, to wrest a feeling of surprise from the differential between the already known and the new set of conditions. In the minor comedy of the series, the components of the image behave like highly reactive free radicals that can fuse with almost any other component that comes their way in unpredictable ways. *While the catchphrase closes down or resolves intensity into a satisfying punch line, comedy in the minor key opens up and increases the intensity of the comic event.* On many occasions, the series goes to some narrative and aesthetic lengths to perform a well-known joke or character stereotype in an entirely new way and manages to inject the familiar with a certain amount of novelty. This minor twist is the spark to the powder reserve of as-yet backgrounded joy: the topological comedy of *Arrested Development* rides on past amusement to intensify the burst of joy in the present. The two forces of this movement are mutually reinforcing: memories of joy help leverage a present burst of laughter which, in its inventive variation on the theme, leaves a ripple on the surface of the comedic complex that may well up into another surge of delight as it encounters a fellow current running through the show. The result is a nonlinear "archiving of affective immediacy" that feeds the *experiential milieu* of *Arrested Development* (Massumi 2015c: 84). Following Alanna Thain, we might also describe this as an "anarchive" in which the past is constantly stirred up, remixed and reactivated (Thain 2010). What is at stake is not the archive as an orderly repository of information,[12] available for consultation when needed, *if* needed, but how the past—unacted but remembered—continues to shape the present. This dynamic constitutes the singular aesthetic shape of *Arrested Development*.

This time, the term milieu does not refer to the content of the image. This experiential milieu is not the complicated fictional world depicted *in* the series but the relational field of which the series itself is a component along with the viewer, technological devices, etc. I qualify this milieu as experiential to emphasize the field effect, created in the assemblage of various components, as that which is *immediately* perceived or "directly experienced" in William James's words (1996a: 22). This conceptualization is related to current theorizations of *media ecologies*, in which "parts no longer exist simply as discrete bits that stay separate [but] set in play a process of mutual stimulation that exceeds what they are as a set" (Fuller 2005: 1). This excess can come as "an explosion, a passion or capacity," in any case it acts as a force within the world (ibid.). This aspect of an *effect* that *exceeds* the material components of the assemblage is crucial to a concept of immediation because it allows us to think lived experience itself as the arena for the ethical and political project of a media ecology.

Such an approach can create new avenues for television studies, especially the kind that has made its way into the cul-de-sac of narrative complexity. Largely following the structuralist tradition of narrative studies, it focuses on TV series as a discrete object to be analyzed for its structures, for its relation between discourse and story (as the narratological equivalents of signifier and signified). As a result, the lived experience of narrative is oftentimes ignored or reduced to a characteristic of the program itself. Thought in this way, a program's importance resolves itself in its structural components and their meaning. Research can still register that which a program composes for: an effect, a lived experience. But it has difficulty thinking this doing. Consider Jason Mittell's description of *Arrested Development* as relying on an "operational aesthetic" (2006: 35). This kind of aesthetic calls "attention to the constructed nature of the narration and ask[s] us to marvel at how the writers pulled it off; often these instances forgo realism in exchange for a formally aware baroque quality in which we watch the process of narration as a machine rather than engaging in its diegesis" (35). Mittell, too, is struck by the workings of *Arrested Development*. He stands in awe of what he repeatedly calls the "pyrotechnics" of narrative complexity (35, 36). Effects are registered: explosions everywhere. But instead of tracing the ways in which they make their way into lived experience, they are looped into self-reflexivity. Marvel and joy lead right back to the complex narrative structures from which they lifted off. "How did the writers do it?" is a question that engages with the "making of" the series rather than its aesthetic doing, with the components of the media ecology rather than the immediate experience they effectuate. It's like saying that seeing fireworks makes you think about the pyrotechnician's recipe of chemicals. As a consequence, the enjoyment that lifted off the narrative is attributed to the series as its structural element. The vitality of the experiential milieu is reduced to a merit of the series as research object. Enjoyment is reduced to prestige value.

A concept of immediation does not lead back to (narrative) structures and components. It starts from these to see what they bring into lived experience and follows these effects. In the case of *Arrested Development*, the field effect of the nonlinear folding of multiple pasts unfolding into new comic bursts is a feeling of *vitality*. As the series twists and turns its past into novel encounters, the most palpable experiential yield is a steady undercurrent of joyful agitation, a vibrant milieu-wide grin. The corollary for composing the milieu is a heightened attention and elastic perception that allow for nonlinear aesthetic, affective, and narrative tracings across the comedic topology. In this way, the comedy of *Arrested Development* functions as a "social gesture" (Bergson 2009: 20). According to Henri Bergson, the social dimension of comic laughter consists precisely in resisting the "easy automatism of acquired habits" and perceptual "rigidity" through which life, both individual and collective, settles into stale circuits of action and reaction. Minor comedy in its radical freedom throws sticks into these perceptual circuits and "softens down whatever the surface of the social body may retain of mechanical inelasticity" (19-21). Bergson's argument is one for collective vitality: the comic is "a living thing" through which a society "obtain[s] from its members the greatest possible degree of elasticity and sociability" as conditions for "living well" (2, 21, 19). In other words, comedy is a way of life to make more of itself. Thus, if the functional principle of *Arrested Development*'s comedic milieu is a memory of the future, the field effect is comedic *joy* understood as the "self-affirming value of the process itself," as the "immediate experience of a qualitative 'more' to life, a surplus value of life that is lived intensely, such that its very living is its own reward" (Massumi 2015c: 70).

The Anarchival Politics of Joy

In order to grasp the social and political valence of this joy more specifically, it is necessary to determine the "easy automatisms" that *Arrested Development* counteracts. Which perceptual circuits and social rigidities does the show allow us to break with?

It is worth remembering here that the series is about a filthy rich, lazy family and its dubious business practices. The Bluths will do anything and hoodwink anyone (including family members) to make a buck and maintain their standard of living. They are the infamous 1%. In fact, George Bluth Sr. himself presciently contributes to the growing housing bubble: his "light treason" consists in selling prefab homes to Sadam Hussein ("Visiting Ours," Season 1, Episode 6), thus linking the nightmare of the 2008 financial crisis to the other American nightmare, the war in Iraq. After the family business goes down, it comes as a shock to the Bluths that they might actually have to work in order to make a living. When Michael insists that his sister Lindsay get a job, she, who sees herself more as a philanthropist doing charity, can't help but find Michael's obsession with remunerated work "materialistic" ("Key Decisions," Season 1, Episode 4). The Bluths are an example of neoliberalism's self-interested subjects caught up in a cycle of desire–consumption–satisfaction. Their rigid mentality and social ineptitude are the real star of the show: arrested development. The series' politico-aesthetic project consists in moving beyond the capitalist modes of (media) consumption to the extent that the joy it creates as a qualitative surplus value of life is irreducible to the quantitative surplus value of capital.

To clarify this, I will follow Brian Massumi in distinguishing joy from the "infernal alternative" between (deferred) satisfaction and instant gratification (Massumi 2015c: 72). The important difference is that both satisfaction and instant gratification put the self-interested subject center-stage thereby reducing fielded joy to an individual attribute. They consume the vitality of the experiential milieu. Consumption towards the goal of satisfaction drains experience of its anarchival richness, of the perception of unactualized potentials stirring the experiential milieu, because it primes experience for an aesthetic object that is recognizable both in content and form. This holds as much for the Bluths[13] as for our modes of TV consumption. As an example, think of the depleting effects of binge-watching a show like *24*: its real-time aesthetic of urgency is at the same time a lure for sustained consumption and the narrative trick that justifies all of Jack Bauer's unconventional methods of investigation and interrogation in the face of a threat to national security, including torture. In this particular case, the perceptual field is reduced to a kind of tunnel vision that allows for the perfect alignment of media consumption and security politics. Even though *24* is extremely suspenseful, it works from the very beginning towards the resolution of tension in the final, recognizable revelation. For this reason, "consumptive satisfaction is the antiaesthetic of capitalism," no matter for how long it is deferred (Massumi, 2015a: 72). Instant gratification, on the other hand, "is an activity that is entered into for its own sake, and is self-affirming. But it is consuming, not creative" (72). Consider the short-lived fun of casual gaming. Each mini session provides a charge of pleasure that is just as soon lost. That is why the next instantaneous hit is so tempting, even if it requires a micro-payment for continued playing. Casual gaming integrates the mini-pleasures of instant gratification with an economy of micro-transactions. Think Candy Crush.[14] The Bluths are stuck in one or the other of these modes: Michael and George Michael are the sad poster boys for deferred satisfaction; the rest of the family is constantly instantly gratified.

If I suggest that *Arrested Development* and its anarchival joy brush against the grain of these consumption habits, this is not to say that the series operates outside of market dynamics. The point is rather that, while the show was first proposed within the existing business and narrative models of network television, its low ratings and cancellation indicate that it did not function properly under those conditions. *Arrested Development* works at the limits of broadcast television's procedures for the creation of quantitative surplus value the better to enrich the experiential milieu in qualitative terms. Against the antiaesthetic of satisfaction it posits the overfullness of the image, operating on the assumption that an image's vitality cannot possibly be consumed on a single viewing, that in fact it grows the more the viewer engages with the image. This means that the aesthetic field is continuously recharged with potential perceptions, the more so as the viewer develops her sensitivities for perceiving across the entire surface of the image and across the living archive of episodes. Thus, if "capitalism is the process of converting qualitative surplus value of life into quantifiable surplus value," then *Arrested Development*'s ethico-aesthetic project consists in mediating a mockery of the latter in order to intensify the immediate sensation of the former (Massumi, 2015c: 77).

Arrested Development is a situated alter-economy that sends ripples across the smooth neoliberal seas which well up into waves and culminate in a series of "splashes," with comedic joy as the sparkling "foam, feathery and frolicsome," that dances at the crest of the wave (Massumi 2015c: 42 passim; Bergson 2009: 200).

Coming Back

What propels a defunct program into a revival is this anarchival potential to inflect the present's more mechanical habits, to recharge the perceptual field, and to propose alternative, directly lived modes of thought. Of course, this potential can just as well be captured for the purposes of telling the same old story within the same old format to encourage the same old modes of consumption. One could show that is what happened in the case of *24*'s revival. Though shortened from a slightly outdated (and more expensive) season model of 24 episodes to a twelve-episode "event season," the show still follows American hero Jack Bauer in real-time as he saves the world once more from terrorists and traitors. And, picking up the theme of drone warfare, Jack Bauer shows us in half an action-packed day that unmanned aerial vehicles are indeed evil weapons in the hands of evil people but can safeguard the geopolitical order when operating under Western democratic control. *24: Live Another Day* is a zombie of post-9/11 security politics.

Anarchival memories of the future do not repeat the past but create an opening for the unacted to ingress in the world. One of the things *Arrested Development* sparked *after* its cancellation is a wiki page on which fans collectively map the major and minor comedic traits of the show, to enrich future viewings of already existing episodes.[15] The growing online fan community relied on post-broadcast distribution through DVD and Netflix. Inversely, the encyclopedic mapping that wikis enable and foster rewatching. New modes of distribution as well as watching and fan activities are mutually beneficial. *Arrested Development* belatedly took advantage of this. It can be said that the same complexity that sealed the show's death on broadcast television is also what gave it its unexpected afterlife.

More importantly, though, the show functioned differently when it returned for its fourth season on Netflix. Instead of comfortably settling into the new, seemingly optimal Netflix distribution model, *Arrested Development* explored the limits of what is possible within the changed media ecology of TV. This becomes evident in the way the show's writing harnesses Netflix' strategy of publishing entire seasons at once. Usually, this model is thought of as targeting viewers and inciting binge-watching, although writers have taken this development into account and adapted the writing conventions for television (see e.g. Klarer 2014). *Arrested Development* pushes this development to its limit when it largely abandons linear narration altogether: if all the episodes of one season are available at the same time, why insist on linear succession? For example, the calamitous events immediately following the ending of the third season are recounted seven times throughout the entire fourth season,[16] each version offering the perspective of a different Bluth family member, each proposing a new, slightly different beginning to the same line of events. The show stretches a scene of about five minutes in length across its entire season and meticulously pieces it together as it moves through it again and again and again. This also means that by episode five you are hardly any further in terms of narrative progression than you were in episode two. You are literally still watching the same scene (and then some). Therefore you might as well watch them out of the suggested order. This is arrested development in the times of Netflix: the show challenges the received conventions for writing, distribution and reception to intensify both the stasis of its plot and the nonlinear foldings of its topological comedy (not without frustrating numerous critics and fans). In this way, *Arrested Development* recharges its anarchival practice with futurity, giving the fourth season itself several curious afterlives: Only days after its initial release, a first chronological re-edit of the entire season appeared online. Such re-edits are anarchival in their profound engagement with the source material, the meticulous process of re-mapping it towards coherence, and the animated fan discussions they give rise to. In the meantime, creator Mitchell Hurwitz is himself preparing a re-edited version of the season, complete with new voice-over narration, also in preparation for what's next.[17] Even though this may constitute a return to linear narrative progression, it is still the working of the anarchive, not least because such a comprehensive re-edit by the original showrunner is, to my knowledge, unprecedented in the history of television. The anarchive is what generates the force to transform itself in the most unexpected ways. It is the potential that stirs in and around media, a potential to act in the world, to enable new immediate encounters. As a concept, the anarchive is indispensable to a theory of immediation, which does not focus on what media mean or signify but wants to come to grips with what they do, how they inflect life. Did you cry or laugh? Were you scared or angry? And which other feelings were there that aren't as easily pinned down but nonetheless color the fabric of experience? These stirrings are the workings of the anarchive; the work of a concept of immediation is to bring them into thought.

Notes

1. In his *Essays in Radical Empiricism*, William James proposes that, "[t]o be radical, an empiricism must neither admit into its constructions any element that is not directly experienced, nor exclude from them any element that is directly experienced" (1996a: 22). This chapter is an attempt to take the direct experience of media as a starting point and see where else that can lead thought in the field of television studies. The argument proposes that it can lead to the politicality of immediation or what will later be called an anarchival politics of joy. This consideration of the relation between aesthetic experience and ethics/politics is informed by the philosophy of Félix Guattari and in particular his book *Chaosmosis* (Guattari 1995: esp. 98-118).
   For a theory that takes aesthetic experience as its starting point, the distinction between art and non-art is secondary. Provided that all its "elements" and singular conditions are accounted for, any experience counts for a radical empiricism, be it of "art," "media," or another aspect of reality. This chapter considers television art on the grounds of its rigorous composition for singular aesthetic experiences.
2. All examples mentioned here originally ran on the US networks mentioned in parentheses. For the announcement of the *Twin Peaks* revival see: http://www.sho.com/video/33371/a-special-twin-peaks-announcement
3. Williams famously based his conception of flow on his confusing experience of American broadcast television: "I can still not be sure what I took from that whole flow. I believe I registered some incidents as happening in the wrong film, and some characters in the commercials as involved in the film episodes, in what came to seem—for all the occasional bizarre disparities—a single irresponsible flow of images and feelings" (2003: 92).
4. See Feuer 1983, Corner 1997, Uricchio 2004, White 2004 and Lotz 2007.
5. Histories of television are oftentimes concerned with institutions, technologies, genres and formats. When individual programs are considered, they usually stand in as tokens of the same (conceptual) type (see e.g. Eco 1994: 85).
6. There are some older cases which show that this practice was not unheard of in earlier decades: *Dragnet* returned in various incarnations; lieutenant *Columbo* came back from an eleven-year hiatus in 1989; *Perry Mason* was rebooted after seven years off the air in 1973. In comparison to the above list of contemporary examples, it is clear however that the number of revivals has increased remarkably in recent years.
7. Generally, this holds for the film and television industries alike. For cinema, Elissa Nelson notes that "[e]ver since 1987, the majority of film revenues are earned in ancillary markets, not at the box office" (Nelson 2014: 62). It is interesting to note however that, at least in the case of Netflix, streaming technology connects much better with the television industry whereas DVD rentals were more aligned with the film industry: "As streaming became a bigger part of Netflix's business, so did TV shows. Studios were more

reluctant to license movies for streaming, and fans were more likely to watch TV series on Netflix when they didn't have to rent DVDs. (According to the company, TV series made up 18% of its DVD rentals at most but about 70% of its streaming traffic)" (Poniewozik 2013).

8. Poniewozik once more: "There are enough channels that someone else can pick up your show, as TBS did with ABC's *Cougar Town*. It can be revived by popularity in DVD format or online, as were *Family Guy* and *Futurama*. It can be brought back by Netflix, as was *Arrested Development*. And now, as happened with *Veronica Mars*, fans can bankroll a comeback themselves" (2014: 56).

9. http://arresteddevelopment.wikia.com/wiki/First_Time_Viewer's_Guide_to_Arrested_Development

10. For stills from both episodes, see http://arresteddevelopment.wikia.com/wiki/The_Ten_Commandments.

11. For a different use of the foreground/background relation for comedic ends in *Arrested Development*, see Vermeulen and Whitfield 2013.

12. In fact, the various distributors of *Arrested Development* are unable to even agree on what would constitute the orderly archive: The order in which the DVD box set lists the episodes differs slightly from the listing on Netflix.

13. The intimate theater of *Arrested Development* exposes the dysfunctionality of the neoliberal economy in the face of the passions. What undermines the ideal of growth is self-interest itself. To pose the world as a resource for a subject's satisfaction in no way requires the subject to engage with the world creatively. None of the Bluths (besides Michael) have an interest in their company except to bleed it dry. A little more money for another kick: When some of the company's frozen assets are released, the family's money habits kick in: Lucille's priority is to treat Buster's clicking jaw; GOB and Tobias invent a fake coffee company, Gobias Industries, to get their hands on the money; Lindsay needs some cash flow to entertain an extramarital affair which is meant to boost her self-esteem ("Whistler's Mother" Season 1, Episode 20). Money is conceived as a tool that makes the material world available for individual consumption for the purpose of satisfying individual needs.

14. For an investigation of the relation between casual gaming and modes of consumption, see Heaven 2014.

15. See http://arresteddevelopment.wikia.com/ and try the "random page" button. See also http://recurringdevelopments.com.

16. The events at the Harbormaster's Lodge are shown in epiosdes 2, 3, 5, 7, 10, 12, and 14 of the fourth season.

17. See Pretentious Film Majors 2014. In July 2016, it was reported that Hurwitz had finished the re-edited version which consists of 22 shorter episodes instead of the original 15 (Schneider 2016). As of writing (August 2016), it is not certain if and how the re-edited version will become available to audiences.

Thomas Lamarre

Nothing Doing: Xu Bing and the Nonsensuous Life of Chinese Characters

> ...nature also writes, albeit in gibberish.
> *Nakatani (2009: 8)*

Xu Bing's installations are renowned for their production of "nonsense writing," that is, for extracting operations from Chinese characters in a manner that defies conventions for what is sensible and intelligible in writing. Xu Bing, apparently in all seriousness, glosses such "nonsense" with the Chan Buddhist notion of *shengyu* 生语 or "living word." If the characters in Xu Bing's installations can be said to be living words, it is because they afford an experience of what is nonsensuous in the everyday experience of characters—while we are used to characters being visible and audible, we do not normally experience what happens *between* seeing and saying the character. In this paper, I look at various installations in which Xu Bing uses techniques of abstract resemblance, such as pictographs (characters that resemble things) and psuedographs (fake characters that resemble actually used characters) in order to provide an experience of *nonsensuous similarity* or *semblance* prior to and beyond resemblance. The challenge of his recent installation, *Background Story*, is that it explores nonsensuous similarity in a new register: calligraphic paintings in which there is brushwork without brushwork, in which actual things appear self-abstracting. Thus his art delivers a profound challenge to received hierarchies for organizing experience, suggesting that things are no less abstract than images or signs, only differently so.

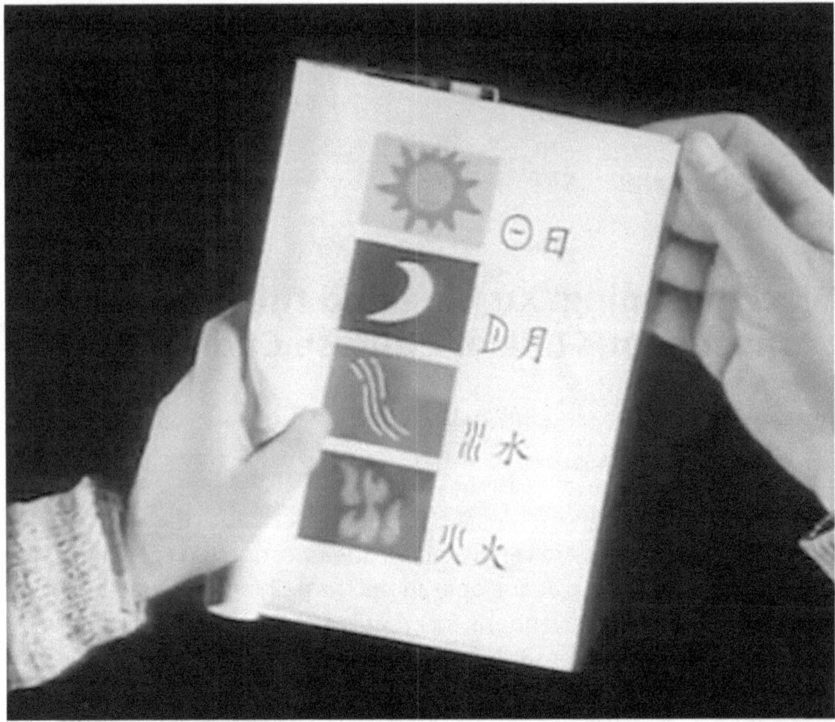

Figure 4. From San shi liu ge zi or "Thirty-six characters" (dir. A Da, 1984)

Living Word

A boy comes over to his father sitting at a desk, shows him a page with four Chinese characters, and asks for help learning them. The father says, "Ah, *xiangxinzi*." The four characters—for sun, moon, water, and fire—are indeed *xiangxinzi* or pictographs, and the page emphasizes their pictorial quality, placing a bold simple illustration for each object alongside the contemporary character and its ancient predecessor, which is written in seal script.

The father remarks that there are many such pictographs and proceeds to draw the characters for sun, mountain, and water on a sheet of paper with his brush, emphasizing their pictorial force to create a simple landscape. He adds characters for trees and then birds. The birds take flight, flapping their brushstroke wings and flitting through the trees.

These are some early scenes from an animated film, *San shi liu ge zi* or "Thirty-six characters" (dir. A Da, 1984), which show how to extract or abstract different potentials from pictographic characters.

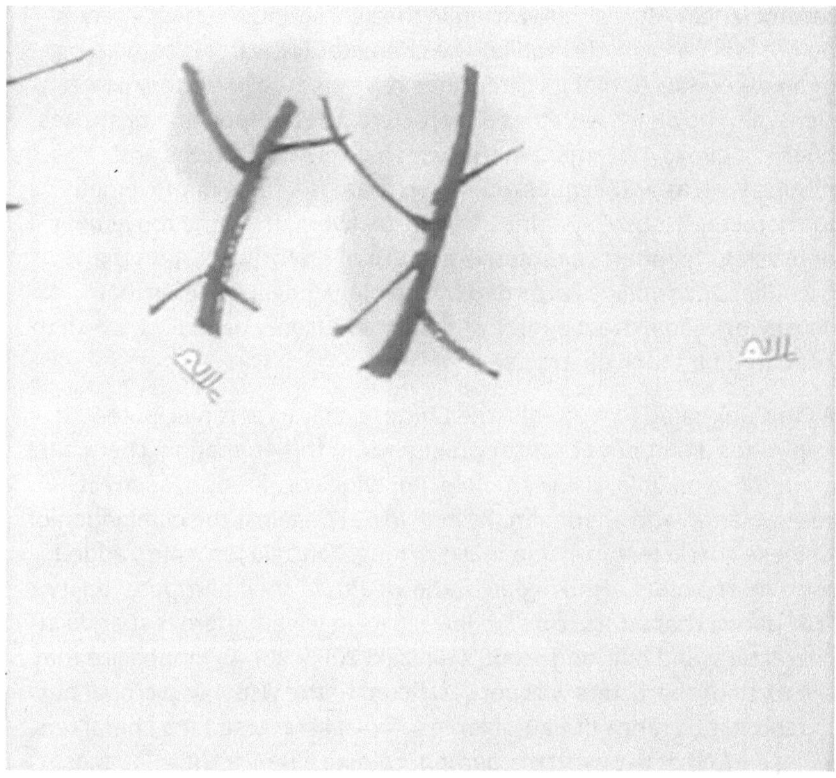

Figure 5. From San shi liu ge zi or "Thirty-six characters" (dir. A Da, 1984)

Visually, it shows them to be abstract resemblances: small, simplified, somewhat distorted or twisted images recalling various entities in the world. Vocally, it provides a sound for the characters: each time a character is written, the boy intones its reading. The animation also shows an orientation toward landscape and narrative: as characters encounter one another, they do not combine to form new words (with the exception of two trees (*mo*) combining to form forest (*rin*)), as is common with Chinese characters. Characters thus retain a sense of mutual independence. Their interactions are those of discrete, autonomous actors or agents. Finally, there is movement. Characters for animals come to life, flitting, swimming, galloping in accordance to their animal type.

Movement, however, raises some thornier questions about Chinese characters. Has the animation extracted a potential for movement from the characters? Or, has it added movement to their abstract resemblance? After all, as written in the seal script, these characters do not feel particularly mobile. The character for water is something of an exception, in that its three lines have a sort of vibratory power. Generally, however, with these characters, the composition of strokes does not evoke movement in the way that certain patterns and motifs, such as arabesques, do. When there is a force of movement to characters, it usually comes from brushwork, from the movement of brush as it imparts a tentative gesture of orientation upon the boundless possibilities afforded by the blank page. It seems that brushwork can extract a force of movement from characters, which this animated film then abstracts.

As this animated film attests, the Chinese character is pluripotent. It implicates a number of sensory registers. In this animation, characters are at once audible, visible, mobile, implying vocalization, abstract resemblance, and animation. Writing in 1917 against the elimination of Chinese characters from Japanese writing, Tanizaki Jun'ichirō, added even more potentials to highlight the wealth of their pluripotentiality: "For poets, characters truly are jewels. As in jewels, there is sparkle in characters, and hue, and scent" (Tanizaki 2005: 26). To emphasize that the force of characters was not restricted to the visual or pictorial but extended to a range of figural forces, Tanizaki reversed the characters *xiang* and *xin* of the word pictograph, coining a new term in Japanese to evoke the overall figural force of Chinese characters: *shōkei moji*, something like *xinxiangzi*, or "figural glyphs."

Such an understanding of characters—as multisensory, pluripotentiated figures—is essential to understanding Xu Bing's aesthetics of the Chinese character. Take, for instance, his installation *The Living Word*, first mounted in 2001 at the Sackler Gallery. On the floor lies a long strip of white board with rows of Chinese characters written in the manner of a traditional scroll, and at one corner, the contemporary simplified version of the character for bird (*niao)* is lifting off from the white paper space, extending into a series of characters gradually transforming into older versions of the character that come closer and closer to its ancient pictographic form, and finally taking flight as an abstract resemblance to "bird" emerges.

As the contemporary character for bird undergoes this half-historical half-mythical transformation, it also moves through the colors of the rainbow, its initial black giving way to violets, indigos, blues, greens, yellows, oranges, until red birds soar skyward. Color adds dimension

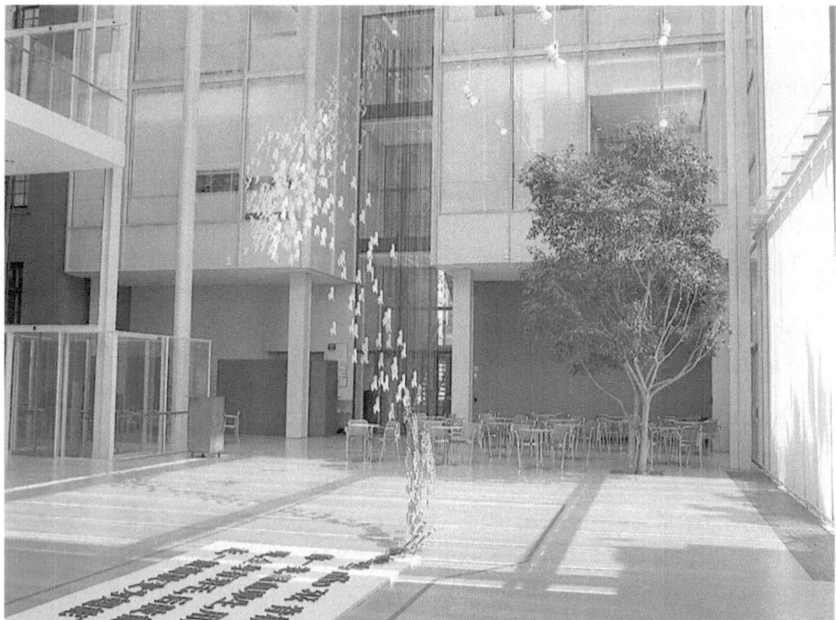

Figure 6. Xu Bing, The Living Word, 2001 (Courtesy of Xu Bing)

as well: the relatively two-dimensional space of writing upon paper shifts into the multidimensional space of characters in flight. But the dimensionality of the array of characters is less volumetric than it is multiplanar, for the characters are flattened cut-outs and are arrayed in layers.

In many respects, this installation recalls the animated characters of the film *San shi liu ge zi*: a flat black and whitish space of writing transforms into a boldly colorful animated space where layering imparts a sense of mobility and dimensionality. There is something equally naïve, even childish about the pictographic word *niǎo* coming to life in Xu Bing's installation. Isn't this play with pictograms just a game for children, and one that appeals to outmoded fantasies about Chinese writing, amusing perhaps to those without any literacy in characters but rather silly for those who do?

Yet, in this context as in other installations, Xu Bing in all seriousness glosses his work with the term "living word" or *shengyu*, and refers us to Chan Buddhism. If the characters in such artworks are living, it is because they imply multiple potentials, multiple sensory experiences. They are synesthetic figures. As such, to grasp what is at stake in this child's game with a pictogram, it is essential to think beyond the logic of pictograms, that is, of abstract resemblance, whereby the character is taken as an abstract representation of a concrete entity out there in the world. Although Chinese characters, at least some of them, can indeed stage an abstract resemblance to things in the world, such as birds, turtles, waters, trees, and stones for instance, that is not all they can do. It is not all they are doing in Xu Bing's installation, even if pictography is highlighted in it. His installation stages the logic of pictography with its emphasis on resemblance, but stages it in a manner that dramatizes what Walter Benjamin, and more recently Brian Massumi, call *semblance* or *nonsensuous similarity* (2011: 105).

Semblance in characters is precisely their pluripotentiated vitality, which in temporal terms and ontological terms can only be described as prior to and beyond resemblance. This is why Xu Bing evokes Chan Buddhism, which often is grossly characterized in terms of a sense of the illusory nature of reality. Reality is not so much an illusion, however, in the sense of a shallow or hollow fiction, but an abstraction. Similarly, Xu Bing's series of bird characters, as they mutate and soar skyward, affords an experience in which actual birds, real concrete birds out there in the world, are abstractions already. An actual bird is no less abstract than a bird glyph, but differently so. One might say that an actual bird is a more concretized abstraction, but an abstraction nonetheless. Both a bird and a bird character are equally yet differently real. Actual birds may indeed be said to be more objective than bird characters. Characters tend more subjective than birds, to the extent that writing is as much "in here" as "out there." But Xu Bing does not posit a dichotomy, a dualist opposition, between objective and subjective. In his installation the word is stretched between two poles, two movements of abstraction: at one pole, the black and white flatness of the written page with its tendency to fix positions and meanings, and at the other, the dimensional transformation with its tendency to run the spectrum of colors into the vanishing point of blinding light. The pictograph happens between the two extremes.

The Living Word thus stages the duplicity inherent in characters, and in words in general. Indeed, Xu Bing's works do not posit an opposition between words and characters: he consistently glosses *zi*, that is, "glyph" or "character" with the term "word," and vice versa. Glyphs, characters, words—these are sliding overlapping zones on a spectrum. *The Living Word* stages the double existence of characters by offering an immobile section of the process of pictographic transformation.

You perceive all the phases of transformation at once. A flock of bird-character variations hovers in air, one end swirling up from the black character on a field of white and expanding, one end tapering skyward and disappearing into brilliant light. The flock of variations is seized between its capture within the black glyph at one end, and at the other end, its release into the light of the heavens, a vanishing brightening point of color against sky, light melting into light. You begin to sense that the movement is not in one direction only, from the black character toward heavenly light. The bird character is also being sucked down from the sky into the dark script upon the paper field.

The variations on the character for bird are arrayed in a spectrum between these two abstract tendencies, figured as black and white, rather like what Deleuze and Guattari figured as the black hole and the white wall. In Xu Bing's installation, the white wall is not the white wall or walls of the gallery, but the expanse of heavens. The two tendencies of the installation also recall those of color as pigment and color as light. If you mix a full spectrum of pigment colors, you'll get black. If you mix a full spectrum of colors as light, you'll get white. The event of the bird character happens between earthly pigment and numinous light.

A paradox emerges. At one end, as the bird character becomes more bird-like in its resemblance to an actual bird, it reaches a vanishing point. It becomes most abstract when most concrete. At the other end, as the bird character loses its resemblance to an actual bird, it becomes less concrete, more of an abstract object. Abstraction and concretization or "concrescence" happen together. This is how Xu Bing's installation stages something before and beyond resemblance. Pictography is the lure, the point of departure, which affords an experience of something non-sensible or non-sensuous about the character, its semblance. This semblance is not only below the threshold of consciousness. It is also below the threshold of sensation, sensuousness. It is at once non-conscious and non-sensuous. This is precisely what Massumi calls *immediation*: "You are consciously experiencing the semblancing of experience—its double order; your double existence—that normally remains in the nonconscious background of everyday life" (Massumi 2011: 166-167).

Xu Bing likens such an experience to the living word of Chan Buddhism—what you do not normally perceive in a character, precisely because you tend to pay attention only to abstract resemblance when you read, is equally real. Semblance is as real as resemblance, but its reality is ordinarily pushed into the background in the act of reading. The experience of the living word is an experience of the double existence of the word. The living word thus embodies paradox, not contradiction, and its process is double-sided, two-faced, or duplicitous, not dialectical in the usual Hegelian sense (although it may be considered dialectical in a broader sense). Escape from resemblance and capture of semblance appear as polarized extremes of a single double-sided process. The pluripotentiality of characters, then, is never fully captured, nor does it ever entirely escape.

Such an experience sticks with you. As Massumi remarks in the context of another installation, "You feel yourself thinking-feeling differently as you exit the gallery and walk down the street. The feeling of perceiving perception's occurring to itself stays with you" (2011: 166). Indeed ordinary Chinese texts start to feel rather odd. You can't course through the lines of characters in the same way. The text takes on a new sense of depth, for something is occurring in its background for you. You are "tarrying in its nascency." Such an experience, as Massumi remarks, "is powerfully suggestive, but nonspecifically. This *should* make a difference. *Could* make a difference. But *how*? *Which* difference?" (Massumi 2011: 167).

Clear Mirror

In all the different versions of the installation *A Book from the Sky* (1987–1991), three long strips of scroll paper, with even rows of tidy characters printed across them, are draped from the ceiling, sometimes describing one long graceful arc, sometimes undulating into as many as four arcs. Light from above shines through the paper, setting it glow. Below the unwound scrolls, as if in response, rows of books lie open on a square platform, their pages arching at the book's spine, creating the impression of smaller, echoing undulations.

Their bindings are sewn with string, in the traditional manner, and their pages are printed with regular columns of characters. The installation thus sets forth a relation between two traditional formats for Chinese texts: above, swooping from the heavens, are the unwound scrolls, below are the bound books, firmly laid on the ground, pages open. Because the scrolls are unwound, and the books open, the characters printed on them seem to echo one another. Is it a matter of the same text presented in two formats? What is their relation?

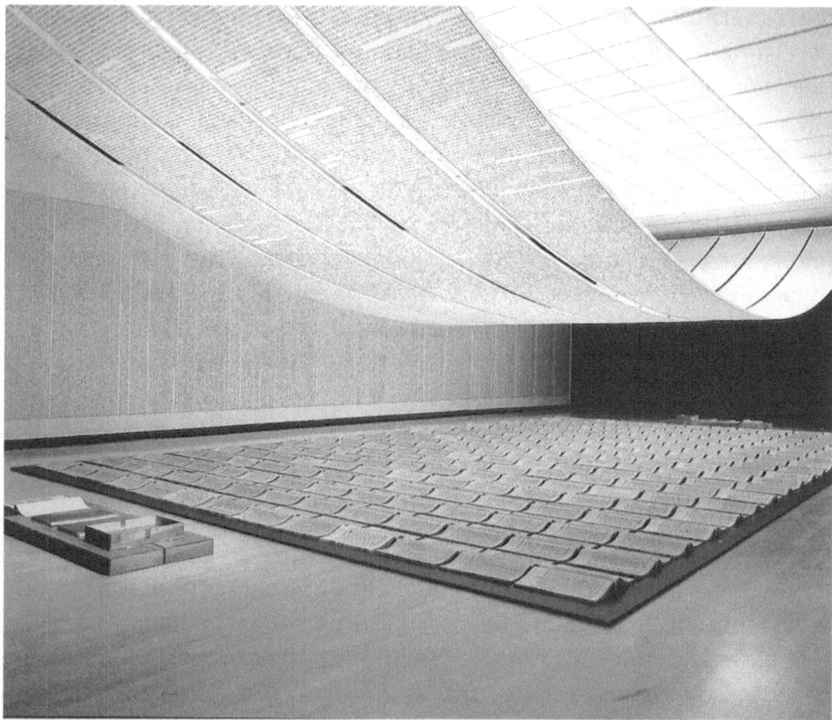

Figure 7. Xu Bing, A Book from the Sky, 1987–1991 (Courtesy of Xu Bing)

The presentation, the open books and scrolls, thus enjoins you to read the texts, but as you try read the characters, you find them unreadable, indecipherable. Depending on what languages you are accustomed to reading, you may assume that the characters belong to another language, one that uses characters differently from Japanese, older forms of Korean or Vietnamese, or received forms of Chinese writing. The characters, however, do not belong to any of these writing systems. They are invented characters or pseudo-glyphs, meticulously organized to appear readable. The moment when you realize that these characters are clever tricks or fakes is the moment of shock of the installation, the moment that stops you in your tracks, forcing you to move even closer to the pages, to figure out the trick. The shock is, these characters have no meaning, they are meaningless nonsense, and they are no one's characters.

Commentators often describe the experience in terms of a general existential experience of meaninglessness, or in terms of the particular meaninglessness of the apparatus of writing of the Chinese State.

Such interpretations are not wrong, especially in light of the Chinese government's response to the installation, and yet as Hajime Nakatani points out in his discussion of Xu Bing, such interpretations tend to see writing only in terms of instrumental functions, and to adopt a familiar yet dubious communication model in which the character is supposed to convey meaning transparently, without its materiality or agency getting in the way (Nakatani 2009: 8-9). Yet what *A Book from the Sky* stages is the material orientations associated with different media—scrolls, books, and characters—that orientate readers prior to and beyond signification. Of course, such meaning is not only in the physical materials. Materiality is also in the experience of materials, working with and passing through materials. Here it is useful to build on a distinction made in French between meaning as orientation or direction (*sens*) and meaning as signification. *A Book from the Sky* offers an experience of mediality of media, of material orientations and directions, without signification.

It also offers an experience of immediation, of a sort of nonsense or nonsenuous orientation that cannot be parsed from the physical orientations alone. The immediation here emerges in the multiplication of senses, directions, orientations, as the installation orientates its readers in a variety of ways and in different registers. There are bookish expectations for reading down the page, right to left, and there is something like a table of contents, and even diacritic marks. There are scroll-related expectations, as the text unwinds, spooling forth its columns of characters. There is the guidance implied in the list of sections and with diacritic marks. There are also character-related expectations that make them appear imminently readable, intelligible. As such, if the texts are said to be meaningless, it is only in the register of signification, for they present the reader-walker with so many directions and orientations as she ambulates around them. Wu Hung (1994), for instance, describes its writing in terms of signifiers without signified, and as forms without content. At the same time, this "nothing" or "nonsense" is full of meaning, offering a plethora of meaningful orientations and directions. This is a full void, to borrow the Chan term. The void of signification is full of meanings.

The installation might also be said to afford an experience of the immediation of reading, bringing to the fore what recedes during reading. When you read, you tend not to see all the aspects of text, at least not in a highly attentive way, consciously and perceptually. You feel its presence, follow its directions, but you don't need or want to be aware of all its material determinations, which might be called passive determinations or "underdeterminations." *A Book from the Sky* brings to the fore these otherwise passive presences, highlighting their agency. It thus forces an experience of one of the paradoxes of reading: meaning is not in the words or on the pages. Nor is it in the mind of the reader. It is both in text and reader as it were, distributed across them, at once objective and subjective. Meaning happens with and through words but is not in them as such. We might think of it in terms of three levels of experience, or more precisely, in terms of what Peirce called Firstness, Secondness and Thirdness (see Massumi 2011: 92-98). First, a stroke of the brush draws a bold black line of ink across white paper. This is Firstness. But that line is really a surface, and there are now two surfaces, white (page) and black (stroke) with a virtual line or edge between them, at once separating and connecting them. White and black mutually oscillate, each potentially the ground for the other's figure. The white is thus active in a new way, which is Secondness. As soon as the black stroke (let's say it is drawn horizontally across the page) is read as the character "one," the activity or eventfulness of the oscillating contrast is lost. The character stands forth in space as if stepping out of time like an eternal form, a general type. The more strokes are added, the greater the tendency toward Thirdness, in which we no longer attend to eventfulness, to the active separating and connecting of two surfaces. The eventfulness is still present, still active, but by habit we abstract or extract a form, a character, a word.

Within a certain tradition of Chan or Zen art, fondness for a single energetic calligraphic line drawn vertically down a white strip of paper, or for a not entirely closed circle, strives to reactivate the Firstness and Secondness overlooked by habit, now activated in technique. Neither the vertical line nor the circle is an actual character, which allows the oscillating contrast or "pairedness" of two surfaces to come to the fore. In other words, we have meanings in the sense of orientations (a page with edges, a tentative up and down, right and left, and a direction of movement of the stroke), but they are non-sense in that the habits that encourage us to add, over and above the contrasts, a form or word, are thwarted or suspended. This is one way of activating the nonsense of characters, making them into living words.

In *A Book from the Sky*, Xu Bing adopts a different way. As in *The Living Word*, he works with abstract resemblance, exploring how the operations of resemblance entail an experience of semblance. Whereas *The Living Word* uses the pictograph (abstract resemblance to actual things) as a point of departure, *A Book from the Sky* explores the operations of another kind of character, *xingshengzi*, which combines elements for pronunciation with a general typology. This classification dates back as at least as far as the ancient dictionary *Shuowen jiezi* compiled by the scholar Xu Shen in the Eastern Han dynasty (25-220 CE). Xu Shen offered "Six Laws of Character Formation" (*liushu*), classifying characters (*zi)* in accordance to six basic patterns, among them the pictographs discussed above. Pictographs, however, constitute only a small portion of characters in use. The great bulk of characters (eighty to ninety percent) are what Xu Shen called *xingshengzi* in which one component tends to provide the sound, while another indicates a generic form, pattern or quality. For instance, characters with a "fish" component generally refer to various kinds of fish, such as tuna, abalone, snapper, and so forth. Or a "hand" component often appears in characters related doing something with the hands, such as pushing, pulling, lifting, and so forth. To this general type is added a second component that indicates the sound or vocalization for the character. The result is a double capture, a cross-modal capture, in which seeing and saying work together to produce Thirdness, a semantic form hovering over the character elements. These characters are today commonly called phonetic-semantic compound characters. While the two elements of the character provide meanings, these meanings are loose general orientations not fixed significations or semantic forms. The significations are learned by rote, and the double cross-modal capture becomes habit.

The characters designed for *A Book from the Sky* evoke the operations of such compound characters, because Xu Bing uses actual elements that are commonly combined in actual characters. Yet his combinations are non-existent: although you feel you can almost pronounce them, almost detect a general type, and almost read them, these characters cannot be read. They are fake characters or pseudo-glyphs, non-existent combinations. They are nonsense, non-sensuous. As with *The Living Word*, however, this nonsense is full of sense, full of potential directions. The installation conjures forth your immediate character sense. The nonsense character is full of potential vocalizations and generalizations, just as the books and scrolls on which they are printed are full of readerly orientations. The nonsense character similarly activates the immediation of reading, but in the register of the printed word. It does so by staging an abstract resemblance to the phonetic-semantic compound character, but the resemblance does not hold. In this failure of resemblance, some commentators see a dramatization of the emptiness and futility of regimes of capture, and in particular the State regime of capture. Again, however, this emptiness is quite full, full of potentials, immediate, as it were. Such potential is always there but we do not notice it due to habits, enforced by State education and policy. Of course, we can never exactly perceive these potentials; nor can we not perceive them. *A Book from the Sky* plays on the edge where such potentials are reactivated. As such, it does not rest content to say in a nihilist fashion: Look, hear, the State is empty and futile, an imposition of meaning upon meaninglessness. Rather it shows that regimes of power actually capture something, which might be activated otherwise. It is already here activated otherwise. This is a politics of semblance.

It is easy to become caught up in the puzzle-like qualities of Xu Bing's pseudo-characters, on the edge of resemblance. At the same time, the installation literally stages semblance: the earthbound books, arrayed squarely, literally mirror the scrolls hanging from the heavens. The earthly book comes from the sky. But what is this relation between earth and sky? The installation evokes traditional cosmologies wherein Chinese characters are patterns mirroring the celestial order of things, expressed quintessentially in the movement of asterisms. Particularly important is the logic of the mirror, made explicit in the original title for the installation, *Xi shi jian—shiji mo juan* or "Analytic Reflection of the World: Final Volume of the Century." The act of mirroring, then, is not neutral. In its insistence that the reflected image is never an illusion precisely because the nothing of the mirror is in fact something, a nothing that is always doing, Xu Bing's true mirror runs parallel to Foucault's account of heterotopia, which systemically unravels the utopian take on the mirror.

For Xu Bing, the mirror does not produce illusions, nor does it only offer resemblances. It is not a utopian representation of our reality. Instead, the "clear mirror," as it is traditionally styled, entails a sort of analysis, to the extent as it enables an exploration of form. It elucidates true form. Simply put, what shows in the mirror is a true form or a truth of form. In folklore for instance, a demon disguised as a human will appear as a demon in the mirror. In effect, the clear or true mirror reveals the (ontological) priority of movement over form. Similarly, the terms virtual and actual derive from the logic of the mirror, but even if the virtual is a reflection of the actual, it is not a mere resemblance. Its abstract resemblance entails semblance, something that is at once actualized in the actual object and generated by it. I have thus far spoken of Xu Bing's use of Chinese characters—both pictographs in *The Living Word* and phonetic-semantic compounds in *A Book from the Sky*—in terms of staging abstract resemblance (to actual things or to actual characters), but it would be more accurate to say that his installations are interested in the logic of mirroring, in the virtual of perceptual experience, that is, the immediation experienced through semblance, and the movement prior to form.

Brushwork

One of the striking features of Xu Bing's use of characters is its avoidance of the more kinetic and gestural possibilities of brushwork, long established in traditions of Chinese calligraphy. Wang Xizhi (303-361) and his son Wang Xianzhi (344-388) are generally taken as key figures in an epochal transformation of calligraphic styles that at once elevated calligraphy to an art and established the three standard styles of script, which have dominated calligraphic practice ever since: *kaishu,* regular or stiff script; *xingshu*, semi-cursive or running script; and *caoshu*, fully cursive script. Wang Xizhi excelled in all styles but gained especial renown for his semi-cursive calligraphy. Where as prior calligraphic styles tended to impart a sense of balanced distribution of the character around a central point, cursive styles open the kinesthetic potential of writing with the brush by imparting a center of motion to individual characters that differs from the center of balance. Cursive writing thus imparts a greater sense of individuality in movement to characters, making them feel as if they were coming alive, leaping and dancing up from the page. The fully cursive script pushes this kinesthetic possibility to new limits. Xu Bing's calligraphic style, however, tends to avoid such possibilities: the script for characters in *A Book from the Sky* is that of print rather than calligraphy. It derives from Song dynasty typeface. Two other installations deploying calligraphy, *Square Word Calligraphy* (1994-96) and *Landscript* (2001, 2002) deserve closer attention, for they afford insight into the implications of Xu Bing's avoidance of kinesthetic characters in brushwork.

Square Word Calligraphy, in its many variations, centers on an invented script in which English, German, or other European-language words (words normally written with the Roman alphabet) are written in the manner of Chinese characters, the letters composing them appearing as strokes and elements of characters.

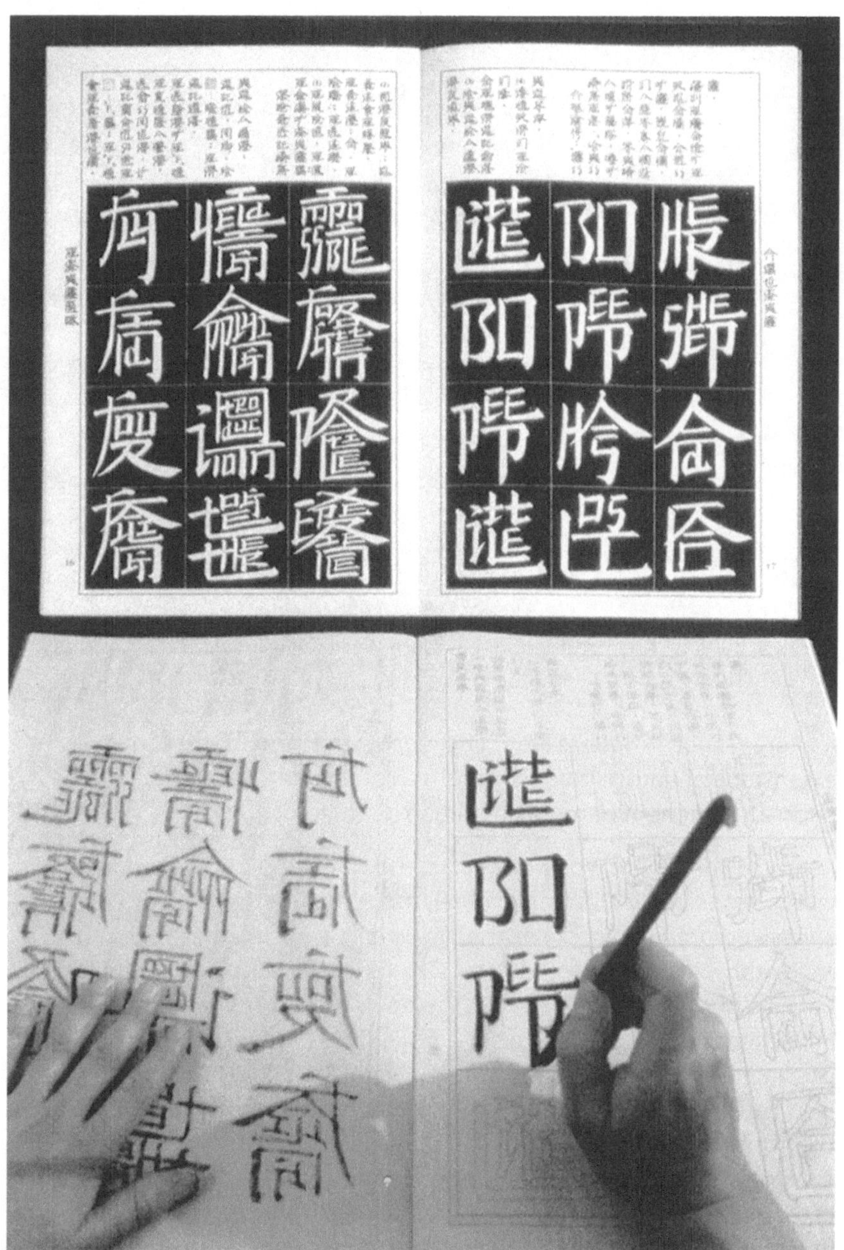

Figure 8. Xu Bing, Square Word Calligraphy, 1994-96 (Courtesy of Xu Bing).

True to Xu Bing's take on writing, the installation also provides a cosmological framework for the elements of these square words in

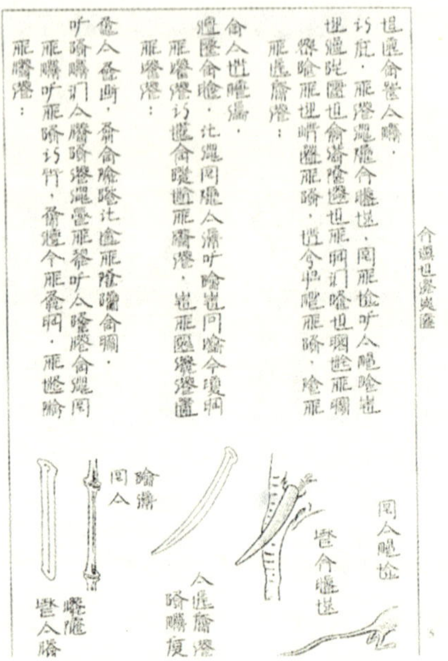

Figure 9. Xu Bing, An Introduction to Square Word Calligraphy, 2000 (Courtesy of Xu Bing).

An Introduction to Square Word Calligraphy: the strokes are shown as extensions of nature, to derive from a curved elephant tusk, a duck's neck, a segment of bamboo, a human hand, for instance.

As the term "square word" suggests, the calligraphic style for these words is decidedly stiff and angular, more reminiscent of printed styles and pre-cursive styles than is usually associated with Chinese calligraphy, that is, kinesthetic cursive styles. What comes to the fore here, as in *A Book from the Sky*, is the double cross-modal capture implicit in script—to see is to say—but such a double capture is only possible with careful initiation and painstaking education. Both installations, *A Book from the Sky* and *Square Word Calligraphy*, force a confrontation with nonsense, that is, nonsensuous semblance, at once evoking and foreclosing the pluripotentiality of characters. Characters can do so many things, and yet here they are, reduced to a simple double capture that yokes vision to audition, seeing to saying, sound or voice to eye. Where *A Book from the Sky* stages the monumental cosmology of books from which regimes of power extract such narrow possibilities, *Square Word Calligraphy* offers a ludic and even ludicrous

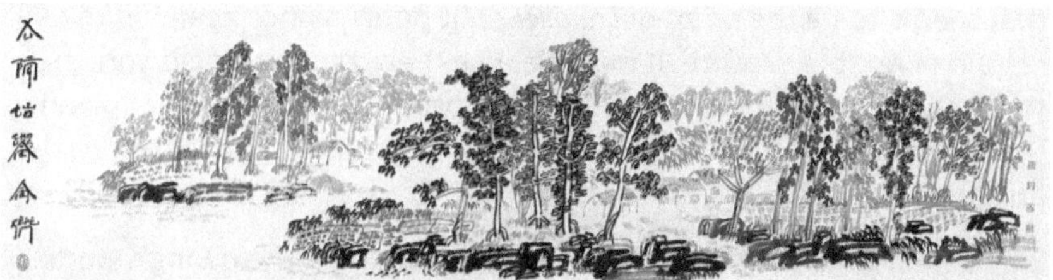

Figure 10. Xu Bing, Landscript, 2007 (Courtesy of Xu Bing).

performance in which Orientalist fascination with Chinese writing is paired with an apparatus of disciplinization and a desire for mastery.

Landscript similarly seizes, with a kind of naïve literalness, upon a possibility suggested by traditional styles of landscape painting in which brush strokes associated with calligraphy are used. Such calligraphic styles of painting become prominent in the Song dynasty (960-1279), reaching new levels of expressiveness in the landscapes associated with "literati painting" and the Southern School, and in some contexts with Chan Buddhism. In literati painting, calligraphic forms of characters were sometimes the source for a particular landscape element. The leaves of a specific kind of tree might be drawn with a calligraphic variation of the character *xin* or heart. But you are not supposed to read the word heart into the tree. It is the expressive distinctiveness of the heart character calligraphy that matters, as contrasted with the calligraphic distinctiveness of other characters, in a manner that recalls the expressive interplay of characters individuated calligraphically in cursive scripts. In *Landscript*, Xu Bing literalizes the movement of calligraphy into painting, rendering a tree with the character for tree, and rocks with that for rock, and the door of a house with that for gate, for instance.

In contrast with literati painting, the characters in *Landscript* are supposed to resemble actual trees, rocks, gates, fish, grasses, and so forth, but the resemblance is abstract, and the force of calligraphy is used to push characters toward likeness. In fact, two characters are used for each leaf in some of the *Landscript* paintings, *ye* and *zi*, which are not pictographic at all. Other leaves are drawn with the character green (*qing*). But leafiness is extracted from them. At the same time, the characters for ducks (*ya*) do not look very much like ducks. Pictography, then, is combined with logography in which characters do not resemble what they speak, at least not without the force of a calligraphic landscape style that pushes them in that direction. Indeed, that seems to be the point of *Landscript*: it puts us once again on the terrain of double capture. It makes sense then that the brushwork in these landscapes, while vigorous and expressive, is not geared toward the kinesthetic possibilities of calligraphy but primarily toward forcing an abstract resemblance while evoking the character's vocalization.

Liu Yuedi makes a similar observation, remarking that Xu Bing's works place so much emphasis on the structure and formal unity of each character that they lose a sense of the *qi* or spirit between characters relating one character to another, which is essential to calligraphic art. Liu concludes, "Even if the *qi* of calligraphy is broken, the *yun* [rhythm] of character has survived" (Liu 2011: 107). In both installations, *Square Word Calligraphy* and *Landscript*, the force of brushwork is directed into the rhythmic quality of each character, imparting a high degree of autonomy and energy to it. While each character is in relation to other characters, the overall force of composition is not like cursive calligraphy, in which each character has its kinesthetic signature, rather like a gait. Instead, Xu Bing's brushwork makes for characters that seem to vibrate in place. His characters do not feel on the verge of galloping or flitting about: even in *The Living Word*, in which the *niao* character takes to the heavens, the installation offers a flock of immobile autonomous characters, as if a series of immobile sections had been taken of a transformation. The rhythm or vibratory energy is not in the calligraphy but in the characters themselves. Movement is not added to characters from without. Rather potential movement resides in even the most inert character.

Of course, it may be argued (and I would agree) that cursive calligraphy is not about adding movement to characters but about discovering it within them. Nonetheless, Xu Bing does not take that route, perhaps because the acquisition of cursive styles is such a long process, entailing years of training and cultivating the styles of masters. Rather, in keeping with his notion of art as a mode of everyday living, the techniques and materials featured in his installations are accessible, often with an aura of naïve play, child's play, and usually with a flair for nonsense, for nonsensical puzzles. The nonsense of Xu Bing's installations, however, is not devoid of meaning, a form of nihilism. As we have seen, nonsense entails a puzzling encounter with the nonsensuous life of characters, which is at the same time a multisensory existence, akin to synesthesia or a union of the senses, a vibratory whole. This nonsensuous life is precisely what happens between different sensory experiences of the character, but is not experienced consciously or sensuously. Xu Bing

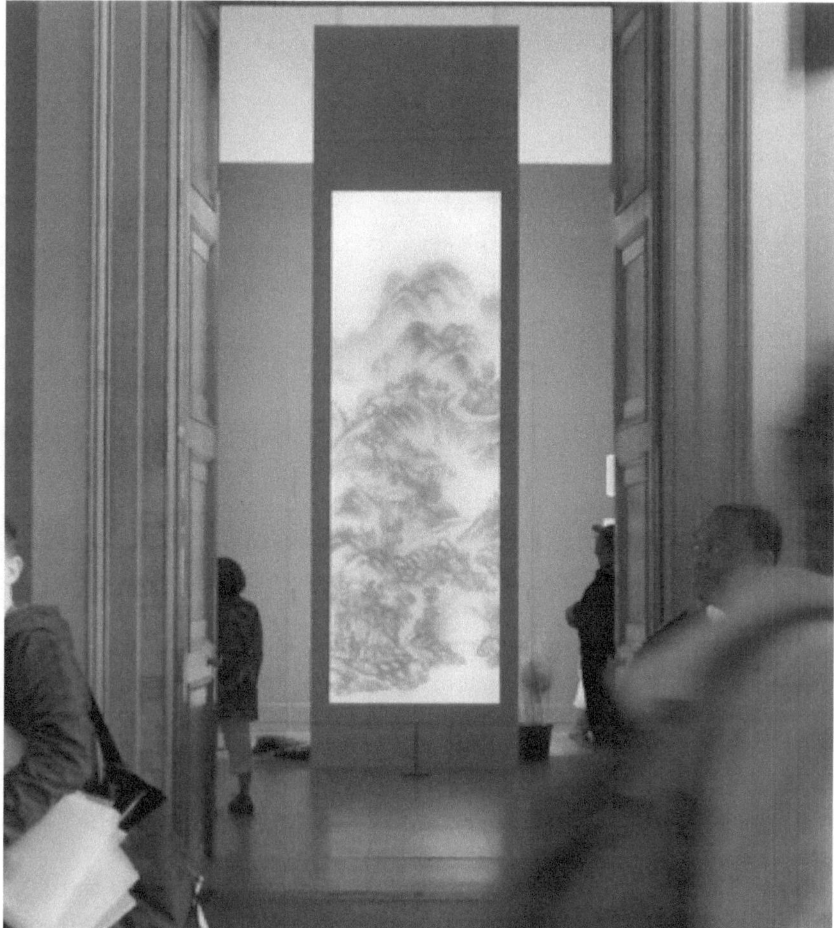

Figure 11. Xu Bing Background Story, 2004-2012 (Courtesy of Xu Bing).

is fond of working with characters that present their readers, viewers, or users with something visual and audible or vocal. Conventions and habits for reading characters encourage us to combine the character's visual pattern and voice in an intelligible fashion. We thus see and hear the character and yet we do not perceive what happens between seeing and hearing. Xu Bing's installations, in different ways, generate an experience of characters in which we become aware of the contingency of the relation between the visual and audible dimensions of the character. In *A Book from the Sky* we feel that both dimensions are there but they do not come together. In *Landscript* and *Square Word Calligraphy*, we feel both dimensions but they are fused in ways that

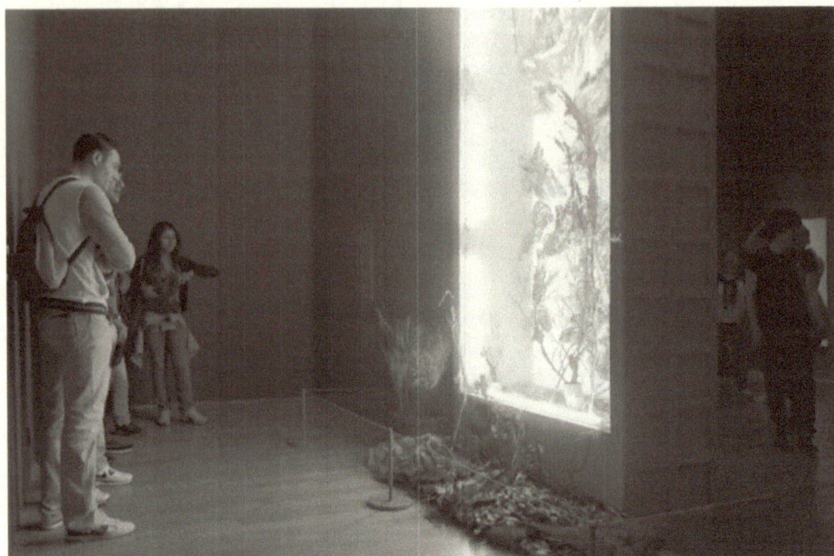

Figure 12. Xu Bing Background Story, 2004-2012 (Courtesy of Xu Bing).

run counter to conventional usage, defying double capture. If we feel that such character play is nonsense, it is because we experience the nonrelation operating between sensory dimensions of the character. We experience, however momentarily, what is always working with and through characters but is not perceived as such. We experience the nonsensuous multisensory potentiality of the character—what makes characters sensible and intelligible to begin with. Even if we do not see it or hear it when reading characters, we experience this nonsensuousness. We experience the "nothing doing" of characters, the nothing that is always doing.

One of the challenges of Xu Bing's installations is the demonstration that this "nothing that is doing" is not in the characters, that is, not in their physical aspects. It happens with and through characters. It is in their eventfulness. As such, in light of Xu Bing's tendency to center his works on characters, his series of installations called *Background Story* is particularly interesting, because it does not use Chinese characters at all. Instead, in the seven variations on *Background Story* in various museums around the world between 2004 and 2012, Xu Bing strives for "nonsensuous similarity" to well-known Chinese landscape paintings (see Harrist 2011). In the most recent variation, Background Story 7, which took place at British Museum in London in 2012, you first see it down a gallery corridor: what looks to be a Chinese

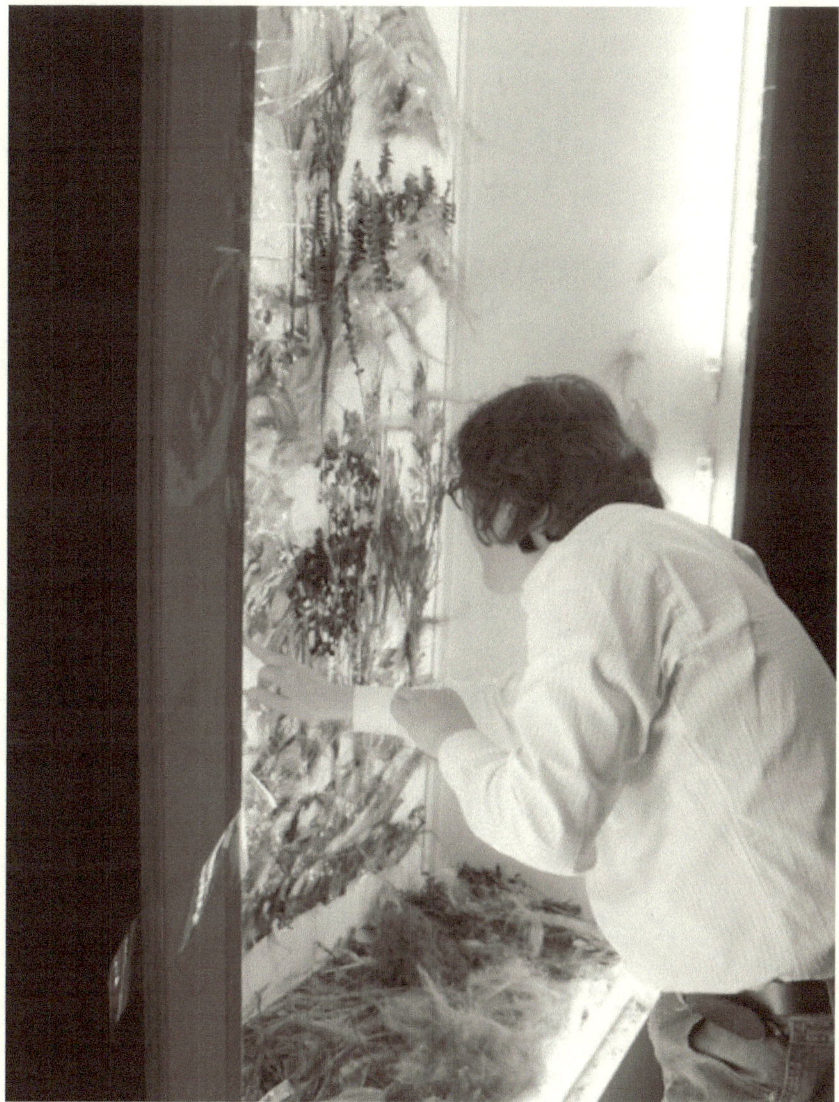

Figure 13. Xu Bing Background Story, 2004-2012 (Courtesy of Xu Bing).

scroll with delicate and meticulous brushstrokes of ink to produce a contemplative landscape.

Yet it glows, and as you approach, you gradually see that it is a lightbox with scroll-like dimensions. The effect, however, is still that of Chinese ink painting. A very close look at the surface shows that it does not in fact use ink or brushwork at all: the resolution of the shadows cast upon

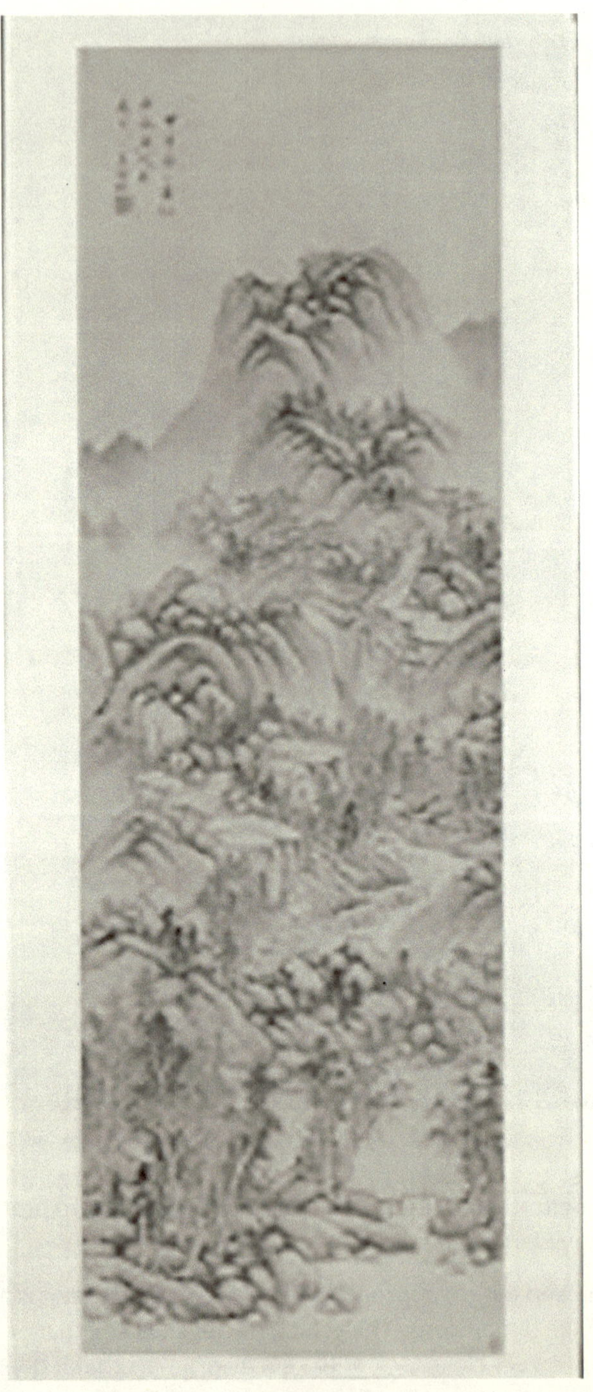

Figure 14. Wang Shimin, Landscape, 17th-century (Courtesy of Xu Bing).

the sheet of frosted glass becomes crisper and clearer. But it is not until you look behind the lightbox that the techniques are fully exposed

Bits of what look to be grasses, twigs, and other detritus or debris (which materials are found around London, such as corn husks, hemp fibres, and other plant materials) are taped directly to the glass or sometimes held in place with clay, fibre, or wire.

A pile of materials is strewn below, and at the base are more heaps of detritus, things that might be found in the streets, like a potted plant, thrown out to desiccate. The shadows cast onto the frosted glass by these materials with the use of backlighting produces a landscape painting that resembles a well-known painting. Indeed the model is hanging on an adjacent wall, a 17th-century scroll by Wang Shimin.

In sum, like Xu Bing's other installations, *Background Story* sets up an abstract resemblance but in order to produce an experience of nonsensuous similarity or semblance.

Oddly enough, commentators often describe the use of rubbish and lights to produce the feel of a Chinese landscape in terms of illusion. But Xu Bing's version of a landscape is no more an illusion than Wang Shimin's. The shadows cast by plants, for instance, may be said to look like brushstrokes. But the shadows are no more illusions than ink marks. The logic of Xu Bing's technique is not one of exposure of illusion. If anything is exposed, it is technique, which provides a reminder that the effect of art, the force of landscape painting, does not lie in the materials. Everything is technique, or rather, technique is everywhere. Everything is abstraction. Indeed, by using natural materials, however desiccated, mangled, and lifeless, *Background Story* reminds us that a leaf is as abstract as the word or sign leaf. Both are equally real and abstract, but different so. Likewise with brush strokes and shadows, they are equally real and abstract, albeit differently so. The point here is not the frequently cited yet highly reductive gloss on Buddhism: the world is illusion. The point is that things are concretizing abstractions, in process, always caught up in a two-fold process of transformation. Techniques can serve as a "clear mirror" to examine form, to explore the virtual, the semblance or nonsensuous similarity that at once enables and is generated by the emergence of actual existence. Instead of thinking in terms of illusion, Xu Bing encourages thinking in terms closer to "awakening-to-self," with his clever and astute staging of the moment of surprise, and a sense of things falling into place, that may come with an experience of nonsensuous similarity.

What is to be done with the awakening-to-self that the mirror of art technique activates? The world of global art and art criticism tends to encourage an impoverished understanding of self: either you're an individual or you're a national, and usually both in quick alternation. The nation or national culture is construed as a container for the individual, and as the frame for understanding art. Artists then are compelled to present themselves in those terms. In an interview about Background Story, for instance, when asked whether art that does not use traditional materials is still Chinese art, Xu Bing is encouraged to respond in a national culturalist manner: "Chinese art is not only made with water, brushes and ink; any culture's art can use these things. It is not different materials that determine the characteristics of a nation's art. I feel that the most important element is the country itself and its people's inner character and spirit. It is related to a nation's physiological rhythm, nature, and interests" (Xu: 2012). But if such rhythms and interests can potentially be found in cornhusks tossed in a rubbish heap in London, then it may be time to extend the question of nonsensuous similarity to understanding Chineseness well.

Little Absolutes

Addressing the question of what difference Xu Bing's artworks make, commentators often favor one pole over the other—escape from resemblance, or capture of semblance. Xu Bing's works have frequently been interpreted as critiques of the capture of writing by the State apparatus, or even of the capture of expression by the heavy hand of tradition. Xu Bing himself speaks of his confusion and discomfort over State-led initiatives to reform Chinese writing, introducing simplifications of characters and then retracting them and offering yet others (Xu 2001). An apparatus of capture can never harness potentiality once and for all, but must capture it again and again. In the case of State-led transformations in characters, it is the mutability stemming from the pluripotentiality of the Chinese character that resists once-and-for-all capture. Capturing the semblance of words thus turns into a series of captures, sequential captures: simplify, retreat, simplify. Still, because the nonsensuous background cannot be eradicated, the political regime and the writing system do not readily mesh. A great deal of effort, in the form of sequential captures, is needed in order to make the dynamics of writing mesh with the dynamics of a political regime.

In the context of the ancient State, Deleuze and Guattari call such a process *overcoding*, which forces the pluripotency of writing into a biunivocal coding. With Chinese characters, such overcoding takes the form of an adequation of the character's sound (its reading) and its visual form. Recall that eighty to ninety percent of Chinese characters are ones in which one component indicates its pronunciation, while another component indicates its general classification or specification. This is why contemporary linguists insist that Chinese characters, in their daily operations, are best described as logographs, rather than pictographs or ideographs. For instance, the character for dove or pigeon combines the bird radical with another character pronounced *ge*: the sound signals "dove," while the bird radical prevents confusing this ge with other words pronounced ge (elder brother, song, to split, etc). The production of such logographs is a prime example of the biunivocal operations characteristic of the overcoding that Deleuze and Guattari associate with the ancient State.

Historically speaking, the capture of the character's multisensory pluripotent semblance does not end there. As Deleuze and Guattari indicate, the modern capitalist State tends to decode this overcoding while applying new axioms to it. The prior overcoding remains as an internal limit to this two-faced process: it provides the point of purchase where decoding worms its way into the overcoded codes, while preventing the decoding from going too far, from releasing non-overcoded or non-recoded codes. Writing is thus prevented from pushing to its absolute limit. The modern capitalist State leans heavily on its internal limit (the biunivocal logograph), which makes writing slip back into a mode of existence axed on its relative limit—Chinese characters become rationalized logographs, just one system of writing among others, a relative and relatively modern system. The increased rationalization of Chinese characters to make them adequate to the modern State—phoneticization and simplification, not to mention new forms of education and literacy—entails a process of decoding the prior overcoding of characters, while applying new axioms. So it is that, in the name of rationalization for mass literacy, the capacity of the character to stand alone as an autonomous object, a simple and rational logograph, comes to jive with the ambition of the modern State to arrive at a simple rational mode of communication, one in which the message will sustain its autonomy and not lend itself to transformation, reinterpretation, or misinterpretation, that is, the polyvocal.

This is precisely where Xu Bing's art strives to make its difference. Commentators typically call attention to its potential critique of State power. As one volume presenting his installations comments, "Like *A Book from the Sky*, *Ghosts Pounding the Walls* is intended to reflect the futility of human effort and the meaninglessness of China's cultural icons" (Erickson 1991: 26). Nonetheless, commentators have not only tended to simplify Xu Bing's art, but have also tended, by extension, to simplify the operations of the modern State vis-à-vis writing. Debate has gradually settled on the status of "Chinese culture" in Xu Bing. Commentators without literacy in Chinese (or in Chinese writing and painting) have stressed a message about the nihilism of the State and tradition-bound China, whereas critics with Chinese literacy have insisted in response that Xu Bing does not see Chinese traditions of writing and painting as empty or futile in a nihilist way. In fact, Xu Bing's works, for all their insistence on an encounter with the emptiness of monumental projects and institutionalized forms of expression, do not condemn or reject so-called Chinese traditions or Chinese cultures. His art works meticulously through techniques and concepts associated with the literati tradition in particular. As such, the latter stance on Xu Bing is surely the correct direction to take. Nonetheless, Xu Bing's recourse to Chinese traditions exacerbates rather than resolves the questions posed in Massumi's account: Chinese traditions *should* make a difference and *could* make a difference, but *how*, and *which* difference?

Such questions are calculated as a challenge to the bid for transcendence that so frequently comes into play as soon as something like "Chinese traditions" enters in the mix. When Xu Bing is construed in terms of a modernist or postmodernist renewal of traditional arts, interpretations of his art swing to the other pole, singing the virtues of traditional forms of expression, and seeing in his evocations of Chan Buddhism, traditional ink painting techniques, scrolls, and calligraphy, for instance, the possibility of transcendence, and a particularly Chinese transcendence at that. His art has also been challenged in such terms, as Tsao aptly does, characterizing his contribution as "not much more than an addition to the late capitalist global portrait of a postindustrial world," whose ambiguous local-global positioning will allow Chinese audiences "to misread the situation as a *Chinese triumph*" (Tsao 2011: 28).

In sum, Xu Bing's works have conjured up a familiar but intractable problematic: What is the relation between traditional techniques and modernist or postmodernist critiques? A problem arises because accounts of Xu Bing have tended to associate the traditional with the local and to place the particular (Chinese) in opposition to the global and the universal (West), and to the modern. Consequently, as Tsao indicates, the resurgence of the traditional or local can be imagined in terms of a triumphant entry into, or overcoming of, the modern or global. At the same time, insofar as the modern is defined as perpetual rupture with or critique of the traditional, the condition for the triumph of the local or traditional is precisely its negation. This is why evaluation of Xu Bing becomes polarized: at one end, there is the modernist critique of tradition, and at the other, traditional arts appear to be surging into the modern or postmodern, to the delight or dismay of the critic.

Such interpretations spur important reflections and debates. Yet a problem arises when the local is assumed to be a specific place or site that is confined, immobilized, and fundamentally opposed to the global or even the general, and when, as a consequence, the traditional and the local are conflated. Such a stance ignores that the local can also be a source of general concepts and practices. Because the local is traversed by and exposed to global flows and general concepts (which are constitutive of it), it always has the potential to move beyond its location, to take on a global or general mode of existence. The literati traditions from which Xu Bing's art draws both techniques and concepts cannot be confined to China or Chineseness, any more than Chinese characters can. In fact, his installations conjure forth and depend on prior regional and global circuits of Chinese techniques and concepts. In his recent installations *Background Story*, for instance, Xu Bing includes Japanese painters of the literati tradition.

The double bind extracted from Xu Bing's art by critics implies an initial subordination of the local (Chinese) to the global (West), followed by an overcoming of Western domination, with echoes of postcolonial paradigms. The resultant particularization of China invites a form of cultural nationalism and national sovereignty, to be enjoyed by Chinese and non-Chinese alike, which completely overlooks or suppresses the contemporary reality and history of Chinese sovereignty, situating it prior to its formation. If one wishes to acknowledge the genuine historical asymmetry between East and West without reincribing it within endless deconstruction, and without retroactively applying it to the tension between literati traditions and contemporary global art, one might well begin with cosmopolitanisms, competing imperialisms, and rival universals, which demands a practical articulation of what Gayatri Spivak calls "other Asias" (2008).

If I have introduced a rather complicated series of terms from Deleuze and Guattari—coding, overcoding, decoding, axioms as well as the internal limit, relative limit, and absolute limit, I have done so in hopes of arriving at another way of assessing the geopolitical implications of Xu Bing's games with the nonsensuous semblance of Chinese characters, some way more in keeping with the challenges posed both by Spivak and Massumi. Let me return to the putatively local and traditional paradigm deployed in *The Living Word*—the Chinese pictograph—with such terms in mind.

In *The Living Word*, the pictograph operates as anything but a territorially confined or spatially bounded paradigm. Put another way, the pictogram in Xu Bing presents a character-territory or character-refrain, but one that is not overcoded, not territorialized into a biunivocal machine. The series of bird characters, rising from the page to soar into the heavens, produce a dwelling in space and time. For all that the sound and the image remain together, they are not yoked into a logograph, not overcoded into a signifying machine. Their territory is a rhythm, a temporal and spatial coding. Now it is true that Xu Bing arrives at this character-refrain or code-territory through a decoding of the State form of the Chinese character. He works through the overcoding implicit in Chinese character, and overcoding usually serves as an internal limit to the modern processes of decoding and recoding—simplification, rationalization, and phoneticization. Xu Bing thus loosens the ties that bind sound and image, that prioritize form over movement. Thus the character no longer functions as a relative limit, as one writing system among others. It pushes toward an absolute limit, where it would become completely unhinged. Such a gesture runs the risk of pushing toward transcendence. Xu Bing's works however, when most effective, produce an utterly localized transcendence. The living word becomes like an instance of what William James called the "little absolute."

James contrasts the little absolute to the grand absolutes of the Hegelian theodicy: variations are relative to an absolute (a non-relation) but one that is so infinitesimally small that it is not known, perceived, or sensed, even though it is nonetheless experienced, being integral to the

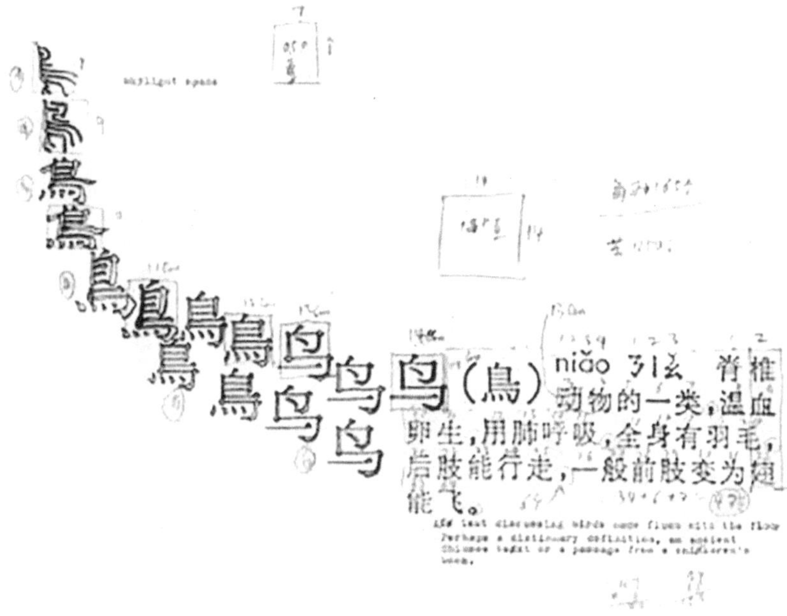

Figure 15. Xu Bing, Sketch for The Living Word (Courtesy of Xu Bing).

experience of the character-in-variation. This little absolute that makes for semblance is active at both poles: at the pole where the character is captured in ink-blackened form within a dictionary, assigned a place and given a definition, as the plan for *The Living Word* conveys so lucidly, and at the pole where the character wings up into skylight. The paradox is that capture and escape are not *substantially* different.

They are, however, different in relation and thus *actually* different in effect and in history, forming different modes of existence in relation to a little absolute that is sometimes called Chinese writing or brushwork because that is where its semblance is experienced. This semblance is analogous to the territories or refrains in Deleuze and Guattari's account—a stopping on movement that produces a localized transcendence, but its localization is not territorialized. Is such an experience of the semblance of writing not precisely where Xu Bing strives to track the eccentric movements of other Asias—in the immediation of Chinese characters as little absolutes?

Second Movement

The More-Than Human

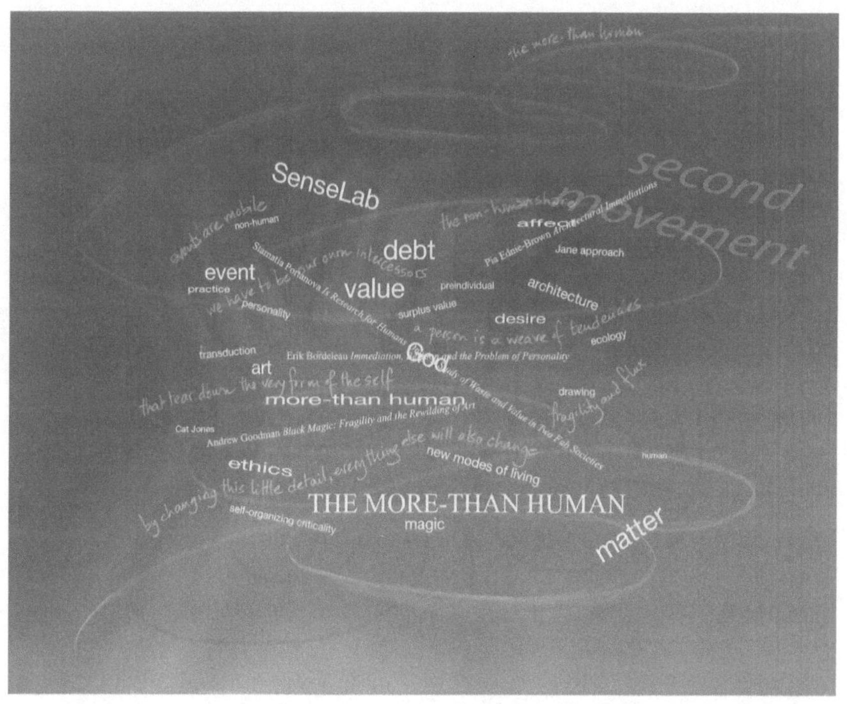

Erin Manning

Prelude

By changing this little detail, everything else will also change.

Mediation keeps things in place. It keeps an order, organizes a hierarchy, names the terms. It's between, not of or with. And so the points from which the mediation occurs sit still. And yet, they never really do. This is what immediation teaches us. Take rewilding. Andrew Goodman writes: "Rewilding emphasises the potential of dynamic and complex ecologies with intensive capacities to collectively experiment with flux" (Immediation 1, 134). Rewilding, while connected intrinsically to a practice of shifting the dynamics of a given natural environment by seeding it with species that alter the balance of its ecology, is also a term that could be given to the work of immediation itself. Indeed, all rewildings are immediations, as Goodman points out.

Immediation is always a practice. Its work is to express the shift in conditions of experience. Stamatia Portanova wonders about the concept of the useful in this context. Does the useful as an evaluative category not require mediation? What would the concept of immediation do to the very idea of value? How would it rewild the "wasted effort" of living, that share of experience which never seems to count even though it always makes a difference?

The question turns around the more-than human. Being moved by thought, Stamatia Portanova suggests, is a more-than human experience, unmediated by the usual tendencies to make experience count. Being moved by Avery Green, an architectural personality, similarly suggests an account of experience that troubles the human-centeredness of our accounts of value.

The more-than human is an emphasis on two things: 1) the very concept of the human as usually situated in experience tends to obfuscate the non-human share that also populates the human, 2) the event of experience cannot be reduced to a human account of it as though the human were the conductor of all worldly events.

It's about moving beyond the idea that human intentionality orders experience as it unfolds. A more-than human approach would begin elsewhere, proposing that the human is continuously rewilded by experience unfolding, is more a tendency than a formed entity. How we compose in the event is who we are, here, now.

Events are mobile. They are choreographed by edgings into determinacy that leave openings for shifts in speed and scale. The event of a forest rewilding shifts the ecology by altering the field of relation. What is reached when the ecology becomes self-sustaining is less a state of identity than a quality of dynamic form. Goodman speaks of self-organizing criticality, suggesting that within the poised state of a rewilding there nonetheless exists a continuous capacity for change: "Here while the proportions of ranges of events may be statistically analyzable and 'predictable,' the timing of any individual event is non-linear and not predictable, and thus at any one point in time all potential future events are still open to actualization and the richness or thickness of the virtual is preserved" (Immediation 1, 144).

Charles Sanders Peirce gives us a definition of personality that carries the force of a self-organizing criticality. He writes: "personality is some kind of coordination or connection of ideas ... This personality, like any general idea, is not a thing to be apprehended in an instant. It has to be lived in time; nor can any finite time embrace it in all its fullness. Yet in each infinitesimal interval it is present and living, though specially coloured by the immediate feelings of that moment" (Peirce 1992a: 331).

Pia Ednie-Brown sees style in the concept of personality. What is the style of this singular rewilding? How does it do the work of immediation? What kind of dynamic form does it call forth?

Avery Green's dynamic form cannot be limited to her architectural boundaries. She is also a proposition, and a fabulation. Her individuation exceeds the shifts of her inner walls to include the solitude of the transindividual who composes across her. Her talent goes far beyond the work of mediation we usually associate with houses. Avery Green immediates not only at the level of everyday living, she composes across all diagrams of life-living. That is to say: Avery

Green is not only the object, she is the process, the force of form that touches at the nerve of architecture itself.

The concept of the useful re-emerges. Ednie-Brown writes:

> All the same issues can be raised in relation to buildings: they generally have a responsibility to be useful and to serve some purpose, but they offer much more to the event than instrumentalised servitude. The aesthetics of their presence, as still and unmoving as they may seem, is no less relationally involved and affectively powerful than the activities that a building makes possible. Buildings may mediate through their instrumental role, but their presence operates with an open immediacy—becoming part of individuating processes well beyond themselves. In the context of architectural practice, the degree to which mediation and immediation operate together becomes vivid. (private email correspondence with Ednie-Brown January 2019)

Portanova might respond: "In particular, we could think of the notion of a "wasted effort," and of the delicious Dionysian joy that comes with it." For architecture is replete with "wasted effort." Think of all those drawings, "piles of torn-edged, diaphanous, yellow leaves marked with graphite thoughts." Think also of the traces left by earlier inhabitants, their marks lost to all except those who lingered long enough to perceive them:

> During demolition we found drawings of girls, by a young girl, on the studwork under the particleboard wall lining. The drawings were dated 1955 and the 11-year-old author was named. Across all those years that my young daughter and I lived with Avery (in her pre-named days) we had no idea how many other girls were hidden under her skin. The more I work with Avery, as we move together through a field of mutual, and at times quite radical transformation, the more I am finding that just as some mysteries or secrets come to light, new ones are generated. (Immediation 1, 190)

This drawing returns us to the personality, and with it to Avery Green's own rewilding, changed as she certainly is by having been fabulated into being. Érik Bordeleau writes: "The person as temporal contraction or duration doesn't necessarily involve a sense of intentionality or humanness" (Immediation 1, 171). If the person is always more-than, a personality a weave of tendencies always in metastability, what we are left with is a sense of a certain inheritance, but not an identity per se. This may be the work of the more-than human, to teach us how to address the complexity between durations and scales. For in the scale of the right-now, a house might seem like a house and a person like a person. A forest might seem like a forest and a wolf a wolf. And it's unlikely we would see anything other than waste in waste. But all is not occurring in this duration aligned to our human scale and sensibility.

"From the perspective of immediation, the person as subject most often appears like an unnecessary or at least secondary form of closure and limitation," writes Bordeleau (Immediation 1, 174). Immediations proposes times not yet felt, immanent to the events they call forth. These times not yet felt include us but they are not composed by a subject that would dwell outside them. From this perspective of mutual inclusion what emerges is much more complex than the form it seemed to want to take. It is no longer waste we see, but the force of value reoriented. It is not simply a house, or a human, a forest or a wolf. It is an ecology always slightly out of equilibrium, always slightly out of sync with itself. The potential of a relational field in transformation is precisely its capacity to immediate in ways that bring to expression new forms and forces of existence. From here, new modes of living can be invented, and with them, new ways of wasting effort.

Stamatia Portanova

Is Research for Humans Only? A Study of Waste and Value in Two Fab Societies

What was Hegel's ultimate project? According to Jean Hyppolite, it was the fusion of being and sense, without the intercession of any intermediate element (Hyppolite 1987: 4-5). This project led his whole philosophy to disclose the identity existing between the being of the world and human sense, a revelation constituting for him the highest form of experience.

The philosophical project of this article is to think beyond the dialectical union of the world's immediacy and human mediation, conceiving instead the possibility to blend both the rigidity of being and the limits of the human into a "becoming of the non-human." This blend will be achieved through the concept of 'immediation', a notion whose precise definition will be the aim of the whole article.

Introduction

Revealing the non-human elements and forces that run alongside and inside human beings is a recurrent aim of many theoretical and practical projects, most of which directly aspire to completely demolish the monolithic ontological partition standing between the passivity of raw matter and the agency of "vibrant life" (not only human life). In these projects, the definition of the non-human therefore aims at resolving the even larger dualism that still opposes inorganic matters to living organisms, a dualism promoting the biological predominance of the living over anything that "does not breathe." In fact, "the quarantines of matter and life," Jane Bennett writes, "encourage us to ignore the vitality of matter and the lively powers of material formations" (2010: vii). These powers are for example suddenly brought to the foreground when the trash generated by our production and consumption activities does not stay "away" in landfills but generat[es] lively streams of chemicals and volatile winds of methane" (Bennett 2010: vii). So, she continues, "How to describe without thereby erasing the independence of [these] *things*?" (2010: xiii, emphasis added). First of all, if we really want to give back to matter its autonomous vitality, it would be best to question any residues of a Hegelian human mediation, not least the very notions of "thing" and "object" so densely populating Bennett's and many other contemporary theories. Matter is composed of things, of objects (and therefore, inevitably, of subjects), but only in "our" objectified subjective picture of the world. It is thus an intention of this article to accept the neo-materialist suggestion of Bennett and others, and take seriously the vitality of non-human bodies, their capacity not only to intervene on human trajectories but also to develop trajectories of their own. At the same time, it will be indispensable to introduce and develop "immediation" as a concept that can start questioning the perception of these material bodies as lively (and, in the case of trash, potentially dangerous) "objects," while disrupting the metaphorical relation (sometimes a fight) established on equal terms between "us people and them things." Through immediation, the humanly limited understanding of experience as an elaboration of data (or "objects of perception and knowledge") will be amplified by putting data in relation to feelings, as "It is by reference to feelings that the notion of [immediation] obtains its meaning."[1] Feeling, in its turn, will not be simply considered as an emotional human content (joy, sadness, etc.) but, as Alfred N. Whitehead suggests, as that quantum of energy, that vectorial transfer of energy which physics exemplifies as a material mediation between bodies (Whitehead 1967b: 116). The material mediation of feelings between occasions of experience is a very different concept from the epistemological mediation of objective perception conceived by Hegel as a way to affirm the human predominance in the world. It is, in fact, a mediation which ultimately does not mediate between preexisting entities but "immediates" their constitution. Under this light, the aggressively democratic knowledge of the "trash-thing" as an objective datum or a matter of fact in life, and the accompanying emotions of fear or disgust elicited by it in the human subject, can be complemented by an "immediated feeling" of waste as energy in excess: as Georges Bataille would put it, not a danger for humans but a "luxury" in nature. In the light of the environmental emergency that is affecting the Earth, such luxurious and excessive definition of waste certainly offers itself to many criticisms. For this reason, an ethical explication of this idea will be developed in the chapter. But the final outcomes of this conceptual turn should be: first, a capacity to think these issues without putting the human point of view at the centre, which still dominates questions of sustainable production and consumption, and then, as a consequence, the theorization of a different ecological sense.

This enterprise will be undertaken in what could be defined as a "con-fi" (or conceptual fiction) scenario: without preoccupying ourselves too much with distinctions between a scientific, an artistic and a philosophical point of view (at least for the present moment), let us imagine a research lab, equipped with test tubes and all the other usual paraphernalia, extending its activities over a time span of almost two hundred years, from the 19th century to our present. This setting might appear somehow awkward to the reader since spaces devoted to research in the Humanities are usually not conceived as labs inhabited by people wearing white coats and peering at colourful tubes. Instead, such spaces are often envisioned as populated by respectful browsers of printed pages that, for the majority of humans, are the functional equivalent of waste. A possible way to explain this unexpected lab scenario might be to consider waste as a substance for thought, a mental compound composition deriving from a basic "conceptual molecule." The idea of a conceptual molecule, in its turn, transposes Gilles Deleuze and Felix Guattari's notion of a "conceptual persona" into our times. Conceptual personae, the two thinkers explain, are points of view that set the conditions for a philosopher's thought and introduce their concepts. (Deleuze and Guattari 1994: 51-75). Accomplished movements of thought can only take place through the acrobatics of these personae which, moving like crystals or germs of thought, become a thinker's agents of enunciation. Adapting this idea to the present time, we can conceive immediation as a thought molecule (rather than a persona) to be synthesised, and from which it should be possible to generate a different feeling, perception and concept of waste. This adaptation allows us to leave the theatrical conception of philosophy as an animated plane populated by personae, transferring the very conditions of thought into a lab.

The whole experiment happens in three phases, which could also be thought of as the main moments characterizing the duration of philosophical research and writing: 1) collecting the informational specimens and synthesising them into a conceptual "immediation" molecule; 2) using the molecule to generate an "immediated" concept of waste; 3) immediately testing the results.

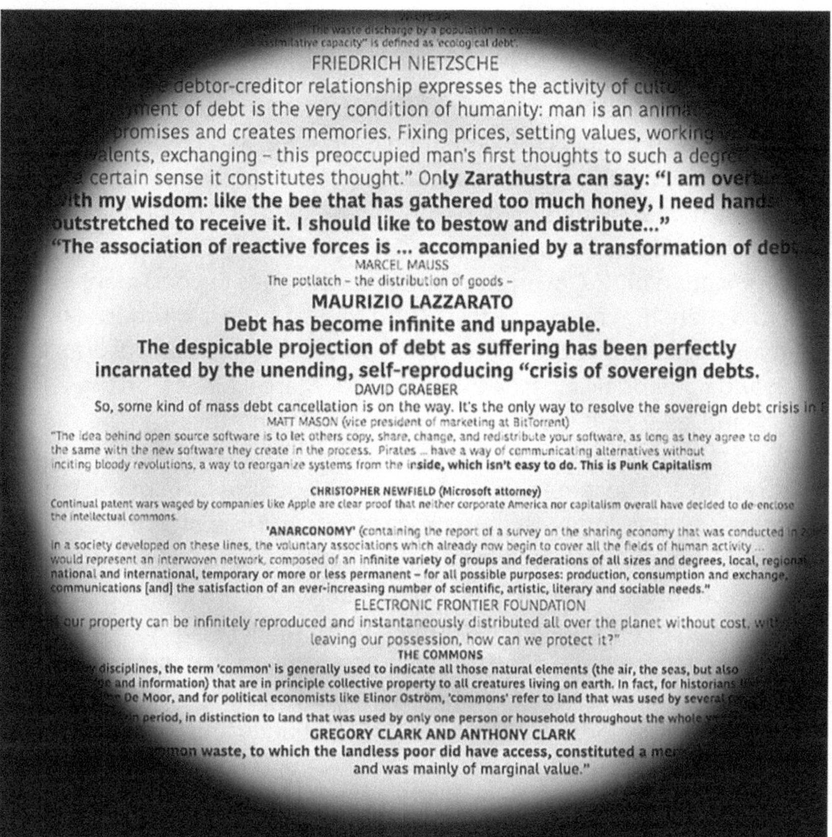

Figure 16. Verbal petri dish Image by Anna Munster

Phase 1: The Immediations Molecule

Our lab has several test tubes disposed on its sterile tables. Each tube has the name of a different "researcher" written on its label, and is filled with a not so rare, and yet quite precious material: they contain bits and pieces of information, conceptual and factual specimens ready to be analysed and synthesised into a complex molecule. The data, as soon as the tubes are opened, quickly pour out in the shape of volatile word assemblages resonating through the whole room. Now let us imagine ourselves in the act of collecting the verbal material from these tubes, and of inoculating it on a verbal petri dish (the blank page).

Once put on the dish, the informational fragments appear logically disconnected and stylistically dissonant, as they certainly do not reflect whole ideas or systems of thought. After analysing them, we understand that the best reagent to be used in order to synthesise them into a coherent "immediation" molecule is the notion of "value".

"Wikipedia tells us that waste is a human debt, towards nature and towards other humans. From Friedrich Nietzsche, we know that the first mental product deriving from debt-based modes of human relation is "value", as the repayment of debt has always been the precondition for the determination of value. (Deleuze 2006: 135). Only Zarathustra, the personification of the "overman" (the one who goes beyond man) is able to donate his knowledge freely and to distribute it without asking anything in exchange. Therefore, he creates an infinite immeasurable value and no debt. (Nietzsche 2008: 54). For Marcel Mauss, on the other hand, every gift received (for example the matters that the Earth puts at human disposal for production and consumption) has to be repaid and becomes a debt (for example, in the form of waste); nevertheless, this compulsion to repay is felt by virtue of a "force" which is not humanly determined but contained in the thing given, a force which compels the recipient to make a return (Mauss 2011: 9-10). From its human determination through debt, value becomes a material energy coming from the gift itself. But, according to Nietzsche, there is a moment in human history when debt becomes unpayable, and this moment coincides with the birth of Christianity and the invention of "guilt." In the Christian conception, guilt is the requirement of an infinite suffering by the human, which is only able to pay the interests on the new incalculable and transcendental value of debt (Nietzsche 2008: 157). In contemporary societies, the transcendental nature of the god-creditor (but also of the "planet-creditor," the "society-creditor" and "the State-creditor") has been acquired by money itself, or capital, the economic surplus value in the name of which, as Maurizio Lazzarato and David Graeber argue, debt becomes inextinguishable, and guilt is internalized (by individuals, but also by whole societies and States, or sovereign powers) (Lazzarato 2012; Graeber 2012). The moral basis of the debtor-creditor relation, as the most fundamental form of human mediation, is thus definitely put into question. The sharing economy or sharing culture, as a culture of the gift, on the other hand, is starting to delineate a new socio-economic model (or, as Matt Mason defines it, a "punk capitalism") where the capitalist compulsion to profit is combined with higher moral values such as creativity and altruism (Mason 2008: 8). In fact, one of the features of this new environment (the "anarconomy," as it has also been defined) is actually represented by so-called "innovation ecosystems," a new business ecology which replaces the old concept of the private firm, and in which the value of the company increases by including other companies, but also groups and individuals sharing their own products (Newfield 2013: 7). According to political theorist Michael Hardt, productive value is indeed maximized through sharing (Hardt 2014: 349). This maximization, though, can only happen through a considerable lowering of costs, thanks to the free work of many and despite the preoccupations of some (such as the Electronic Frontier Foundation) with the right way to find a value and compensate collective work (Mason 2008: 4). Beyond the evident confusions, beyond the differences of approach and even the superpositions between those who support free sharing in order to exploit and make a profit, and those who believe in its revolutionary potential to do away with capitalism itself, the main idea that sustains this system is that of the "commons." A common property (such as air, water, information, or Zarathustra's freely bestowed wiseness) has values of subtractability and excludability that can vary according to different social dispositions and needs (Verhoeven 2015). Since pre-capitalist antiquity, in fact, the Commons have been mainly conceived as non-excludable common goods (more specifically, "common lands") appropriated by autonomous self-managed collectives of land workers. It is interesting that the land of marginal value, not officially claimed by anyone and cultivated by landless peasants, on the other hand, has usually been defined as "waste land."

After the synthesis, the conceptual molecule, which in the end has emerged as a molecular concentrate of the "commons", seems to strangely reveal contradictory qualities: it is too densely packed with facts, ideas, concepts, from the measurement of value through debt, to the sharing culture as a problematization of value, from the birth of Christianity to land enclosures. At the same time, the molecule appears to be quite diluted, the notion of "waste land" as common unclaimed property of no value, for example, being too far from Nietzschean disinterestedness. The outcome of the first experiment phase is therefore not positive, if tested for the creation of a coherent and innovative conceptual molecule that can change our conception of waste: from a dangerous ṭhing (Bennett's landfills), the latter simply changes its status and becomes a useless and recyclable piece of the environment (the waste land). Perhaps as a consequence of this conceptual limit, the sociopolitical and economic practice of the commons still conceives and produces trash as a valueless substance to be either discarded or put to new use (even if only in the form of "data trash"). The commons, in the end, are not immediations, as they seem to be still motivated by a Hegelian desire to make the world coincide with human sense (or, in the same way, with human need).

What are the dominating aims and desires of scientific, cultural and economic research in contemporary societies? Running the risk of oversimplifying, we can recognise two tendencies that (as the sharing economy is showing us) are not necessarily oppositional but contrapuntal. On one hand, we see the constant urge to make more money and extract a surplus profit from all available resources, as a way to honour the divinity of capital. This is "capitalist desire." But on the other hand, as Tiziana Terranova writes, there is a parallel, increasingly spread-out tendency towards "acknowledging that growing food and feeding populations, constructing shelter and adequate housing, learning and researching, caring for the children, the sick and the elderly requires the mobilization of social invention and cooperation" (Terranova 2014: 388). We could call this "common desire." A consequence of this second social tendency is that all the main biological and inorganic materials (water, land, air, or "matter") are defined as collective human property, something to be well disposed of in order to avoid the current situation of resource shortage and distribution inequality, which are among the biggest problems faced by our species of human proprietors. In this process of material redistribution, "the many redefine what is necessary and valuable, and how to achieve it" (Terranova 2014: 388). Economically re-evaluating waste into a new source becomes then another necessity for the contemporary human.

In fact, to these two tendencies it is possible to add (at least) a third one: immediated desire. What if the above issues were addressed from a non-human-centred point of view, one where the universal man, the natural owner of matter and of the inalienable right to its property, was finally put into question? As already mentioned, many contemporary research projects are inspired by this kind of desire. An example, as we have seen, is certainly Bennett's aspiration to "highlight the active role of *nonhuman* materials" in our life, and her conceptualisation of a desire which is not simply of the theorist or of the researcher but of things themselves: thing-desire or, as she calls it, "thing-power" (Bennett 2010: 2). Going much beyond the recognisable identity of an object as being inextricably coupled to a subject, the thing appears when the object reveals its otherness, that never objectifiable depth from which, for example, a credit card suddenly looks uncanny to its possessor, or a sardine can buried in a trash heap loses its muteness and says something to us. The ontological operation accomplished by such theory is, in other words, the equation of things to bodies, on the basis of their common tendency to persist (a definition which Bennett obtains from Spinoza's "conatus"). It is in this sense that Bennett's things stop being objects of human knowledge and begin to show what they can be and do by themselves: the independence of the "it" is not an epistemological effect of the human's cognitive failure or of the object's recalcitrance, but is an ontological definition of the thing's active capacities. Under this light, the world can be seen as a giant deposit of more or less useful, more or less dangerous, more or less powerful things (a vision in line with the whole conception of the "common good," which in its turn resonates with Mauss's anthropological analysis of things and their force or capacity to make us indebt ourselves). And yet, this "thingy" vision does not really free itself from a real anthropocentric tendency to affectively, cognitively and theoretically appropriate, economically exploit, use or reuse the world at will. In order to at least tend towards such liberation, we should question the very existence of such a thing as a sardine can, for example in the perceptual sphere of the fly quickly covering the trash heap with its little legs.

If we look more closely at these pre-supposed things through the lens of a speculatively materialist philosophy, we find that, as Whitehead writes, "The most general term 'thing'—or, equivalently, 'entity'—means nothing else than to be one of the 'many' which find their niches in each instance of concrescence" (Whitehead 1967b: 211). A thing is always part of a collective "concrescence," a term whose etymology comes from the Latin *concrescere*, to "grow together," and which is used by Whitehead to indicate process, or the way in which experience reaches its unity as "the many become one, and are increased by one." (Whitehead 1967b: 211) What all this means is that each instance or moment of experience is an individual thing, and ultimately there are no things but only concrescence, or acts of growing together. And what is it that grows together in experience, if not things? Recognising the abstract metaphysical nature of such analysis, Whitehead nevertheless argues that the apparent singularity of an entity (the vision of "this" or "that" sardine can) presupposes a plurality of components (physical and conceptual data, emotions and purposes, affective tones, a subject and object that emerge and do not preexist), none of which are to be exclusively attributed to the human or to the material element of the experience, but all belonging to the experience itself. At the same time, these components are indistinguishable from their growing together, as they constitute not a thing but an actual occasion of experience, the real atomic entity in Whitehead's philosophy. In this sense, the overcoming of the human point of view is not given by an overlapping of human being and thinghood, or by the horizontality of the "us-it" relation. Rather, this overcoming coincides with an operation that transforms a multiplicity of objective data into an experiential complex "which is concretely one." According to Whitehead, this operation is performed by feeling, the latter being defined by the philosopher as a transference of quantitative emotional energy from cause to effect, or from past to present. In this way, Whitehead's cosmology makes the objectivity of materialism shift into an "organic realism," a point of view where a world of "fluent energy" finally replaces one of "static stuff." This fluent energy is constantly in transfer or, which means the same thing, is always felt, but this does not imply the existence of preexisting subjects and objects of feeling, but only a mutating energy, from which sentient subjects and objects emerge. It is important to remember here the non-anthropomorphic nature of feeling, at least in the Whiteheadian sense of the term: feeling, or prehension, is a non-human affective response, the immanent affective ground of all perceptions (physical prehensions) and thoughts (conceptual prehensions). The stone feels the water it falls into, and shifts its temperature and texture accordingly.

Returning to the conceptual specimens collected on our verbal dish, we can follow again the process of value-production which, from the notion of debt as a primordial human form of value measurement through to the necessity of repayment, goes through the accumulation of capitalist surplus value, and then through its redistribution in the sharing economy, to arrive to a commons-based idea of value re-production (in the sense of a production or creation of new values). This process of "valuation" (value creation) appears now, under our new organically realist lens, as a selection or a filtering of forms of energy, or feelings (from the preference for economic calculation to moral obligation) that shape the relational space between giving and receiving humans and given things. The same fluent energy takes on always different forms while flowing across that relation, progressively morphing from a feeling for money to a sense of community. At this point, we are finally able to synthesise a possible new definition for our philosophical molecule: immediation as the energetic metamorphosis, mutation or modulation, the shift in feeling that creates different occasions of experience, without the need for any human means but only for that capacity to feel which is proper of matter itself. Conceiving the world as a process or a continuity of occasions linked through the energetic modulations of feeling, our immediation molecule can thus do away with the rigid Hegelian conception of the world as the historical evolution of a Pure Being perfectly coinciding with human consciousness and reason.

Phase 2: The Substance of Waste

One of the main examples of how immediation, or immediated desire, can be experienced, is found in Bataille's writings. In particular, his reconsideration of the problems of human production and consumption (or the economy) inside the larger framework of matter and its energetic expressions seems very much in line with our reflections so far (Bataille 1991: 20). As Bataille writes, the energy transmitted by the sun to the planet Earth is always in excess, as the most perfect embodiment of a disinterested donation. This energy is in any case too much, and "It is [only] to the *particular* living being, or to limited populations of living beings, that the problem of necessity presents itself" (1991: 23). Wealth, or energetic excess, characterises what Bennett calls "vital matter." This material vitality is deployed by living beings to feed their own growth and, Bataille explains, once this process is completed, the remaining energy is simply dissipated without any profit. The act of dissipation, which is performed by nature in several ways (for example through reproduction), seems to go against the basis of any rational economy and against the continuous implementation of productive forces. According to Terranova, in fact, "what characterizes a capitalist economy is that th[e] surplus of (...) energy is not simply released, but must be constantly reabsorbed in the cycle of production of exchange value leading to increasing accumulation of wealth by the few (the collective capitalist) at the expense of the many (the multitudes)" (2014: 387). And yet this cycle, she continues, leads nevertheless to the periodic widespread destruction of accumulated wealth in the form of psychic burnout, environmental catastrophe and war, the creation of hunger instead of satiety, food banks next to the opulence of the super-rich. Against these energetic blockages, what needs to be reclaimed is therefore not merely more power to produce and consume but also to dissipate, to waste energy, a luxury to be extended, or returned, to all beings. A democracy of waste, a luxurious commons without any subjects and objects, and therefore without any residues of production and consumption.

But how could this possibly be realised, without falling back into the vicious circle of capitalist consumerism and recycling? How could new forms of experimentation work with the notion of dissipation but from a different, non-human and organically material, perspective? At this point, it would be interesting to try to understand whether the classical notion of economic value and productivity still enchaining all forms of research in the scientific, artistic and even philosophical fields (their possibilities and outcomes) to the imperial mechanism of utility (and debt) can dissolve itself into and through the notion of waste as a necessary luxury, without implying the squandering of quantities of fossil-fuels or solar power or of any other resource. Let us think for example of dance as a form of energy research. In dance (or, as Erin Manning describes it, the relational movement of at least two bodies), the energetic excess economically described by Bataille as material luxury and biological fuel, is intensively felt, as Manning writes, as a "preacceleration," the feeling of the imminent motion waiting to take a direction, the body's way to already and still vibrate in unison with the world created by each of its steps (Manning 2009b). This intensive flow, always active in the stillest of bodies as a not-yet motion, a motion on the verge of expression, passes between bodies, and is aesthetically modulated, or "wasted," into the movements of a dance. In such research processes as tango, contact improvisation or even ballet, subjective utilitarian or functional consciousness is at some point postponed and all the elements involved (humans, clothes and shoes, floors, music, air) let themselves be simply instructed by the movements of energy, rather than by a predetermined aim. A different individuation of living and non-living ecosystems emerges, where the research activity acquires a lived and felt, rather than a merely performed and evaluated, nature. For the researcher, this implies beginning with a question that is a real opening, an interval that will activate and compose the process, and using that space to let the energy of bodies and movements take its own trajectory. Only in this way can research compose an infra- and trans-institutional ecosystem, an ecology of human and non-human experiences that are never externally informed but always immanently in-formation. The ontological and ethical presupposition of this conception is, indeed, that events have a privilege over products, objects and goods, and experiential ecosystems have precedence over established economic systems.

Phase 3: Testing in the Labs

But the final aim of our research experiments, as already anticipated, is to contrapuntally examine two research labs, testing them against the immediated concept of waste as a common luxury, while also verifying the latter's ethical sustainability. In order to do this, it is now necessary to get out of the lab and direct our theoretical point of view onto some concrete examples. First, we will pay a visit to the Biohack Academy, an education programme of the Waag Society in Amsterdam that teaches its participants how to use biological applications and grow their own bacteria or fuels, food, filaments, fragrances, pharmaceuticals, and fungi "at home," using only Open Source hardware, a FabLab (Fabrication Laboratory) or a Maker/Hackspace.[2] With this kind of personalized biofactory, it becomes possible to experiment with the production of a biogas or the purification of water, realizing various potentials that diffuse the gift of biotechnological knowledge across an ecosystem wider than the institutional and corporate bio-industry, and beyond the capitalist logic of debt. In this open fabrication environment where information, tools and life are shared, we are curious to explore whether the materials themselves, air and water and information, are not simply put to use (or re-used) as commons or, in other words, as passive objects endowed with an economic or productive value, but become, with their properties and their energies, actively involved in the process.

In a bio-hack lab, the routine procedure comprises the gestures of thinking, testing, watching the results and sometimes, inevitably, failing. When we get to the lab, we meet a citizen scientist who is thinking about calorie restriction as a form of biological stress that could be used as a method for prolonging life. The scientist decides to test his thought on a colony of worms but, as it can often happen, the experiment fails, which means the death of the worms. Some other researchers would certainly burst into tears for such an event, since as we are told, they tend to do so even at the unexpected death of their pet bacterium. Nevertheless, once dead, the worms are disposed of in the appropriate containers and become waste.

After a few days, we attend an international Bio-Commons Lab organized by Rural Hub in Salerno (Italy), where a group of bio-hackers is discussing the important issue of the Bio-Commons (to be intended either as a potential institute or simply as a license to be designed, or as both), in which digital commons (hardware and software) and biological knowledge are combined as free material to share in a legally protected way.[3] The digital infrastructure of the Bio-Commons, it is collectively agreed upon, needs to be open source, democratic, efficient, universal, decentralized, convenient, and accessible to everyone, while also being safe and secure. But at some point, someone shifts the direction of the discussion, and starts to talk about patents as weapons, or as a form of protection against multilateral corporate and competitive interests: not willing to take risks and be exploited, they support the idea of decreasing the openness of the whole project. We do not understand: is all this about market survival, or about undermining the system and providing free bio-technologies for everyone? This kind of lab environment (Salvatore Iaconesi, who is also present at the meeting) explains, is in fact often inhabited by a population of practioners such as makers and the new digital craftsmen of the DIY, hackers and collaborative innovators, engineers, designers, artists, scientists, all people that gravitate from the world of corporate business to that of alternative organisations. A whole creative class which has already been absorbed by the industry, as "Creatives are transformed in precarious research labs (startups, incubators, fablabs) [that] typically promote optic fibre, sensors, robots and all of the other products, services and approaches of the industry financing the initiative" (Iaconesi 2015). Despite the increasing usefulness of bio-tech hacking, the people involved in the research fall into the ambiguous in-between zone of the capitalist start-up and in the too human logic of value expressed by open source culture.

In another room, Ruediger Trojok from the Karlsruhe Institute of Technology is talking about the bad management of the antibiotics distribution by corporate pharmaceutical companies, and about the issue of increasing bacterial infections. It is prospected that, with a Bio-Commons license protecting and regulating the private use of wetware, hardware and software, (almost) everyone should become able to grow their own personalized phages (antibiotic cells) at home. At this point, we remember the dead worms left in the bin as victims sacrificed to the health-war: even in a bio-hack lab, it is still an issue of "us" against "them with a biological status proportionate perhaps to their size." A neo-materialist war between bodies, objects, things that are more or less frightening and dangerous to each other. When looked at from this point of view, bacteria therefore seem to be operating a rebellion or "a revolution without politics" in labs, a revolution without subjects and without principles of decision. We are increasingly surrounded by bacteria, we are told, and "[I]n the moment of right/s the commons [the universal human right to health, as the justifying foundation for research and experiments of all kinds] is already gone in the movement to and of the common that surrounds it and its enclosure" (Harney and Moten 2013: 18). In this situation, the main preoccupation will need to consist in avoiding (and potentially curing) that thing which is an illness or, in other words, the attack of a collective aggregate of bacteria.

The inefficacy of such an objectivist vision in the biotechnological research on illness is well identified by a more general statement by Latour. According to him:

> It is generally accepted in the various sciences dealing with complex collective behaviour [such as biology] that there exist some fundamental differences between the individual and the aggregate levels.... In 2-LS social theory, the most current approach to handling the distinction between macro-structures and micro-interactions consists in establishing a first level of individual entities, then adding to them a few rules of interaction, in order to observe whether the dynamics of interaction lead to a second level, that of aggregation, which has generated enough new properties to deserve to be called a "structure," that is, another entity for which it is possible to say that "it is more than the sum of its parts." (Latour et al. 2012: 2, 6)

Taken individually, bacteria are things without rights, easily transformable into waste, and not even easily recyclable. Collectively, they become a dangerous object to be fought without wasting any time. And yet, "By presupposing that there exist two levels, [biologists, like all "social" scientists] might have solved too quickly the very questions they should have left open to inquiry: What is an element? What is an aggregate? Is there really a difference between the two?... To dramatize the contrast, we," Latour writes, "claim that there is more complexity in the elements than in the aggregates, or stated a bit more provocatively that 'The whole is always smaller than its parts.' " (2012: 2). To the scientific approach based on 'individual-aggregate' or 'micro-macro' object dualisms, Latour opposes Tarde's alternative notion of the monad, neither a part nor a whole but a point of view. Each monad is an envelope encapsulating a content, or a series of properties. In this sense, there remains no real ontological difference between a person, a place, an institution, an event, a society and, we could add, a bacterium and an illness because, "In our model agents do not interact with one another, ... they 'are' one another, they 'own' one another, since they share many attributes or properties" (2012: 7). What we materially share with bacteria, what we lend and borrow from them, is the Bataillean idea of an energetic surplus to dissipate. By recognizing our positioning on this common field, it becomes possible to shift our point of view to an immediated conception of biological research. From the focused visualization of the scientist looking into a microscope to have a clear vision of the minuscule individuals, and then to be able to prevent or fight their collective behaviour, we can deviate our attention towards that energetic flow which runs between us and them, and which (as bacteria seem to know very well) needs to be wasted in some way. For example, through those useless bodily movements we humans call dance. Do any bio-hack labs exist which possess this kind of sensitivity? Are they willing to open another possible future for science? The first test ends at this point, with the idea of the bio-hack lab as a research environment where human conceptions of value and waste are still tied to the notion of the commons, and therefore not immediated enough. The potential for this kind of research to develop new sensibilities is, nevertheless, enormous.

After our bio-hacking incursion, one day we encounter by chance a blog post that catches our interest. The post was written by Paolo Venturi, and discusses some crucial aspects of sharing culture (Venturi 2014). In particular, it explains how instrumentality is one of the main dimensions on which the practice of sharing (such as the information and bio-material sharing of bio-hack labs) is often based, while the possibility for non-instrumental actions becomes increasingly scarce. And yet, the article goes on, what is generally considered as "wellbeing" for the human species appears as directly proportional to the quantity of time employed in non-instrumental activities, a time which, as social research is paradoxically finding out, is constantly decreasing. Corroborated by a series of well documented and referenced sociological studies, the article rekindles our interest in the idea of a non-functional movement and, consequently, of a non-instrumentally spent time. And it comes to our mind that the second location for the testing of our luxurious concept of waste could be the Immediations event of the SenseLab European Hub.[4]

This event (which is still running) is comprised of a series of micro-events held in different locations and connecting different practices. The micro-events are part of a wider scheme, an international project initiated by the Montreal-based SenseLab. Every SenseLab event, in the words of Brian Massumi and Erin Manning, is a research-creation event in which the coming together of people from different backgrounds happens alongside conceptual work and creative practice.[5] The event does not have any predetermined goal, but differently from the happening of improvisation as an unconstrained interaction, the experiential format of these events is given by the respective ways of coming together, of people but also of practices, concepts and techniques, all coworking along a reciprocal sensitivity to the properties of what is occurring. In this spirit, at each of the European SenseLab meetings, the preexisting tendency has been to create the conditions, through a series of enabling conceptual constraints (such as thinking the urban fabric in a non-metaphorical way, or working with water from a philosophical and micropolitical perspective), for a new experiential time of the city to emerge through the encounter. Preceding the actual physical meetings, the main activity has always been constituted by skype-facilitated reading sessions. Practical potential and material knowledge have then been woven to the conceptual inputs and to the movements of thought elaborated during these sessions and, once in locus, they have become something more than they were intended for, helping to develop propositions for collaborative techniques. An example: in preparation of the Zurich get together, which was held in April 2014, from the reading of Virginia Woolf's *The Waves* we moved to thinking about the rhythm of water and of words, and then to conceiving subjectivity as always being in a fluid state of subjectivation. From the same text, we also learnt about the vital role, in every subjectivation process, of those small moments and tiny events which Deleuze and Guattari define as "haeccities" (1987: 260-265). And then, in Zurich, something happened. Now, since another crucial constraint for SenseLabbers is to remain outside of the logic of reporting and representation, instead of trying to literally describe what happened we will simply sketch one of the little moments or "haeccities" that occurred while we were there.

Walking in a city garden, one day we encounter a red rope sculpture, a big and intricate net catching both the attention and muscles of its

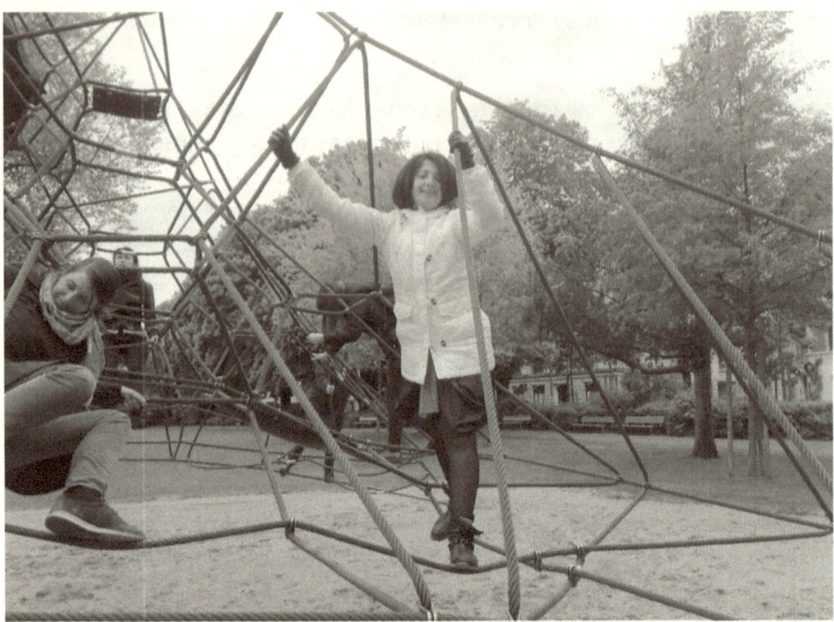

Figure 17. Red rope haecceity. Image, Stamatia Portanova

viewers with an immediated gesture. As soon as we see it, we start climbing, playing with it and taking pictures, putting it all of the different uses that such a versatile object can lend itself to. Apart from its actual usefulness (because entertaining children and adults, and stealing them a smile is certainly not a minor therapeutic task nowadays), the main property gradually emerging is that of an incredible capacity to adapt itself to our various bodies, each with its own size, shape, weight, height, elasticity, training, agility.... All this might not sound like anything of particular value. But let us think of the many motions and postures that could develop from such an encounter, from standing in freeze frame to be photographically captured, to walking and bending and jumping, and then let us think of all the feet and hands and knees and brains mobilized. Let us also look at all this through the eyes of a whole-day-sitting-alone-in-the-lab researcher, and let us imagine their wonder: a lot is actually going on. The mood changes, even the most blocked and immobile ones start to feel acrobatic in their brave attempts at coming to terms with the many hidden possibilities of elasticity. Suddenly, the city is transformed into an experimental motion lab. A choreographic fab(ulatory)lab. After leaving, we realize it was neither the rope nor us, but the whole spacetime woven for the duration of the event that really bounced and stretched and floated, giving to that corner of the city for that moment a different environmental configuration. The memory, of course, stays with us, inciting many reflections, allowing for the technique of philosophical research and writing to take on new intensities and new forms. Thus, in the second lab society, attention has moved from the observation and handling (and appropriation) of organisms/bodies as isolated things, to a more horizontal relationality that goes through the idea of energetic dissipation and practices of bodily movement.[6] Would it be possible (and desirable) to connect these two different sensibilities in some way, in a sort of future lab to come?

Conclusion

Our experiment started with a philosophical thought, and with the same tone it must conclude itself, while also continuing our reflection on the philosophical value of waste in research. From the neoliberal pragmatism of the useful, of scientific research that has the production of economic and cultural value as its real final aim, we have arrived to the event of playing with a rope. In this vision, the economically-conceived waste of actions, or of thoughts, or of time (as with philosophy itself, that great time-waster, and the only mode of thought perhaps brave enough to suggest a combination of bio-technological research and choreographic experimentation), does not need to be redeemed or reevaluated. On this point, it is of particular interest to think of Manning and Massumi's idea of a "pragmatics of the useless," giving value to what is not already valued as productive in contemporary capitalist societies (Manning and Massumi 2013). In particular, it is possible to think of the notion of a "wasted effort," and of the delicious Dionysian joy that comes with it. It is of course not a lack of value that is attributed in this sense to actions and efforts, but what is at stake is a rethinking of value in itself, and a questioning of the conventional economic and moral senses we, as human beings, usually give to it. The useless, as Massumi explains, is never passive and nihilistic, but already reveals the value, the force of research as an open, speculative, non-object-oriented and imaginative process. This kind of approach unleashes the intensity of research as a non-human-centred or non-human-mediated process, a process that, like philosophy itself, is only attached to the joy of being moved by thought.

What is important to highlight is the fact that pragmatic uselessness in research events is the plane from which new modes of subjectivation and of relationality can very concretely and usefully emerge. From this kind of lab society, in fact, comes a significant replacement of the key notion of debt with that of a disinterested gift, which is now intended as the disinterested act of paying the right attention to differences, to the various bodies and properties implied in all our relations, those same bodies and properties that still represent a hindrance for contemporary algorithmic and financial capitalism, and are at best to be simply dismissed, or eliminated as waste (think of the tons of local fruits thrown away each year in the name of profit, and think of all the wasted efforts of unknown artists trying to produce some work and to survive with no financial support). "Waste" is really such, of course, only in markets, where the very notion of value is totally submitted to a logic of quantitative in-equivalence and debt repayment: would it be possible for the unknown dance performer to repay the services of the prestigious doctor with her work? Under this light, all kinds of play with what is excessive and wasted (wasted efforts, wasted matters, wasted ideas), generously bestowing it without expecting anything in exchange, become vital not only for political critique but for creation, and therefore research (intended in the sense of an excessive and Dionysian political economy, as that conceived by Bataille). In view of a radical redefinition, as in Terranova's words, of what is necessary and valuable. Or, in Manning's words, "To remain as unintelligible to instrumental ways of working as possible.... In a sense, we have to be our own intercessors, our own free radicals, making sure that we don't get bogged down in what we think is expected of us, but build instead on the force of what we can barely imagine..."[7]

Notes

1. The original text from which this citation was extrapolated uses the term "immediacy" instead of "immediation." The term has been replaced on purpose, in order to highlight the semantic conjunction of the two concepts in this context. For the original, see Alfred N. Whitehead's 1978: 155.
2. This Academy was not attended by the writer in person. All the relevant information and data (such as about the worms experiment) were collected by following the online lectures uploaded on their video channel, available at https://vimeo.com/channels/biohackacademy
3. The Bio-Commons Lab was attended personally by the writer, and all the information presented in this article was collected through direct participation and discussion.

4. I attended the Immediations event of the European Senselab, and all the information presented in this article was collected through direct participation and online discussion.

5. See the video of Erin Manning and Brian Massumi's presentation for Public Humanities at Western "For a Pragmatics of the Useless: Propositions for Thought" (2013).

6. The word "society" is used here in the sense Whitehead refers to: a nexus of entities with a social order, not limited to the human, but even comprehending the physical states of matter. For a definition, see Whitehead 1978: 34.

7. This quote was extrapolated from one of Manning's posts on the online SenseLab hub.

Andrew Goodman

Black Magic: Fragility, Flux and the Rewilding of Art

> To grow nature is to encourage more of it. That's not easy to do. More nature means less control. Less control requires a certain kind of faith ... do you see the natural world as needing modification and improvement...? Do you view humans as a small part of an unbelievably complicated and fragile system, or do you view us as commanders?
> *Barber (2014: 19)*

Introduction: Ecology and Art

The recent "Rewilding" ecological movement has proposed radical new ways of conceiving of the care for the environment, challenging the "bottom up" and anthropocentric approaches favoured within much current environmental thinking. In rewilding experiments, rather than target the careful nurturing of fragile and endangered flora and fauna within an environment, or the large-scale breeding and reintroduction of species or replanting of forests, or focus on close supervision and regulation by trained park managers, "keystone species" such as wolves, bears or beavers are introduced into degraded environments. This has been shown to have a surprisingly far reaching impact on an ecology's overall "health," affecting all aspects from other predators, large and small fauna, and the development of microclimates and diversified flora, through to soil and water health (Monbiot 2014: 81, 84-86). Rewilding emphasises the potential of dynamic and complex ecologies with intensive capacities to collectively experiment with flux. This contradicts the perceived environmental necessity of ongoing outside intervention to predetermine acceptable outcomes (83), which places value on system stability (denying the very fragility that may in fact be a key to novelty). Here, rewilding is an ecological practice squarely addressing the field—not through control but through an understanding of the capacity for self-organization that exists within complex systems in certain states.

In considering instances of rewilding and its radical effects on ecologies—interesting in themselves as they are—I want to here interrogate what might be learned from these experiments. Aside from the wonder at these displays of the force and power of "nature" inspire (with potentially romantic and sublime aura), can these events be thought in a broader sense, beyond the detail of wolves, beavers and literal environmentalism, and thus could this concept have potential for a "rewilding" of art? That is, if we are concerned with a kind of art that might be thought of as participatory in an expansive sense of the term—one that involves more than a simple conversation between a participant and an object, or between two or more already composed and stable participants—an art that we might even choose to call "ecological" in its encouragement of a complex set of relations forming and reforming immanently between, within and across various components of an event, can this type of "ecology" be rewilded? Can indeed, "ecological" art be more than just a metaphoric label, loosely applied as the term "relational" often is, to a broad range of practices that think beyond the object[1]—can an art event in fact become a literal intensively organizing dynamic system?

How can we think or push participation outside of investments in control, identity and outcomes and into a more radical concern for the field *in its ongoing emergence*? By this I mean that to approach a "wilder" state, perhaps such art needs to think more about enabling the conditions for emergence of complexity—the prehensive capacities of ecologies to intensively evolve their own motivations or, as Erin Manning has termed them, their "minor gestures" (Manning 2016: 1). This, I would argue, might be linked to the concept of "immediation": a concern for the primacy of the event, for "affective field[s]" that generate "an immediate in-bracing of multiple bodies in an event and in differential attunement" (Brunner, Immediation 1, 276). As with processes of rewilding, processes of immediation might be concerned less with linear cause and effect and more with the excess of any direct causality (that must always also be in play), an excess arising from "the complexity of those relations, from interference and resonance effects between the formative factors" that creates a "margin of play in an event" (Massumi, Immediation 1, 281). That is, as I will argue, it is not exactly the wolves or beavers themselves who instigate these dramatic shifts in the ecological health, but the inventive, forward looking trans-subjective events that experiment with collective individuation-ing (wolf-*and*-deer-*and*-grass-ing, and so on) that continue to transduce forces flowing through the field, immanently create new relational complexities.

Here I attempt to extrapolate abstract principles from rewilding by considering such systems as examples of state systems, organized through intensive differentiation (DeLanda 2002: 14-16), in order to bring in research from the physical sciences on how in certain conditions such systems move towards novelty rather than entropy: studies on self-organizing criticality, far-from-equilibrium states and radical cybernetics concerned with expanded dimensional capacities. I then speculate on what might the role of an artist be when we attempt to think the potentials and tendencies of a relational artwork through enabling such dynamism of the field to be foregrounded? What might such an art look like and what intensive motivations would it attend to? What transindividual collaborations might evolve? Here this is thought through an examination of Cat Jones' *Somatic Drifts V1.0* a work that grafts human and plant life into new collective experiences: a strange hybrid of therapy, participatory art and black magic. For, as much as rules or conditions can be abstracted and quantified, both rewilding and Jones' artwork remain also magical: mysterious, alien and fragile, operating beyond the reach of the human participant, instead entertaining on an environmental scale, flowing through and around the human, with little concern for discrete boundaries. To paraphrase Gordon Pask, when we think on an environmental level, we must think not of systems composed of discrete things with inputs and outputs through which they communicate, but must recognise that the magic all happens on the plane of the field: as system level composition of potentials (Pask cited in Green 2001: 681).

Black Magic

> Since ecstasy is a communication with what is sacred, remote from ourselves, it is a communication with others too. There is no such thing as private ecstasy.
>
> *Lingis (2011: 169)*

What is black magic? Firstly, it is a *practice* rather than a thing, an adventure-into—rather than a method—an ecstasy of fields drawn into relation. Black magic is conjunctive, a practicing of intersubjectivity, an inter-specialization—a dislocation from a body that implicates "not one but several bodies and energies flowing in and out of one another across borders" (Taussig 2006: 141). It is flux, transition: an encounter with a wilderness that is the feeling of a "more to come" rather than an arrival.[2] It is a wilderness that comes from no longer being a thing, but the flow between things, their circulation, the force of their becoming-other. This is a wilderness that is as much found in one's own black heart as in the world, in a speculative moving beyond oneself—a transindividualization in the midst of individuations[3]—self organizing, metastable, autonomous and anonymous: a collective immediation with the event, the wilderness of the field.

But as well as enacting this flow, black magic is also a game or play that is a fluidity between belief and scepticism, a trickery that gains its strange power through the display and revelation of deception, through making perceptible the "fault line" in and between such distinctions. That is, it enacts a continuous movement between treachery and its reveal that is the shaman's technique: to involve confessions of fraud whilst inventing new trickery to confound and question this exposure, to hide and reveal simultaneously without resolution (Taussig 2006: 144). This is a fragile and paradoxical event whose magic is in the flow of ideas and other energies, in the *event itself* becoming "plastic and protean," suspended in "becoming other" (140).

Rewilding

> Instead of finding stability and harmony wherever we look, we discover evolutionary processes leading to diversification and increasing complexity.
>
> *Prigogine (1980: 2)*

George Monbiot's book *Feral: Rewilding the Land, Sea and Human Life* charts a series of instances in which the return of a top predator to an ecosystem enlivens and reinvigorates the environment far beyond linear causal chains, and he makes the argument that the loss of such "keystone" species (both extinct mega flora and existing species such as bears, whales, wolves and so on) is as least as responsible as a general loss of diversity and habitat for the degradation and entropy of these once dynamic natural systems. The controlled reintroduction of beavers into certain rivers in Scotland and Wales,[4] for example, changed and most importantly, diversified the surrounding area, creating variations in the river flow through the elaborate lodges they built, ditches and hollows in the banks, the felling of trees to create surplus wood and cleared areas, and through all this created habitat for a much wider variety of wildlife including fish, bats, ducks, voles, insects and soil microbes, as well as reducing flooding and soil loss through erosion (Monbiot 2014: 77-82). Similar reinvigoration was seen when wolves were reintroduced into Yellowstone National Park, where their arrival reduced the deer and antelope numbers that had led to erosion and modified the grazing animals' routes, allowing tree regrowth, the return of numerous species dependent on these forests, including bison, beavers (with accompanying diversity in river ecologies as above), bears and small mammals. This continued throughout the system down to soil health and nutrient distribution, with some areas now being intensely fertilized by the deer in their restricted safe havens, while other areas received less nitrogen, all allowing a greater diversity of fauna to flourish across the newly variegated terrain. As Monbiot argues, previous attempts to curtail the damage caused by deer through culling not only failed in this aim, but also provided none of the flow-on benefits the wolves provided (84-86).

The key to this success is not a move from bottom-up to top-down planning or organization, as the success of the wolves might imply. Top-down organization is highly problematic, it might again suggest anthropomorphism: that humans, as the top of the food-chain, are the necessary component, or worse, neo-Darwinism and a capitalistic "trickle down" economic model that sees the free market as the most dynamic and viable system.[5] Rather, looked at as a system-level problem, one can see that the wolves add or motivate key factors in the "system" of the wilderness. Firstly, one could say that they add "dimensions" —new levels on which interactions can take place between the components, new *system level* capacities for interaction, beyond the individual capacities of any one component. Secondly, they help to activate a metastable system, where there is a greater tension or competition for resources and thus components of the ecosystem are subject to multiple complex forces in this competition that allow nonlinear shifts to occur: a far-from-equilibrium system. Rather than attributing the new dynamism to any one species, this abstraction of the events might suggest these more promising and useful explanations that emphasize relationality, complexity and flexibility as the root cause of the newfound health or wilderness. Such system-level complexity is the third factor in consideration, the evolution of self-organizing capacities that are achieved at a point of system criticality.

Dimensions & Trophic Diversity

> Unity is not uniformity, but is coherence and diversity in collusion
>
> *Pask in Frazer (2001: 645)*

As Monbiot points out, clearly the success of rewilding is based on its emphasis on process rather than outcome (thus it is not really about "conservation" at all), emphasizing the necessity of promoting dynamic and deeply interactive environments (2014: 83). Monbiot argues that such systems are activated by an increase in "trophic diversity" leading to "trophic cascades." These, he states, occur when the animals at the top of the food chain—the top predators—change the numbers not just of their prey, but also of species with which they have no direct connection. Their impacts cascade down the food chain. (84)

The use of the term "cascades down" here perhaps demonstrates something of a misunderstanding of non-linear events and the special system-level capacities that might override local causalities. Greater trophic diversity, being an increase in diversity of potential energy-exchange relations, is however clearly a key factor (83).[6] When, for example, a particular animal increases the number of food sources it can exploit, and in turn can be exploited as a resource by a larger number of other components of the environment (remembering that fauna are, eventually, food for flora as much as vice versa), the overall entanglement of components, and therefore the system's flexibility and adaptability is increased as is its heterogeneity.[7] This increase in ways in which an environmental component[8] relates to the world around it might also be thought of in a larger sense as an increase in dimensions that, in Peter Cariani's terms, enlarge its "life-world" (Cariani 2008: 3).[9] Dimensions might be thought of as capacities for a component's interaction and differentiation within a system, its expressive possibilities, or, as Manuel Delanda states, "the number of relevant ways in which [a component] can *change* (these are known as [a component's] *degrees of freedom*) (DeLanda 2005: 13). A component species with increased dimensional capacities has a greater number of potentials that it is attracted towards, the conflict between these "attractors" —future states—charges greater potential differentiation (that is, differenciation): more (and more diverse) processes in which the species can engage with the field. Thus thinking in dimensions is not, as Delanda points out, about the consideration of individual static properties of objects or components, but instead a way of thinking the potential complexity of a system in process (14).

At its simplest, whilst the sheep or deer, for Monbiot, potentially erode and drain their environment of energy by interacting in a relatively mono-dimensional manner (eating everything in their path indiscriminately), the beavers eat some wood, leave other species alone, create eddies, pools and banks in rivers that once flowed relatively uniformly. In turn this creates new opportunities and problems (dimensions or capacities) for all that they interact with, and cause diversification (a particular tree species can grow here but not there, a fish can breed in this part of the river but not that section, and so on): there is a cascade, but not necessarily of direct relation, rather of exponential system-wide complexity seen as both ongoing positive and negative differentiation, with the system held in states of process or immanent states of development. These potentials are forward driving, if sometimes contradictory on the level of individual actualization, held together on a virtual plane as the undifferentiated potential of the system—as a multiplicity. As a multiplicity, this potential is without essence, it has no "unified and timeless identity" (DeLanda 2005: 26). There is no essential "wolfness" to perform, there is what the wolf does, how it interacts—what it is in a process of becoming—and this is always subject to potential change, a genesis immanent to the genesis of its world and organized through the negotiations between the evolving dimensional capacities of the wolf and the emergent dimensional capacities of the field of which it is a part.

These additional dimensions add new planes in which the components can potentially interact, and the ability of a system and/or numbers of its components to develop new dimensions gives it a level of 'autonomy' as Cariani terms it, as new intensively organized rules, actions and potentials can evolve (2008: 3). Dimensional change problematizes existing relations: they require a new flexibility—a new immanence to relations—in order to survive, and the event that develops is this very exploration of the field's new capacities to intertwine. Increases in dimensional capacities then might be the first step in creating a more complex system that is *immediating* (an ongoing event of exploration/ evolution of field or system capacities) rather than *mediated* (a renegotiation between components).

As in some of Gordon Pask's experimental art/science cybernetic ecologies[10], the dynamic wilderness post-beaver/wolf reintroduction is dynamic in a radical way because it does much more than encourage further individuations of a species' capacities. At a system level it goes back to a step before this stage, and demonstrates a capacity to autonomously develop the potential and motivations out of which such special individuations (and differentiations) might arise—to develop new dimensions. As Cariani terms it this is a truly "creative" rather than "adaptive" emergence: less concerned with creating new combinations of interactions within available dimensions as the former is, and more with the "expansion of the possibility space" (2008: 9).[11] This, I would argue is at the basis of the intensive dynamism of rewilding, the opening up of new dimensional spaces that is a charging or priming of the ecology's capacity to develop "minor gestures" (Manning 2016: 1-2 and passim) —a tuning of the field towards its future differentiation that is felt by the ecology itself—an immediatory process by which "fields of relation agitate and activate to emerge into collectivities" (Manning, Immediation I , 276).

Far from Equilibrium Systems

> The laws of nature, which no longer deal with certitudes but possibilities, override the age-old dichotomy between being and becoming.
>
> *Prigogine and Stengers (1996: 155)*

This exponential increase in intensive (actualized) differentiation and (potential) differenciation changes the nature of the system in a fundamental way that might be crucial to its newfound wilderness. The "rewilding" might be that the system as a whole as developed from a relative stable organization to an unstable system of organization—a far-from-equilibrium state. In the eroded sheep paddock where all is subsumed by the vociferous and uncritical appetite of the animal grazing without competition,[12] perhaps one could argue that this is an ecology in an entropic cycle. That is to say it tends towards a minimal energy state, while still being, of course, in many ways a complex ecology. While this tendency towards entropy might, as in classical physics, be seen as the "natural order" of all systems, Prigogine argues otherwise, stating that in far-from-equilibrium (FFE) systems behaviour can move instead towards a greater relationality and complexity (1980: 88-89), as components "acquire new properties" and become more active (Prigogine and Stengers 1996: 65).[13] Whereas the sheep maintain similar relationships in a relatively stable (if entropic) system, the presence of wolves not only encourages difference to arise (new feeding habits, redrawing of safe habitat boundaries for herbivores, increases in bird species, variations in forest density and tree species, and so on), but here difference is also preserved—accentuated even—through ongoing capacities to further differentiate differences (the preservation of potentials) that are, DeLanda states, characteristic of FFE systems (2005: 73). These emergent differences are tensions that drive the circulation of energies. This might be closer to the drive towards novelty that Whitehead designates as the driving appetite of the universe, rather than the entropy of classical physics that struggles to explain the nonlinear nature of events such as rewilding.

As a FFE system, a rewilding ecology operates in an intermediate position 'between a deterministic world and an arbitrary world of pure chance' (Prigogine and Stengers 1996: 189), moving beyond linear causal chains events. Here events that occur are never the result of clear trajectories, but always one (or more) of the many potential options, and causal chains are complex and system wide, and always themselves in a process of development and differentiation, held in tension (that is, quasi-causal). The arrival of a particular bird species to the river where beavers have been returned, might, for example, be related to (though not entirely contingent on) the increase in wood debris on the riverbanks that provide habitat for insects that become a food source, and/or the reintroduction of opportune tree and shrub species in cleared spaces that provide shelter and nesting materials, and/or the beaver's lodge that provides pools in the river in which further food sources (fish and insects) thrive. At the same time the bird's droppings might fertilize the river, providing food for insects and small fish (allowing larger fish to thrive and an opportunity for otters to feed), eggs hatched might provide food for scavenging mammals, the disturbance of the leaf mulch created by the search for food and building materials might create new conditions under the trees allowing fungi to grow and new insect species might arrive to colonize this growth, trees may thrive on the new microbiological activities around their roots, and so on. The evolution of aspects of the system is, or becomes, increasingly symbiotic (composed of parallel and interdependent individuations) —the birds need the insects as the insects need the birds. Potential in the system for new developments (habitat, food, symbiotic relations) continue to arise, bifurcate and disappear: energy continues to circulate. Individual species of bird, fish, tree and insect may thrive or decline as the conditions constantly evolve and change or diversify, affecting many other elements in the ecology, as a series of 'fluctuations and local instabilities' (64-65) that knit together over time in complex tangles of local and non-local connection. In an ecology operating in such a FFE state, small shifts resonate throughout the system (42-44) in unpredictable and productive ways, opening both new actualizations of relation and also always increasing the potential for further diversification and entanglement. Here the 'system' is in itself a series of *relations and potential relations* between components— not the components themselves—and as an assemblage of relations (actual and virtual) it develops its own emergent characteristics and properties (Bak 1997: 51): it is in flux, adaptive and remaining charged through the ongoing 'potential energy due to [the components'] interaction' (38-39).

Over time such a system might have many small or catastrophic shifts or losses as it continues to diversify and evolve potential, but as a whole can remain in this unstable and productive state. Without contradiction, such a FFE system is both fragile and robust. It is fragile on an individual level, in terms of the loss of the certain futures of clear linear trajectories of a stable system (where the sheep consume everything and the system—the intensity and potential of relations—degrades), and in the fact that the system as a whole never ensures the survival of any particular component, only the exchange of energies. It is robust on a level of collective individuation in the metastability that allows the system to accommodate ongoing differentiation, adjusting system-wide to accommodate new relational factors. Thus as the wolves clear the grassland of deer, trees, birds and small mammals begin to reinvent the area into new, varied and resonate systems of relation.

Self-Organizing Criticality

> The critical state is the most efficient state that can actually be reached dynamically.
>
> *Bak (1997: 198)*

FFE systems such as the dynamic rewilded ecologies are more than simply complex—as all systems when studied closely enough have many scales, relationships and causal chains. Complexity, Per Bak argues, is in itself not a cause of intensive self-organization, but merely an observable 'local manifestation of a globally critical process' (1997: 112) (again the necessity of thinking field effects, system level capacities and expressions). Rather, such system's dynamism and vigour are due, according to Bak's arguments, to the FFE system reaching a 'poised state': a point of, as he terms it, 'self-organizing criticality' (SOC), where the required range of events and dimensions of relationality are potentialised (48, 45-46). Here while the proportions of ranges of events may be statistically analyzable and 'predictable', the timing of any individual event is non-linear and not predictable (12-14)[14] and thus at any one point in time all potential future events are still open to actualization and the richness or thickness of the virtual is preserved.

Once a system has reached a state of SOC this might be recognized not because the range of potential events actualize in a predictably linear order of events over time leading to greater complexity (the arrival of wolves leading to small local shifts in flora and fauna numbers, then larger local changes, then forest-wide shifts, and so on), but instead because a state is reached whereby all sizes of shifts and developments are potentialised. In this newly critical state a small shift may lead to very large changes echoing quasi-causally through the system (a few trees removed by beavers leading to associated birds, insects and fish thriving as outlined above, these birds bringing in seeds of berries, leading to bears reappearing and associated shifts caused by their hunting of fish and mammals and the fertilization of soil through droppings and carcasses left, and so on), and also larger changes in individual species may not directly or immediately have any noticeable effect, though like any event it opens new potentials (as a bird species is chased out of the riverbank habitat through competition for resources the overall ecology remains relatively unchanged, but their replacement species has slightly different feeding habits opening at least possibilities for shifts in fish and insect numbers and types, and further potential differentiations in the system as new characteristics might be developed in one particular location)[15]. Each event may cause local, system wide or little change but it is always an act of differentiation and associated differenciation, and this is a new system-level virtual dynamism that operates on an additional and autonomous dimension, a metastability based on system-wide contingency (Bak 1997: 59).

In this contingency, cause and effect are enfolded, immediating and in flux. Each event enriches—rather than 'adds to' in the sense of classical physics (DeLanda 2005: 172-173)—the system dynamics not by necessarily causing an immediate or recognizable reaction or chain of events, but because it adds new potentials across the system. It is perhaps on this level of the virtual that SOC systems are most dynamic, saturating a system with potential, each actualized differentiation adding further to the multiplicity, the virtual plane on which the system is immanently and intensively organized. It is here that the global dynamics or capacities emerge from the potentialising effects of components' interactions. Once a rewilded ecology reaches SOC, you can no more explain its behaviour by examining the capacities of the wolves than you can by understanding the worms or rivers (though all these capacities oscillate or resonate with the system), or by summing all the capacities of all components into an algorithm, if such a thing was possible. Rather, system organization evolves an independence from component properties (Bak 1997: 50-51, DeLanda 2005: 171) that is immediatory: a potentialisation of all relational dynamics that allows for ongoing exploration or freedom of expression of evolving wolf-ness, worm-ness, beaver-river-fish-ness drawn from this saturated potential[16], while at the same time understanding that each of these explorations is also folded back into the ongoing potential of the system.

SOC is of course not exactly a state that is 'achieved', but rather an always-emergent state, a robust criticality where not only are components' properties emergent, but the 'rules' or relational capacities themselves are also emergent (Bak 1997: 110) (its system level capacities immediated by emergent component expressions and visa versa[17]). Thus SOC is very likely not achieved as soon as wolves and beavers are introduced (though undoubtedly they do immediately cause changes to the ecology), but eventuates once (or if) the flows of energy and relational entanglement reach a limit—a critical tipping point into a new global dynamic.

How do the wolves or beavers tip ecologies into this state? SOC does not necessarily or simply arrive simply through pushing more energy into a system—add more sheep to a degraded paddock and it will simply degrade further. What critical states require, according to Bak, is a surplus of energies that continue to circulate through the system, and in doing so cause an intensive problematisation of energy (50-52). Perhaps here Simondon's concept of transduction provides a clearer explanation of what might be occurring in rewilding. Transduction is a process by which disparate entities and forces are integrated into a system of relation through the ongoing negotiations and transformations of energy flows and individuations (Simondon 1992: 315) and in doing so the system evolves the 'dimensions according to which [its] problematic[s] can be defined' (313). The incoming energies that Bak proposes are required to reach a self-organising critical state, and which are provided by the introduction of the wolves or beavers, create tensions or incompatibilities within a previously relatively stable system that require new negotiations and developments. There is a circulation and transformation of the force of the wolf's movements, its eating habits, territorializations and the affectual power its howl to the moon has on other animals, as shifts and developments to accommodate such forces occur throughout the flora, fauna and geology. That is, these new disjunctive forces problematize the existing system, moving it into 'criticality'—partial and provisional resolutions that are ongoing, keeping the system in productive or creative tension as components move outside themselves (their previously defined capacities and relational expressions) to continued and collective becomings, generating new relational systems between previously disparate elements (311, 315)[18].

If this ongoing transduction of energy added to the system is key, then it is this the force of these transductions that immanently organizes relations (a concretization in Simondon's terms, where components' individuations become interdependent) and its ongoing input and flow (in terms of the reintroduction of species, the growth of diversity, and the input of force from one species or micro-environment into another) that keeps the system in a critical or problematic state (Bak 1997: 50). But transduction also emphasizes that in a FFE system it is the ongoing flow and problematisation of force that organizes, instigating individuations of flora and fauna in response, not a fixed set components that forces respond to: it is the field that is the self-organizing criticality, not a specific set of animals (never the wolf or beaver, despite their role in shifting the system to this state).

Transductions, as Brunner says, 'cut across the disparity of the physical, biological, mental and social' at an affective plane (Brunner 2012: 6). Thus while energies and their transductions can be thought most obviously as the redistribution of biomass—through the continued conversions between energy and biomass—it might occur also with energies on other planes: movements and territorializations (the pulse of the refrain of a species, the magnetism of a nesting pair, the tensions of invasion); speeds and flows (water running, pooling and stagnating, lines of ants, flight paths); surfaces (colours, textures and densities that reflect the sun's rays, earth crust splitting as seeds germinate and fungi bloom); and sensations and perceptions (sounds that vibrate ears and diffract off surfaces, smells exciting nostrils, touch that triggers imagination)[19]. All of it is the energy of flux: of diversification, splitting, novelty arising, of an excess in the field that must be dealt with, circulated, distributed (that is also perhaps the development of an excess of capacities within the system to deal with these flows) —a flux that organizes and generates dimensional capacities whilst remaining far-from equilibrium.

Sacrifice

> The destruction that sacrifice is intended to bring about is not annihilation. The thing—only the thing—is what sacrifice means to destroy in the victim. Sacrifice destroys an object's real ties of subordination; it draws the victim out of the world of utility and restores it to that of unintelligible caprice [...] it passes from the world of things which are closed to man and are nothing to him, which he knows from the outside—to the world that is immanent to it, intimate.
>
> *Bataille (1997: 210)*

In no way are the wolves and beavers merely catalysts calling an already primed environment into action. Rather, they are intertwined and nascent within every particle and potential of the new field: beaver-treeing, water-beavering, wolf-deering, grass-wolfing, microbe-beavering and so on. Just as the animistic gods always are, the wolves and beavers are embedded in the heart of the extended potential—eruptions of the other-(future)worldliness of every component—a parallel series of collective individuations that move the ecology forward. To where? Perhaps to a new intensity—new degrees of differentiation—lived across new planes. It is not a question of triggers, nor of dominance, but of sacrifice: sacrifice of individual rights for collective re-beginnings. Wolf and beaver do not mediate the environment, they enter into movement[20], embedded as the spirit of the ongoing field-wide immediation.

What is sacrifice? Fragility and flux. As the Shaman sacrifices her own truth to the conjunction of spirit and physical world (sacrificed to the flux between dimensions), how does the wolf sacrifice wolf-ness - as this wolf-ness takes on new conjunctive meanings— (first to become a pack animal rather than lone wolf, then to become wolf-and-pack-and-deer, wolf-and-pack-and-forest), how does the beaver sacrifice itself to the excesses of its lodge—an expenditure beyond any utility—then to become beaver-and-lodge-and-river, beaver-and-lodge-and-fish, beaver-and-lodge-and-soil microbiology. Wolf becomes spirit (potential, future-being) of the plain/forest, beaver becomes spirit of the river/flow, a heterogeneity in which the shaman/wolf/beaver does not dominate its subjects, but is rather lost, brought to the surface as points of contact between things (Taussig 2006: 153) as it is also secreted into the very field, connected on a charged collective plane of potential—becoming its very essence, its spirit, taking on a new fragility of being. It loses its place in the order of things, its fear of dying as a thing in that order, a sacrifice in which it is never isolated but negates the individual in favour of a contagion, a dangerous 'intimacy' with all (Bataille 1997: 214-215).

The motivation of the Shaman—which is not a perspective owned by her, but an environmental appetite that passes through her—is a collective conditioning, the addition of new planes of potential, newly layered dimensions of relationality. In both black magic and sacrifice this journey, this '*more*' is the important bit (more than the novel conjunction, instead the very act of transition), the intertwining, complexify-ing, unbalancing that is a system held in a fragile state of intensive, generative emergence and gathering.

Somatic Drifts V1.0

> "Fluidity" to me suggests mimesis as a sort of streaming metamorphicity rather than a replication as with a photograph [...] this is magic of contagion and not of likeness.
>
> *Taussig (2006: 140)*

In Cat Jones' work *Somatic Drifts V1.0*, participants are taken through a curious journey both into and beyond their body boundaries[21]. Using a range of sensations and the processes of perception the participant's gestalt is put aside, at least temporarily, in favour of a new intimacy: new relations with the artist, the plants, their own body, with a field of potential, and ultimately with a larger expression of a collective individuation. In brief, after the artist gives a careful explanation of the pragmatic physical process to be undertaken[22], the participant is asked wear a pair of headphones (through which they hear both the artist's voice and tonal drones) as they lie on a black platform. Above the participant is a screen on which a life-size and (sometimes) real time projection of their body looks down on them. Throughout the process this projection is manipulated—often split down a central line of the body—so that sensations experienced in the body do not always correlate with what is seen above. This is combined with the artist making a circuit around the body (first in one direction, then the other), gently stroking body extremities, in a touching that moves between synchronicity and a-synchronicity with the touch shown in the projections.

At first the right and left sides of the body in the projection are swapped, and the participant is asked to move around and experience the discontinuity between what is seen and what is felt in moving and in being stroked, then one side of the body replaced with an image of that side of the body filmed earlier in the process to create a new discontinuity. As their body adjusts to each new projected metamorphosis, a new challenge is initiated: half the body is replaced with a different body of the same sex, then a whole other body, back to their own body and then to a body of another gender. At each stage the artist performs a circuit of gentle touching, mostly synchronised with the projection in which her hands are seen touching the other bodies. Next, while a participant's eyes are closed, a beach spinifex grass

(*Spinifex sericeus)* is placed in their hands and they are asked to smell a scent of wet earth. As a participant opens their eyes Jones touches one side of their head, while in the projection this side of their head is replaced by the image of the spinifex. Then the actual plant is removed. The video shows their reflection as half plant, half human, then fully plant, as the artist again moves around the body making contact (again the artist's hands are shown in the video touching both body and plant). Finally the projection returns to a live feed of their body and they are able to return to some sense of solidity.

During these later stages participants lose spatial orientation—they feel strongly that the spinifex in their hand is in fact on their head—and they feel themselves suspended perhaps in a state of transition as their sense of their own body fluctuates and shifts to something well beyond the human: not exactly a becoming-plant, but more an intense body-plant individuation. Yet this is not done through persuasion or through hypnosis. If the process is in itself based on mirror therapy for phantom limb pain, it has here been taken into another realm, one that puzzles the clear world of the cognitive scientist[23]. And, unlike a Lacanian mirror stage this is a mirroring, that reflects a greater potential for the body, its saturation with the field rather than its containment and separation.

Perhaps one could say the artist plays a shamanic role here, tricking the participant through sleight of hand whilst also revealing this treachery (forewarning and explaining), and whilst also adding always-new layers of trickery and forgery of otherness, confusing any revelations of technique. This might be a game that all enter into: a literal field of play. It does not require blind faith or belief, just as it is not hypnosis. Its power does not lie there, but perhaps willingness and shared enjoyment in such continual fabulation[24]: tricks, deceptions and semblances that create a 'continuous movement' across many planes of becoming (Taussig 2006: 128).

How is it that Jones is able to achieve this poised or critical state in the bodies of participants that allows such movement—creativity and play—and sensitivity and attention to the rich potential of the field in which these bodies become immersed? Here, after making a few more general observations about the artist's technique, I want to return to the physics that I have argued underpins rewilding: dimensional flexibility and invention, far-from-equilibrium states and their capacities to dynamically organise flows of energies.

The technique explicitly plays with both such conceptual and physical shifts between stable and unstable states, so that the participant shifts between forming a picture of their body (both a sensory and conceptual image of what is and is not a part of the body) —that is less a representation of the participant's body, more of a parallel individuation, entwined and complicating—and again and again experiencing the disturbance of these boundaries. This the artist describes in terms of states of 'congruence' (when the perception and conceptual image of one's body correspond), and 'incongruence' (a gap between self-image and perceptual evidence), that through experimentation she has found to be a essential part of the process, as the body seems to quickly adapt and accept each new dismorphic image and restabilise itself[25].

Jones introduces a complex succession of sensorial and perceptual factors into the event that create new relational resonances of both connection and new eruptions of difference within the system. Not only does this operate in the series of connections and disconnections between the participant's sensation of their body and the image they view of their body mixed with other bodies and plants, but there is, for example, the act of the artist laying hands (and plants) on their body that creates congruence and incongruence. The pattern of touching creates a direct affectual connection between surfaces that at once defines as it breaks body boundaries, that connects the image of hands moving on a foreign body to the feeling of the hands on the actual body, that then contradicts this connected movement with touching that is asynchronous to the projected gestures. How is it exactly that this touch of the artist's hand on another's body can be felt so keenly on the skin of the participant, experienced both emotionally and as an affectual force? To view this merely as perceptual confusion or misplaced projection seems to me to sell it short. Is it not that *Somatic Drifts* engages a system or circulation of mutual feeling or prehension binding and extending components (just as the water, trees, plants, fish feel with the activities of the beaver)? This affectual force reaches—resonates—across planes, activating minds, bodies, senses, feelings. Such resonances across differences are perhaps the echoes of the minor gestures that activate this fielding of experience, existing only in the immediacy of the event, belonging not to any one body but the forward moving generation of difference of the system(s) of the event and its components into being something-else or more than themselves.

As it brings bodies to their surface through touch, the process of *Somatic Drifts* also shifts the manner in which it splits and connects to other entities the parts of the participant's body, at times connecting one side of the body back on to itself or to a series of other bodies (of increasing degrees of difference), or splitting half or all of the head from the body, or a hand. In this the *process itself* that is undergone is subject to the same shifting and re-combinatory status as the bodies are: as one cannot settle into a secure sense of oneself (or oneself as some strange new hybrid) in this art event and one cannot settle into a concept of how the techniques will unfold, so that here technique moves closer to a technics that is itself imminent and open. There is perhaps here also some relationship to Feldenkrais techniques, in the splitting of the body down the centre, the unbalancing and then reconnecting of the two halves (a mereotopological system addressing parts rather than wholes that consume and erase the differences between parts): the careful attention and close focus on individual parts and the larger sense of connectedness, the re-combinations of sensation, perception and mental processes, and the demonstrable power of the imagination in reconfiguring neural and nerve pathways. Here the rewilding that Jones' work performs on the bodies of participants does not address the mind as an ecology with inputs and outputs to and from the nervous system, as cognitive science might. And, just as it does not address the mind as a whole but as a series of mutable, overlapping and developing parts, so the body is not addressed as ecology interfacing with the environment, but a series of parts that are co-emerging with the ecology: one's head-with-plant immergences, one's left side-another's right side immergence, eyes-skin surfacing and so on. These energies are generated and felt from the perspective of the field, not to be seen or understood from outside the event, preceding and producing these new bodies rather than emerging from them as a collective becoming of components (artist's hand-shoulder-image-gesture, movement-smell-tone-touch and so on, each a complex emergence that does not act out a rewilding of a particular body but searches to immediate a new and tenuous relationship of forces). In this it addresses the field as the only ecology that counts, as the habitual becomings of relatively closed and stable system systems are opened and made fragile again.

Through these and other technics, perhaps Jones' work succeeds in opening a gap between the immediacy and excess of sensation (touch, smell, movement and proprioception and vision), and perception. That is, the transition between the event of sensation and its comprehension and placement within a logic is stretched and enriched. The gap between the felt qualities of the contradictory sensory experience (feeling a hand on one's shoulder while seeing the same hand on some else's shoulder, feeling a clockwise movement of touching while seeing it performed counter-clockwise, the sensation of one's head contradicting the vision of the fantastic plant-head that then resonates also with the sensation of one's plant-hand), and the acceptance of this new logic that allows the participant's body to begin to feel stable again is delayed, so that, as Manning says of immediation, it draws 'attention to how the stakes of experience occur in the immediate interstice of its coming to be' (Immediation I , 276), and immerses the participant in this feeling. In *Somatic Drifts* there is a particular care and attention to these technics of moving between relatively stable and FFE states, that so that this transitioning is preserved and felt, achieved less through a slow shift between the two states (though certainly the degree of otherness of each new image, perception and sensation grows) than an episodic series of sudden plunges back into creative transition[26].

This gap between sensation and perception is accentuated by the sheer quantity of sensory experience that creates an excess of energies in the event, beyond the limits of (human) perception. That is, when pushed beyond limits of perception that can be contained within a gestalt a new system of relation concretizes that problematizes the limits of a single body, and is instead held between the components as a system of both actual relations of sensations and a shared potential to circulate these sensations. This might be a redefinition of the dimensions of the event, as it takes on this new, if temporary, system-level 'gestalt' that is decidedly transindividual. In this the excess sensation re-composes and re-potentialises the field, as attention and care move across many planes that become transpersonal—affective, neurological, sensorial (touch, smell, sound), intellectual, muscular, social (their skin against the skin of the artist, their eyes on the body of another & the artist's eyes on their body). Rather than removing extraneous input and energies as in a scientific experiment that seeks to establish clear causal links, this flooding of the body with sensations that in their excess quantity, incongruence and differing qualities cannot ever be completely contained within the logic of perceptions is employed by Jones as a 'psychic tension', a relational overload and incompatibility that is rich with potential individuation (Simondon 2007: 4, 3). Perhaps this sensory overload that pushes the event FFE can be thought of as the excess energy that the system circulates and transduces (gesture to touch to vision to concept and so on), in order to achieve its dynamic or critical phase where new immanent connections can occur and a new flexibility moves component parts beyond individual trajectories. Thus, if it encourages a fragility of self, this is not merely the cost of the increased affectual flow but perhaps the very gesture that provides the condition for the flow.

Beyond simply exploring the capacities of the body, this process might be thought to allow new cross-form plasticity: new dimensions on which capacities might be expressed to develop. Jones' work moves beyond simply prompting the body of the participant into a FFE state of individual confusion or sensory overload, and emphasizes the body's co-individuation with other components within the field of the event. The participant's body not only pulls towards self-other hybrids that might resolve as a discrete body, if a strangely modified one, but pulls towards a new collective 'vital complex' in which the affectual force of becoming circulates through all aspects of the event's potential (Simondon 2007: 3). The ecology that is activated here is not just a body-mind ecology, nor just a combination of bodies, but of the held spaces between—resonances—the tensions within a problematized but open system in a state of individuation. These resonances might motivate, as minor gestures, the event's new dimensions —its new and forming relational planes[27]—or, if they already existed perhaps they are intensified, their expressive capacities expanded and brought to the fore. Thus the process emphasizes the affectual circulation of energies in the field and brings to attention the potential of ongoing individuation beyond stable individualities, it also now overlays with collective individuations: with the operations of a field of energies that organises and expresses itself (Simondon 2007: 4).

In these technics intensive difference is generated and preserved—a key factor in creating a FFE state—as parallel impressions of congruence and incongruence exist together to create a paradox: keeping the event at a critical, intermediate state somewhere between stasis and a chaotic loss of connection and collapse of self. Or rather, if from a process-based philosophy view of the world this is always the nature of events/ecologies, then it is that here such a state is perhaps heightened and brought to attention. This continued problematisation or incongruence might perhaps be thought of as a critical state, with its accompanying characteristics of heightened creativity (an ability to make novel connections) and the related capacity to organise on a system level in ways beyond and outside the boundaries and capacities of individual components that preserves this creativity as the participant's body continues to individuate, moving further and further away from its original conceived form.

To me this work cannot be explained in terms of conversations between plants, humans and images, rather it needs to see the transindividual nature of the forces at play and their primary role in the potential individuation of plant, human, image, thought and hybrids of all these components, and therefore needs to be thought in ecological terms, as a dynamic field of relations and its immanent capacity to connect a series of disparate components into a meshwork of flows. It seems to me that even as scientists are studying Jones' work to unlock its 'secrets', cognitive or other scientific explanations are never going to be able to satisfactorily explain the event unless they are prepared to abandon classical physics and embrace the radicalism of thermodynamics (or even further, the radical empiricism that would acknowledge thought as an actual event in the world (James 1996a: 18)). Nor can this necessarily be thought purely from one position—that of the participant. Just as the rewilding of the wolves is not a conversation between wolf and deer, but an ecological movement that is an event immanent with the individuation of all components—the grass, worms, berries, wind, river flows, rainfall—*Somatic Drifts* might be thought of as a 'fielding' in which new motivations can be found at this system level and it is these minor gestures that pull the components forwards towards new collective individuations, and it is in this creation of such minor gestures that the system achieves a 'wilder' state. Perhaps then this work has to be considered to at least some extent in terms of the movements, feelings and affective speeds that all components (artist, participant, plants, sound vibrations, projected images) enter in to. And so perhaps we should also not forget to ask what the plant feels—does it feel its own transitions to plant-humaness? And what does the artist feel —a becoming plant, a becoming participant? All here are caught up in the immediation of the event.

Rewilding and Immediation

> Perception is not of a human nature as such, but part of a "worlding": the unfolding of relational events.
>
> *Brunner (2012: 4)*

Rewilding is not conservation but something more radical and essentially creative. Reintroduction of wolves or beavers unsettles a system in ways that may be catastrophic for individual flora and fauna (deer population, a particular tree species that the beavers clear), but that also utilizes increased component fragility to organise new system-level vitality as the system of flows of affectual energies undergoes individuation. It is precisely this fragility that brings *Somatic Drifts* back from the sideshow and takes it beyond the understanding of the cognitive scientist and to a darker place. It is a fragility born out of the suspension in felt states of transitioning, in the immediacy of collective individuations, layered, competing, excitations of difference: not a new plant-human hybrid identity, but a collective moving into the flux, resonating with pasts and transducing towards new futures. Rewilding then might be exactly this suspension in the fragile act of transitioning, the experience of this process as it opens up to multiple possibilities, a world of problematisation and partial solutions. *Somatic Drifts* might be seen as a technics of both rewilding and immediation not because it suspends bodies in the FFE state in which they achieve a personal fluidity or dynamism, but because of its insistence that the participant reaches beyond their own body in a continuing act of co-composition with the field. Such rewilding is fuzzy, vague in that it is saturated with potential, always evolving on the virtual plane in parallel to the actualised novelty—a wolf or participant individuation that is now comprehensible not on its own but can only be understood as part of a collective immediation of the system.

If one might say that there has been a turn in recent years in towards thinking participation and relation in art on an ecological level, perhaps it is possible to say that artworks such as *Somatic Drifts* rewind a step from this. That is to say, such artworks might be concerned not primarily with developing potentials that allow a dynamic and complex meshwork of relations to actualise or be expressed, but with creating the conditions for the field of the event to evolve its own potentials: its own new dimensional planes or capacities beyond the control, interest or desires of the artist. Rewilding is less about conservation than returning an ecology to a state where it can immediate, and it is not simply a priming of an existing potential within a field, but a different milieu of relation that erupts from a field in a critical state—where there is an ongoing 'conditioning [of] the event's emergence' (Massumi, Immediation I , 281).

Here perhaps what is important is not so much that the participants (or beavers or wolves) gain a greater range of expressive capacities within a system, though this may be true, but that the system as an ongoing event increases its expressive capacities and dimensions. Such a system might exhibit self organising and far-from-equilibrium properties that allow it to enfold its web of relations such that the rules or structure governing these relations remains immanent to the (re)expressions of those relational forces: whole and parts not adding up to each other but caught in a system of immanent self-production. It is this that I want to name both a rewilding and immediatory process that Cat Jones' work engages with exploring 'the potential of the preindividual field [that] is relational and can only be expressed relationally, through and with others' (Massumi, Immediation I , 284).

Notes

1. Some of which may be quite limited in their understanding of relation: Relational Aesthetics, for example, with its very fixed and limited concept of relation as a human-centered social construct, or much interactive art with relational conversations limited to those between preconceived and clearly demarcated participants and technical objects.
2. "We are expectant of a more to come, and before the more has come, the transition, nevertheless, is directed towards it." (James 1996a: 78).
3. The "transindividual is neither interior nor exterior to a body, but the continually folding and unfolding limit between inside and outside" (MacKenzie, 2002: 137).
4. It perhaps needs to be noted that these experiments concentrate on the reintroduction of species into environments in which they quite recently were indigenous, having been forced out by farming and loss of habitat. Clearly the introduction of non-native predators—such as cats into the Australian bush—can have quite catastrophic effects on flora and fauna.
5. See Per Bak for just such a disappointingly naïve conclusion championing neo-capitalism and the automated stock market with its non-linear causal chains and associated peaks and crashes (1997: 183-192). While far-from-equilibrium systems are of interest here they have their limits as ideal systems for all situations, being truly an-ethical (bluntly concerned only with the health of the system as a whole and without regard for the survival of any particular species or individual). In thinking any such system in which we might wish to live/experience, it remains necessary to also consider the ethics of care and attention across these other levels: this perhaps

is a compromise that Cat Jones' work, as discussed later in this chapter, attempts to address.

6. "Trophic" however only refers to the eating habits of species, and clearly the relational connections go much deeper than this, including, for example, aspects of habitat (micro-climates, competition for nesting materials, refrains and so on).
7. This emphasizes the ad-hoc nature of evolution: where survival is not based on "fitness," but on the ability to adapt and make do in changing conditions. For example, see Varela 1992: 185-207.
8. I use the term "component" here rather than concentrate, as Monbiot does, on particular marquee or key examples of flora or fauna to emphasize that the greater flexibility and complexity applies to all aspects of the environment, whether microbes, water, leaf-mulch or wolf.
9. Although Cariani does not use the term, this might be thought of as its capacity to feel in a Whiteheadian sense of the term.
10. See for example, the self-organized development of new sensory capacities (an "ear") in one of Pask's chemical computers (Cariani 1993).
11. See also Luis Mateus Rocha on the capacity of self-organizing systems to develop new dimensions, (2001: 822); and John Collier on systems with emergent dynamics as a third level of autonomy beyond autopoiesis (2008: 14-16).
12. Monbiot is particularly critical of the desolation caused by sheep farming, this of course is at least as much to do with the problems with sheep farming methods—monoculture approaches with blatant disregard to the long-term health of ecosystems—as it is to do with the omnivorous appetites of the sheep themselves. For an alternative approach see, for example, Permaculture design methods for sheep grazing, which emphasize a greater level of diversity of feed sources and a more complex integration of the function of components of the system (Mollison 1999: 442-446).
13. Indeed, equilibrium systems might be almost "mythical," convenient abstractions of the complexity of real interactions (Green 2001: 674). See also Bak 1997: 1-31 and Serres 2001: passim.
14. Bak uses many examples of SOC found in the natural world to explain this, including the example of earthquakes, where the proportion of minute, small, medium and catastrophic sized quakes that will occur can be charted logarithmically as probability using power laws (a quality expressed as a power of another property), but it can also be shown that there is no direct linear relationship over time between sizes of quakes (small quakes do not directly lead to larger and then catastrophic events) (24-7, 85-6).
15. A SOC can accommodate sudden dramatic shifts in relational dynamics, long periods of what looks like relative stability and what appears to be relatively linear flows of causal chains. And while these events may look local and linear when examined individually, there are always aspects that are

globally organized. It may be that the evolution of SOC (rewilded) ecologies could be as effectively triggered by the introduction of a new insect, shrub or the reinvigoration of water flows in a river system as by the large predators championed by Monbiot, and that these self-organizing dynamics have simply not yet reached a critical state, or have reached SOC but have yet to trigger major, observable effects. See, for example, Charles Darwin's writing on the significant role of worms in archaeology and non-human scales of action (1881: 176-229; 305-313).

16. 'One does not act freely, one acts freedom out' (Massumi, Immediation I , 284).

17. It is a mereotopological system—composed of parts that are not fully contained within a 'whole' that sums up or defines/restricts these parts' futures, a FFE system that is not defined by any final stable state but rather is caught in ongoing immediation, intertwined events that co-compose without losing their singularity. See Portanova 2013: 79-80.

18. See also Adrian MacKenzie on transduction as a partial resolution to internal differences (2002: 50).

19. It might be important to remember here firstly that while SOC 'organizes' energy in a system, it does not organize it towards any particular end, rather towards an immanent state of maximum relationality and openness to exchange energies, and secondly that SOC can be used to 'explain' some qualities of complex relationality, other qualities of the system remain free—in other words it is functional across some but not necessarily all of the dimensions in which a system is active.

20. 'To go into nature is to leave stabilized and sedentary existence and enter into movement.' (Lingis 2011: 79).

21. See "Somatic Drifts V1.0", for the artist's documentation of this project. Cat Jones, <http://catjones.net/2014/05/27/somatic-drifts-v1-0/>

22. This explanation is used to try to circumvent the possibility of hypnosis or suggestibility leading to the shifts.

23. In mirror therapy for phantom limb pain the patient's healthy arm or leg is mirrored to replace the damaged or missing limb, and in many cases with this visualization they are then able to 'reset' or control the painful nerve impulses that seem to be emitted by the missing limb. Cat Jones' work is now being studied by pain researchers in Australia to try and determine how she achieves such body transformations well beyond the general techniques and understanding of cognitive science.

24. The pleasure in magic, Taussig writes, is both in the denial of trickery and also the bringing to attention or sharing of the knowledge of such trickery and the collective enjoyment of trickery (2006: 150-151).

25. This ability to accommodate such disturbances and reconfigure might indicate that bodies themselves are already at a point of self-organizing criticality, with capacities to incorporate new differences without dissolution.

26. This might be thought of as a 'punctuated equilibrium', which, as Bak argues, is characteristic of what happens in nature, with relatively stable periods punctuated by shifts into FFE states when vast creative and system-level ecological shifts can occur (Bak 1997: 29).
27. Relation is 'an aspect of internal resonance of a system of individuation' (Simondon 1992: 306).

Erik Bordeleau

Immediation, Bergson and the Problem of Personality

In 1914, Henri Bergson gave a series of conferences as part of the Gifford Lectures in natural theology entitled "The Problem of Personality." For those who have discovered Bergson's oeuvre mostly through Deleuzian scholarship, this title might come as a surprise, and even more so when considering that Bergson understood the question of personality, alongside William James, as *the* central problem of philosophy, toward which "all philosophy gravitates or ought to gravitate" (1914: lecture I). Bergson's interest in the notion of personality is closely related to his concern about independent will, free acts and the affirmation of an active and practice-based pluralism. As such, it is a key element of his reluctance towards philosophy's tendency for systematicity. For the Greeks as well as for the Moderns, Bergson writes in his introductory lecture, "to philosophise has usually meant to unify"; and for this reason, philosophy has always had difficulty "finding a place for personality, that is to say, of admitting real individualities possessing an effective independence, each of which would constitute a little world in the bosom of the great world" (1914: lecture I).

This insistence on real and multiple individualities disrupting systematic rationality hints at the fact that the problem of personality is, in the last instance, inseparable from the question of how fully expressive free acts come to existence. Freedom for Bergson is indeed always a freedom to create and as such, it naturally finds its chief paradigm in the figure of the artist. In *Time and Free Will: An Essay on the Immediate Data of Consciousness*, first published in 1889, Bergson for example states: "In short, we are free when our acts spring from our whole personality, when they express it, when they have that indefinable resemblance to it which one sometimes finds between the artist and his work" (1950 : 172); and 25 years later, the Gifford Lecture conference ends on a very similar note: "Each of these personalities is a creative force; and, in all appearances, the role of each person is to create, exactly as if the great Artist had produced other artists as work" (1972 : 1086, my translation).

For some of our contemporaries, this metaphysics of creative freedom might feel somehow obvious—something like the default condition of being "creative" within the neoliberal world with its constant requests for innovation and self-renewal. But what is perhaps less expected is that the problem of personality for Bergson is fraught with rather deep theological and religious implications. But how does it matter nowadays? More than a hundred years after Bergson's Gifford Lectures, the question of personality appears indeed singularly outdated, not the least in the context of a theory of immediation that insists on ecological relationality and that, following the tenants of vital materialism or immanent realism, aspires, among other things, to make us more sensitive to the presence of *impersonal* affects circulating between beings. Classically, if we take Locke's definition, a person is a creature that can consider itself as itself in different times and places. In a similar vein, Whitehead defines personality in terms of the capacity of sustaining the realization and embodiment of certain types of value. He thus explains "the tendency of the transitory occasions of fact to unite themselves into sequences of Personal Identity" (1951: 688). But isn't striving to be such a "consequent" person nowadays akin to a voluntary and self-inflected reduction of one's own amplitude of the soul, to put it in a theological fashion along with Deleuze's Leibnizian definition of damnation? For if Deleuze didn't believe in things, as he once stated, he certainly didn't believe in persons neither.

The realist interest in whole, accomplished or exemplary persons seem, at first sight, somehow foreign to research-creation practices' interest for subjectivity in its nascent and mutational state. But for reasons that I hope will become clearer through this article, I believe there is an unsuspected relevance (not only regarding the history of ideas, but also on a speculative level) in revisiting the often overlooked theological or religious dimension that has nurtured essential components of the work of pragmatists like Charles S. Peirce, William James, Henri Bergson or Alfred N. Whitehead—especially with regard to how it concerns our ways of practising pluralism, intensifying relationality and actively relating to futurity. Yet I'm aware that opening up this kind of inquiry is fraught with potential misunderstandings and difficulties. Let me very briefly outline the general coordinates of the situation in which I find myself launching this line of study. As a speculative pragmatist involved in many different ways in research-creation practices, I think that the question of how to believe in the world and foster an ethics of speculative trust is a crucial one, on which depends, among other things, the effective production of transversality. This option of thought differs greatly with the way the so-called "return of the religious" has been thematized in recent years. There is no place here for any form of substantialist nostalgia and clear-cut transcendence. Otherwise, as I happily stand in the Jamesian open space, I often feel that chilling "spin of closure" hegemonic within university circles (Taylor 2007: 549), especially in the form of the negligence of the critical academic, a form that, as Harney and Moten acutely put it, professionally excludes "the prophetic organization of the Undercommons" (2013: 31). But all in all, I largely agree with William Connolly that "the philosophy of a world immanent to itself," supported by the idea and practice of immediation, "does not correspond to the philosophy of 'closed immanence' Charles Taylor discusses and criticizes in *A Secular Age*". (Connolly 2011: 38)

In "La méthode de dramatisation et la question 'Qui?'", an article recently published in an issue of the *Inflexions* journal about radical pedagogies (Bordeleau 2015), I started exploring how, in the philosophy of William James and Alfred N. Whitehead, theism has been praised for favouring a sense of active personality. In the context of this article, I would like to push this philosophical inquiry in the surrounds of (process) theology further, by bringing into focus Bergson's complex understanding of the notion of person. As for James and Whitehead, Bergson's treatment of the question confers a crucial importance to activity. The evolution of the concept of person throughout his work culminates in *The Two Sources of Morality and Religion* (1935). There, he defines what is immediately communicative in a person's emotional experience as a "call." How does the problem of personality concern the now of immediate affective experience? And how to understand Bergson's claim that enthusiasm, *as a call*, constitutes persons?

My prospective guess could be stated as follows: for Bergson, the philosopher of duration, intuition and creative enthusiasm of the body, as Massumi has recently put it in *What Animal Teach Us about Politics*, the im-mediation of the person through intense or mystical emotional experience (to use Bergson's vocabulary) isn't exactly congruent with the affirmation of impersonalization and involuntarism that has dominated some segments of contemporary media and cultural studies, to which Bergsonism has contributed to no minor extent. Conceived of as temporal and ethopoietic contraction, Bergson's concept of the person culminates, I will argue, in the definition of a non-discursive *exemplary immediation* that is intimately related to this divine feeling that Peirce once called evolutionary love.

James and Whitehead on the Person

The influence of William James on Bergson's ideas about religion, mysticism and the importance of personality, as it will appear fully only with the publication of *The Two Sources* in 1932, is well established. In a passage of the preface to the French edition of *On Pragmatism* (published in 1911) that prefigures much of what he will develop in his last book, Bergson writes:

> Souls filled with religious enthusiasm are truly uplifted and carried away: why could they not enable us to experience directly, as in a scientific experiment, this uplifting and exalting force? That is undoubtedly the origin, the inspiring idea of the "pragmatism" of William James. For him those truths it is most important for us to know, are truths which have been felt and experienced before being thought. (2002: 269)

Pragmatism for Bergson finds its subjective source in an energizing enthusiasm that breaks open the limits of daily experience and allows for novel concerns to be approximated through philosophical inquiry. If *The Two Sources* is dedicated to the study of (mostly Christian) testimonies of mystical experience, we know that more generally, the problem of personality as introduced by James and Bergson takes place within a wider shared interest for non-conscious and anomalous psychic experiences including hypnosis, mediumship, experiences of conversion and so forth. James, Gabriel Tarde and Bergson were all members of the Institute of Psychical Research in Paris, established in 1900. As Lisa Blackman explains in "Affect, Relationality and the 'Problem of Personality'", an article in which she explores "the forgotten historical antecedent of contemporary work across social and cultural theory that is being described as 'vitalist'" (2008: 27), "the problem of personality was framed in this milieu through concepts derived from spiritualism, studies of hypnotic trance, and psychotic hallucinations and delusions" (33).

There would be much to say about how the studies in "the varieties of religious experience" have contributed to the formation and complication of the question of how to hang together amongst our many selves and thus achieve "personal" unity.[1] But what I'd like to focus on here is how James' argument in favor of theism has influenced Bergson's later conception of the person as transformative emotion. What's at stake is the ethopoietic function of the belief in a personal God, or in God as a person. What difference does it make to be engaged in a relation with a personal God instead of conceiving of the universe as an impersonal cosmic flux, for example? Isabelle Stengers sharply highlights the ethical urgency that animates James' plea for theism: "The question that lies at the heart of William James's theism seems to be: what God is susceptible, today, to bring into existence saints *that are those of our times and not living relics*?" (2011a: 67) James' answer couldn't be clearer: what is needed is a *personal* God, not a selfless conception of the universe. This involves to envisage God as something exterior, or rather as someone with whom we enter into relation and who can never be reduced to being a part of oneself. It is in this sense that for James, arguing against what he calls infratheism, God is to be conceived under the form of a "mental personality": "God's personality is to be regarded, like any other personality, as something lying outside of my own and other than me, and whose existence I simply come upon and find." (James 1912: 122) Or again:

> The more perfect and more eternal aspect of the universe is represented in our religions as having personal form. The universe is no longer a mere *It* to us, but a *Thou*, if we are religious; and any relation that may be possible from person to person might be possible here. For instance, although in one sense we are passive portions of the universe, in another we show a curious autonomy, as if we were small active centres on our own account. We feel, too, as if the appeal of religion to us were made to our own active good-will, as if evidence might be forever withheld from us unless we met the hypothesis half-way. (28)

This preference for a personalized figure of God as means of activation is quite remarkable. It bears to my view unmistakable combative inflexions, and it is perhaps one of the reasons why many people nowadays prefer to stand away from such a polarizing spiritual option.[2] Nevertheless, it seems to have been widely favoured among early day pragmatists, often in open opposition to "the monstrous mysticism of the East" (Peirce 1995: 339)[3] and its bend toward contemplation and passivity. I can for myself say that the habit of envisaging the world as composed of myriads of actors and of foregrounding its intrinsically narrative dimension does hold a potent activating and somewhat anti-depressive effect! [4]

In *Religion in the Making*, Whitehead makes a similar argument: "The extremes are the doctrines of God as the impersonal order of the universe, and the doctrine of God as the one person creating the universe" (1996: 135). His preference also seems to go, even though he takes great care in distancing himself from any form of Christian substantialism, for the personalist option, insofar as it gives a better account of the contingent aspect of evil, and concomitantly, encourages a sense of what he calls "active personality":

> Buddhism is a metaphysic generating a religion. In respect to its treatment of evil, Christianity is more inclusive of the facts. It derives the evil from the contingent fact of the actual course of events; it thus allows of an ideal as conceivable in terms of what is actual.... Buddhism, on the whole, discourages the sense of active personality, whereas Christianity encourages it. (1996: 125).[5]

The question of God in Whitehead's philosophy is an extremely complex one that unfolds mostly within a speculative rather than religious register. In a passage of her *Thinking with Whitehead* that was added in the English translation, Stengers discusses Whitehead's Jamesian inheritance around the question of a personal God in these terms:

> Whitehead presents himself as the philosopher who comes after William James. It is thus permissible to wonder to what extent Whitehead is not also the heir to James's God.... If the speculative God, derived from the adventure of rationality, is not able to satisfy the vital need that James's God answered, how does Whitehead inherit this need? ...
>
> For me, it is crucial that Whitehead did not speak of his God as a person or a personality, and that the reversal of the physical and mental poles suppresses any possible relation of consanguinity between him and us." (2011a: 491-492)

Whitehead's God, Stengers subtly argues, belongs to an adventure of rationality distinct from the adventure of the spirit. If Whitehead's God indeed *saves* the world, I agree that it is first and foremost as an answer to the requirement of his metaphysical scheme. It is hard though to completely exclude religious and personalist considerations from the picture, if only because he himself brings them back in so readily. In a late article dating from 1941, "Mathematics and the Good" Whitehead discusses his conception of deity by contrasting it with that of Spinoza, Leibniz, Buddhism and Christianity, all in the same breath (Whitehead 1951). This text, and another one from the same year entitled "Immortality," shows Whitehead's concern for offering a well-tempered and balanced account of how the "activity of finitude" must always be thought of in reference to the "unbounded universe."[6] For Whitehead, the way we deal with finite patterns—through mathematics for example—bears an intrinsically ethical component. Hence his reference to the great religions to *illustrate* our relation to finitude, and more precisely to the way Christianity has conceived of goodness "in terms of active opposition to the power of evil, and thereby in terms of the limitation of deity" (1951: 675).

The ultimate evil of the temporal world, Whitehead sustains on a metaphysical mode in the last pages of *Process and Reality*, is that the past fades; accordingly, the main religious problem is "the question whether the process of the temporal world passes into the formation of other actualities, bound together in an order in which novelty does not mean loss" (Whitehead 1978: 340). Perhaps this rigorous and depurated formulation of the problem of salvation is to be understood only as an analogy, as he suggests a few pages later: "The image—and it is but an image—the image under which this operative growth of God's nature is best conceived, is that of a tender care that nothing is lost" (346).

Whitehead's God does not create the world: he saves it. That being said, it is interesting to note that this salvation process coincides with the fact that, as "the lure for feeling, the eternal urge of desire" (Whitehead 1978: 344), Whitehead's God is indiscernible from the multiple feelings that aim at him. The "divine feeling," Stengers notes, as a perpetually increasing experience of contrasts, "implies the feeling of an *individual completion in its living immediacy*, that is, qua *appeal to the future*" (2011a: 476, my emphasis). For we are facing the dire paradox of a world that desires the freshness of novelty yet is haunted with the fear of losing the past. The idea of a salvation of the living immediacy of individual realization and self-enjoyment—"in everlastingness, immediacy is reconciled with objective immortality" (Whitehead 1978: 351)—that simultaneously (and erotically) appeals to novelty is summed up in rather intricate terms in the penultimate paragraph of *Process and*

Reality. Strangely, the explanation makes use of the term of person (a few lines before, he was speaking of "enduring personality"): "In the sense in which the present occasion is the person *now*, and yet with his own past, so the counterpart in God is that person in God" (Whitehead 1978: 350).

When reading Whitehead, we have a strong sense that what he refers to as person or personal identity has very little to do with individuals as we commonly understand them. It is a historical tendency within a society of molecules, an inflection that orients and unifies in relation to the realization of values (the latter term to be understood as the intrinsic nature of an event). We will see that Bergson's use of the term conveys a similar feeling. In "Immortality," Whitehead offers a synthetic and elucidating summary of his conception of God and its relation to personality that is worth quoting at length:

> The world of Value exhibits the essential unification of the Universe. Thus while it exhibits the immortal side of the many persons, it also involves the unification of personality. This is the concept of God.
>
> [But it is not the God of the learned tradition of Christian Theology, nor is the diffused God of the Hindu Buddhistic tradition. The concept lies somewhere between the two.] He is the intangible fact at the base of finite existence. (1951: 694)

I'm not sure to what extent Whitehead's considerations about salvation and finitude find resonance in Bergson's work. If Heidegger was right in pointing out that there is apparently no sense of the irreparable or the irrevocable in Bergson's work, it is perhaps, as David Lapoujade aptly suggests, because "he reverses its destiny in order to replace it with a sense of vocation" (2010: 15). This vocational aspect of Bergson's philosophy—its calling or appealing aspect, if we take the word vocation etymologically—is indeed of foremost importance. In all cases, the divine feeling and its appetitive dimension of futurity as understood by Whitehead bears close proximity with how Bergson conceives of emotion as an activating convocation and uplifting call as we will now see.

The Person as Temporal Contraction

The concept, or rather, the *dispositif* of the person, as Roberto Esposito frames it in his genealogies of the concept,[7] has a long and complex history. It is intimately intertwined with the Christian onto-theological interpretation of being as sub-stance and is a core element of the roman juridical system. The concept of person and its derivative, the "human rights" (*droits de la personne*, in French), are so common and deeply embedded in our habits of thought that we often overlook their religious dimension. Juridically speaking, the term person expresses the dignity of the rational human being in her consciousness.[8]

Bergson first approaches the problem of personality mainly through a discussion of Plotinus's conception of the (human) soul. Plotinus is the creator of the doctrine of hypostasis, which marks a deep ontological mutation that opens the way to the modern understanding of personality. It coincides with the Christian doctrine of Trinity, which can be summarized as: one God, three hypostases. The doctrine of hypostasis deals with the philosophical problem of individuation. It is an attempt at explaining how things come into existence. The ontological mutation at stake here is that this process of individuation has been more and more readily conceived of as a process of subjectivation. This process is highlighted by a rather curious yet crucial historical fact: the term hypostasis, which it would only have been natural to translate by substance if only this term had not already been used to render the Greek *ousia* (being), has been translated by *person*. The philosophical use of the term person is thus rooted in theology, and its technical use was epitomized in Tertullian's formula: *tres personae, una substantia*, in reference to the distinctions recognized by Christian theology within the Godhead. Originally, the term person comes from the Greek *prosopon*, mask. It suggests, as Clement C.J. Webb explains in his *God and Personality* Gifford Lectures of 1917-1919, "that the being so designated has a part to play in some kind of social intercourse, such as is represented in a drama; and that of such social intercourse no mere animal but only a human being is capable" (Webb 1919: 36).[9] This demeaning reference to the "merely animal" gives us an important indication as to why the concept of the person is certainly something to be overcome instead of promoted for many thinkers today.

As an ontological process, the doctrine of hypostasis is that of an effectuation or *realization* that happens through a personal figure. For Agamben, who dedicates a whole chapter of *The Use of Bodies* to the subject, "the 'personal' character of the modern subject" (2014: 179) originating from the Trinitarian onto-theology, still holds sway nowadays and only a truly modal ontology could emancipate us from it. Agamben's whole philosophical endeavour seeks to undermine the subject/object metaphysical divide; as such, he is very critical of the notion of personality, preferring to explore the clandestine grace of *genius*, the impersonal zones of non-knowledge and the commonly intimate *use* of bodies. Agamben's *homo sacer* project patiently retrieves the history of metaphysics (paying a specific attention to its theological dimension) in order to de-activate it or render it "inoperative".

Bergson's discussion of the problem of the soul in Plotinus also aims at breaking free from the metaphysical divide. But unlike Agamben, who in this respect stands closer to the involuntarist Deleuze, he does not refuse the concept of the person. On the contrary, drawing from his philosophy of continuum and duration, he reclaims it *against* any subject position. "The philosophy of Plotinus, Bergson states in his Gifford Lecture, may be taken as the vey type of the Metaphysics which we are eventually led to when we look upon internal time as pulverised into separate moments, and yet believe in the reality and unity of the Person." (1914: Lecture III). The metaphysical perspective attributed to Plotinus simply enacts the immanent logic of language, which Aristote has, according to Bergson, "formulated once and for all": "The subject, because it is named as such [par cela qu'on le nomme], is defined as invariable; the variation will reside in the diversity of states that will be successively attributed to it" (Bergson 2003: 73).[10] Camille Riquier summarizes the consequences of this entrapment of duration in the subjective presuppositions of language (*hypokemeinon*, sub-ject or what lies under, can also in all rigor be translated as what pre-supposes): "The person only becomes a subject through a loss of its personality, since it converts itself into a stable support from which predicated qualities are subtracted more than they are added up to it" (Riquier 2007: 202, my translation).

How then to conceive of this tentative wholeness called personality? Like time, suggests Bergson, the person as a prospective and open totality can only be the object of an elusive and implicit knowledge rooted in immanent practice. But against Plotinus who argued that the acumen of personality is to be found in contemplation, for Bergson the person—and *a fortiori*, religion as well—is all about *action*. The person, vector of novelty on the edge of the present, can't collect the sum of itself from a self-assured and pre-constituted position. It is a continuous forward movement that gathers all of the past in the present as it engenders a future. It is precarious and mobile, and the continuity of its interior life can never be fully objectivized. In short, for the Bergson of the Gifford lectures, the person is essentially a matter of *temporal contraction*.

The person as temporal contraction or duration doesn't necessarily involve a sense of intentionality or humanness. It sometimes simply suggests the "truly primitive and immediately given" dimension of an experience, its implicit wholeness as it precedes any philosophical explication. The structure of address or agentivity immanent to certain experiences—their dramatic force of conviction as James puts it—is what Bergson calls in *The Two Sources* "fragmentary personalities" or the transmutation of an event into "elementary personality." (1935) These characterizations seem closely related to what Latour calls quasi-subjects. Yet, already in the conferences he gave in the 1910's, it appears that the central issue at stake in the problem of personality revolves around the conscious and voluntary *effort* of being a person. The sense of active personality Bergson is passionately after only finds its full (religious) expression many years later with the publication of *The Two Sources*. But in order to understand the specificity of Bergson's conception of the person and how it relates to his more general endeavour, one crucial transitory element still needs to be foregrounded: emotion.

Emotion (here understood, following contemporary affect theory nomenclature, as impersonal affect) is the pivotal element that ensures the passage between the person understood as unitary duration and the person understood as vocation or call. We know that for Bergson, duration can only be felt; the immediate data of consciousness are but emotions. At this level of analysis, as Lapoujade puts it, "we are no longer "beings," but vibrations, effects of resonance, "tonalities" of different frequencies" (2010: 9; my translation). This register of experience corresponds exactly to the pre-personal lived immediacy and "activist sense of life at no remove" (Massumi 2011: 1) favoured by occurrent arts and immediating practices. Bergson's philosophy as a whole reads as a conversion to this register of felt duration. It appeals to transform our perceptions by *naively* turning toward experience in the making, the world in its constant worlding. In the classical understanding of conversion, the multiple elements of the soul aim to be unified in a superior One; but with Bergson, conversion happens instead by placing ourselves entirely within the processual movement.

Or again: for Plotinus and the Alexandrines, says Bergson, things come out of God by procession and reintegrate him through conversion.[11] Inversely, for Bergson, following Spinoza, it is not necessary to enter into a movement of conversion that returns to original unity; rather, in order to "know perfectly," one has to coincide with the very movement of procession. Conversion for Bergson and Spinoza is therefore the act of coinciding creatively with process itself—and this essential grasping happens initially at the affective level. We participate in the movement of what is in the making insofar as it affects and moves us.

This affective involvement in the world's becoming is intrinsically related to active futurity. As Lapoujade nicely puts it: "If there is a sense to the future and if it can be engendered, it is from emotion and from emotion only" (2010: 23). And this brings us to the crux of the problem of personality as understood by Bergson: in what way does engendering futurity require a personalization of emotions? Wouldn't it be just the opposite, that is: doesn't the crucial moment of creative evolution reside precisely in a creative *involution* towards impersonality, unconsciousness or animality? The situational openness to which Brian Massumi appeals to in his latest books for example, whether he defines emotions as a personal and narrativizable *containment* of affects or defends an anti-representational politics of the animal's enthusiasm of the body, clearly points toward this second option (Massumi 2014; 2015a). Within the speculative pragmatist horizon broadly conceived, the most fruitful divergences and contrasts concern, I would argue, the ways in which we craft, induce and conceive of our relation to futurity. If God (or religion) is introduced in the equation, as in the case of Peirce, James, Whitehead and Bergson, we end up with a personalist or unifying gesture that, more often than not, involves rather unsettling and passionate celebrations of the evolutionary power of a love that, as Whitehead tenderly reminds us, "finds its own reward in the immediate present" (1978: 343). Inversely, Deleuze, in the wake of Nietzsche, prefer to think of becoming and futurity in a schizoanalytic fashion, away from the person, invoking dark precursors and embracing the multiplicity of forces conjugated at the fourth person singular that tear down the very form of the self.[12]

One effective and graphic way to approach this (mostly literary) divergence in orientation of thought—ascending and descending, one might say—is through how these authors relate to magic and passivity. In *A Thousand Plateaus*, Deleuze and Guattari wrote some wonderful lines about becoming-sorcerer and becoming-imperceptible; and their invocation of the outside often involves a transformative suspension of the will that culminates in *What is Philosophy?* with the contemplative "mystery of passive creation, sensation" (Deleuze and Guattari 1994: 212). In contrast, the personalist option introduced by Bergson in his later philosophy derives from his stated preference for action. "Complete mysticism is action" (Bergson 1935: 193) he writes; and discarding the contemplative mysticisms of the East, he maintains that the true mystics—the Christian mystics, therefore —are also great men of action. This mode of existence is also, immediately and exemplarily, a moral exhortation and an appeal, as we will see shortly. In parallel, Bergson also presents the process of personalization as an evolutionary progress towards distinct relationality. This is made particularly clear in his discussion about the emergence of the fabulatory function.

Technically speaking, the fabulatory function is related to the elaboration of what Bergson calls "static religion," which is a reaction to protect the humans against the depressive powers of their intelligence. It is superseded by the emergence of dynamic religion, propelled by mystic transductivity oriented toward openness. Fabulation is a form of active characterization. Its specific delivery is that of transforming individual entities into personal ones. Bergson's paradigmatic example is that of the transformation of spirits into more and more personalized gods. This "gradual evolution of religion towards gods of increasingly marked personality, who are more and more definitely interrelated (Bergson 1935: 151) is opposed to magic, presented by Bergson as a refusal of the individuation of the event and a return to an impersonal essence. The power of fabulation resides for Bergson in the capacity to generate "efficacious presences" (167); as such, it is closely related to the "essential function of the universe," which Bergson defines in the very last line of *The Two Sources* as a "machine for the making of gods" (275).[13]

But we shouldn't overvalue the role and purpose of the function of fabulation in Bergson's account, insofar as for him, it is dynamic mysticism, not fabulation, which is the ultimate source of moral improvement for the earthbound. The mystic appeal to the person is of a different nature than fabulation's pragmatic of address. For beyond the function of fabulation, Bergson finds the superior power of what I would tentatively call here *exemplary immediation*.

Exemplary Immediation

> Undoubtedly philosophy can only consider the mystical soul from the outside and from the point of view of its lines of probability. But it is precisely the existence of mysticism that gives a higher probability to this final transmutation into certainty, and also gives, as it were, an *envelope or a limit to all the aspects of method.*
>
> *Gilles Deleuze (1991: 112)*

Emotions, these "differential elements of freedom" as Lapoujade defines them in his study of Bergson, constitute, as we have seen, an essential element in the effective production of futurity. As such, they could just as well be called "affects", following the general use of the term in the realm of affect theory. No doubt, Bergson's philosophy is affect-friendly; and the general aim of his philosophical endeavour could certainly be dubbed immediationist. But Bergson, the philosopher of immediate felt duration, also requires a concept of emancipating personality that differs quite substantially from the image of thought that presents emotions as the result of the psychological capture of affect in the interiority of a subject.

From the perspective of immediation, the person as subject most often appears like an unnecessary or at least secondary form of closure and limitation. And interestingly enough, one would be most justified to argue that this position is precisely that of... Bergsonism itself:

> life as *movement* alienates itself in the material *form* that it creates; by actualizing itself, by differentiating itself, it loses "contact with the rest of itself." Every species is thus an arrest of movement; it could be said that the living being turns on itself and closes itself. (Deleuze 1991: 104)

Isn't a person just such alienated material form, a self-enclosed "arrest on matter" that separates from the vibrant core of creative evolution? And yet, this characterization would fall short of taking into account the importance that Bergson confers to the ethical effort of being a person, or more precisely, to the fact that for him, emotions must be accounted for in a "personal" way—the technical meaning of this word still needs further elucidation—in order to become fully integrated in the world's processual advance. This requirement certainly doesn't change the general orientation of its philosophy toward openness; in fact, the appeal to the person involves a form of individual completion or self-enjoyment that concerns precisely how to generate an active relation to futurity. But it does bring to the fore a pragmatist complication that challenges post-humanist sensibilities, which more often than not prefer to avoid *The Two Sources* altogether, and not without good reasons. The book indeed reads as a fairly old-fashioned idealization of "great men" that seem to pay too heavy a tribute to the intellectual and moral preoccupations of the time. But I think it also develops a stimulating and non-moralist approach to ethopoietic exemplarity, on which I would like to bring further attention here.

Pursuing Bergson's general critique of detached and contemplative (pure) intellectuality, *The Two Sources* poses a simple yet crucial diagnosis: "philosophy (…) has scarcely succeeded, so it would seem, in explaining how a moral motive can have a hold upon the souls of men." (1935: 51) It is in order to answer this particular problem that Bergson will dedicate numerous years of his life to an extended study of different forms of mystical practices. This study will lead him to conceive of mysticism as nothing less than a philosophical method: "If mysticism is really what we have just said it is, it must furnish us with the means of approaching, as it were experimentally, the problem of the existence and the nature of God" (1935: 206).

Bergson's conception of the mystic soul puts great emphasis on embodied soulful exemplarity. It bears in this regard great proximity with how Peirce conceives of the exemplary introduction of qualitative "divine" difference in the world:

> If a pragmaticist is asked what he means by the word 'God', he can only say that just as long acquaintance with a man of great character may deeply influence one's whole manner of conduct, so that a glance at his portrait may make a difference … then that analogue of a mind … is what he means by "God" (Peirce 1955: 376).

Accordingly, the presence of the mystic exceeds the moral obligations of what Bergson calls reproductive or closed societies. It represents a form of ascensional movement, a "pure aspiration" that can potentially move individuals and collectivities beyond their confines and limits. For Bergson, the mode of existence of the mystic is that of an enthusiast and somehow irresistible call that exerts an uplifting effect on its congeners:

> It is the mystic souls who draw and will continue to draw civilized societies in their wake. The remembrance of what they have been, of what they have done, is enshrined in the memory of humanity. (...) If we do not evoke this or that sublime figure, we know that we can do so; he thus exerts on us a virtual attraction. (1935: 68)

In Bergson's account of ethopoietic exemplarity, calls and persons refer circularly to each other. In opposition to the "*impersonal* moral requirements" established by society to ensure its steady reproduction, Bergson describes the virtual attraction exerted by the mystic souls as "series of *appeals* made to the conscience of each of us by *persons* who represent the best there is in humanity" (1935: 68).[14] What is particularly fascinating in my view about Bergson's account of the virtual power of attraction of what he also calls "privileged personalities" is that it is immediate and non-discursive:

> Why is it, then, that saints have their imitators, and why do the great moral leaders draw the masses after them? They ask nothing, and yet they receive. They have no need to exhort; their mere existence suffices. For such is precisely the nature of this other morality. Whereas natural obligation is a pressure or a propulsive force, complete and perfect morality has the effect of an appeal. (1935: 23-24)[15] The mystics for Bergson are traversed by the élan vital, the creative process of fertile duration. As such, their personal effort, their effort to be a person coincides, by "living contradiction," with the "creative effort that created a thing which is a species, and turns into movement what was, by definition, a stop" (1935: 201).[16] Defining the existence of mystics as an immediating and transformative call that simplifies, intensifies and unifies subjectivities raises the question of the nature of that call and of the form of address it generates. Not surprisingly, Bergson argues that what makes this call efficacious is the infra- or supra-intellectual emotion it is susceptible of arousing in an individual or a collective. The mystics incorporate and bring to a superior degree this divine feeling called love. And love, or at least love as it is theologically treated

within the "superiorly" active Christian tradition, involves a personal address. Let's move with circumspection here. "Love, Peirce writes forcefully, is not directed to abstractions but to persons" (1955: 362).[17] Love is a relational power that creates persons, persons that are immanent to the field love co-individuates. This claim brings us back to James' passionate plea for a personal God, which is, at the end of the day, is no more than a reassertion of theology's most fundamental claim. Interestingly, Bergson here introduces a subtle gap in which he qualifies the mediating situation of philosophy with regard to the fullness of the mystic's truth:

> The philosopher could soon define this nature, did he wish to find a formula for mysticism. God is love, and is the object of love: herein lies the whole contribution of mysticism.... What [the mystic] does state clearly is that divine love is not a thing of God: it is God Himself. It is upon this point that *the philosopher must fasten who holds God to be a person,* and yet wishes to avoid anything like a gross assimilation with man. He will think, for example, of the enthusiasms which can fire a soul, consume all that is within it, and henceforth fill the whole space. *The individual then becomes one with the emotion*.... (1935: 216; my emphasis)

Mysticism and theology both celebrate the identity of God and love. What is at stake then in the intimate coincidence of the two terms *for philosophy*? Why is it that philosophy's task at this precise point consists in holding God to be a person? Everything happens as if the philosophical rationalization of the mystical experience requires the introduction of a mediation in order to testify for the exteriority of thought, although it is most definitely a vanishing mediator of sorts that is destined to be im-mediated in the mystical experience itself. Following the other pragmatists, Bergson thus seems to say: the personal God is the form most akin to induce and express the inherently addressed and transformative relationality of love. It is in this perspective that one should read, in concordance with Whitehead's idea that God is indiscernible from the multiple feelings that aim at him, Bergson reminding us that "the mystics unanimously bear witness that God needs us, just as we need God" (1935: 219). Ethopoietically speaking, this divine image of reciprocal love works as a pragmatic and dramatizing formula for futurial activation.

Conclusion: Immanent Planning in Person

> Sometimes, I now think I'm just a social media addiction masquerading as a person.
>
> Hang on to that personhood, though—you can't remain on Facebook without it.
>
> *Jacob Wren and a friend, discussing on Facebook*

In the introduction of his inspired study around mysticism and philosophy in the work of Bergson, Anthony Feneuil wonders why the philosophical explication of the formula of mysticism requires the concept of person. The answer he provides reads as a solid summary of the core issues at stake in the problem of personality as presented by Bergson. It is worth quoting at length:

> ... if God gives himself in the personal relation one entertains with him, then he is not known in his *quid*, but in his *quis*: he is not known conceptually but *personally* ... in the term *love*, the nature of God is only given through his person. *Love is the proper name of God*: it designates him in the relation we can entertain with him, without ever inserting him in the conceptual network of our discursive knowledges. And if God only gives himself as a person ... then this donation cannot possibly be conceived of independently from the one *to whom* he gives himself. (Feneuil 2011: 145-146)

The problem of personality points toward the incorporations and paradoxical closures involved in the effective practices of opening to the outside. The spiritual work on oneself invoked by the Christian mystics is characterized by the possibility to become organisms-that-person through an intimate relation with God qua love. For the philosopher, this experience translates in the requirement to hold God to be such a person. As we have seen throughout this article, the preference for the recourse to an activating personal address to the divine runs deep in the work of many pragmatist thinkers of the turn of the past century. For most of us, this ethopoietic option appears rather foreign and exotic and it is not that easy to see how it could concern us today. As for myself, I think this study might offer an unexpected yet rigorous starting point from which to interrogate our very manners of thinking, figuring, announcing and relating to speculative futurity. The ways by which we generate, tend to and eventually curb collectively our carrying enthusiasms away from default neoliberal narcissism is an essential component of how we orient ourselves in the world. In this regard, what Bergson says about the communicative an energizing signature of the mystics' presence applies just as well to transindividual collectives. They too can be exemplary in the immediating sense of the word we have defined before, that is, relationally and without necessarily referring to predetermined rules or codes of conduct. Isn't exemplarity intrinsically relational, always event-based, always an event in itself? Exemplary immediation is an integral component of a modal ontology's ethics. In the end, I think we can push exemplary immediation even further into transindividual and political matters and think of it alongside what Stefano Harney and Fred Moten say about *planning* in the undercommons and the "futurial presence of the forms of life": speculative and exemplary immediation conceived of as an "ongoing experiment with the informal, carried out by and on the means of social reproduction, as the to come of the forms of life" (2013: 74).

Notes

1. In Process and Reality, Whitehead states a similar concern for what he calls the "living person" or "living personality": "Our own self-consciousness is directed awareness of ourselves as such persons. There are limits to such unified control, which indicate dissociation of personality, multiple personalities (...) what needs to be explained is not dissociation of personality but unifying control, by reason of which we not only have unified behaviour, which can be observed by others, but also consciousness of a unified experience." (1978: 107-108)
2. William James' brother, the famous novelist Henry James, describes this (irremediably?) agonistic situation with eloquence: "Life is, in fact, a battle. Evil is insolent and strong; beauty enchanting, but rare; goodness very apt to be weak; folly very apt to be defiant; wickedness to carry the day; imbeciles to be in great places, people of sense in small, and mankind generally unhappy. But the world as it stands is no narrow illusion, no phantasm, no evil dream of the night; we wake up to it, forever and ever; and we can neither forget it nor deny it nor dispense with it." (James 1912: 292)
3. In *American Pragmatism: A religious Genealogy*, Gail Hammer suggests that Peirce was contemporary to a renewed interest in Buddhism: "He sometimes expresses the sentiment that the heart of the Gospels is equal to the Buddha's teachings on selflessness and compassion." (2003: 118)

4. For a detailed discussion of this question in the context of Bruno Latour's recent work, see Erik Bordeleau (2015).

5. In a slightly different, more metaphysical register, Whitehead argues in favor of an activist philosophy that leaves aside the posture of quietism that rightly derives from the conception of a self-sufficient world created once and for all. For when facing such a world, Whitehead says, "the best we can say of the turmoil is: 'for so he giveth his beloved—sleep.' This is the message of religions of the Buddhistic type, and in some sense it is true." (1979: 343)

6. "Among philosophers, Spinoza emphasized the fundamental infinitude and introduced a subordinate differentiation by finite modes. Also conversely, Leibniz emphasized the necessity of finite monads and based them upon a substratum of Deistic infinitude. Neither of them adequately emphasized the fact that infinitude is mere vacancy apart from its embodiment of finite values, and that finite entities are meaningless apart from their relationship beyond themselves" (Whitehead 1951: 675).

7. In *Terza persona* (2007) and *Le persone e le cose* (2014), Roberto Esposito aims at revealing the biopolitical separation that runs through the concept of the person and thus producing a formal and operative distinction within the human between a rational and voluntary part on the one hand, and an immediately biological and animal part on the other. For Esposito, the apparatus of the person produces a metaphysical stripping (scarnificazione) of the body. Following this philosophical diagnosis, Esposito reclaims the body as a site of resistance that must be conceived of beyond (or rather, below) the dialectics of personalization and depersonalization.

8. It's interesting to notice in this regard that the very notion of "human person" as used in the discussions about human cloning has posed some serious difficulties to Chinese translators. In their attempt to establish a common international legal frame, they decided to introduce a neologism, wei geren, instead of the more usual shehui ren, "social person," in order to make apparent "the religious connotations that certain Chinese philosophers attribute to the Western conceptions" (Delmas-Marty 2007: 827-830).

9. Webb also recalls that "the history of the notion of personality" was "marked by the stress laid successively on incommunicability (among the Schoolmen), self-consciousness (since Descartes) and on will (since Kant), as characteristics of personality." (1919: 10)

10. It is quite fascinating to notice that Agamben's ultimate analysis of what he calls the "ontological apparatus" adopts exactly the same strategy as Bergson's and focuses on the "linguistic presupposition at work in the ontologic interlacement of being and saying (Agamben 2014: 155-178). It would be interesting to contrast Bergson's idea of continuum and duration with what Agamben's conception of the anthropogenetic history that surges from this ontological interweaving.

11. In *Creative Evolution*, Bergson uses the same terms (procession and conversion) in his discussion of divine causality in Antic philosophy: "Aristotle (...)

shows us in the movement of the universe an aspiration of things toward the divine perfection, and consequently an ascent toward God, while he describes it elsewhere as the effect of a contact of God with the first sphere and as descending, consequently, from God to things. The Alexandrians, we think, do no more than follow this double indication when they speak of procession and conversion." (1998: 341, my emphasis). https://archive.org/stream/creativeevolutio00berguoft/creativeevolutio00berguoft_djvu.txt

12. In this regard, Lapoujade notes that "when Deleuze searches for his own account a time of the future, it is not to Bergson but to Nietzsche that he refers to, the only true thinker of the future to his mind." (2010: 17; my translation)

13. The formative, delirious and cosmical dimension of fabulation is also suggestively described by Deleuze: "(...) fabulation – fabulating function – does not consist in imagining or projecting an ego. Rather, it attains these visions, it raises itself to these becomings and powers. (1997: 3) Or again: "It is the task of the fabulating function to invent a people (...) that is a possibility of life" (4).

14. The italics are present in the French original but have been seemingly forgotten in the English translation.

15. In the original french version, we actually read: "Ils n'ont pas besoin d'exhorter; ils n'ont qu'à exister*; leur existence est un appel*" (Bergson 1967: 30) (my emphasis).

16. Or again: "In our eyes, the ultimate end of mysticism is the establishment of a contact, consequently of a partial coincidence, with the creative effort of which life is the manifestation. This effort is of God, if not God himself. The great mystic is to be conceived as an individual being, capable of transcending the limitations imposed on the species by its material nature, thus continuing and extending the divine action. Such is our definition" (1935 : 188).

17. A few lines later, Peirce adds up a quite compelling characterization of the passionate relation to abstractions that gives us another view on the importance of the problem of personality for the pragmatists of that time: "Suppose, for example, that I have an idea that interests me. It is my creation. It is my creature... it is a little person. I love it; and I will sink myself in perfecting it" (1955: 362-363; emphasis mine).

Pia Ednie-Brown

Playing Person: An Architectural Adventure

World Play

> In play, you don't bite, you nip. The difference between biting and nipping is what opens the analogical gap between combat and play. It is the style of the gesture that opens the minimal difference between the play gesture and its analogue in the arena of combat.
> *Brian Massumi (2014: 9)*

As you read these written words, on some screen or page somewhere, they are to some extent involved in the act of mediating between whatever it is I am trying to say and whatever meaning you might glean from them. As anyone who writes comes to realise, they will do an imperfect job—for meaning is not simply "conveyed" or moved seamlessly from one place to another. This is linked to the fact that words do not simply mediate—they also have an immediacy that acts in the moment of your reading—now—as the act is taking place. This event will inflect the meaning of any assemblage of words I might have strained to compose into clear form. One could see this as interference—the pesky potential for misunderstanding. However, this would be to risk overlooking every other potential of words.

Let's think for a moment about the eventfulness of just one word: "word." When spoken (with an Australian accent at least) "word" voices the sound of having "erred"; the act of being mistaken, quite fittingly, inflects potential background associations. It rhymes with "heard," "nerd," and "turd." Visually, it is almost a "sword," and nearly a "world." In all these ways and so many more, the word "word" (along with all other words) both finds precision and blurs into a cloud of slippage, association, variation—and potential. The way in which that potential unfolds in events will be modulated by, say, the style and tone of the essay in which the word helps flesh out ideas. They take part in a complex of qualities; the complexion of events. It matters what is said or written, but *how* this is done matters at least as much. And, as we step from a word to concepts, the cloud of potential gets thicker. What, after all, can we make of the concept "immediation"? If immediation is a concept that is hard to define, this may be because that cloud of potential is very thick indeed, and attempting to fix a definition would be counter to it's aims.

As Brian Massumi has pointed out, "We are not born into 'the' world. We are thrown into worlding" (Massumi 2011: 110). Here I am approaching immediation as a problem of worlding *in such a way* that every thing becomes open to eventful potential—come what may. The world plays. Immediation pertains to *how* we play; to our style of worlding. This is not always fun and games—we can't always know when the world play will bite—when a playful nip might flip into combat and sink in its teeth. The question then becomes: what techniques can we assemble that can both support an attention to immediation, and help to hold potential open—in a playful place?

This essay—however it unfolds for you through the event of reading—has been written as a way to explore this question through a very particular (architectural) project, and with a few specific concerns in mind. The first concern is a desire to usher attention away from a focus on human activities—which largely dominates in explorations of collectivity—in order to offer inanimate characters, such as buildings, a more active place at the table of events. The degree to which they tend to be cast into the background impacts on our capacity to acknowledge and work with their on-going immediating activity. The second, related concern is to allow inanimate, ostensibly human-made artifacts to become less defined by human ownership or authorship, such that we might have a better chance of taking their powers of immediation into account, and to work with them in amplifying these capacities.

What's In a Name?

The story here begins with a house—the partial demolition, renovation and extension of a centenarian Victorian brick terrace that I came to name Avery Green. This act of naming was a technique I was keen to

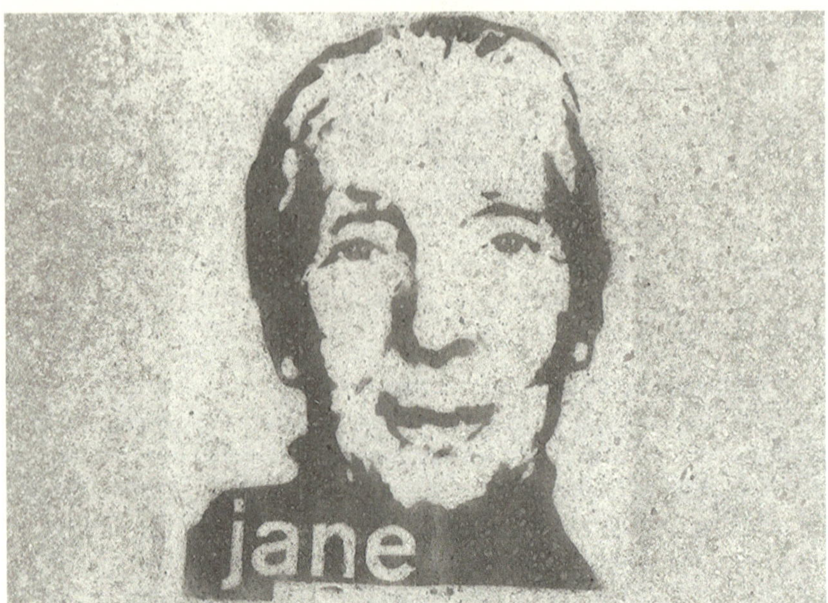

Fig 18. Jane. This stencil art of Jane Goodall was found on the concrete surface of a bicycle path, about 1km from Avery Green. It has become an emblematic image for The Jane Approach. Photograph by Pia Ednie-Brown, 2015.

explore as a way to experiment with approaching the house as a non-human *person*. Both the naming and the personing are full of dangers—and may seem to risk moving towards an emphasis on the mediations of identity—to the pre-categorised, pre-determined categories of recognition. I hope to eventually show that the risk of these techniques was worth taking.

These techniques were part of an experiment in assembling an approach, which I have also named: the Jane Approach. The Jane Approach offers approaches for the development of Avery Green, while Avery Green offers a highly situated, material specificity through which the Jane Approach can also be developed and articulated. This approach takes flight through emphasizing speculative experimentation, while becoming grounded through explicitly material acts of making and extremely specific, situated exercises of imagination. Jane and Avery are sisters, having an intimate relationship in that they continued to inflect one another as they developed together.

The Jane Approach is named in reference to a series of Janes: Jane Goodall, Jane Bennett, Jane Jacobs.[1] All three attend carefully to the

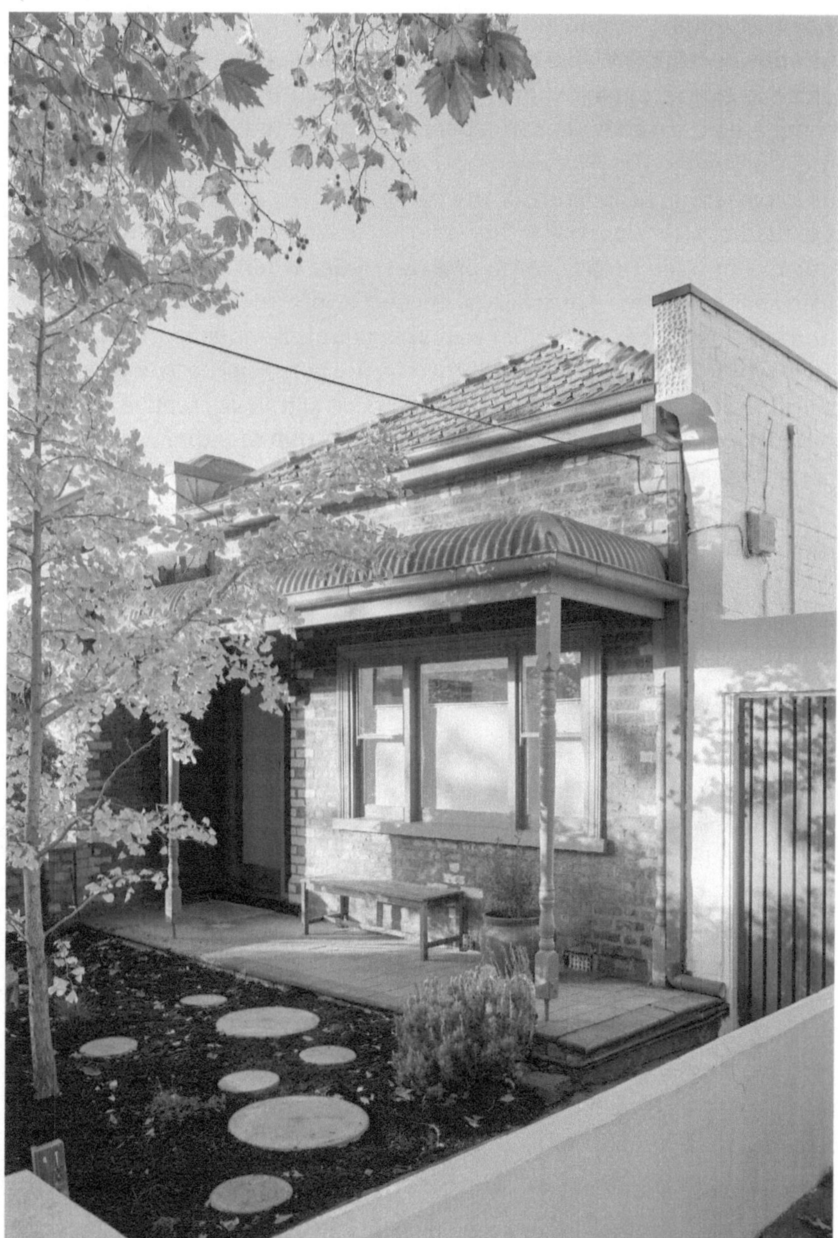

Figure 19. The face of Avery Green. Photograph by Lucas Allen, 2016.

potential—or living, situated eventfulness—of non-human animals and things, such as chimpanzees, cities and trash. Their approaches all move against the grain of dominant assumptions about what is worth attending to, and all open up complex ecologies in places where top-down, reductive approaches had been favoured. The works of these extraordinary women have some beautiful affinities and complementary attributes that become highlighted and amplified as they come together. Working through such a contrived coincidence of affinity—around the figure of the name 'Jane'—is not about limiting the field of attention, but rather offering it some admirable anchor points—or open sites to which one can return when feeling lost. What I am calling the Jane Approach is, of course, informed by many other unnameable forces, and other namable people's endeavours, not all of which are called "Jane." Ultimately, the Jane Approach is about drawing attention to the co-creation implicit within all creative activity by working with coincident correspondences that together generate something new. Its also a way of saying that the approach is not "mine": this is not "my" creative process and despite being "my" creative project, Avery Green is not simply owned or authored by me. "I" simply made a difference as part of an ecology of differences inflected through the Jane Approach.

Playing Person

> To live with someone for a long time requires an element of fiction—the selective use of facts to craft an ongoing story. Also the suspension of disbelief: we must believe a story is real while we are in it, and the same goes, Tess thinks, for a marriage. She used to admire people who described their marriages as open, who told each other about every indiscretion in thought and deed. But what she noticed now was that without editing, or at least a little magical thinking, those relationships had ceased to exist, because their participants simply no longer believed in them.
>
> *Anna Funder (2015: 32)*

Approaching a house as a person involves an element of fiction, and perhaps some magical thinking. Resonating with Anna Funder's observations about marriage in the quote above, this approach is aimed at building up the strength and richness of relationship with a house. Hand-in-hand with personing, naming is an ancient technique through which we can identify and recognize a singularity without claiming to contain or know it in any entirety. Personal names are different to categories of things; to be called, say, "Eliza," sustains a kind of evocation that is different to being called something in general, like a "person," even though there are many Elizas (just as there are many Janes). If we call the family car "Daisy," the specificities of that car and the degree to which it becomes part of the family, moves closer to the foreground, out of a backgrounded status of being, say, a "Toyota" or a "car"—a generic brand or type of thing.

Arriving at the name Avery Green involved a process of feeling around trying out names that arose in relation to her qualities, her history, and the inclinations growing through the design process. It some ways, where it fell was another co-incidence of events. She had other first names—"Eleanor," "Ava"—and for a while her surname was "Evergreen." The various names were tested out over time, tried on and measured up, discussed with others, googled, felt out against ideas growing inside the design project, etc. Her name settled into place only because at some stage it became documented in a recorded lecture (Ednie-Brown, 2015b)—which became her proxy certificate of naming.

When Jane Goodall famously named the chimpanzees she studied, she was criticized for being unscientific. However, this naming was integral to her recognition that as much as there are traits that are indicative of chimpanzees in general, every species is only constituted by relations between many instances, differences, and variations found across individual characters. Goodall's insistence on working through the particular to the general is also integral to the approach of Jane Jacobs—who found it important as a way toward dealing with the kind of problem that a city is: that is, an organized, irreducible complexity. The kind of problem that a person is, I would argue and Jacobs implies, is of the same nature (Jacobs 1992: 447). When Jane Bennett more recently suggested that it might be worth running the risk of anthropomorphizing (Bennett 2010: 120)—which Jacobs does for the cities she cares for—she was, similarly, understanding that this act of qualitative linking can foster a vibrant recognition of the vital connections between us and other things.

Naming the house and exploring her as a person, is in part an act of anthropomorphizing. But the approach is not tied to the human in as much as not only humans are named or considered to be a person. Most dictionary definitions of "person" refer immediately to humans, but it has broader reach. In legal contexts a person refers to a body or assemblage that has rights, responsibilities and interests ascribed to them. This can include firms, labour organizations, partnerships, associations, corporations, etc. In 2015 a legal battle sought to attribute personhood to two chimpanzees, Leo and Hercules, held as experimental subjects at Stony Brook University. In 2012 the Whanganui River in New Zealand was recognised as having legal personhood.

So, a person is not always human, but it is also notable that many humans were not always considered to be a person—slaves, women and children have historically been considered to not have legal personhood, for instance. If we now consider this past to be abhorrent, my provocation here is that there are ethical reasons for taking this shift even further in reconsidering the status of buildings in a related way. Houses are generally considered to be property, like wives used to be. In a time where houses are increasingly considered to be an investment, rather than simply homes, there is good reason to rethink the nature of our relationship with our home, house, and by extension, buildings in general. Most importantly, however, this is a call for an ecological broadening of attention—in a manner that takes seriously the presence of persons beyond the human, particularly in terms of the more behaviorally, qualitatively inclined idea of personality.

If naming points evocatively to an identification of something, the concept of "person" points to both its particularity and its generality. Charles Peirce claimed that "a person is only a particular kind of general idea" and "every general idea has the unified living feeling of a person" (Peirce 1992a: 350). The person is already transindividuating, well poised to be a trans-species, trans-entity concept that can feed into Jane Bennett's ethically inflected thesis on enchantment, where she argues for interspecies and intraspecies crossings (Bennett 2001: 17) and for extending these crossings to "nonhuman animals, the wind, rocks, trees, plants, tools, machines" (29). She suggests that the magic of these crossings "generate what might be called presumptive generosity toward the animals, vegetables, and minerals within one's field of encounter" (30). In forging a certain crossing for Avery Green, through her naming and personing, I have found Bennett's claims to hold weight. As a designer, it helped me to more expressly or closely attend to the personality of the house within the maelstrom of design and construction process, and to focus on ways of working with her as an entity that is utterly beyond me—a complexity unto herself. The house became something to care for as a person by attending to her personality—with a sense that decisions related to issues like

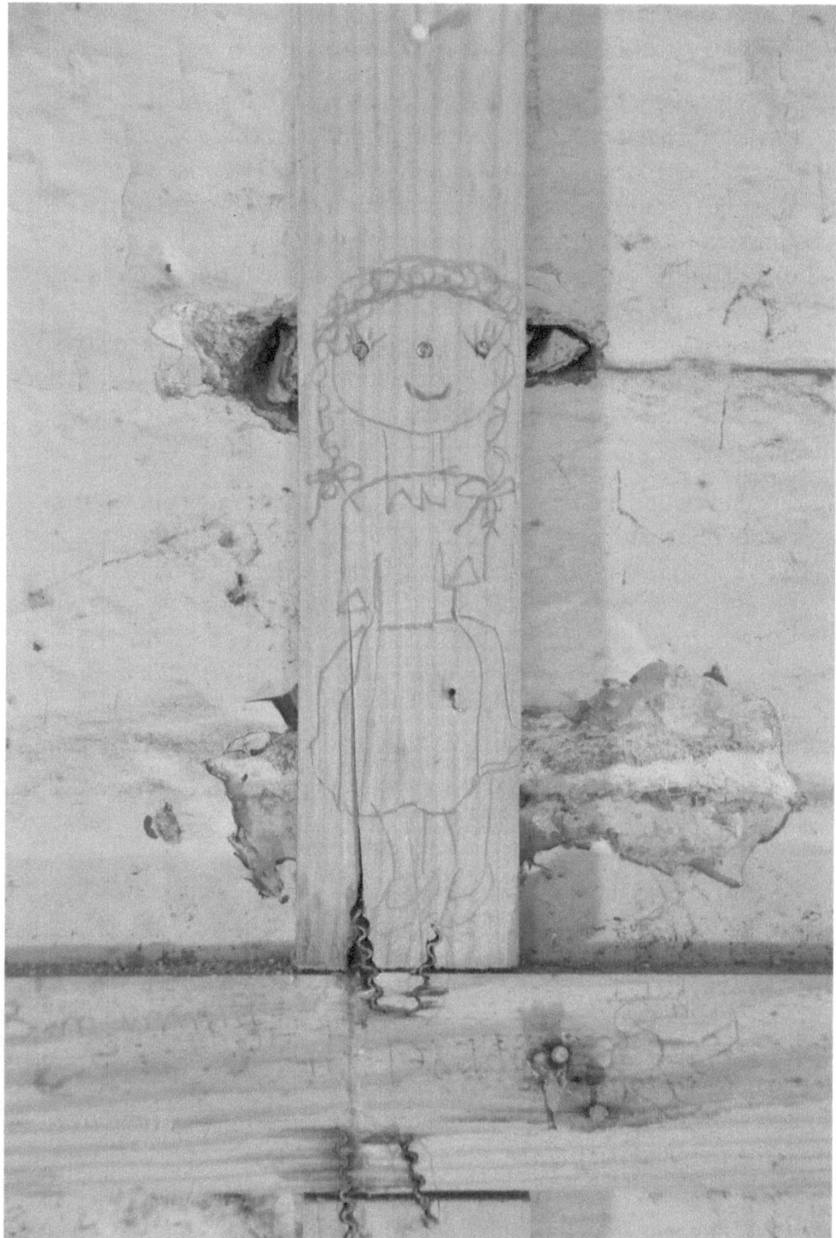

Fig 20. One of the pencil drawings found during demolition on the studwork under the particleboard wall lining. Photograph by Pia Ednie-Brown, 2015.

the quality of materials, the relational work of colour, the relative placements and connection between elements within her, were not just about what some human person might like, but what might work for Avery.

"What might work for Avery" was of course something could only be known in the midst of her on-going individuation. There were broad characteristics that were clear from the start: she is a brick Victorian terrace house, built around the turn of the century, and as such fits into an architectural genre. But like all houses, she is not like any other house. A stylistic mongrel—her Victorian façade was ripped off in the 1950s and replaced with a more broad-windowed street address, and a number of Victorian details were replaced by modernist-deco styled features. A timber frame kitchen and bathroom had been added to her rear, which had gradually decayed to the point of being structurally unsalvageable.

During demolition we found drawings of girls, by a young girl, on the studwork under the particleboard wall lining. The drawings were dated 1955 and the 11-year-old author was named. Across all those years that my young daughter and I lived with Avery (in her pre-named days) we had no idea how many other girls were hidden under her skin. The more I worked with Avery, as we moved together through a field of mutual, and at times quite radical transformation, the more I found that just as some mysteries or secrets come to light, new ones are generated.

Collective Solitude

> In affect, we are never alone.
> *Brian Massumi (2015b: 6)*

In her 1971 book, *In the Shadow of Man*, Jane Goodall discusses the impact of having been at the Gombe Stream without human companionship for a considerable period. It was after being removed from the demands of human interaction, that she was able to connect with the personalities that are everywhere, immediating with us. She reflects that:

> ...had I been alone for longer than a year I might have become a rather strange person, for inanimate objects began to develop their own identities: I found myself saying "Good morning" to my little hut on the Peak, "Hello"

> to the stream where I collected my water. (van Lawick-Goodall 1971: 50)

Goodall's comment points to the way in which companionship operates well beyond the human-with-human variety, and even beyond the human-with-animal. Companionship becomes a multifarious potential of her worlding. Despite the degree of interest in the more-than-human, the non-human, etc. experiments in collectivity largely involve groups of human people as a default. I am often left feeling that we talk too much, and that there is a great need for more attention to less perceptible movements, which the clamor of human interaction will often obfuscate. There is more work to be done exploring creative activity aimed at generating emergent collectivity in which we don't rely on groups of human people to mobilize the event. This leaning away from human-sociality, or what we could call "multi-human" relationality, is related to Gilbert Simondon's theory of individuation and his concept of the collective. As Muriel Combes' book on Simondon's philosophy of the transindividual clarifies:

> The collective is not to be confused with the constituted human community; it can only happen via that which is neither the constituted individual nor the social as an entity; it arises rather through the preindividual zone of subjects that remains uneffectuated by any functional relation between individuals. The interindividual relationship even constitutes an obstacle to the discovery and effectuation of this residual preindividuality, or at least it provides a cause for avoiding it ... for the subject to become engaged in the constitution of the collective, first of all, means stripping away community, or at the very least, setting aside those aspects of community that prevent the perception of the existence of preindividual, and thus the encounter with transindividual. (Combes, 2013: 37-38)

Apparent solitude becomes a paradoxical passage toward the collective and transindividual because it becomes a milieu that, while no less densely populated with relations (Combes, 2013: 37), is cleared of the habitual regimes of relationship that come to constitute communities. In this clearing one is opened up to the otherwise less perceptible, an entering into the "more-than-one" through a more immediate access to the preindividual. The "more-than-" and the "pre-" of the individual are slightly awkward ways of referring to a level of existence that is very hard to name in its own terms. Another awkward way of approaching it is in terms of *connectivity*, or how things become mutually constituted through forming connections. The "pre-" and the more-than-" are what we might call "deeper" levels of mutual connection—operating abstractly and affectively. If open to the encounter with the transindividual, an apparently cut off or isolated condition that one might call "solitude", becomes transformed into a milieu that can amplify immediation—thereby enabling that "deeper" or more abstract level of connectivity to flow.

Via Simondon, we can think about immediation as an entering into this level of connectivity. Mediation, then, becomes an issue of operating at a different level—that of the individual and the inter-individual—where relations have become partially assembled into forms, shapes, and identities and the relations between those assemblages. The process of individuation, then, *is where these different levels are all-at-once*, as part of a polyphonic disparity. For Simondon, the individual is a metastability: never stable, complete or simple in its dimensions, and is always part of an ongoing process of individuation, which can be considered as a:

> partial and relative resolution manifested in a system that contains latent potentials and harbours a certain incompatibility with itself, an incompatibility due at once to forces in tension as well as to the impossibility of interaction between terms of extremely disparate dimensions. (Simondon 1992: 300)

This incompatibility is an important aspect of the metastablity of the system, because it means it can never be a simple or non-complex unity. In harbouring disparity, the individual—as an individuating process—operates as a collective. The collective nature of the individuation is tied into its "environment," or milieu. Always inseparably folding out of and into its milieu, it is always both less than and more than whole, such that completion or closure is impossible. This link to environmental milieu is important and, as Simondon writes: "Individuation, moreover, not only brings the individual to light but also the individual-milieu dyad" (Simondon 1992: 300).

Simondon wrote of individuation as a process relevant to both living and nonliving entities, albeit with some distinctions. The primary difference is that "the living being conserves in itself an activity of permanent individuation," (305) whereas the non- or semi-living is the *result* of an individuation. As a crystal forms in a saturated solution of copper sulphate, this is a process of individuation, and the crystal itself becomes a result of that process. But even when the individuating process comes to an end, activation or reactivation via ongoing engagements are always occurring, even if imperceptibly. Regardless of their relative stability, things are always "eventing"; always immediating in manners that carry their past forward and gather forming futures. One of the key implications here is that all things have collective lives, never being closed, complete, or separable from the world around them, even while (and arguably because) they can be distinguished as entities unto themselves. As discussed above, even "solitude" is a collective activity, and a condition that can allow for a clearer realization of that collectivity.

A desire to resist the habitual tendency to understand artifacts as tied to and limited by human authorship is at stake in this call for more exploration of collectivity minus the inter- or multi-human. Under names such as "architect," "artist," "philosopher," artifacts are "authored," but even while they are being made they are never simply determined or owned by an author because the depths of relationality in the event of making well exceeds the individual, which is always part of the individual-milieu dyad, as Simondon might put it. This is where and why entering deeply into examining actual, specific cases of creative production becomes important—because it can reveal the irreducibility of the creative process. In the same way that explorations of collectivity tend to fall, by default, into groups of human people, the idea of "co-creation" tends to call up multiple human individuals. However, co-creation is not simply about many human people creating together—"creation" is *always* co-creation—even when there is only one human person, or no human people involved. The garden around my home, for instance, is a product of ongoing co-creation whether I actively garden or neglect it for long periods of time. With or without me, it grows, dies, evolves. Clearly, my involvement or lack thereof makes a difference, just as the involvement of an "author" in any act of production is in no way inconsequential—the point is simply that there are many differences being made.

Co-creation operates across levels—mediation and immediation, individual and preindividual—in that, in as much as all creative processes are also individuating processes, it harbors heterogeneous dimensions and a polyphony of levels and phases. Human involvement in creative, individuating processes both contributes to and is pulled around and exceeded by a dense thicket of relational forces. Once "finished," the emergence of an artifact enters a different register that is even less beholden to individualized authorship. This remains the case even though it may carry ontogenetic traces of a style of authorship with which it came-into-being, and even when those involved in its emergence might feel a specific attachment unavailable to others. Those traces are not unlike the qualities of a parent one sees in a child, and those attachments are not dissimilar, I would argue, to the connection one feels to a friend with whom you have shared a transformative experience. You never own that friend, but each of you are partly constituted by and connected through a shared, significant event. The buildings an architect ushers into being can be understood as her good friends or her extended family, rather than "her projects."

Drawing Out; Individuating

> And what is a habitat? It's an intricate, complicated web of interdependencies.
> *Jane Jacobs (2000: 21-22)*

Most of us would have had experiences in which group activity becomes an energizing force. However, many will also know of group situations that dulled energy, suppressed potential, and/or produced conflict that can become destructive. This is similar to the difference between feeling (unhappily) alone and feeling more deeply connected, or transindividually engaged through solitude. Both personal and collective histories offer us examples of affirmation and negation. In this sense, the on-going task of finding ways to foster affirmative, emergent collectivity is always relevant. This same problem also bears upon any generative or creative process.

This task motivates my interest in the dual and complex tangling of mediations and immediations in relation to architectural drawings and models. This becomes most accessible through ways in which architectural drawings played an active role in the individuation of Avery Green and the way in which related multifarious and fluid movements came to unfold across the construction process.

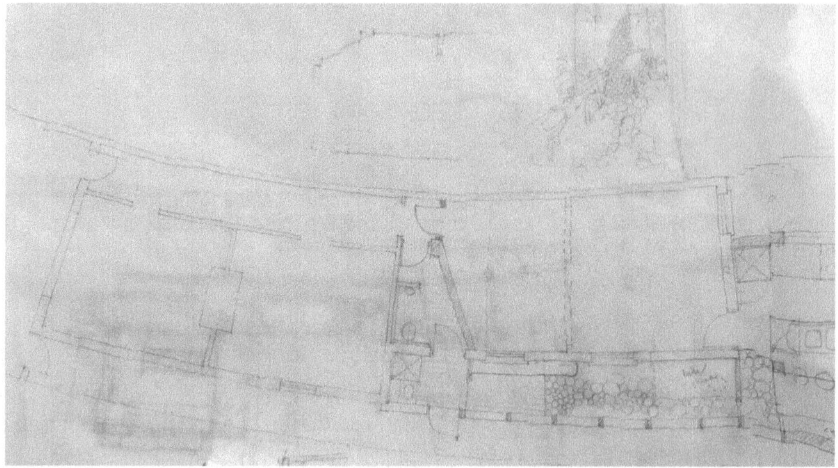

Figure 21. Panorama of Avery Green design sketches. Photograph by Pia Ednie-Brown, 2015.

Before Avery was named, drawings that dreamt of altering this house accrued sporadically over a period of about 8 years—generally on yellow tracing paper. Piles of torn-edged, diaphanous, yellow leaves marked with graphite thoughts, bear witness to the many potential excursions and forms I imagined the house might move toward. In 2013, a different ecology of image-making-imagining technique arose during a three-day residence with the experimental architecture of Arakawa and Gins' *Bioscleave House* on Long Island, New York. I spent time writing letters to this house I was with—in an effort to approach an architectural presence more creature-like than most. This was interspersed with photographing the house as a technique through which the house spoke back to me. In the process, the panorama function of the iPhone became an unexpectedly useful extension of the power of photographic description.

At first, they seemed simply like a good way to capture the sheer expansiveness of the interior. However, they became particularly interesting when, due to an inadvertent deviation from the assumptions of the software, significant "glitches" were generated. By walking with the camera, rather than staying in one spot and panning around like a well-behaved perspectivally-defined observer, the software was forced to make sense of and stitch together the data differently, in ways that both interfered with and reassembled the usual perspectival logic of the image. In other words, the resulting panorama images

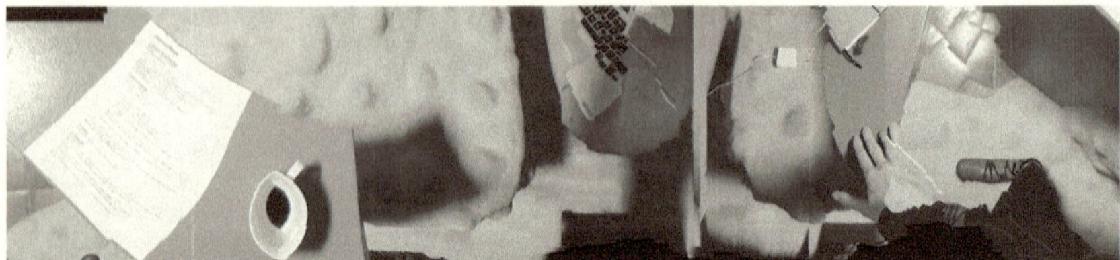

Figure 22: Panorama photograph taken with the Bioscleave House (Arakawa and Gins), New York. Photograph by Pia Ednie-Brown, 2013.

literally became a simultaneous collapsing and reassembling of the way the house was "pictured." The *Bioscleave House* is designed to invite perceptual/experiential collapse and reassembly, and a strange resonance appeared between the glitchy panorama and the experience of the house. The "collapse" of the logic of the photorealistic image, as well as the operational logic of the panorama software, call out to the way in which the house destabilises habits of perception and common assumptions about our potential relationship with architecture. Rather than archiving an experience of the house, the images entered into an "anarchiving." At the same time, these panoramic images had leapt quite explicitly from mediating, or representing the house, and into an immediation with it. House, panorama software, my directional movements of the phone camera and the resulting images became an ecology of mutual affects as they inflected with one another, creating an event through their immediating, resonating coinciding.

This residency led to more play with the panorama function of the iPhone to explore ideas of experiential discontinuity within continuity, bleeding into Avery Green. I made a series of glitchy panoramic images of the yellow trace drawings—these were done in the backyard to catch the light, and where wind and flies intercepted, often adding to the buginess of the images. Here, I had in mind a different issue to the perceptual/experiential collapse and reassembly inherent to the *Bioscleave House*. The Victoria era—alive in the background of Avery's architectural style—was when the greenhouse typology evolved. It has been argued that this was when the very idea of "the environment" emerged (Taylor 2004). Through the design of her extension, I ushered Avery into recalling the Victorian desire to bring nature indoors, into controlled environments. In stretching the bathroom out into something strangely long and skinny (one meter by seven meters), I imagined cracks appearing in that corridor-cum-bathroom, like glitches in a panorama image gone wrong, letting the outside seep in to create

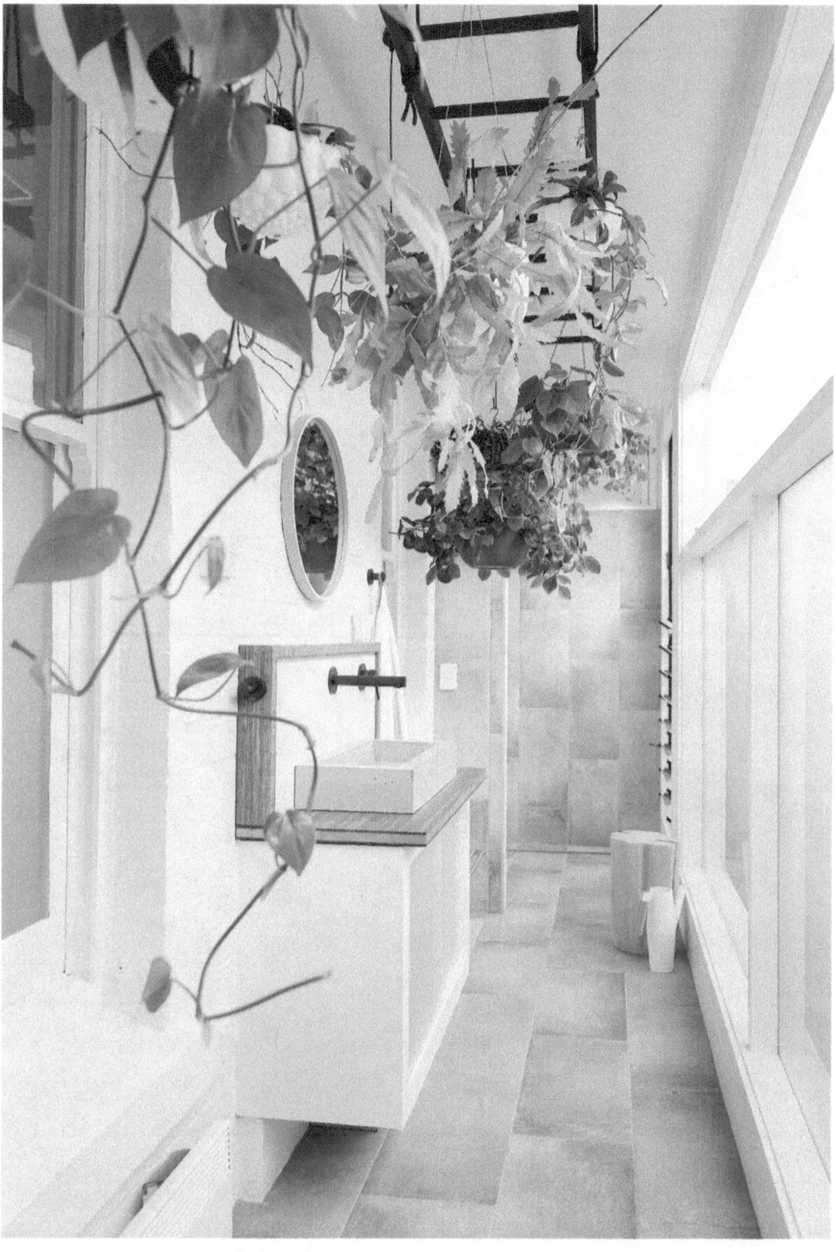

Figure 23. The greenhouse-bathroom-corridor of Avery Green. Photograph by Lucas Allen, 2016.

a greenhouse-bathroom-corridor. This was about a different type of reassembly than the *Bioscleave House*—a hybridization of tropes

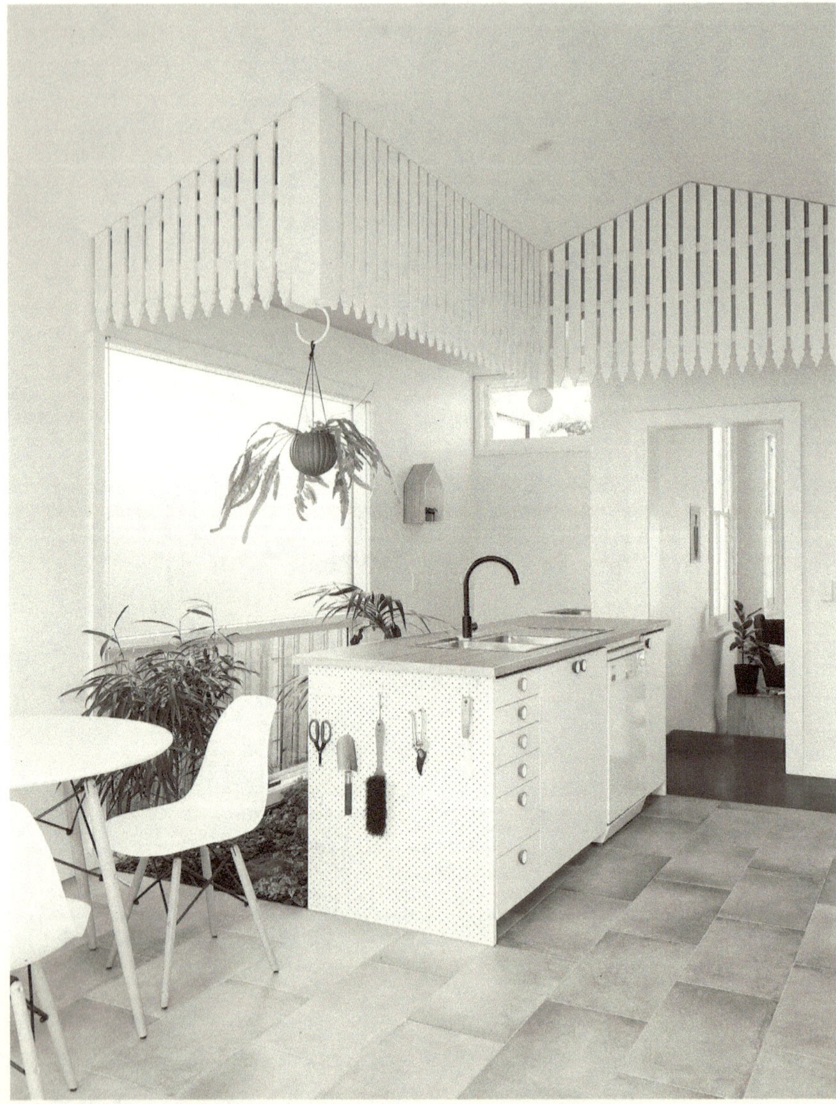

Figure 24. Avery Green's kitchen, with floor garden and upside-down picket fence. Photograph by Lucas Allen, 2016.

or types, rather than one referring back to human perception. This cracking-open bled into the kitchen, where a garden was introduced into the floor, above which an upside-down picket fence is now hung. The ceiling became a landscape and garden. The extension as a whole became a twisted terrain wrapped around brick shoulders. This twisted

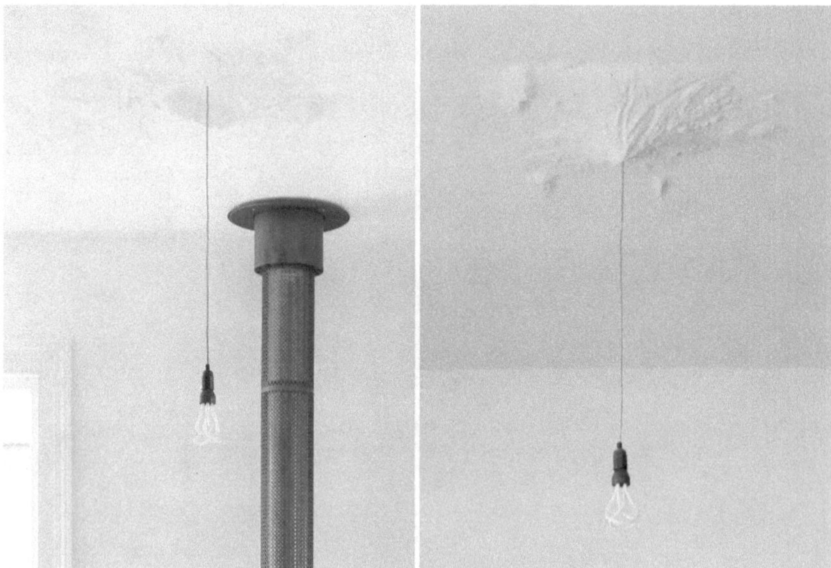

Figure 25. Avery Green's ceiling roses transmutated into upside-down volcanic mountains. From photographs by Lucas Allen, 2016.

wrap was stitched back into the main living space where Victorian ceiling roses transmuted into upside-down volcanic mountains.

In 2014, I exhibited *Architectural Animality: drawings out for a walk* (Ednie-Brown, 2014)—a collection of drawings exploring the design process. A role of the group exhibition, called *Trace: Architectural musings*, was to explore the nature of the act of architectural drawing. Coming to this with an interest in how the non-representational or immediate operates with and through the representational task of architectural drawings, I spent a good part of a week in the space assembling the work—having arrived with a series of large prints of the glitch panoramas and a range of other objects, but no clear sense of how they would come together.

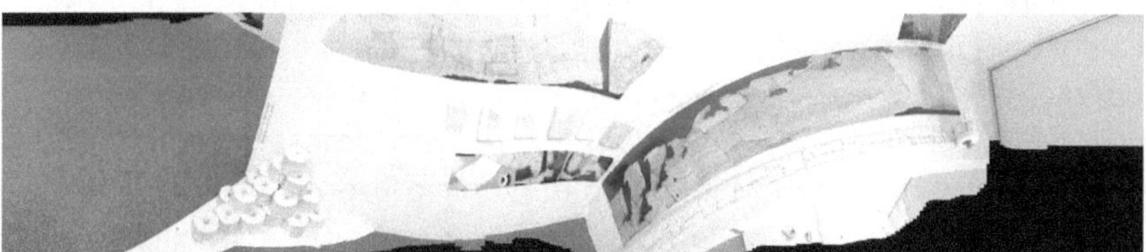

Figure 26. Panorama photograph of 'Architectural Animality: drawings out for a walk'. exhibited as part of: Trace: Architectural musings, Leonie Matthews & Amanda Alderson (curators), Mundaring Arts Centre, Western Australia, October 3rd-November 9th, 2014. Photograph by Pia Ednie-Brown, 2014.

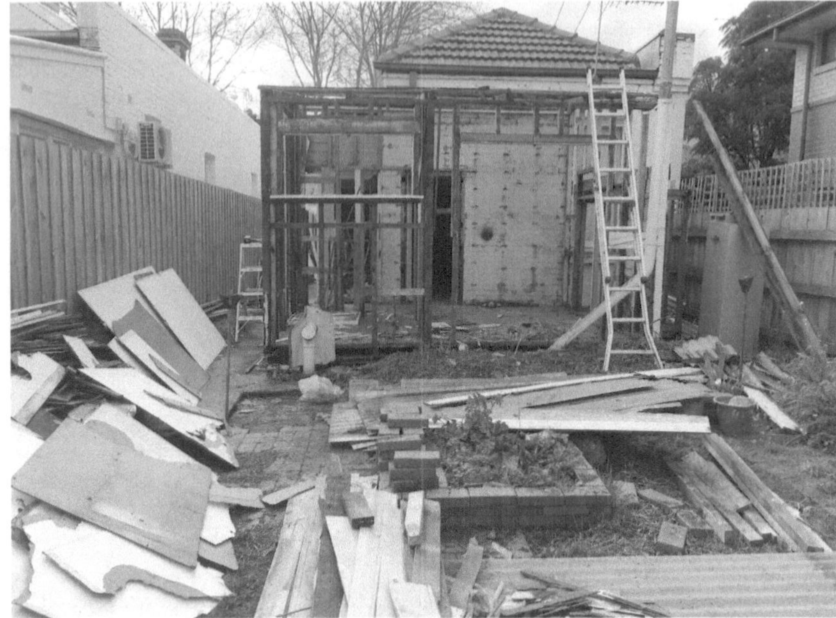

Figure 27. Avery Green during Demolition phase. Photograph by Pia Ednie-Brown, 2015.

The hope was that this process of assembling would enable more than a display of drawings *about* an architectural project. Rather, I was interested in how the act of exhibiting might feed back into the design process—becoming part of the individuating process and enabling the exhibition itself to more emphatically immediate as well as mediate—like taking Avery for a loopy walk outside the space of her design (into a solitude of sorts), to return with something that would feed into her.

The exhibited drawing-assemblage visually agglomerated a variety of stories: the panoramas, the greenhouse stretch; architectural drawings on toilet paper; the influence of a giraffe. Later, in the midst of construction, I discovered that the carpenters often referred to the cavity built into the floor to accommodate the planter as the "crocodile pond." There were animals abound, and an animality seemed to keep rearing its playful head. This little fabulated zoo almost impishly stretched out her individuation and personing through an ecology of materiality (brick–stone–timber), vegetality (plants), animality and humanity.

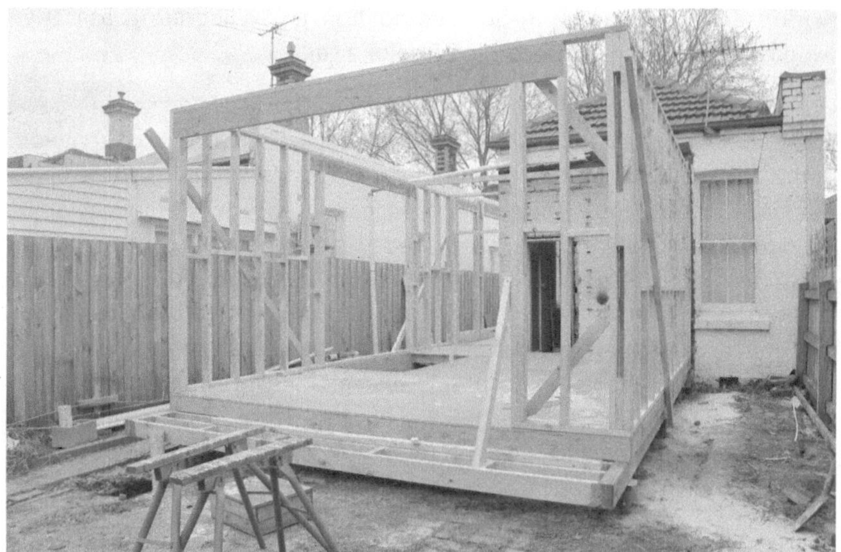

Figure 28. Avery Green during construction. Photograph by Pia Ednie-Brown, 2015.

In 2015, in preparation for council approval and detailed drawings, I took the drawings for Avery into Rhino software—another beast. Instead of the diaphanous yellow tracing paper, I accrued cascading digital files of translucent, zoomable images, capable of measurements to more decimal points than is perceptible, let alone constructible. Her development in this idealized, glassy, swimmable space of drawing immediately preceded the almost shocking opacity of her sheer physicality.

Pulling off the back of the house—opening walls, heaving cabinets out of their places (the nails that held them in place hanging off them like the roots of weeds), levering cladding off in heavy, dusty, flaking chunks—her spatial condition became as elastic as putty, something like the disorienting zoomability in Rhino, but only after infinitely more heaving effort and brute force. She transformed daily—vistas opened up and pockets of space that were previously secrets to one another became suddenly, sometimes violently connected. The south facing window of the old brick house had been tussled into a dank corner—the kitchen wall had run over and hidden the end of its stone ledge, and then a rude asbestos alcove stuck out—blocking what a window can do well: provide a view. As the barriers between that window and the world started to open up through demolition, it was liberating, as if the window was waking up, becoming free of a cage.

Until this point I felt as if I had been playing with my design stories alongside Avery, but as I pulled her apart, her weight and force arrived at the party, physically leaping into play. Around this time I also read Jane Jacobs' book, *The Nature of Economies,* which operates as a dialogue between five characters. Theory is brought to life through characters in domestic scenes and environments, where the events and scenographic shifts in which the dialogue occurs start to both illustrate and enact issues under discussion. Jacobs tells us that her approach is about bringing "rarefied economic abstractions into contact with earthly realities" (Jacobs 2000: ix). She does this through an enactment of the very multi-levelled tangle of mediation and immediation, abstract, individual, interindividual: the all-at-once of individuation. The broad thesis of the book is that economies are not metaphorically like eco-systems but are operationally equivalent, as understood via complexity science as dynamic systems: economies individuate. The idea of "economy" is often traced back to "oikonomos," derived from oikos, "house," and nemein, "to manage." Economies and ecologies are complex, dynamic systems—like a house.

This ecological complexity becomes all the more screamingly evident when you open up a house to transformation. In the midst of Avery's intensive, individuating transformation, everything felt delicate and vulnerable—wherein the apparently stable, static entity of 'a house' was opened up as a vibratory, contingent and mobile assemblage.

The complexity of the process of construction and the interdependencies pressing upon single decisions was often almost overwhelming, as I became part of an intensive process. Architectural projects are a choppy, polyphonic sea of interdependent factors: council and building regulations, soil problems, time constraints, the specific expertise of tradespeople, the dynamics between trades, amongst so many other forces. Materials arrived, heavy and demanding. They were cut, deployed, and the excess discarded. Rubbish heaped in ungainly piles, weather intervened, mountains of dust flew and settled in blankets, timber warped against the grain of architectural assumptions of linearity. The budget heaved, recalibrated, swelled. Detail after detail after co-determining detail demanded attention ... it was indeed a complex ecology that immediately challenged many presumptions of authorship, amplified by directing a priority of attention toward the needs of Avery's personing.

The Personality of Things

During Avery Green's intensive transformation, The Jane Approach lingered and matured, quietly prodding Avery's development. The construction work may be complete, but these sisters still have a long way to go before their work together is done. Their collective processes are easier to perceive when they are explicitly in the process of development or construction, but as they settle, what do they become? How does their processuality remain alive in immediacy? A tentative answer to that question is that their individuation or emergence is inflected (and anarchived?) *into* the qualitative, processual dimensions of their being: such as personality and style.

"The house the vortex built" had been the name of a paper I thought might emerge well before building work on Avery Green commenced. The maelstrom of making did not feel as "neat" as a vortex might imply, but the force of a form beyond but inclusive of me-Avery-and-everything-else seems an accurately vague way of describing it. Perhaps this force was a force of personality, drawing on Peirce's notion that:

> personality is some kind of coordination or connection of ideas.... This personality, like any general idea, is not a thing to be apprehended in an instant. It has to be lived in time; nor can any finite time embrace it in all its fulness. Yet in each infinitesimal interval it is present and living, though specially colored by the immediate feelings of that moment. (Peirce 1992a: 331)

If personality is "some kind of coordination or connection of ideas" then style[2] is the *way* in which these many lived complexities are coordinated and connected. Personality becomes Simondon's being: "Being itself now appears as that which becomes *by linking together*" (Combes, 2013: 17). This "way" of linking together goes to the heart of how a personality individuates—how things incompletely "hold together" into those metastable assemblages of internal disparity that come to stand as individuals/structures.

Cities become a useful example: getting off a plane into a new city we are often struck by a very particular feeling—a specific quality

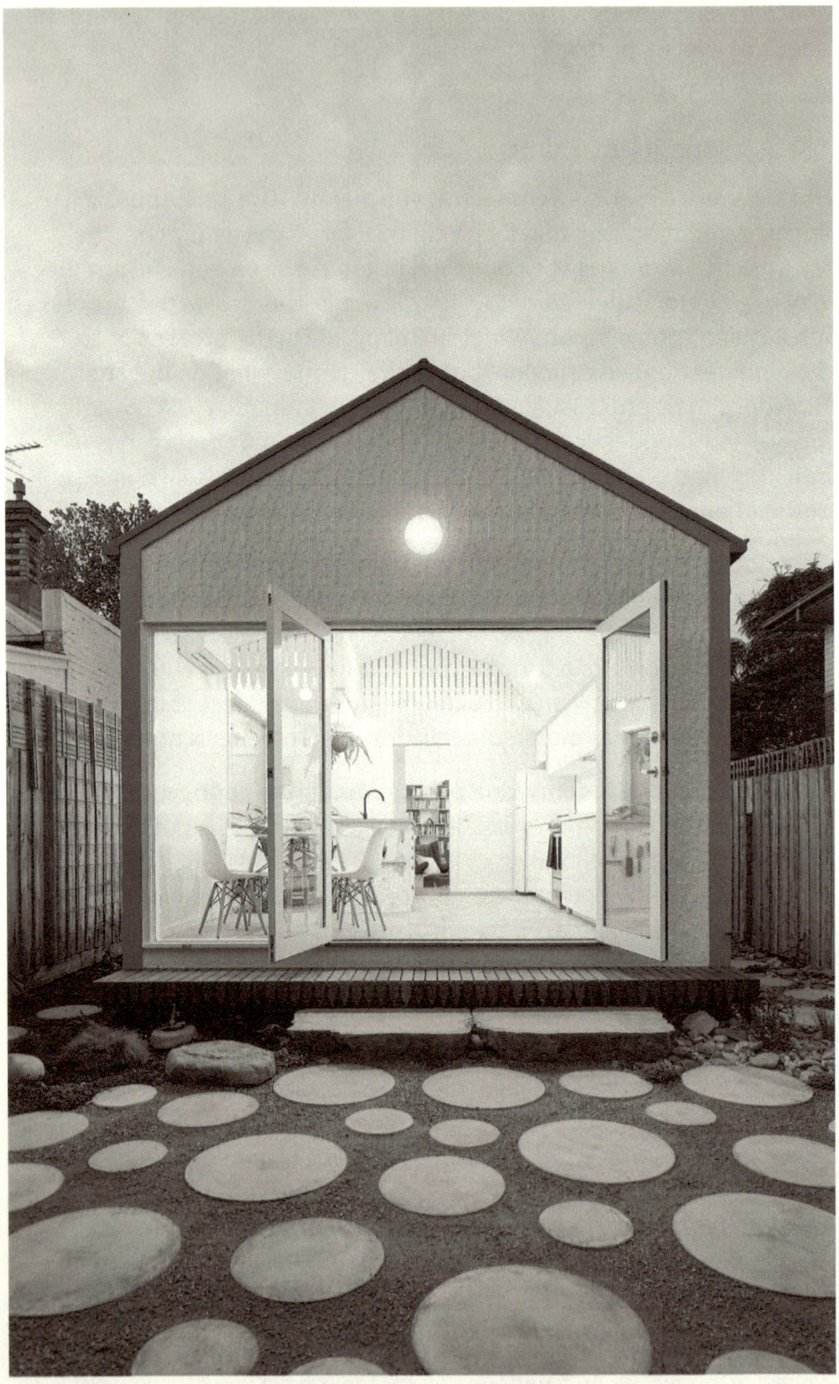

Figure 29. Avery Green's twilight. Photograph by Lucas Allen, 2016.

"in-the-air" that permeates with a quiet but palpable force. Could this be understood as a personality that can't be fully apprehended in an instant, but is nevertheless "present and living"? Similarly, arrive at and enter a house and what is colloquially referred to as the "atmosphere," the "energy" or feeling of the space, etc., point to this accretion and effervesce of behavioural tendency: style and personality. We will often recognize the style of a person's walking before we recognize the person: style precedes but develops through personality—one is the other's "way." Together, they exceed the individual while emanating through it, becoming the constitutive, qualitative "flavour" of individuation, in which acts of mediation and immediation bleed into one another across the tangle of levels.

Importantly here, and to return to a suggestion made at the outset of this exploration-through-writing, immediation might be about a style of worlding. All manner of personalities will find different ways of worlding toward eventful potential. Naming, personing and seeking out collective solitude are techniques that won't work for everyone or every event; playing person is not everyone's world play. Along with the muliplicity of events, there is an infinite play of techniques that can support an attending to immediation, helping to hold potential open in its playful place.

Notes

1. I want to thank and acknowledge architect and PhD candidate Anna Tweeddale, who introduced me to a few of Jane Jacobs' works I hadn't known about. It was through our conversations that the idea of The Jane Approach emerged.
2. Style is understood here as a textured patterning that arises through an accretion of behavioural tendency—a kind of variational consistency that is compositionally abstract.

Third Movement

Ecologies of Practices

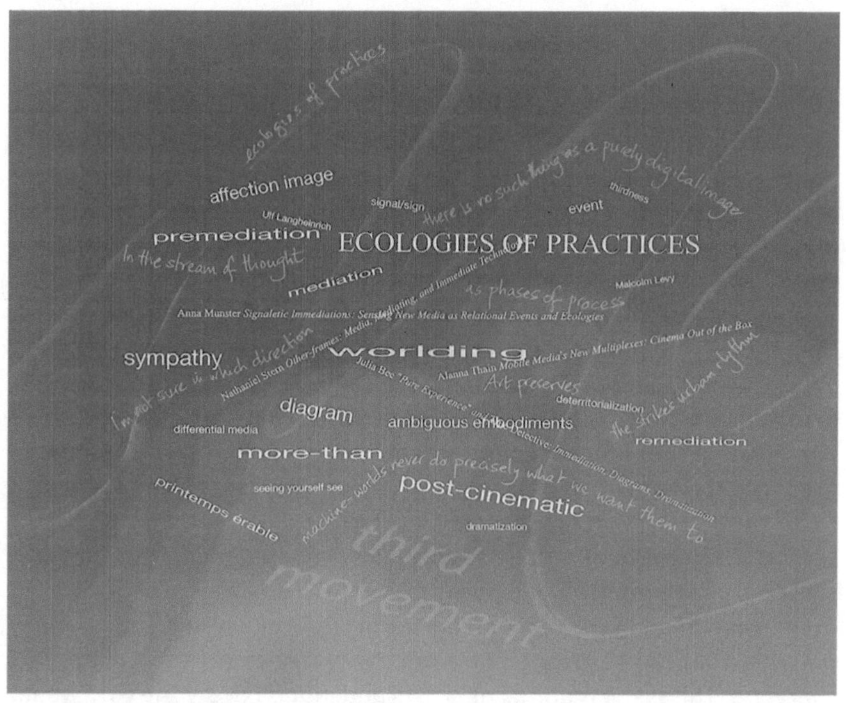

Bodil Marie Stavning Thomsen

Prelude

To be moved by, to linger on and to stay connected to the ecologies of immediation's practices is different from what Jay David Bolter and Richard Grusin (1999) refer to as practices of "immediacy" in mediated representation. The question of "how" this difference is experienced is attended to in this chapter. In Bolter and Grusin's *Remediation*, a media-framing intended for immediacy aims for transparency and the impression of direct or "authentic" experience of reality. Often this strategy involves that media-framings are obscured or "naturalized." Even though an awareness of immediation's practices might be experienced by way of, for example, condensed affective responses in real time immediacy, it is important to stress that a practice of immediation rather designates a creative awareness toward potential events contained within a changing whole of experience. Immediation thus refers to the virtual potentialities of events. Perceptions and sensations from the position of subjectivity are embedded and thus secondary to the unfolding of events. This said, an awareness or prehension of an event's immediate unfolding contains a creative potential that can be grasped on a pre-individual, affective level by everyone. This is the material of artists and indeed everyone who would care to activate immediation's ecologies of practices. Being aware of our surroundings, as an all-encompassing environment or habitat inseparable from the sensation of our own body-thought-feeling could be a giddy or life-changing experience. But even on an everyday level of experience, a practice of immediation actually guides our every move in our connections to past or future events even if they go unnoticed on a cognitive level of experience. Without thinking, our feet recognize in a singular event the touch of a well-known ground and by our every move, we're widening and renewing the scope of our move and thought. The experience of being in the world is an experience of time and space on an immediate level of experience. Our bodies yield to an illness or to a sudden gust of wind before we know of it. Nevertheless, we're able to access this experience as a thinking-feeling experience of what happens. A glimpse of coming events or an ability to suddenly approach a long since passed expression in the eyes of another belong to the ecologies of practices that everyone could exert. Immediation opens the potentiality for change in the moment of catching a glimpse.

Being on the immediate side of what happens means to let go of "any excess over the real" (Combes 2013: 11) and to question an outspoken connection of thought, identity and being that nourishes the idea that a critical position is the answer to all challenges. Such an approach to the world is limited and limiting in the perspective of immediation. Things often happen unnoticed by a critical position that equals thought and identity. What goes unnoticed and is often only accounted for afterwards is the force by which something happens and is expressed. Even within theories of expressive, real time media forms offered by Television, Video, the Internet, Games and Augmented Reality the relational and affective aspect of communication as expression is not really taken into consideration. One reason for this could be that "mediation" stays the focus of the research questions posed—and thus the shaping mattering of media often becomes the object of study. Questions of "information," "communication," "transmissions," or "channelings" doesn't vary much from this, although this point of interest often tries to consider a broader media ecology connected to studies of culture and society.

The scope of the term "immediation" includes the non-human in the human and reaches philosophically beyond the studies of "immediacy" connected to representation or framing in media studies (cf. "re-mediation," Bolter & Grusin 1999; "pre-mediation," Bolter 2010). Meanwhile, an awareness of immediation puts demands on these studies, since ecologies of immediation's practices also implies media. In this third movement of the book, Nathanial Stern shows how Malcolm Levi's works bring immediation forth by showing media as matter, waste and un-controllable amounts of failures in data. By focusing of how media always takes part in geophysics and thus can never be exhaustable to its representations, Stern underlines how media-ecologies play a significant part of a contemporary relational ecology.

In a different mode, Anna Munster explores the "durational dimensionality" of Ulf Langheinrich's film, *LAND* (2008), as a shared affective and rhythmic terrain of technological and human ecology. The work is "barely [an] image" in a traditional sense, since it is more loaded with "texture and kinesthetics" [than] "opticality." (Immediation I, 229) The experience of this work underlines the signaletic space as an open-ended experiential field of expressive energies that both intensify visual elements and devisualise them. Or rather, *LAND* creates encounters or (in)formations of visual perception-expression: you don't exactly see but drown in an "immedia event". Consequently Munster reads this work as an invitation to dephase the 3D illusion of depth and thus reach experiences of immediation beyond the seen.

In the following article Alanna Thain digs into and questions a post-cinematic approach by her own practice with "a guerilla, bicycle powered outdoor cinema throughout the city of Montreal," named *Cinema Out of the Box*. By moving the cinematic experience to new shifting contexts, environments' and publics' experiences of a city-body relationship can change. The not-yet of immediation becomes vital: "Immediation names the sensational stretch of potential that doesn't yet know its own limits, touching and transforming what falls within its purview. The immediacy of immediation signals the urgent liveliness of the art event, immediacy as a "still happening" in the midst...." (Thain, Immediation I, 243). Her approach to cinema thus reaches beyond its mediated framings, and toward its (with Guattari) "disjunctive" forces, when attention is distributed both "inside" and "outside" the frame—and toward the edges of perception as connected to the event of seeing.

In Julia Bee's article on the credit sequence of the TV-series *True Detective* she considers the variation of the dissolving frames to be a kind of "dramatization of experience." Even though this intro is highly mediated to create an experience of immediacy, Bee reads its micro-shifts as a process of emerging and fading of images—abstract and concrete at the same time—that dramatizes "an emerging ecology of experience itself" in relation to William James' notion of "pure experience." So this process of becoming-image becomes "an immanent image-perception in the sequence itself," and in this way the moving, transitional event of experience becomes a dramatized or performed practice of immediation that as an experiential ontogenesis enables an affective opening to the series.

Nathaniel Stern

Other-Frames: Media, Mediating, and Immediate Ecologies

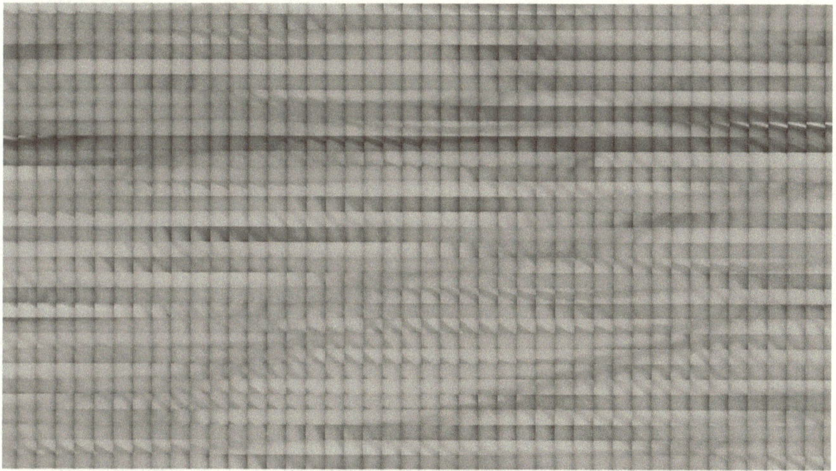

Figure 30. Malcolm Levy, Video Stills in Lightbox, 2015, montage 55cmx44cm, Judisches Krankenhaus Berlin, image courtesy of the artist.

There is No Such Thing as a Digital Image

Or at the least, there is no such thing as a *purely* digital image. Our machines are built and programmed so as to box in and grid out pictures as thousands of tiny and perfectly legible squares. But at the level of the pixel, there are always mis-takes, mis-steps, and mis-representations that occur when translating from coded image forms to the printed page or screen. With print, the ink might clot or dry slightly differently in a given region. A minor imperfection on the paper may cause a divot and thus a variation in its pulp-and-pigment versioning. There could be a surge in amperage that causes the printer head to overshoot. Or, more visible and known to us in the everyday, a colour of ink could run out, or an ink valve could need cleaning. On screen, there are variations of light reflecting and refracting in and around what we see. Not all liquid crystal (the "LC" in LCD screen) responds to electrical current exactly the same; and dead pixels remind us just how fragile our computers, data, and images are. All of these real-world elements—referred to as "analog" since the advent of the digital—create imperfections in our images: a glitch, a bad print, an inconvenience of ink or cleaning, having to go into shade, or needing a new printer or screen. But they also reveal that our expensive and ideal machine-worlds *never* do precisely what we want them to.

In fact, there is no such thing as "digital." If nothing else, Malcolm Levy's *Other-frames*, an ongoing series of art prints and videos, perform how digitality is a construct, and a precarious one at that. At the level of the microprocessor and smaller, there are no zeros and no ones sent in perfectly timed sequence as data. Each "bit" of digital data, every "one" and every "zero" traveling from point A to point B across copper and silicon circuitry, is in actuality *somewhere* around five volts, and *somewhere* around, well, *not* five volts. These imperfect groups of electrons are cleaned up for noise, then thresholded at around 2.5 volts for an approximate value. We are consistently told that digital images never degrade. This is mostly correct ... except for when we actually *do* anything with them. Each time data is copied or moved, transformed and re-saved, or transferred from one place to another, there is a risk of some kind of failure. Why do files and hard drives fail? Because they are *messy*. It is so easy to forget that most drives in existence are little better than our tape decks from the 1980s: rust filings shifted around by magnets in order to store information. It is certainly accurate to assert that it's more efficient to store only two forms of datum (mostly on and mostly off), and create complexity from large quantities of those ones and zeros, in relation to another. For this reason visible degradation is more rare in the digital age. But once an error presents itself, one does not simply perceive a bit of noise in their content, per degraded video- and audiotapes of years gone by. A seemingly minor misreading/miswriting of a bit or byte—caused by anything from cosmic rays or electromagnetic waves to background radiation or simple aging—can remake an entire file so as to be illegible, and this new, "bad" version is the one copied over, identically, forevermore. We've all had this experience several times, usually with an all-too important Microsoft Word document that has been "corrupted" by nothing more than its own materiality. Levy's work re-members—that is, embodies again—the *materiality* of our digital machines. Computers and processors, he shows us, are just as chaotic and noisy and *substantial* as their analogical predecessors.

As I write the first draft of this text, I am looking at a still from one of Levy's videos on his web site, with the simple denotation *Sao Paulo Graffiti (series 2) 3*. It is a semblance of a landscape, with a sky the colour of reeds, and an occasional purple tinge that seems to ripple from left to right, sea to shore. There's a trail of amplified colour near the center and moving upward, where the sun may have risen or set. The road, like the sky, zooms by horizontally at high speed nearer the bottom of the page, but it somehow still feels like it's in slow motion. This passage careens across almost half the image—though I'm not sure in which direction—and leaves vestigial traces of grays, deeper purples, turquoise, a diminutive smudge of green. On the other side of the road, the bottom of the print (is this closest to us?), the reed-like streaks appear again, as if they want and need to trickle into a stretch of purple, just beyond the frame.

It is strikingly beautiful.

As Levy's elusively descriptive title suggests, this image—which gallery viewers experience both as a light box print, and as part of a video—was shot in Brazil, using a camera pointed at graffiti encountered by the artist while traveling in the Villa Magdalena area of Sao Paulo. But it is not an image *of* Sao Paulo, at least not in the traditional, photographic sense (a "photo of graffiti"). As with all his works, Levy's capture is achieved by focusing his lens on a specific surface, then rapidly jerking his camera around for between one and ten seconds. It's simple enough, but what happens at the level of the chip, which the artist reminds us is more accurately described as an image-sensor, is somewhat magical.

There are two types of mainstream image-sensor: a CCD (charge-coupled device) or CMOS (complimentary metal oxide semiconductor), each of which converts light into electrical signals in different ways. In both cases, light is focused through a lens onto an array of either capacitors or photodetectors, each corresponding to a pixel in the final image. For a still or video camera, this is a two-dimensional array, whereas in a scanner it would be one-dimensional. A CCD is actually an analog sensor, where the capacitors in its array convert light coming into each location into a proportional amount of electrical *charge*, then store that charge for a short amount of time. There is also a charge amplifier in the device, which later converts each individual charge into a proportional amount of *voltage* (Janesick 2001). This occurs pixel/charge by pixel/charge, via shift registers that move the charges one at a time through the other capacitors towards the amplifier, like a queue. What this means is that in a full HD (high definition) camera of 1280 x 720, every charge is read in by its individual capacitor, and while the first in line (the capacitor closest to the amplifier) is immediately converted to voltage, the last has to move through every single capacitor, over 900,000 movements/changes, before that conversion. For digital use, each voltage is only then sampled through an analog to digital converter (ADC) somewhere off the sensor and elsewhere in the camera.[1] Each pixel's assigned number value will be its colour information, usually 32 bits (ons and offs) per tiny square.[2]

Beyond this, there are compression techniques to save storage space; for example, a JPEG image (Joint Photographic Experts Group) will store only the difference between two adjacent pixels, rather than storing three bytes of data for every single pixel.[3] Compressed video files will often additionally apply compression that looks at the same exact pixel in space, then calculates and saves only its difference *over time*, meaning, across multiple frames of the video.[4]

The CMOS works with the same principles. But as opposed to the CCD, it is a digital device that uses an active-pixel sensor (APS), combining photodetectors and amplifiers together. Here an integrated circuit houses an array of APSs, each *individually* converting light energy directly into voltage, then data. The multiple converters may sound like a better option in terms of speed, but they cannot all "snap" at the same precise moment, and there is potential for more variety in their conversions, since each is essentially a different "machine."

Levy's movements with his cameras, in short, overload both kinds of sensor. Neither array and subsequent conversions and movements can keep up with him. He challenges the chip's sensibility, its ability to sense and make sense. "CCD sensors are more susceptible to vertical smear from bright light sources," causing blooming effects "when the sensor is overloaded," whereas "CMOS sensors are susceptible to undesired effects that come as a result of rolling shutter," the latter because a CMOS sensor captures images one a row at a time, rather than grabbing an entire frame as a singular moment with all its active pixel sensors at once (Pradeep 2011). Though the CMOS is more commonly used today across the field from DSLRs to mobile phone cameras, this is because it is generally easier to manufacture rather than it being superior (or inferior) to a CCD. Its rolling effects can include image wobbling, skews, smears, and partial exposures. Levy says that in the case of both CCD and CMOS, one sees "multiple examples where the concept of the sensor, as a controlled process, is problematic from the beginning" (Levy 2015). The captured "information"—which as laid out above is actually the movement of light, charge, voltage, numbers, etc., coupled with photodetectors, capacitors, circuits, filters, prisms, etc.—is literally transformed anew at every capture, every shift, every conversion, every compression, and more.

Levy himself can wax lyrical about the inner-workings of ADCs and semi-conductors, serial pixel transfer and circuitry, all invoking the physical presence of metal and electrons, silicon and plastic, as a veritable minefield of potential problems for that never-perfect photo capture we aspire to for our holiday vacation album. His is not the description of the flawless digital machine, the impressive megapixel count, letter-number combination motherboard (G5! i7!) that somehow abstracts and makes infallible the conversion of our memories into Facebook pages, ready for consumption, again.

On the contrary, Levy reminds us that such jargon is just a strategy to have us *buy more stuff*. Most digital camera sensors capture a spectrum of colour and light smaller than traditional film, which is then artificially enhanced to please our eye. The detail of film is greater than most large megapixel counts can offer—so we get pixilation instead of grain— and, an equivalent to film cameras, most current digital camera limitations are from the quality of the poor analog lenses mounted in *front* of our image sensors, rather than the pixel counts inherent to them. Furthermore, the outcomes of minor errors and corruption actually have a greater potential to entirely destroy an image once in digital form, rather than "ruining" only part of where film may have been overexposed, for example. Here I'm not praising the analog over the digital, but rather arguing, along with Levy, that no manner of tricks with code, hardware, or language can get us away from the fact of *matter, and its immediacy*. Despite what we and our commercial industries desire, our media devices do *not* produce pure mathematical abstractions of our experiences; they are not perfect memory conversion machines that mediate and store *only* that which we desire to see and remember, in front of the lens. Our media, like us, are immediate. Like all matter, they are always ongoing, always changing, always in relation: events.

Levy is avowedly inspired by structuralist filmmakers from the 1970s. These artists more or less turned the film camera on itself. In response to Hollywood's over-commercialization, they made films that study the apparatus of the camera. "Each film is a record (not a representation, not a reproduction) of its own making. Production of relations (shot to shot, shot to image, grain to image, image dissolution to grain, etc.) is a basic function which is in direct opposition to reproduction of relations" (Gidal 1978: 4). Here avant-garde practices produced abstract films that purposefully framed and amplified the properties of film and camera: grain and scratches, pans and zooms, saturation and exposure, weight and counterweight, and more, were accented as always present, presenting, and eventful. Levy follows their work by mapping and imaging the analogies and idiosyncratic inner-workings, the sensations and perceptions, of digital and computational media apparatuses.

Some of Levy's stills look like dramatically shot architectures, others as if abstract expressionist painter Mark Rothko had made a photographic contact sheet. I see Caribbean roller coaster motion blurs, and unicorn hairs under a microscope. Video game skylines after bedtime, and drunken firefly time lapses. Green lagoon waterfalls, and dark and dirty rainbows streaked by coarse, dry paintbrushes. But Levy's works are none of these things; his process is not to take images *of* something, or *from* somewhere. They beg the question, What is mediated, and how?

Media theorist and cultural scholar Richard Grusin wants there to be a rethinking of media, and more importantly, mediation. In his 2015 paper for *Critical Inquiry*, "Radical Mediation," Grusin argues that "mediation operates not just across communication, representation, or the arts, but is a fundamental process of human and nonhuman existence" (Grusin 2015: 125). Here mediation does not stand "between already actualized subjects, objects, actants, or entities" but is rather "the process, action, or event that generates or provides the conditions for the emergence of subjects and objects, for the individuation of entities within the world" (137-138). Mediation is, for Grusin, all of relation: experience, ontology and re-presentation, generation and transformation, and how they all work together in the continuous making of what *is*. Grusin's ideas around media and mediation are most interesting if followed along his trajectory of publications from 2000 to the present day.

In Grusin's most well-known book, *Remediation: Understanding New Media*, written with J. David Bolter, the authors claim that new media not only mediate information, but mediate (implicitly *old*) media as well. For example, and simply, the Internet changed newspapers, and since remediation can go both ways between new and old, each continues to change the other, both in content and form. And all mediation is always *re*mediation, is always changing and translating experiences as well as connecting them. Remediation is composed of both immediacy and hypermediacy, and Bolter and Grusin initially wrote of these in relation to mass media and the Internet. Immediacy was imagined as Virtual Reality and other media platforms that were more directly experienced themselves, rather than mediating other things; hypermediacy was the propagation of communication across various platforms, "the multiplication of mediation among sociotechnical, commercial, and political networks" (Grusin 2010: 2). After the events of 9/11, a now-writing-solo Grusin saw a shift in how and what was remediated. Remediation became constant and unfiltered connections (immediacy via Twitter and Facebook, for example), which are saved, sold and securitized as information for commercial or governmental use (hypermediacy).

This shift lead Grusin to the core concepts in his 2010 book, *Premediation: Affect and Mediality After 9/11*, where the notion of premediation is that media and mediation create affects and moods in the present, that make possible new futures. In the context of mass media, potential meaning is often attributed before something takes place. When a Republican pundit or Fox News anchor says, "If Obama attempts to provide any form of amnesty for immigrants through executive order, it will be illegal; there must be approval from Congress," he or she sets up a question of legality, and the possibility for a lawsuit, without knowing any of the details of the yet-to-be issued executive order, and whether or not it will indeed be legal. The event is mediated before it occurs, packaged and delivered to those who will respond accordingly; this premediation creates a collective readiness to act on an event before it even takes place, making a cascade of new (potential and actual) events unfold.

Now, Grusin's research easily moves from mass and digital media to the everyday. Premediation, he argues, exists as part of every encounter. We continuously generate a "multiplicity of potential but never fully formed futures which will have real impacts on life or action in the present whether those futures actualize themselves or not" (2015:

142). In other words, we are always already planning, acting with, and re-acting to, the virtual—a not-yet future, full of potential and possibilities—and those plans, actions and reactions have an impact on the present, and thus the future that will eventually actualize, regardless of if that future is any of those we had imagined in the first place. Here Grusin begins to rethink mediation (and its inherent premediation) as relationality, as "all connections" which involve "modulation, translation, or transformation." It is "not derivative of but co-present with creation" (138, 142). And thinking in this way requires revisiting the *im*mediate as something quite different from how he and Bolter initially defined it. What about direct and embodied experience that is not (yet) coded by humans, not seen and understood with any form of (human) semiosis? Is that "mediated"?

Grusin posits out two new approaches to immediacy and its relation to mediation. First, he recognizes that there is always *also* an *immediate* (affective) experience of things that are mediated, or mediating, or indeed of mediation itself. We of course directly experience media—whether devices, news, language, or other forms—a before we understand and internalize them. And so the "radical" in "radical mediation is its immanence, is immediacy itself—not the transparent immediacy that makes up half of remediation's double logic, but the embodied immediacy of the event of mediation" (2015: 132). It is affective, an unqualified and fully embodied response to experience, which of course impacts how we will later qualify that experience. If our palms are sweaty, our heart is racing, and there are butterflies in our stomachs, we may not yet know if we are angry, scared, or aroused (perhaps more than one at once), but our bodily response will certainly play a role in how we eventually move-think-feel-act.

While hypermediacy's proliferation of media may seem to be at odds with this version of immediacy, Grusin more or less argues that we experience media such as blogs, Tumblr and Instagram immediately as well. The idea here is to move away from mediation as a secondary category of representation that acts only after subjects and objects, humans and nonhumans, have been categorically defined, and to rather understand mediation as contact and relation, immediacy and understanding, always moving together.

The main parallel Grusin draws for radical mediation is with William James' radical empiricism. He directly quotes James' "A World of Pure Experience" and simply replaces a few words. Here is James' original quote: "To be radical, an empiricism must neither admit into its constructions any element that is not directly experienced, nor exclude from them any element that is directly experienced. For such a philosophy, *the relations that connect experiences must themselves be experienced relations, and any kind of relation experienced must be accounted as 'real' as anything else in the system*" (James 1912: 22). And here is Grusin's modified text, where he replaces "relation" with "mediation," and "real" with "immediate": "the mediations that connect experiences must themselves be experienced mediations, and any kind of mediation experienced must be accounted as 'immediate' as anything else in the system. Where James is concerned with the empirical reality of relations, [Grusin's] concerns start with the immediacy of mediation" (2015: 127-128). Mediation is not neutral, not reproducing meaning, but "actively transforming human and nonhuman actants, as well as their conceptual and affective states" (130). It is therefore ontogenetic, an incipient process that is not reducible to technology or communication, matter or media, alone. Nor is it, for that matter, reducible to an exclusively human endeavor. Mediation is, in other words, always already mediated, and *also* always immediate.

This brings me to Grusin's second relation between immediacy and mediation: "for radical mediation, all bodies (whether human or nonhuman) are fundamentally media and life itself is a form of mediation" (2015: 132). In other words, mediation is not, and never has been, a discretely human practice. Grusin uses as illustration here Charles S. Peirce's example of a sunflower and its representamen (a concept which Peirce places in his category of "thirdness," which he later refers to directly as mediation). The flower turns towards the sun, an act which *makes* it a *sun*flower, and both makes and calls the sun, the sun (Peirce 2009: 274). Here, the sunflower is exhibiting a "point of view," a kind of perception and semiosis that understands and responds to its environment, as it "sees" fit. And if *we* see the world in this way, then all "activity is mediation ... there is no discontinuity between human and nonhuman agency or semiosis" (Gruson 2015: 140). We—and this "we" is a large and relational cross-section of technology and information, kids and adults, rabbits and trees, keys and locks and more—are always already media, mediating, *mediation*, always already immediate, immediating, *immediation*.

As a media theorist, Grusin of course puts mediation and media at the center of his work—just as "being" would be at the center of a philosopher of ontology's writing, experience at the center of phenomenology, perhaps process and relation at the center of mine. And each could be complexified anew in the way Grusin does for a contemporary context: inaugurating becoming, relation, the nonhuman, and affect can develop ever more intricate systems, in much the same way Grusin shows media and mediation to (also) be non-object-based and immediate. But, in the case of ontology for example, Jean-Luc Nancy argues that putting being before becoming (or being-with) will always put stasis before movement and relation (2000: 4). Phenomenology rarely moves outside of human experience and subject-object hierarchies. And beginning with mediation at the center (within a media-framing), with immediacy, hypermediacy and other such concepts unfolding out from there, perhaps portrays these terms and concepts as too operational, and knowable; they are in danger of becoming almost graspable "objects."

What if we *began* with the immediate? With affect and relation, pure experience and movement? This is almost exactly what Grusin is calling for. He asks us to redefine mediation so as to include immediacy. He pushes beyond the human, beyond human experience, beyond media, to understand an entire ecology of events, each feeling the influence of other events, becoming anew through a multiplicity of encounters rich with both information and thinking-feelings. I would, however, shift focus away from media and mediation (and their many counterparts), and towards immediation itself (and its purposeful ambiguity). The former can always be complexified, but the latter is in-itself unknowable, and so needs not ever *be* complexified. The immediate is unactualized and atemporal. It is sensed and felt, but never understood. And I am arguing that immediation's forces are central to mediation (and becoming, and experience, and much more), rather than the other way around. Immediation is transformation without meaning, potential without quantifiable possibilities.

So then what do Levy's images do? If they were to mediate the immediate, then that mediation would no longer *be* immediate (other than each image's inherent immediate experience, à la Grusin). If they are images *of* one thing or another, then we are assuming discrete objects to be extant and preformed. Levy's work rather calls attention precisely to immediacy, to the ungraspable potential of "stuff and things," and how they relate. And because it avowedly does so with what is traditionally thought of as (new) "media" and what that mediates, it also brings to bear the continuity of media and immediacy's relation. Levy amplifies the constantly evolving individuations that emerge from (and also *as*) "we," between the known and mediated, and its immediacy, between the quantified ones and zeroes of the digital, and its purely analogical actualization.

For the video *Shanghai Future Cities Model 3*, Levy focused on a miniature design model for what the largest city in the world might eventually become; this is located in the Museum for Urban Planning in Shanghai. His other sites featured as part of this ongoing series so far include Passages Jouffroy in Paris—which was the inspiration for Walter Benjamin's *Arcades Project*—and the Judisches Krankenhaus Berlin—which was a Jewish hospital throughout World War II. These choices are, of course, never absent from the videos and prints. The spaces, Levy's motivations for choosing them, his gestures with the camera, his amount of sleep or exercise, what he had for breakfast and his plans for napping later in the afternoon, his inspiration from the structuralists, his busy schedule and son's daily needs, and more, are all folded into every sequence. But Levy intentionally magnifies the impact and implication of the digital apparatus in this series.

Shanghai Future Cities Model 3, a 59-second video, begins as a pool of bright blue, oceanic light, that seems to cross-fade from image to image, like glowing slivers projected through an overhead aquarium. Five seconds in, blurry brownish-green algae sprout from the sea floor, followed by diagonally traveling, tan-coloured cubic creatures, that stretch into grainy, banana taffy pieces, as they crawl to disappear beyond the upper left quadrant of the frame. Before long, there is nothing. And I don't mean a white emptiness or fading to black, but rather no-thing that I recognize—merely an amorphous mess of moving, thinking, feeling intensities of colour, shape and vibrancy. Greens and browns, pinks and reds, clouds and starships, boats and amoeba, dissolve and reappear in a gorgeous cascade of rotating life and non-life. Every-thing throbs in and out, between rhythm and syncopation.

After capturing his rapid motions with the camera, Levy imports the distorted videos into his computer, slows their speed down more than 20 times their original, and quantizes the files by restricting the range of data, before re-rendering these videos as something new. Using a combination of free and commercial software such as Processing, After Effects, Final Cut Pro and PhotoShop, among others, he blends frames, analyzes, extracts and amplifies colours, grains, shapes and movement; he interpolates and cross-fades, then exports once or many times more—as high resolution physical prints, and as new image sequences ready for playback.

The majority of *work* in this work is not done by the artist. It is done by the image-sensor, and by the sensing image. Levy does not intend for this or that colour or shape, does not purposefully glitch with this or that software. What he has done is capture the inner-workings of the camera, *with* the camera; he creates an encounter with, a mediation of, the immediacy of what it is and does. He then enhances each image as it *tells* him to—pumping up the volume on its already extant intensities. Here again is immediacy, an attunement to his affective and embodied response around the mediation present in each encounter, and all the encounters—past, present, and future—that are presenting themselves in the event of his editing. By intervening in or disrupting or making visible what the chip is and does, what the chip is not and cannot do—and what each image is and does, what they were and potentially could be—Levy is more or less making CMOS and CCD selfies.

"It's not a bug, it's a feature."

Every Image, Everywhere, is More than What We See

In a painting, in a photograph, we know there is a before and after to that still, an inside and an outside to that frame. An astute viewer thinks about not just the context of the image, but also of the artist, their perspective and tools, the camera, the paint, the paper, the ink, the time of day and the cultural and scientific influences of the age. Through memory and cross-modal perception, we can feel the vastness of the room behind Diego Velázquez's *Las Meninas*, taste the "petites madeleine" cookies made by Marcel Proust's grandmother; smell, touch, long for, extend into, placate...

But what of Malcolm Levy's *Other-frames*? What do these images sense, when the image-sensors that help to create them are beyond sense—or at least beyond the perceptible? What do these artworks do when they show us something outside either what we or our cameras can perceive? The question here is not "Why does it matter?" but "How does it matter?" and" What is implicated in that mattering?"

Perhaps another analogy is in order. N. Katherine Hayles calls our everyday abstractions—taking the "world's noisy multiplicity" into the cleaner forms of language and math, for example—the "platonic backhand" (Hayles 2008: 12). Here we simplify and theorize in order to understand, and sometimes change, the world around us. She considers this a good thing. Thinkers from ancient Greece to and beyond Claude Shannon and his theories of information (on which modern computers are based) all require this kind of conceptual engagement (Shannon 2001). The problem of the "platonic forehand" emerged only more recently, where the over-simplified abstraction of the backhand is forced onto a view of reality, "privileging the abstract as the Real and downplaying the importance of material instantiation" (Hayles 2008: 13). In other words and in context, we overlay a false digital perfection onto a messy reality, then pretend that *is* reality—and the consequences for doing so could be dire.

It was not long ago that we ignored what our cars output in the form of carbon, and we still pretend our environment is not telling us, loud and clear, that it is changing. Today, we think not enough about the lithium ion and plastic, silicon and super-conductors, in our laptops and phones and yes, cameras. What war-torn countries do they come from, and how did they get *there* in the first place? Where do they travel to and from, and who assembles their various parts? What do they do in use, and what do they do as waste? At stake, whether in our everyday interactions or on a large scale, are the very relationships between humans and the natural world on the one hand, politics and commerce on the other.

In his short "Forerunners" thought-in-process book, *The Anthrobscene*, Jussi Parrika elegantly, and frighteningly, interweaves various narratives surrounding the "materiality of media technology," its "growing waste problem," and the relationships between them, and with "energy and power" (Parikka 2014: 35). He begins via Antonio Stoppani, discussing the many cycles of the earth's crust and core, its bowels erupting and crawling outward, sinking and resurfacing, amassing deposits and waste and life and death. Where, he asks, do the mass amounts of tin, cobalt, palladium, silver, gold, copper and aluminum in our everyday devices come from? How are they "made," over millennia, in a geological sense, via large-scale schisms and faults, fossils and deposit formations? What will be "made" from our techno-waste, in that same geological time scale, as opposed to the business-as-usual frame of the quarterly report, or the tax year? What will become of 50 million mobile phone screens in fifteen years? In 50 years, 3000, or 3 million? It is madness to assume we are not subject to the earth's movements over time (that the raw materials for our technologies do not come from such movements), and conversely that we are not contributing to these movements and makings, more and more, on a massive scale. Of course geology contributes to nation-spaces and technological possibility, to biology and the potential for civilization; and inversely, of course the laws and demands of those nations, the usage and waste from our devices, the qualities of life, non-life, farming, and industrialization, interrelate, together and with the Earth, both now and in the very long term.

The relation between our experience of media (art) and immediacy along the lines Parikka writes about could perhaps be called an "aesthetic of the immediate," following anthropologist Eduardo Kohn. In his dissertation, *Natural Engagements and Ecological Aesthetics Among The Ávila Runa Of Amazonian Ecuador*, Kohn discusses how the Runa practice this. An aesthetic of the immediate has the "concomitant effect of inculcating an attitude toward experience in nature that encourages people to focus on their immediate perceptions. It encourages people to engage in the world of experience with Zen-like mindfulness to the moment" (Kohn 2002: 70). The Runa tell stories, use sounds, engage in "the creative use of poetic language" to help one another practice being "attentive to the immediate forest experience" (72-3). By "immediate" Kohn conveys a kind of "lived process"—one that is not knowledge, but "knowing," not meaning, but "meaning-in-the-world" (29, 72). And by aesthetic, he proposes a "system that attaches particular values to experience in ways that affect experience" (70). Overall, we are asked to concern ourselves with, both, the immediate and immediated materials, times and spaces of the habitats we are a part of (both in the present, and in the *presented* geo-timespace of the Earth), and also the media and mediated languages, poetics and natures of that encounter. Art and media think and promote knowing; they can gift meaning-in-the-world beyond human timescales, or beside the immediate.

Levy's digital print, *Palm Islands Apartments*, appears to be an asymmetrical grid of over 200 sequential shots that could present trees, windows, mountains, televisions, shops, people, lights, roads, solar panels, mice, wheels, microchips and/or nothing at all; and the "point of view" could be from space, under a microscope, via a GoPro webcam on a skateboarder's helmet (while he zips around then does a kick flip), while driving a car, and/or via an accidentally hand-covered lens. Taken individually, as my eyes scan each of these "shots," their inner-images make me feel queasy and uneasy, see a zig-zag of tans, blacks, greens and browns, silver frames and unnatural outlines that force me to squint and wonder, shake my head and look away. And together, when I pull back and try to experience the whole as a singular image, I feel the tectonic shifts of malls, and light breezes against green palms; I tilt my head to try and make sense of the image's "time" via the "sequence." Is it fast or slow? Man-made and technological, or natural and geological? What is *my* relation to *it*?

Levy's work has us encounter the "double bind of technical materiality and conceptual immateriality" (Parikka 2014: 7). He shows us our technologies were designed to have us forget their materiality, their imperfections, their inner workings and mis-workings, and where they come from in the world, as well their impacts on the world around us: psychic, social, and environmental. He asks us to think outside of human temporality, to remember the nanoseconds of the machine, as well as the millennia of the earth, which, Parikka reminds us, "surpasses a time scale we are used to in media studies" (39). Implicit in each image is everything before, and everything after. Earth and animal, politics and, of course, labor—its "processes, exploitation, and the dangerous conditions that characterize also the current persistence of hardwork alongside persistence of hardware" (48). Malcolm Levy's *Other-frames* bring movement, change, and continuity between humans, nature, and politics, media and immediacy, into to the foreground. What if *all* of us *always* listened to computers and cameras, to battery packs and electrons, to the material politics of translation and difference and more, with the level of care Levy affords them?

Do I experience *all* of this in *every* single one of Levy's works? No. But what each piece invites us to do is listen to, and look at, and feel for, and move with, *more* than just a *human* ecology, in a *human* timescale—more than just a (human) mediated image, in its most traditional sense. With *Other-frames*, Levy is not an expert craftsman that produces only what he sees in his mind's eye. Instead, he disrupts encounters between abstraction and materiality, between mediation and immediacy, between the supposedly digital (technology-based and modern) space and its alleged counterpart, the analog (imperfect, unrefined, natural, perhaps uncivilized or primitive). He methodically breaks down these mythic opposites by showing how they are always already together, and augments their intensities so as to wind up with powerful works of art, which acknowledge and engage with—indeed magnify—their ecological relations.

Here "human-nonhuman collectives ... share experience" (Bennett 2010: XIX). Objects and things and matter are "vivid entities not entirely reducible to the contexts in which (human) subjects set them, never entirely exhausted by their semiotics" (5). Levy rather *synthesizes* digital and analog, matter and sign, time and stasis. From the ancient Greek for "with" and "placing," synthesis refers to a combination of two or more entities that together form something new. Levy's work frames and amplifies always already synthesized digital-analog-sign-matter "assemblages [that] are living, throbbing confederations" (24). He reminds us that every-thing matters—personally, politically, economically, socially, environmentally. These images, this imaging, our viewing, all ask us to experience, and practice, attuning to machines and the earth and *their* habitats, in addition to ourselves and our own.

It is Stunning and Terrifying All at Once

The "media of geology/metals" and the "geology of media" together create a kind of "geophysics of media culture" (Parikka 2014: 44-45). The earth is a resource, and also needs resources, just as much as technology is a resource, and also needs resources. Each of matter and media engages in short- and long-term mobilization; each mediates, is mediating and immediate. And together they turn from many long and interwoven pasts, into far-off and not-yet imagined futures. Parikka reminds us that the technological device "never dies, but remains as toxic waste residue, and also that we should be able to repurpose and reuse solutions in new ways" (41). Malcolm Levy's *Other-frames* do something quite similar. They do not reveal the ghost in the machine. Rather, they finally render the possibilities and potentials beyond those human constraints we thrust upon our machines, with micro-control. This body of work does not position digital technologies and digital images as, or on, a grid of known and desired quantities. It rather implores us to take account of media ecologies on a massive scale of time and space, in the durationless moment of the immediate, and then do something *else*. It asks us to do something more.

Other-frames create a passage—a movement and a place to move—for thinking and feeling the relation of humans, nature, and politics.

Notes

1. This assigns that voltage a number value, before storing the complete, high definition charge-voltage-number-pixel range as an image—or rather long sequence of images, since Levy captures video—as a digital file in memory (for example, on an SD—Secure Digital—card).
2. In a greyscale image, for instance, the usual breakdown is one byte (eights bits) of information per pixel, which can be any number between zero and 255. Zero is black, 255 is white, and there are 254 possible gray values between them. For a colour image, there will be one byte of information for each of red, green, and blue, making for the possibility of over 16 and a half million colours in any given pixel. These numbers exponentially increase with images and video of a higher bit quality.
3. This makes the file smaller because of how blue skies, skin tone, or a car's colour will have many similar pixels right next to each other in a large group. It is called "spatial" compression, as it compares pixels in the 2-dimensional *space* of the complete image.
4. This is called "temporal" compression. Digital video standards such as DivX (which is not an acronym but a brand name) and H264 (the recommended codec standard by giants like Apple and YouTube) are both spatially and temporally compressed.109

   To add yet more layers of complexity, the CCD sensor doesn't actually capture separate colour information; instead every group of four pixels will have a physically gridded filter (called a Bayer mask) to remove portions of red, green, and blue from various pixels in each group, in order to read in only light outside those spectra as greyscale, and then hard- and software basically approximate the colour image by putting the puzzled pieces of data back together. The newer 3CCD cameras use dichroic beam splitter prisms instead of Bayer masks, the former of which separate out red, green and blue light. They have, as the name suggests, three separate CCDs that each only convert one of those colours via the aforementioned chain of events (Janesick 2001).

Anna Munster

Signaletic Immediations: Sensing New Media as Relational Events and Ecologies

Ulf Langheinrich's *LAND* (2008) is not so much an image transmission of something but image transmission that does. At a very ordinary and practical level, we cannot enter the space in which the film plays out and just watch, at least not comfortably. The very minimum of requisite audience participation involves doing something to our eyes—we must don the viewing apparatus of red/cyan (3D) glasses so as to resolve the polarization of its channels presented as two separate and displaced fields. And yet this kind of viewing experience is increasingly that of mainstream cinema or even home entertainment these days, which promises to offer us something so oxymoronically different that we are offered "dimension" as an addition to the physical space in which we watch our three-dimensional screen content: "Add dimension to your room with 3D cinema" (LG Electronics 2015). In *LAND*, however, an imperceptible dimension is immanent to the image that differentiates it from the experience design of home entertainment. An actionless and eventful, plotless but durational dimensionality unfolds.

LAND also necessitates a doing-with rather than a doing to. Very little occurs in the course of looking at it over 32 minutes that could easily be narrated or discussed in terms of the transmission of "signs." Indeed, much of the experience of watching the piece comprises trying to work out whether something is happening in front of us or not, where that "in front of us" might be located, and at what point, if something is happening, this something actually begins or finishes. One could walk away from *LAND* feeling that nothing much had taken place at all in spite of the elaborate and obvious technical accomplishment that the film achieves. And yet, something quite transformative nonetheless occurs. Already it is impossible to think and speak of this piece in ordinary media, digital media or art historical terms. It is barely image; its moving elements seem not to propel it onward but suspend a texture mid-air, creating a hallucinatory quality that never resolves optically. An image with texture and kinesthetics, but little opticality. It defies Boris Groys' conception of the digital art installation as productive of a struggle or negotiation between the becoming visible of the invisible (digital data) and the time a viewer is prepared to spend negotiating such a space (Groys 2008*:* 88). *LAND* seems initially to have more in common with the work of artists such as James Turrell in which the process of "seeing yourself see" unfolds.[1] However, *LAND,* for all its hallucinatory edges, takes us out of our heads and away from processes that might be said to originate "in" the human brain or even in the machine vision of the specific technologies deployed. Instead, it helps us think art, media and perception ecologically. Here both the human and the technological operate as activations amid—rather than origins of—rhythmic and affective terrains.

LAND and similar pieces that traverse moving image, sound and spatialisation—Ryoji Ikeda's *Test Pattern no.5* (2013) or Robin Fox's *RGB Laser* (2013 ongoing), for example—are *de*-visualisations, functioning to make the visual itself a kind of nonimagistic element by transducing it into environment or milieu. Here the visual (re)discovers its own nonvisual spectra and these get taken up kinaesthetically through rhythm and movement, and proprioceptively via participants or audience members. Such works offer more in common, at first glance, with online spaces such as *Second Life* in which media become places to simply hang out in; to simply be with mediality itself.

In a large industrial bay that had become part of an arts precinct in Sydney, *Test Pattern no. 5* was projected on to the floor. Nothing but pulses of varying black and white stripes, blinks and flashes, it rolled up and down the space, cutting it up, reassembling it rhythmically and recomposing the cavernous room into a cross between signal noise and nightclub. Unexpectedly, though, people didn't dance much. Instead, they hung out, sprawled across the room with their friends and devices—some working, some chatting. Sometimes someone ran spontaneously around and across the moving image but mostly the atmosphere was languid. Without communicating, without deciding deliberately, the space was inhabited as if it were a new kind of city park emerging via a collective shaping bereft of any obvious design or plan.

In a devisualised milieu, rhythms are activated instead, forming repetitive sequences or refrains. Deleuze and Guattari call the refrain "the being of sensation" (Deleuze and Guattari 1994: 184); blocs of sound, colour, gesture composed in relation to a territory. Guattari, in particular, directs us toward the ways in which the refrain operates as an initial pulsation that folds affect onto itself, and in the process etches the first contours of expressivity (Guattari 1996: 160). This etching is not yet so inscriptive that affect is fully individuated as "an" expression such as a particular feeling about the art experience. Rather, the refrain scribbles affect into communicability, insofar as "communication" here designates only a movement or eking out of affectivity as it carries "sign-particles" (Genosko 2002: 181) that facilitate the passing or sharing of one thing (in) to another. In these media milieu, this might include the passing of screen into floor; excitation into calmness; the passing of variable speeds of lines and sonorous blocs between and across each other. Such media environments do not communicate, then, but rather eke out the conditions for communicability. It is no wonder they are spaces to become social without being overtly participatory in the sense of someone deliberately doing some *thing*. Perhaps this is why people seem to like simply sitting and talking or relaxing in them. They invoke a sympathetic atmosphere across people, media and space, so long as we understand sympathy in a nonidentifcatory mode: "What is felt in sympathy is the *dynamic form* of the *situation*. This is felt not from the point of view of one participant or the other, but from the situational perspective of what, potentially, passes between them" (Massumi, 2014: 77). And this despite their frenetic patternings, their probing of the auditory and optic nerves, the ways in which they seem to fold around their own nonhuman space-times.

The visual elements of such media works are not what are fundamentally up for grabs even if they are nonetheless necessary for their functioning. What matters more is *conjunction with signal*, or rather as I will discuss later, signal's relation with the signaletic. In the kinds of environmental works I am discussing here—and especially in *LAND*—the visual field finds passages *to* and *with* the signaletic. We pass from the visual as a regime of signs (or signal as codified) to traverse it instead as an energetics—entering it through its signaletic mattering. We can—following Maurizio Lazzaratto's reading of Deleuze's concept of "signaletic matter" (2007), Bodil Marie Stavning Thomsen's development of signaletic material in relation to media arts' audiovisuality (2012) and Andrew Murphie's research into signal and convolution in electronic music (2013)—propose that the "signal transmission" of any media always operates in oscillatory relations between molar and molecular processes; between *deterritorialisng* and *reterritorialising* trajectories; between signs/signal and the signaletic.

For Lazzarato, specifically discussing how this operates in video signal and aesthetic practices of video, what is interesting is not so much the molar process of deterritorialisation in which the media artefact is decoupled from its object and/or materiality and in which it also conjoins with the other deterritorialising tendencies of social machines (2007: 283), although these can be considered one pole of signal transmission. The video image, for him, is deterritorialised—decoupled first, from the physical-chemical indexicality on which photographic or celluloid film was inscribed. And, second, decoupled from the necessary processing (developing film) and redisplay (printing the image on paper, the fim on to celluloid) of such physico-chemical media. And for Lazzarato such mediatic deterritorialisation of the video image -which, prior to digitization, had become an electronic pulse rearranging the surface of magnetic tape—is transversally related to the increasing deterritorializing trajectories of post-Fordist or *cognitive* capitalism. Yet in the midst of these molar flows, Lazzarato also alerts us to the ways in which both electronic and digital technologies also transform and compose intensities, forces and fields *at the molecular level*. Picking up these compositional possibilities, Thomsen has argued for a rethinking of not just video signal but any digital media or signal through the ways in which signal's intensities, or its "signaletic material," find a way of becoming felt in a range of reflexive media art works (2012). This locates digital media's aesthetic potential—the possibilities for different and genuinely novel composites of intensities, forces, fields—in the nexus between the molecular and the molar, between the asignifying and signifying; in the possibility, in other words, of transmissible signal as an ongoing modulatory movement, oscillating from the signaletic to sign/signal and back again. For Thomsen, this nexus encapsulates a modulation of *the becoming of time* in signal. For what is increasingly reterritorialized by signal regimes—from broadcast television in the 1980s to current attempts to control signal by licensing the spectrum among a myriad of molar mechanisms—is the *matter* of time, its material currents, processes, movements. Amid the detrritorialization of media from artefact and the inscription of media flows as a medium (whether chemically or magnetically), time is nonetheless *increasingly indexed* by its stratification as "real time." This is a capture that attempts to modify signal so that it adopts the meter of broadcast, webcast and streaming instantenaity, modulating out the instabilities and myriad potentialities of signaletic mattering. For time to become—that is, for it to become potential tendencies other than *real time*—intensities and different durations also need (their) time.

LAND becomes a signaletically-charged environment by developing material conjunctions and intensities within signal/sign *through an intensification of elements of the visual while it is also devisualising.* It multiplies dimensions of and for the visual—the textural, the tactile, the kinaesthetic—but is less concerned with the visible or the optical, and it disregards the opposition between illusion and "the real." In these ways, *LAND* shares qualities with hallucinatory images, which are no less real as events than any other kind of image. Hallucinations are intensifications of images that are immediately perceived as interpenetrated by auditory, proprioceptive, textural, olfactory (and so forth) registers. Such intensifications also modulate the speeds of images, thickening the kind and range of durations. *LAND's* visual intensifications spreading out into a devisualized field/environment, operate not just with matter-flows but with *matter-time* flows and offer us alternate durations whose nonlinearities place us in the midst of signaletic events. Molar (visual) regimes such as real time find themselves modulated by such field-events as *LAND* through processes of *immediation*.[2]

Compared with much mainstream 3D cinema, the spectacle of depth perception via *LAND*'s stereoscopic imaging is only barely sustained. One has to line up this minimal sense of 3D as "effect" against the ways in which objects and action clamor to reach out of the screen for the eyes in narrative and action-driven 3D cinema and television. Here things become super-charged with visibility instead—a visibility so ferocious that the image almost hunts down the eye as it pops out and punches it. This is the third dimension as an inversion of classical perspectivalism where, instead of a vanishing point receding into an infinite horizon, the point inverts outward beyond the screen, penetrating back out into the visual field. A mantra of 3D film making in the last decade has been that whatever is closest to the eyes should typically become the point of narrative focus for the scene.[3] This is all assisted by the possibility of rendering everything infinitely in focus—the infamous infinite depth of field effect of 3D cinema. The depth of field effects used by classical Hollywood cinema, for example—in which backgrounds are excessively blurred against a foreground object sharply in focus, delivered via cinematographic techniques such as dramatic focus pulling—can cause visual confusion in a 3D cinematic field. This ushers in an entirely new set of relations for the classic "affection-image," which Deleuze famously analysed as nonrepresentational cinematic images presenting pure quality (1989: 30). The affection image relies on the contrast between a sharply focused foreground; Deleuze selected the close-up of the face filling the screen in classical cinema, set against a blurred and diminished background. The face as close-up affection image, isolates and removes the face from its context and pulls focus on the qualities that pass across the sur-face instead. But in mainstream contemporary 3D cinema, we have ceded affection-images to purely sensory images—the rendering of everything in sharp focus into depth of field means all objects are constantly vying for attention and exchange in the visual field. The visual field is overloaded and is given temporary discharge via proximity, with whatever extrudes discharging the sensation. The affection-image recedes and its duration is lost in a sensorimotor avalanche.

But in *LAND* it isn't clear what is in focus and what's not. It is uncertain what is extruding from the screen and what receding. Full realization of where the (3D) action and objects occur in its screen space is obscured, folding back into the "event" of its intensive molecular activations and exchanges. Proximity to the "matter" of *LAND's* image is not consistently cued by depth perception but seems instead to both emerge and recede as rhythmic manifold. Just when you thought you had worked out where the "land" is, the landscape has already changed, morphing into a new horizontality, a new feeling of landfall. As a result, the transmission of image in *LAND* produces a strange dance. It is as if its 3-dimensionality happens only after the fact, as if one's eyes were constantly scanning ahead of the unfolding of the image flow itself and as if this very "aheadness" is what, in retrospect, allows a perception of depth to unfold. I think I will begin to see depth emerge as the image horizon lands toward the bottom third of the screen. By the time we reach the bottom third of the screen the image has morphed into another topological configuration that may actually have flattened out. Consequently, *LAND*'s 3D effects arrive somehow before being seen, registering imperceptibly. They unfold as an imaging of something more surface-like, more flattened. Depth perception in *LAND* is experienced as a reminiscence rather than actually seen. This is reminiscent of something you might expect or strive to envision when placing the glasses on your head—that old familiar world of volume. Yet how *LAND's* dimensionality unfolds is quite different to the memory of "depth" and volume in Euclidean space. *LAND*'s dimensional unfolding is more an instance of what Erin Manning, in a different context, calls "the deja-felt": "You experience an uncanny 'deja-felt' or—'deja-unfelt'—a direct experience of difference felt in the act" (2013: 78–79). Manning suggests this "infra-thin" in experience occurs, for example, in movement when, having practiced a technique that has become embodied, the movement of the same technique unfolds in a completely unexpected way. It feels familiar and yet the movement unfolds unexpectedly, in a manner not experienced before.

Instead of seeing objects, action and the spectacle of 3D cinema, in *LAND* you are seeing across this reminiscence and the difference that the image flow's unfolding actually becomes—you are directly seeing intervals that comprise a seeing of what is not seen but cued for in depth perception. This "not seen" is the very process of volume emerging from surface as the eyes scan around objects and project into the future direct experience of that object as if it might sometime be circumnavigated. Here the depth cues occur topologically rather than volumetrically—there is no "around the object" but rather a continuous surface unfolding of depth. Eyes have to continuously cross its surface of differences and produce depth processually rather than as a thing placed already in space. In doing all this, *LAND* produces a direct encounter with its visuality as a coming into formation—in-formation. Not the seeing of vision but rather inhabitation of a nexus in which the visual is both dedifferentiatied by signaletic mattering *and* differentiated by habits of cueing for depth. Drowning, not seeing—you are *immediating*. Or rather, *LAND* and viewers participate ecologically within an *immedia* event.

Make no mistake, such a mode of composing with immersive media environments does not grant privileged access to a "real" for the perceiving subject—the human viewer. A real that has typically been characterised as noumenal or transcendent, existing before or beyond the media ecology conditioning it. Let's establish just what seeing is doing, then, in this particular case. *LAND* uses a low-cost method of producing stereoscopy: anaglyph 3D achieved by means of encoding each eye's image using filters of the chromatically opposite colors red and cyan. Anaglyph 3D images contain two differently filtered coloured images, one for each eye. When viewed through the "color-coded" "anaglyph glasses," each of the two images reaches one eye, revealing an integrated stereoscopic image. Neuroanatomically, the visual cortex of the brain fuses this into a "perception" of a three-dimensional scene or composition. It's easier to see what seeing is doing when this fusion is not taking place—take off your 3D red/cyan glasses and all that uncanny phasing and desphasing of both image flow and duration is lost. Neuroanatomically, perception must also be cued.

With no glasses, you see instead the actual matter of the image fields *as differentials for themselves alone*, refusing both the glasses and (human) eyes and offering up only a kind of endless stuttering chromaticism. Indeed, this is the film's own immediacy. This is the image matter that subtends it. At the same time, when you look through the red/cyan glasses you are looking at the *recomposition* of 3D space sometimes referred to as an "illusion." This is what it means to look at a film—rather than say the chair in front of you—in 3D. Not that one space is real while the other is not. Rather what occurs is recognition that seeing cinematically, doubles the vision. To borrow Brian Massumi's glasses in discussing the question of illusions with respect to the way movement is conjured by a spiralling decorative motif:

> The form naturally poises the body for a certain set of potentials. The design calls forth a certain vitality affect—the sense we would have, for example, of moving our eyes down a branch of rustling leaves, and following that movement with our hands. But that life dynamic comes without the potential for it to be actually lived. It's the same lived relation as when we "actually" see leaves, it's the same potential. But it's *purely* potential. We can't live it out. We can only live it *in*—*in* this form—implicitly." (Massumi 2011: 43)

The motif is static but we can't help but sense the movement about to occur. Likewise, the red/cyan fields converged aren't depth, but we cannot *not* see the perception of depth when we look at these with 3D glasses on.

If the polarised and displaced image fields are what lie "underneath," "behind" or "prior" to our seeing of a 3D film, can we call *this* the immediate? Alternatively, if we see sufficiently and in depth only after we replace the red/cyan glasses, should we call *this* vision the something that is now immediately given in experience, especially since without the glasses it is actually relatively difficult to see clearly at all. What happens to the idea of the immediate when mediation itself no longer guarantees a looking through or at in a geometrically and perspectivally verifiable mode? Or, is what is being transmitted to us no longer readable according to such a framework or regime of depth cues and signs? As Massumi suggests, this thing that we cannot see but cannot *not* see is another dimension of seeing that is there all the time—the abstract dimension: "The reality of this abstraction does not replace what is actually there. It supplements it. We see it *with* and *through* the actual form" (Massumi, 2013: 41). In *LAND,* rather than falling in step with a narrative of illusionism—with the 3D media *replacing* or substituting for "unmediated" vision—stereoscopy itself becomes abstract; an abstraction coming in to form. This is an in-forming made visible by the immediating of intervals across depth and non-depth; between familiar experiences of depth and an imaging in which depth seems to itself recede, composing just outside of the visual field. Immediately, experience composes a strange lagging force that comprises the crossing of these intervals. *This* is the real of this event. As we can or cannot see, such an event unleashes and is constituted by an entire ecology of movement, perception and technics that cannot be easily subsumed within the paradigm of mediation.

Interestingly, the nonconverged red/cyan fields of *LAND (*watching without glasses) are in some ways easier on the eyes. This is not at all the case with most 3D cinematography, which generally demands stereo convergence since its images are based on photorealistic representation. *LAND*, instead does not offer such an obvious resolution but asks us to participate in the event of resolving-unresolving across 2 and 3-dimensionality—a task that is usually relegated to habit. Perhaps I notice these things because, like about 6% of the population, I have what is called "convergence insufficiency"—a sensory and neuromuscular anomaly of the binocular vision system in which I fail to fully resolve the convergence of my left and right eyes views. At certain distances and viewing certain kinds of phenomena, I don't see "an" object, then, but rather its differentials. For me*, then,* the immediate of *LAND* unfolds between glasses on and glasses off, a few inches from and meters away from the screen. I can only proprioceptively and actively engage to resolve its intervals. But this is not to say that we should understand *LAND*'s abstraction of 3D vision in terms primarily of the human subject's perceptual system. Rather it is to suggest that its eventfulness lies with its exploitation of the potential to actualise differently in every iteration of its viewing.

Its eventfulness lies not so much with me or even with anyone's perception in particular, although visual perceptual parameters are an *enabling constraint* of any stereoscopic imaging. Instead, its eventfulness lies in its activation of relations between phasing and dephasing. The concrete and the abstract planes of 3D cinema are out of phase with each other, which is why there is difference *before you put the glasses on and after they have been placed on you.* And this difference is already there prior to you. What is *also doing* in 3D cinema, then, is a constant crossing of the intervals between the differential fields of the image and this takes place as much in the deployment of specific camera techniques in 3D cinematography for registering horizontal rather than vertical displacements of the image being shot or produced. If we want to think about what happens in this out of phaseness, we might also think about the doubled perception of 3D cinema as its polyphasal compositionality.

This is a term I am borrowing from Muriel Combes' reading of Gilbert Simondon's process of individuation (2013). Simondon is concerned with understanding the individual—whether physical, technical, organic, human, social or psychical—as a momentary concrescence brought about by very precise and continuous operations of continuous *individuation. These operations are nonlinear.* As a system, for example, water, changes its state, it contains (at least) two subsystems or phases that have different orders of magnitude—liquid and gas or liquid and solid. The process of change brings these systems into communication. This system changing and its process of transformation, then, can be described as *polyphasal*. The "resolution" of the tensions between phases—or two systems with different orders of magnitude that establish a communication, which Simondon also calls a "mediation" (2009:7)—constitutes a dephasing. Importantly, however, and unlike a dialectics of change, *becoming or individuation or the process of dephasing* also always imply that the energetics of incompatibilities from one system (and/or the other and/or its resolution) is not completely dissipated or resolved in the dephasing. Returning to the relatively simple example of state changes for water between liquid, solid, gas, we must understand that these are not progressive or ordinally resolved phases of water's being. Rather, any of these phases may dephase back into each other again, depending, in part, on both the intensive energetics of the system itself as well as the associated milieu of the specifically individuating water itself. The question of the associated milieu is crucial: is the water above land? Above another body of water?

what is its altitude? What is its proximity to other molecules, gases? And so on and so forth. As Massumi, moving with the different processes of affective politics, suggests, the polyphasal character of phasing and dephasing must be thought nonlinearly:

> Although the phases emerge sequentially, they operate conjointly to form a complex, multilayered formation. The overall process is at once additive and distributive ... dephasing is when things roll back into each other, activated by a virtual cause in a kind of shared potential.... To phase, then, is to unfold differentially—to dephase is to de-differentiate. (2005: 45).

Importantly, phasing and dephasing are not exclusive or ordered in individuation. And this goes straight to the micro-politics of perception with which mainstream 3D cinema and any other "new" technological display of images *and* experimental modulations of the visual field are engaged. The individuation of a becoming environmental of the visual through an immediating event, in which intensifications of the signaletic and nonlinear offer an opportunity for inventing perception, *is as possible to actualise as is its opposite* using just the same technical components, the same perceiver, the same configurations of space. It is thus not in these elements but in the nexus of the signaletic and signal as a regime of signs that the politics of contemporary visualisations will play out. In "object-oriented" 3D cinema in which sharpened volumetric objects extrude for attention, the 3D image fields are only primed for rephasing. They seek to have already resolved any polyphasality outside of processes of perception individuating. The image here must be oriented as an object, pre-constituted and out to get you in a 3D cinema coming at you real soon.

To experimentally modulate such a mediatic and technical ensemble, is to first consider how image, perceiver, signal flow might be inserted into this nexus of phasing and dephasing, by modulating differently; that is, in a way in which one constantly "jumps off" prior to landing, between the signal and the signaletic. This is made possible in *LAND* by immediately experiencing the force of 3D imaging as abstraction—not a force seen as such, but one that is "deja-felt" across intervals, across difference. Strangely, the immediacy of such a media event requires us to inhabit the non-now, to dephase and rhythmically invent a virtual, abstract dimensionality *retroactively* from the actual 3-dimensional percept. And with this invention comes a dance of visuals, swaying signaletically, in more-than real time.

Notes

1. 'Seeing Yourself See' is the subtitle of a retrospective exhibition of James Turrell's work first put together by the Los Angeles County Museum of Art, The Guggenheim Museum, New York and The Houston Museum of Art and currently touring the globe. The catalogue of the exhibition was put together by Michael Govan and bears this subtitle (2013). Turrell's work is usually discussed from the perspective of the ways in which viewer engagement foregrounds the sensory and cognitive processes of visual perception.
2. In this chapter I am concerned with the ways in which real time has been captured by particular kinds of (visual) apparatuses such as 3D entertainment machines/regimes. This is not to suggest that "real time" is itself to be regarded as solely a molar assemblage. In other work, I have suggested that real time can be thickened rather than merely resisted or critiqued. See, for example, a recent paper "Tuning in to the Signaletic: experiements with the imperceptible of real time," (Munster 2015)
3. See for example Kristen Thompsen and David Bordwell's (2009) discussion of the "coming at you" sensation while watching objects and action in a range of 3D Hollywood cinema releases from *Avatar* through to *Harry Potter and the Half Blood Prince*.

Alanna Thain

Mobile Media's New Multiplexes: Cinema Out of the Box

> Art preserves, and it is the only thing in the world that is preserved. It preserves and is preserved in itself (quid juris?), although actually it lasts no longer than its support and materials-stone, canvas, chemical color, and so on (quid facti?). The young girl maintains the pose that she has had for five thousand years, a gesture that no longer depends on whoever made it. The air still has the turbulence, the gust of wind, and the light that it had that day last year, and it no longer depends on whoever was breathing it that morning.
> *Deleuze and Guattari (1994: 163)*

In the city of Montreal, where I am from and where I teach at McGill University, no event has marked my thinking of the ecological art of the encounter more forcefully than the Québec student strike of 2012, popularly known in the wake of the Arab Spring as the *Printemps Érable*, or the Maple Spring. Many people recognize the red square worn by participants, initially meant to convey "*on est carrement dans la rouge*" (we are squarely in the red) as the strike's symbol, as part of a global movement that both sought to articulate a widespread unhappiness produced by neoliberalism and austerity politics, and a means to practice alternatives techniques of togetherness. After years of failed negotiations between student associations and the provincial government over a planned tuition hike, a general unlimited strike was declared in February 2012 by many of Quebec's college and university students by their representative organizations. At one point, more than half of college and university students in the province were on strike in actions that lasted for over 8 months. In that time, students and their supporters proposed numerous tactics to creatively demonstrate that

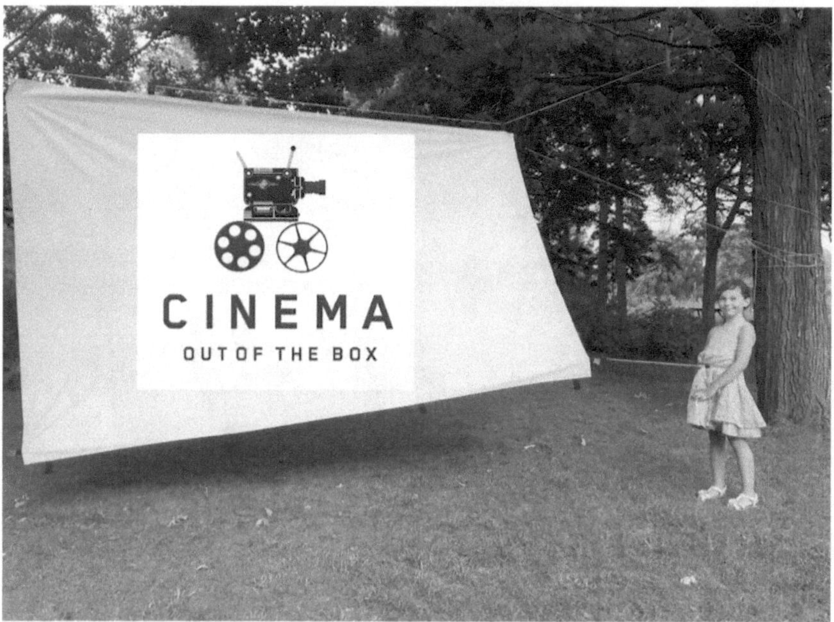

Figure 31. Cinema Out of the Box collaboration with Immediations event on "The Undercommons," a "Disco Soup" in Parc Jarry, consisting of a collective dinner from gleaned and donated foods and a screening of Agnes Varda's The Gleaners and I, July 2015. Photo Credit: Cinema Out of the Box

their protest against planned tuition increases was not simply a matter of local or personal concern, but part of a wide and encompassing effort to reimagine a social space-time. Monthly daytime marches drew the largest crowds in more than a decade onto the streets of Montreal, prompting governmental restrictions on marching without a predetermined route that were largely ignored.

However, the strike's urban rhythm, centered on Montreal, emerged more urgently from the nightly unplanned and unorganized marches that left every evening at 8pm from the strike's symbolic home base, Parc Émilie-Gamelin. This downtown concrete park is bordered by the city bus depot on one side, the gay village on another, the student-heavy Quartier Latin, and the highly active Université de Quebec à Montréal. It is a frequent meeting point for social justice activism in the city, as well as police management of homelessness, sex work and drug dealing. During the more than 100 nighttime *manifs*, Émilie Gamelin launched the strike's nocturnal urbanism, an untimely and punctual political derive. These marches moved through the city in

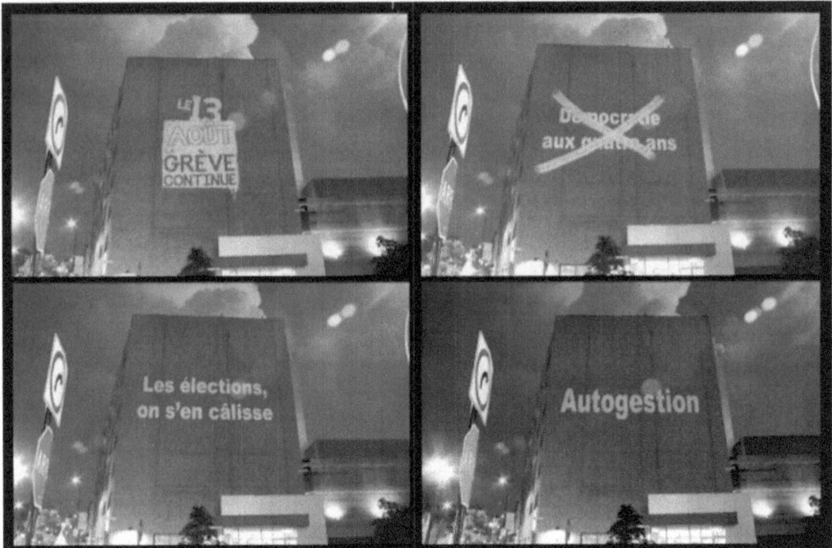

Figure 32. *100th Night Manif*, projections by Nous Sommes Tous Art. Photo Credit: Nous Sommes Tous Art.

creative, unruly ways, activating all of its spaces as territories of political and social potential: on the ground, indifferent to the suggestions of sidewalks and streets as sortings of soft and hard bodies, and in the air both sonically and through, for example, the use of provocative projections to detour vertical surfaces of surrounding buildings from their usual work of advertising.

I make this detour myself as an opening because of the profound effect that the strike had on me, not simply as a educator directly interpellated by the strike's ostensible motivation, but as a citizen moving with and through these activist flows for months on end. In particular, the disjunctive audiovisual ecology of the strike as live performance and embodied archive of action made the entire city for the duration of the strike, once the lights went down, into a zone of immediation: the intensive immersive experience of the unfolding participatory spectacle, immediately doubled by the untimely force of potential as the felt proximately of the "what if?" The strike's call and response—"*avec nous, dans la rue*" (with us in the streets)—laid claim to everything it encountered. As such, the strike threw into question—in a way that has often been identified as its Achilles heel in terms of traditional protest strategies of demand—what counted as part of the political scene. The radically speculative gesture of making common cause, of suspending the city's normative status as container for action and generating an ambiguous embodiment of nebulous limits, has changed for me the way I live the city space, and is the affective context behind my research-creation project *Cinema Out of the Box*.

In that project, I have sought to develop a concept I first conceived while trying to articulate an expanded sense of a cinematic eventness that exceeded the relational diagrams mapped onto discrete arrangement of "production—distribution—consumption," or the purported immobility of spectators as imagined by apparatus theory, without simply falling back onto questions of agency on the part of the spectator as promised by new theories of digital media.[1] Immediation named an experience of starting from the middle or the in-between as the generative condition of a media ecology, one that produced a sensational intensity that relied on, rather than resisted, the ambiguous experience of embodiment itself. Immediation names the sensational stretch of potential that doesn't yet know its own limits, touching and transforming what falls within its purview. The immediacy of immediation signals the urgent liveliness of the art event, immediacy as a "still happening" in the midst, rather than the mark of presence or "liveness" in a non-mediated fashion. In cinema, I frequently felt that it was precisely through the disjunctive force of the cinematic experience, one often theorized away, as through the concept of suture, as disruptive or even dangerous. Part of what I do at the university explores thinking through making in an expanded sense. In the aftermath of the strike, and without really knowing it at the time, I turned to cinema as a site for exploring the potential of the urban commons as a place for generating what I have been calling techniques of togetherness.

The student strike responded to and, through experiments in playfulness and joy, resisted the logic of crisis that permeates our social fabric today. In my work a question I am exploring is: how can cinema as a practice reanimate the potential of the urban commons, precisely through an immediation that fails to know its place? Specifically, how can the contemporary crisis of post-digital cinematic ontology be remobilized to allow for the emergence of productive zones of ambiguous embodiment premised on, rather than nostalgically resisting, the distributed attentions of what Felix Guattari calls the "post-media age"? (Guattari 2008: 61). How can an expanded sociability be generated by and through cinema that includes techniques for a togetherness that exceeds the human, and an opportunistic creation of cinematic movement ecologies, where what moves is not just devices,

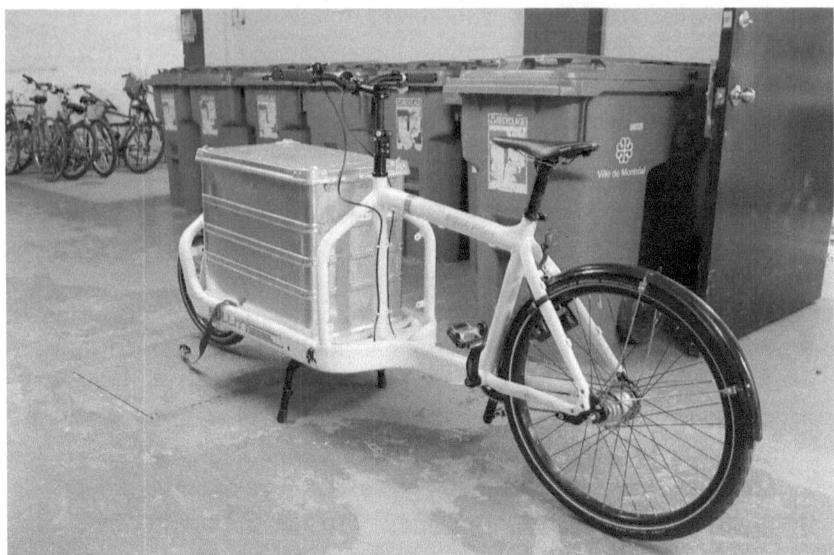

Figure 33 Photo credit Cinema Out of the Box, 2015.

signals or bodies, but a horizon of potential? The ecological art of the encounter that was the movement impulse of the student strike distributed the potential for engagement; in its aftermath, I have sought to amplify the productive ambiguity of immediation in a project that crosses the urban commons with a media ecological approach drawn from the work of Félix Guattari, to understand immediation as an attention to the world-building force of disjunctive attentions.

Territories of Togetherness

Since 2013, I have been running a guerrilla, bicycle powered outdoor cinema throughout the city of Montreal, off the grid and as an ongoing experiment in the potential of the new multi-plexes of mobile media. What kind of folds in space-time and social imaginaries can build an ephemeral cinema out of light, shadow and conviviality? *Cinema Out of the Box*[2] is the research-creation wing of my project "Anarchival Cinemas" that I founded in collaboration with my students at McGill University to develop practical tools for a mobile cinema.[3] The project responds to the contemporary condition of a media defined by mobility—devices that can go anywhere for bodies always on the move. It consists of an energy efficient audiovisual projection system that all fits inside a 4x3x2 foot box, mounted on the front of a cargo bike. The

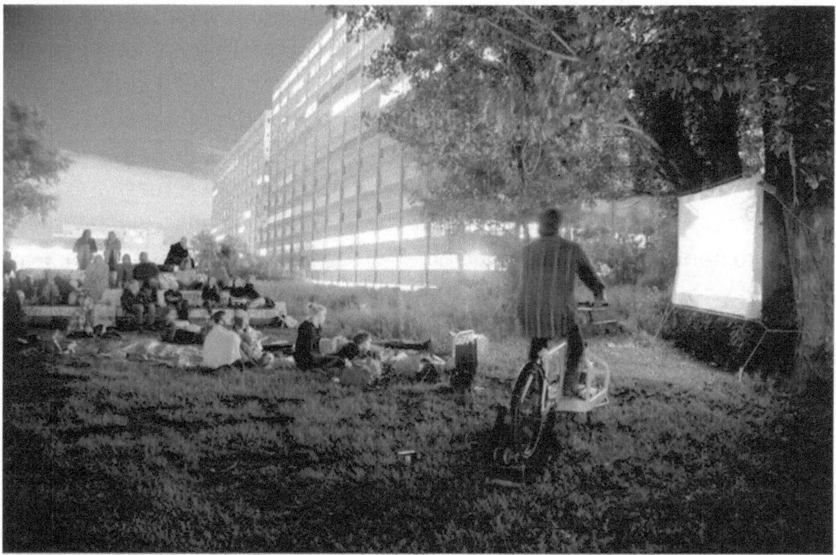

Figure 34. Cinema Out of The Box screening of Green Dream with filmmaker Maia Iatova at the citizen-managed space "Le Champs des Possibles" (the field of possibility), August 2015. Photo Credit: Thomas Kneubühler

initial project proposal for *COTB*, which was funded by a grant from the Sustainability Projects Fund at McGill, sought to do three things: 1) design a portable infrastructure for a mobile cinema that can take the capacity to project audiovisual materials anywhere; 2) develop a year-long screening series experimenting with the potential of this new mobility and 3) find the most ecological and sustainable ways to equip our cinema, focusing in this first year on the potential for bicycle powered generators and low energy customized AV equipment.

Unpacked, the entire system is powered by a battery that is charged by the energy produced by cyclists riding in stationary mode during the screening events. The system relies on audience participation to run, and can be set up in almost any environment. We have held screenings in parks, parking lots, by the side of the railroad tracks, in underpasses in abandoned industrial zones of the city, at the cemetery, under the branches and stars on the mountain on fine summer evenings and more. It moves transversally across questions of the material sustainability of a post-cinematic, post-celluloid, post-digital cinema to ask the question: what remains of cinema when we take it on the road, and what happens to our experiences when we have new contexts, environments, and publics for cinema events?

For some, cinema's new mobility means the loss of a "cinematic specificity," associated with the experience of actually going to a movie theatre (sometimes called the "cathedral of cinema"). But a cursory glance at cinema history reveals that any presumed homogenous institutionality of the theatre space is illusory. It's not simply our mobile devices that are taking cinema out of the (architectural) box. Cinema's territory, both that of actual projections and also of its ability to generate what Guattari calls an "ecology of the phantasm," has always been mobile (2008: 57). Historically, the cinema has been a heterotopic space of social mixing, performative disciplinarity and political potential. Quebec, for example, is home to one of, if not the first, dedicated movie theatre (rather than a theatre adapted to show films alongside other forms of live entertainment) in the world: the Ouimetoscope built in 1906 by Leo-Ernest Ouimet the entrepreneur. Early cinema was influentially theorized as an alternative public sphere by Miriam Hansen, a site of the mixing and social contagion of different classes, races and genders.[4] In Montreal, the Ouimetoscope was a territory that heterotopically reanimated the techniques of togetherness that the Catholic Church at that time dominated through spectacle and biopolitical management of population. Ouimet's Sunday screenings provided citizens a breather from the iron grip of the church, through collective modes of socialibility. At the turn of the 20th century, church leaders in Quebec (hand in glove with the government) were raising alarm over cinema's poaching of audiences for the religious and disciplinary spectacle of Sunday mass, and attempted to invoke their para-governmental authority by banning Sunday screenings (McKenzie 2004: 74). This was resisted both by the public (a 1907 ban instigated by the Archbishop of Montreal led to a protest of more than 10,000 people of a population of around 250,000) and private interests (82). Ouimet, Québec's first movie impresario, was able to remain open by repackaging his space on Sundays as a corner store, selling candy in his lobby; buy a candy bar, get a movie ticket for free. Condemned by the church as the "devil's night classes," cinema's artificial night served a territory for an alternative sociability. While mediation might look to the content of what was screened as the source of concern, immediation explores the effects of the unruly spatio-temporal territories of cinema as a site of togetherness beyond the church's codified regime.

While cinema has been repeatedly declared "dead" over its century-plus of existence, a cinematic *quality* has proven surprisingly resilient as it migrates between media forms, urban ecologies and an "anarchive" of social memory and embodied practice. But as the new mobility of cinema means that we can have "cinematic experiences" in novel and unexpected ways, what are the new potential for collective encounters and compositions that "the cinematic" activates? What remains of cinema when we take it on the road, and what happens to our experiences when we have new contexts, environments, and publics for cinema events? And in the case of *Cinema Out of the Box*, how does its flexible experimental structure activate an experience of immediation, through its ambiguous architecture of media, ecology and embodiment?

Ambience and Ambulation

COTB is a project that emerged directly from my pedagogical practice at my university, through what it means to take a research-creation approach to thinking cinema, and as such is intimately connected with the pedagogical potential of using public spaces. Thinking about immediation through *COTB* requires a detour through the undercommons of university education in Montreal in the contemporary moment. At McGill I teach cinema and cultural studies, but I also take what we call a research-creation, or thinking through making, approach to cinema and media studies. I don't train students in technique per se, but I ask them to tackle basic ideas about cinema through production practice, despite the lack of cinema production on offer at the university. Consistently, the question of how and where to screen such productions has been a central and productive problem in these classes. If the cathedral of cinema has lost its hegemony in movie consumption practices, it was also the case that students chaffed against the implicit restriction that their work was meant to be delivered to a theatrical screen. For instance, in a class I taught on Canadian filmmaker Guy Maddin (that groundbreaking experimenter in "anarchival practices"), thirty-two of my students collaboratively prepared a final performance/ installation, "The Dominion of Forgetfulness" inspired by Maddin's works, snaking through the underground tunnels that linked McGill's Redpath library to the Arts Building. Writing about it, I described it as: "Taking off from Maddin's anarchival practices of memory and cinema in *My Winnipeg, The Dominion of Forgetfulness* proposed a new expanded cinema that both spatially and temporally redistributed the experience of cinema, an immersion not only in a sensationally intensive physical architecture, but also one rich in the immersive sense of time itself." What I didn't write at the time was that beyond the logistical challenges of kitting out a found space with heaps of projectors and amplifiers and lights was the more pressing problem of the lack of access and entitlement to that space for students on their own campus. What kind of permission do you need to occupy a zone of passage for the space of an evening? Someone pulled a fire alarm on us, the trucks came, and the administration wrote the next morning to find out what we had been up to.

McGill University is a campus without a cinema, without an art gallery, and with few official spaces for art. My work with students continually runs up against this not as a limitation, but as a potential. When art is unframed, everything becomes the matter at hand for making. I found myself always thinking about both the practical problem of screening in unusual spaces (like the lack of power) but also what happened when you tried to use these spaces. The question provoked by cinema's movement out of the box is one of the territory made out of time, a refrain function of the cinematic. Something was making itself felt through the errancy and errors of this type of experimental mobility.

In *What is Philosophy?* Deleuze and Guattari write about the territory of art as a function of art's self-standing, one that exceeds the material support of objective existence as much as it escapes capture in subjective modes of memory, embodiment or intention. They write: "the territory implies the emergence of pure sensory qualities, of sensibilia that cease to be merely functional and become expressive features, making possible a transformation of functions" (1994: 184). This self-standing is a form of affective autonomy that I call immediation. Such a territory does not pre-exist; rather its self-standing is made and remade through a refrain function. With *Cinema Out of the Box* during the projection of a film, such emergent qualities might include the wind in the trees, the sound of pedaling, the sweetness of one person offering to take over the work from a breathless rider, a raccoon waiting until people leave to scour the grounds for a midnight snack, car headlights passing across the screen and doubling the projector's beam in a small arcing dance, dogs welcomed along with their owners, dogs doggedly walking their owners past the screening, the mobile media of headphones insulating passing joggers from auditory contagions, mosquitos, cops cruising past or slowing down, the smell of pot drifting across a large crowd, a relay of pitching arms before the film launching ropes into branches to hang the screen,

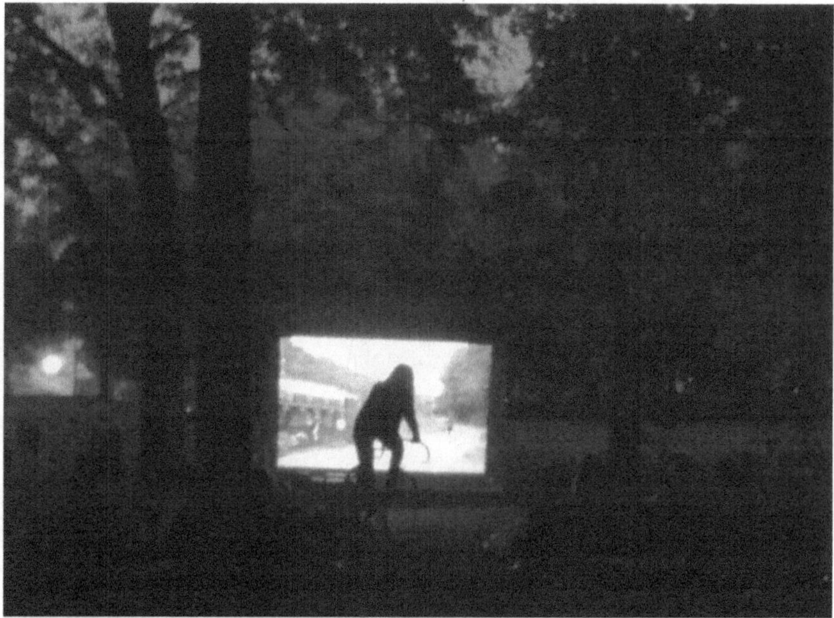

Figure 35. Unknown screening. Photo credit: Cinema Out of the Box.

the self-ushering illuminations of cell phones as people head off into the night after the movie, the lure of brightness or noise that draws people in off of their intended trajectories with curiosity, a shyness that keeps people on the edge of the crowd, uncertain of their invitation, the surround soundscape of urban life edging its way into the film in a novel synchresis, the surprisingly persistent discipline of a theatrical audience, the slow rippling of the screen in the breeze between trees, the luminous intrusions of surrounding buildings or streetlights, the accordion player across the lake unintentionally twining with the soundtrack "proper," the pleasures of anonymity as viewers arrive and leave in the dark, the scent and feel of grass or concrete or blanket under you. The question the format poses more or less insistently, with and through the particularities of programming is always: what counts as part of the show?

The Movement Impulse

One piece of the practical apparatus for COTB was an anarchival relic from a 2013 Immediations event called Three Mile Meal, a collaboration with Boston's Design Studio for Social Intervention (DS4SI) who work to change "how social justice is imagined, developed and deployed."[5] They collaborate with nonprofits to inventively "create new forms of effective social intervention and the exploration of new ways to be interventionists." Working with their expertise, we created public kitchens in three sites in Montreal over three days, travelling between them on bicycles to circulate energy, ideas and experiences and using common spaces: sidewalks, alleyways, parks and street corners. At one site outside a neighbourhood fruiterie, we made smoothies from donated fruit to offer passersby, who often swapped stories in the time it took to blend. For this, we needed a way to power the blender, and I purchased a bike-powered generator online to use for the event. When the event was over, I wondered what else we could do with it, and how it might fit into my challenge of staging new distributed cinemas.

One month later, during a research-creation event I organized called "Time Forms: The Temporalities of Aesthetic Experience,"[6] artist-researcher Sean Smith of the Department of Biological Flow organized "The Acceleration Tour," a race from one work of public art to another.[7] With Mont Royal at the heart of the race's urban trajectory, I asked my former student Tyler Lawson to screen a work he shot on the mountain, *Speeds and Slownesses*, on location.

At the end of the race around the downtown core, the Acceleration Tour ended deep in the forest on this mountain. As we caught our breath, we lived the doubled time of the recorded and the now, the edge of the work bleeding off the screen and fringing the experience. Hearts pounding, it took a while to sync up with the screen and land on site. Time stretched as the tour raced back into our bodies. In this intensive moment, unable to properly focus, we were immediated. Not so much an immersive experience that draws in the edges of perception, immediation insistently asks, could this be part of what is happening?

A movement impulse, of bodies and attention, drives *COTB*. Portable digital technologies raise the potential that the small screen of portable media might produce a cinematic architecture as a creative territory, and as a way to make new kinds of cinematic experiences. In turn this produces new modes of embodiment often and alternately theorized as posing a radically democratic potential for activating individual autonomy, or as producing what Deleuze terms the endlessly flexible dividual (Deleuze 1992, 5). *Cinema Out of the Box* has instead explored the disjunctive and recombinatory potential of these media movements not simply as an artifactual effect of devices, but as a way to reanimate

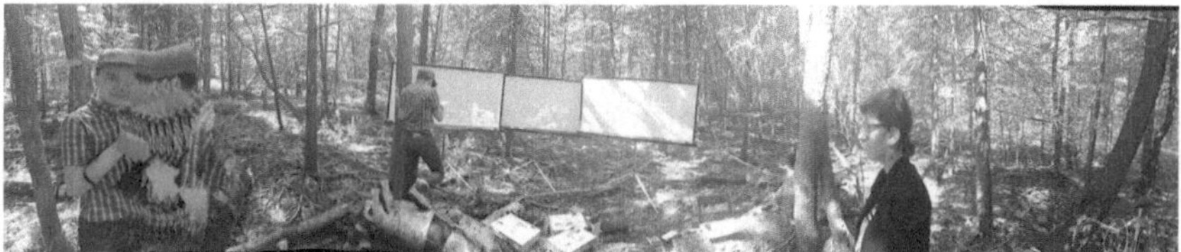

Figure 36. Speeds and Slownesses on Mont Royal during Time Forms. Photo Credit: Cinema Out of the Box

the record of the media archives of text, memories and spectatorial habits we all live. We rely on the histories and habits of bodies, media texts and cinema's ephemeral architecture to somehow produce a self-standing of the cinematic event as a territory, rather than to determine and police spectators who already know what to expect and how to behave.

There are numerous iterations of open air cinemas in Montreal and indeed around the world. In Melbourne you can go to the movies on the beach, if you have cash to get past the gate. In Bologna, "Sotto le stelle del cinema" time shifts history by screening classic cinema in the spectacular historical setting of Piazza Maggiore. London's "Hot Tub Cinema" is exactly as it sounds. Part of a global phenomenon of the festivalization of nominally public spaces, many of these use cinema as a bounded punctuation, precoding the ephemeral environment as container.[8] COTB's uniqueness in Montreal is that it is a fully mobile cinema, that aims not to recreate a bounded space for an outdoor screening, but to draw in aspects of urban, natural and social ecologies to fray the edges of what can count as the cinematic in a deterritorializing practice. We do not need an ever-more finely attuned design that pre-determines what we need, but to invite precisely the experimental and emergent into the heart of our practice. Art, says Deleuze, is neither information nor communication—what he calls the communication of "order-words" that tells you what you need to know. Art is the creation of blocs of space-time as acts of resistance, or counter-information (Deleuze 1994b: 327) As a practice-led research emerging directly from my pedagogy, *COTB* resists the neo-liberal imperative to efficiently stream information and involves instead a slow pedagogy of emergent experience. With screenings ranging from experimental gardens in abandoned lots in Montreal's Mile-Ex, to the "Champs des Possibles" citizen managed urban wilderness,[9] to the cemetery on the mountain, numerous public parks and dead zones such as underpasses, alternative student housing and reclaimed guerilla gardens and in collaboration with community organizers, student groups and the growing crowd of passers-by and regular participants, *COTB* is a practical and continuing experiment into post-digital cinematic practice and the vibrant media ecologies of the city's built environment. Since 2013 we have held more than 50 unique screenings in collaboration with 45 different campus and community organizations and curators.

As practice-led research, *COTB* brings together two concerns: practices of post-digital cinema and the political potential of ambiguous embodiments, such as we experience in our transversal movements within what Felix Guattari terms the three ecologies: the mental, the social and the environmental. This is "ecosophical research":

> At every level, individual or collective, in everyday life as well as the reinvention of democracy (concerning town planning, artistic creation, sport, etc.), it is a question in each instance of looking into what would be the dispositives of the production of subjectivity, which tends towards an individual and/or collective resingularization rather than that of mass media manufacture, which is synonymous with distress and despair. (Guattari 2008: 34)

The refrain function of COTB each time begins with an attempt to find a resonance between film and location (from the obvious, such as screening the cemetery-set *La Rose de Fer* in an actual cemetery, to the suggestive, such as the science fiction dystopia of *Beyond the Black Rainbow* in a post-industrial wasteland under an overpass). We then seek to activate a fragile society of spectator-participants (ranging from a dozen to several hundred on any given night), to explore this resingularization through immediation, a continual calling in and on of the surrounding ecologies to the phantasmatic territory of the projection's space-time. Media ecologies are transversal in nature, sites of partial subjectivities that include phantasms, social sites of collective experience and environmental spaces for the forces of matter as energy. They are not representational in nature but critical sites for heterogenesis, or resingularizations—that is to say, they are, or can be, productive. Immediation signals this emergent urgency of the now that is not simply the present.

Guattari's three ecologies diagram the space of a micro-political practice of ethico-aesthetics. In other words, he did not feel that art was a rarefied experience, but in fact the very stuff of life itself. As cinema loses its distinct edges, we see anew a political potential not of representation, nor of a pseudo-democratic interactivity premised on intentionality, agency and prescribed access, but a constant experimentation in heterogenesis. Behind this thinking for me is an understanding that COTB is an attempt to activate a media ecology that activates three approaches to the commons, as a site of shared concerns.

The first concerns the ecological commons addressed by attention to sustainability, environmental concerns, land use, our shared ecosystems, and bike/ people power. At stake is the question of techniques for living together across human and nonhuman bodies. How to fold participants into our temporary multiplex is essential to the process. One simple way is the bike as lure for both actual participation—we need people to ride to power the projection, and we invite them to do so at the beginning of each show without determining in advance how this will happen—and as a visual and sonic "static" during the show. Logistics demand that the bike be placed at the front near the edge of the screen. You can't help but hear the squeak of the wheel, the murmured exchanges as riders hand off, or constantly catch the movements of the biking out of the corner of the eye. Fraying the edges of attention, the format invites both passive and active modes of participation throughout. When spectators are also co-producers, their motivations, knowledge and skills become part of the production praxis not just because of what they are explicitly invited to do but because of a sense of potential, leading to new ways of interacting and coordinating social and economic life. A new production of learning-by-doing-with then becomes possible, in excess of the habitual expertise we all share as movie-goers.

A second territory animated by COTB is that of the urban commons: what are the spaces in the city that can be activated by tending and that can be open to all? One of the things that we consistently have not done is ask for permission to hold our events, with two exceptions (the cemetery and the Champs des Possibles). About 50% of our events have taken place in "public" spaces such as parks. Parks are theoretically open to everyone and in practice completely regulated. One of the great things about living in a densely-populated city like Montreal, for instance, is that most people in the city centre don't have private outdoor spaces of their own. This means that as soon as it gets warm, people treat public parks like private yards. But for many people, the experience of using a public space, like a park, is one that is highly regulated, and those regulations are unevenly enforced. Technically, we are not supposed to be in many public parks in the city between 12 and 6am. So one of the things we like to explore is the potential to make apparent a commons beneath the public. At a screening of *5 Broken Cameras*, the documentary about dispossession in the West Bank, a man arrived well into the film and began yelling intermittently at the screen, sometimes reading subtitles before tapering off, sometimes simply arguing excitedly, especially during scenes of great violence. As the "host" of the screening, I felt an anxiety about how to act, if I should intervene, and what I would do if his verbal belligerence, so at odds with the culture of discrete sonority of most moviegoers, became something more. I didn't act, but waited, sometimes very distractedly. Ultimately, hospitality is not the right mode for this event, as the territory is not mine. But the screening's ambiguous edges that night included the space that for all I knew was the home turf of this man, who may have been homeless, or high, or excited, or who correctly read the screening's open format as an invitation to engage. How is this not understood as part of the event, and how could future events find ways to open more fully to a society beyond those with the invited confidence of having heard of this on social media?

Lastly, COTB seeks to animate a cultural commons of uncertain ownership: how do ideas, cultures, languages and images that we share in but do not own circulate and what are our claims on them? The immediation COTB seeks to provoke includes, but necessarily exceeds, the memories of an embodied cinematic experience that any single spectator brings with them, an archive of media experiences. The ubiquity of media today is often reviled as the atmospheric pollution of advertising and the inescapable sound bath of media escaping the boundaries of headphones and portable devices. When we screened Spike Lee's *Do the Right Thing*, in summer of 2015, the indiscrete scale and relentless repetition of Radio Raheem's enormous boombox and insistent presence was an ongoing invitation to collective resingularization in the face of racism and police brutality. That screening and Raheem's violent suffocation at the hands of police anarchivally linked up with a mobile media ecology still breathing today in the re-circulation of this film in the wake of #BlackLivesMatter after the murder of Eric Garner. COTB's participatory and ephemeral architecture seeks, in a minor way, moments where "the air still has the turbulence, the gust of wind, and the light that it had that day last year, and it no longer depends on whoever was breathing it that morning" as the promise of immediation's creative and autonomous now (Deleuze and Guattari 1994: 163).

Notes

1. See: Alanna Thain, "Suspended (re)animations: Affect, Immediation and the Film Body". (2005).
2. See: http://mirl.lab.mcgill.ca/?page_id=814
3. *Cinema Out of the Box* has had many guest curators and partner organizations over the years, but I note here Claire Drummond, Steph Berrington, Tyler Lawson and Thomas Pringle as the main student researchers on the project, and Brian Bergstrom as an important and enthusiastic collaborator.
4. See Miriam Hansen's "Early Cinema, Late Cinema: Transformations of the Public Sphere." (1993)
5. Design Studio for Social Intervention website "Mission" http://ds4si.org/mission/
6. *Time Forms: The Temporalities of Aesthetic Experience*, Sept. 18-21, 2013. Organized by Eric Lewis, Stephen McAdams and Alanna Thain, McGill University. http://mirl.lab.mcgill.ca/?page_id=499
7. *Department of Biological Flow*, "The Acceleration Tour" http://www.departmentofbiologicalflow.net/curated-events/the-acceleration-tour/
8. See for example Eleonora Diamanti's work on festivalization and container spaces in Montreal. "Formation et transformation de la place publique montréalaise." (2014)
9. 121 Les Amis du Champs des Possibles http://amisduchamp.com/

Julia Bee

Pure Experience and *True Detective*: Immediation, Diagrams, Milieu

1. Media's Immediation

Production and perception are two concepts used to describe media's relation to the world. In its realist version the concept of perception is based on the idea of a world of stable things represented by "the media." In its constructive version, this world is constructed through the media. Both concepts take "world" and "media" as given yet separated realms. The concept of immediation undoes these dichotomies by intertwining the processes of production and perception and thereby creating assemblages of immanent media.

This becoming of media intermingles, folds and relates with experience. Rather than unmediated *or* mediated, immediation is experienced and it is experience *itself*, as will be outlined below. Media's audio-visual constitution itself consists of experience: media's immanent immediation. In this article I will discuss how media is not detached from experience: it is regarded as form of content as well as form of expression. By thinking through the stream-like imagery of a 'minor' but popular form of media—a TV-series' intro—I suggest the following: Audio-visual media is enfolded in experience rather than experience being represented by media. With William James I argue that experience is the very "stuff" imagery is made of. The metamorphic forms of images of the intro of *True Detective* analyzed here perform processes of audio-visual media becoming as micro-differentiations of emerging experience.

Immediation exceeds the event, differentiates it further (see Manning and Massumi 2015: 147), transfers it as an ongoing process of experience. Assemblages of experience consist of ongoing immediation—of production and reception—rather than subjects experiencing media, which represents a detached world. Immediation runs transversally to the realm of entities. It becomes as emerging perception, it constantly creates micro shifts of becoming something else. The process is the experience, or as James puts it: "The fundamental fact about our experience is that it is a process of change" (James 1986: 89).

Immediation here produces something new rather than represents something given. This relates to recent approaches in media theory: Following Parikka in his perspective on media as the creation of a new space-time, immediation operates not outside or prior to media but from within. "Media are an action of folding time, space and agencies; media are not the substance, or the form through which mediated actions take place but an environment of relations in which time space and agency take place" (Parikka 2011: 35).

Media's immediation changes what is usually perceived as actual stable entities or as mediation in between existing entities. As immanent process in the becoming of media immediation is an ongoing space-time-mattering: It produces assemblages of media as an ongoing material *and* experiential becoming.

The events of immediation exceed and undo media's stable framework. To think media from the perspective of immediation one needs to start with experience:[1] Not just the experience of the observer but of media itself. Experience—in its radical empirical notion developed by William James—is not performed by a given entity. It is productive and of the logic of the event. In the first place, immediation begins with a relation.

2. Radical Immediation

William James' notion of experience can be read as closely connected to experience as event: as immediation. Experience is neither only *in* nor *of* entities but a constant flux and transformation, its wave-likeness as James terms it. But the stream of experience is neither substantial nor homogeneous.[2] Experience is *in* transition, *of* transition and becoming. The "world of pure experience" (James 1912: 39-91) is a constant becoming and transformation of knower and known, subject and object, inside and outside. *Pure experience* as James calls it is the "flux of life" itself (James 1912: 93). Starting with pure experience as non/human does not mean to start with the representation either of human *or* nonhuman experiences, with subjects or objects but with a world full of perception and affection: " ... there is only one primordial stuff or material in the world, a stuff of which everything is composed, and if we call that stuff 'pure experience' then knowing can easily be explained as a particular sort of relation ... " (4).

"Pure" means that experience is not yet dichotomized into subject and object, it belongs to no one yet—it is an immanent field of experience (Lapoujade 2000; Soldhju 2006: 44). It is therefore not purified but virtual:

> It [pureness of experience] marks the processual co-presence of a self-creating subject of experience with what will prove to have been its object, together in the making. "Pure experience" is not in the least reduced or impoverished. It is overfull. It is brimming "virtually or potentially" (Massumi 2011: 10)[3]

Experience is the *more-than* of an event (see Manning 2013). It is an ongoing process out of which subjects and objects emerge and actualize temporarily and retrospectively—branching out from a wave-crest of rolling events of becomings.[4]

James uses the wave or wave patterns like interference patterns ("fringes") to describe experience as changing, becoming, and fading. Experience is not secondary to a conscious subject, or to a subject at all. It is a relation in time.[5] Experience in its transitional becoming, its character of in betweenness, and of betwixtness is not a half-being, but a real virtual becoming of experience.[6] The fabric of experience is primarily a reaching toward or an in between and not as we often think of those states a deficient representation of objects by subjects. Experience is movement, flux, becoming, not of something but with the things (see James 1996b: 7).

Experience makes itself felt in its continuous-discontinuous self-variation, the flux of life that is constantly "off its balance" and "in transition" (James 1996b: 283). It is a non-identical event in its transition, vibration, pulsation, flowing, its growing and fading. In the *Principles of Psychology* James writes of the "feeling of *and*, a feeling of *if*, a feeling of *but*, and a feeling of *by*, quite as readily as we say a feeling of *blue* or a feeling of *cold*" (1950a: 245-246).

Experience consists less in elements than in tendencies, directions, echoes, and coronas, interferences: its so called "fringes" (James

1950a: 259-267) that extend and grow into the next experience or are superimposed by the last.

In the *stream of thought* no dualism between material and mental world exists, it is rather a continuity of things, thoughts and feelings that are describable as scenery or assemblage. We do not perceive book and table, but "book-on-table" (James 1912: 118). This stream, again, consists at the same time in separations and associations that are themselves experienced. They describe the continuous discontinuity of sensation, thinking and feeling in a world of experience: "*But thoughts in the concrete are made of the same stuff as things are*" (37). The continuity of the stream of experience itself *experiences* the discontinuity:[7] experience is relation and relation is experience:

> For such a philosophy, the relations that connect experiences must themselves be experienced relations, and any kind of relation experienced must be accounted as real as anything else in the system (James 1912: 42).

Not only are relations experienced directly, but the fabric of experience constantly transforms itself in a nonlinear way. Experience itself relates elements and builds a consciousness by relating experiences. It co-emerges or results from experiences. Every experience is immanent and processual, it weaves the world and is the weaving itself. It does not need an instance outside of experience, as it productively weaves together experiences: "In the play of conjunction and disjunction the event of experience itself becomes a bridge between past and the not yet happened" (Brunner 2011: 129). To start with the transformative virtual change of experience means taking experience as inventive of relation and as a construction—but that agency is of the event.

As Brian Massumi puts it in reference to James:

> Thought and thing, subject and object, are not entities or substances. They are irreducibly temporal *modes of relations of experience to itself*.... In experience what goes along comes around. The world rolls in on itself, over its own expectations of reaching an end.... The world revolves around its momentous relation to itself (Massumi 2011: 34).

Experience is not built on a pre-existing consciousness or (human) subject, rather subjectivity emerges situational as knower and known in a relation derived from pure experience. That changes perspectives on epistemology. As David Lapoujade describes it, in this view not only the human spectator sees a how chemicals crystallize but chemicals themselves undergo the experience of crystallization: "Insofar as it is pure, experience is not said of us, it is said of the things in relation: it is the chloride and the sodium which crystallize; it is they which can therefore rightly be said to be undergoing the experience of crystallization" (Lapoujade 2000: 193).

Experience *is* the event of "*worlding*" (Manning 2013, 169), that means the world is *of* experiences rather than given in experience. The world "grows" creatively by experience; experience is the "stuff" (James 1912: 4) fabric or "tissue" (57) of the world.[8] Thereby he is challenging the hylomorphic schema of form over matter by introducing the material of experience as directly "physical-mental" (Lapoujade 2000: 194). "There is no thought-stuff different from thing-stuff" (James 1912: 137).

William James' pragmatism is often misunderstood as subjective instrumentalism. But it is a situational ethic, not a normative one. Following what is experienced *really* is the becoming of experience: The wave-likeness of actualization is felt as a process and virtuality in its own right, which is contrary to a positivist empirical approach. It claims a relational reality (Massumi 2011: 85): Experience itself is becoming other, starting from the perspective of a world of experience, not a world of entities, that make experiences in the second place: an "ontogenesis of experience" (Massumi and McKim. 2008: 25).

The concept of immediation takes up William James' notion of experience and expresses it on a different plane of thought.[9] William James notion of "radical empiricism" as well as "pure experience" served as a framework to analyze audio-visual media aesthetics as "ecologies of experience" (Manning & Massumi 2014; for the network as experience-making see Munster 2013). Immediation outruns dichotomies of subject/object and production/reception by composing transversal movements and processes of experience.[10] "Pure experience" is not prior to mediation but enfolded in the becoming of forms of media itself: not immediacy *or* representation but immanence. Usually media is regarded as a force of the formation of experience. A notion of pure experience in a constructivist perspective would belong to an unmediated sphere. Necessarily an unmediated sphere would produce resentments because of its "naïve" point of view.

Experience as event is key for a rethinking of media through immediation: It is the immediation of forms of media, as an emerging ecology of experience in itself—it is not an experience defined from the subject's point of view, i.e. the viewer's perspective. Its beginning is in the midst: neither the media nor the spectatorial subject are the starting point of the pure experience. They are the result of the process. Media apparatuses or subjects are not the only participants of processes of immediation. It is rather an assemblage of perception and production that transverses the entities by relating *and* differentiating them in ecologies of experience. Immediation is the differential becoming of media itself (see Murphie 2014). Immediation is worlding as experience. A world that experiences itself: "Media (and technics more generally) are in constant variation, immanently, as part of the world (as medium)'s ongoing variation" (Murphie 2014: 192), so that "sense, sensation and technics come together to constantly transform all three" (193).

3. Diagrams of Experience

How to conceive of forms of audio-visual media as an assemblage or ecology of human and media experiences if they are not a representation of anything in the world, but a part of a *world of pure experience,* as James terms it (1912: 39-91). Simply turn on the TV: Assemblages of images in which no inside and outside, no foreground or background can be fixed. Images of the Gulf Cost, industrial and petrochemical landscapes, human silhouettes, an interchange of highways, and trucks are pictured through dissolve technique. Oilrigs take shape, a church and a deer evolve and dissolve in a fire. In the optical depth of one image the emergence of new images takes place directly in the former images' contours. In one's perishing another figure emergences. Foreground and background shift constantly and vertiginous through each other: Form and matter, milieu and figure create a rhythm of fading away and taking shape. Landscapes emerge in the outline of human silhouettes. Another contour for another landscape: A factory appears in the silhouette of a face. One becomes an ocean, a face appears in a telephone and when the contours of the phone begin to solve, a street crossing appears.

These images are animated photography: they appear as if filmed by a camera diving through the imagery of the TV-Series *True Detective* (HBO 2014-).[11] This credit sequence, which introduces the series, consists

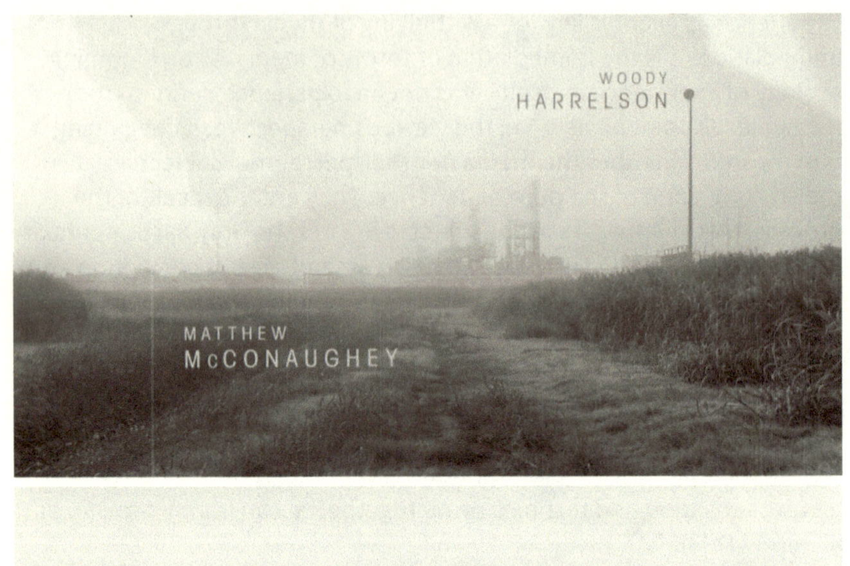
WOODY
HARRELSON
MATTHEW
McCONAUGHEY

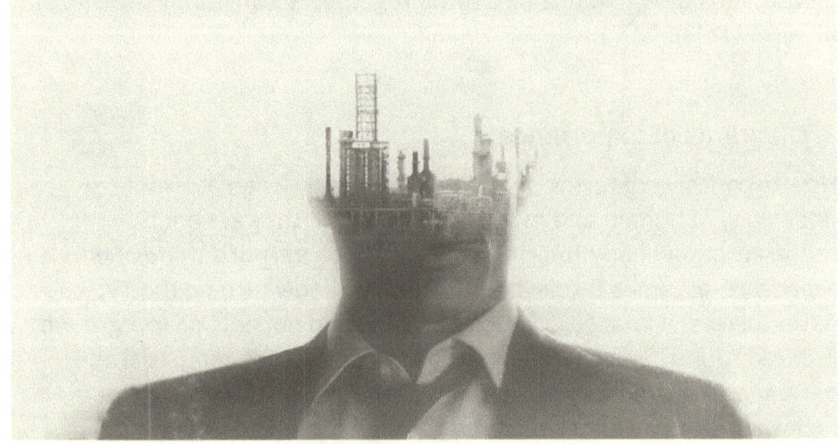

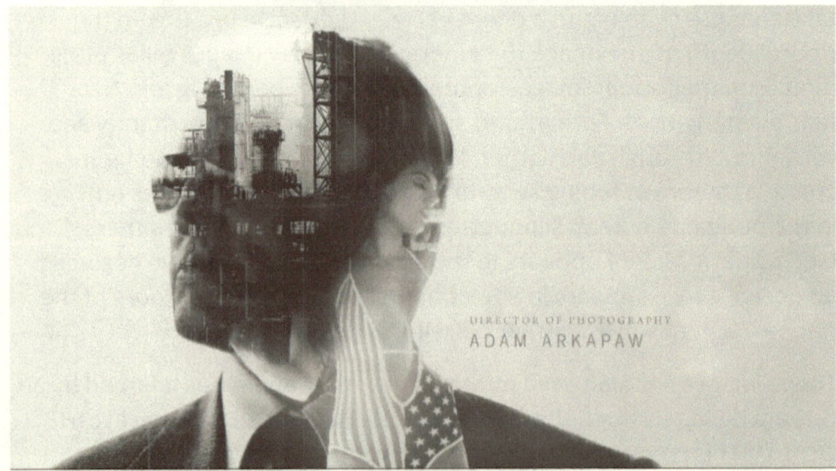
DIRECTOR OF PHOTOGRAPHY
ADAM ARKAPAW

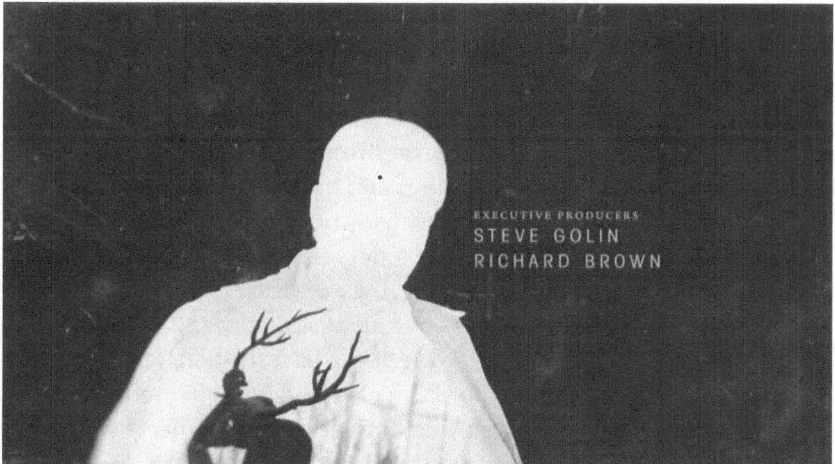

Figures 37-40. Stills from the title sequence of True Detective, season 1, HBO, sequence produced by Alex Gansa, 2014

of visual impressions from the first season. It performs an abstract montage: Milieus, characters and atmospheres from the series are assembled into a stream of excerpts that zap through the show. It is a montage of different layers of animation. Dissolving frames alter and intensify the show's images in the process of constant variation.

With the intro of *True Detective* the thinking about experience becomes thinking *with* experience. The stream of images opens up an immanent way of researching media with media. In the intro, images experience images, they fold into each other and thereby create an ecological experience as well as an experience of the milieu.[12] This is the immediate process of the intro's becoming experience. The process is not simply experienced from the outside, it is experienced *as* process: A process full of micro shifts that intensify the emerging continuity of fading and becoming of images at the very same time.

Oil rigs, industrial landscapes, pollution, shapes of deer and symbols of religious practices are projected with superimposed landscapes. Photography loses its flatness and becomes three-dimensional. Animated by a virtual camera perspective, different media technologies overlap. Photography, 3D animation, and layering animation create a human-nonhuman assemblage as partial double exposure, executed only to parts of the images, which makes them appear as a deepness out of which new images flower.

Silhouettes of human bodies and landscapes, industrial machines like oil refineries, technical devices like telephones as well as streets and trucks merge to a flux where boundaries of objects and bodies become hardly distinguishable. The experience acts like a field that enrolls and enfolds itself alternately. What emerges from what is barely definable: technical devices, industrial machines and human bodies merge with landscapes, fading away the moment they become recognizable. The *how* of the images' emergence is the emergence of experience. It is not secondary to the "entities'" becoming: they *are* their movement or mode of becoming experienced, as their becoming is composed of experience itself. Following James' notion of experience as transition, tendency and relation, what is diagrammed here can also be a (non-)human stream of experience unfolding. Not only do entities or images merge and emerge, experiences are continuously cross-fading through dissolve.

The technique of double exposure of fragmented portraits, "using human figures as windows into partial landscapes" (Clair 2014.) seem to embody an ecological approach, in which figures, machines and environment (technical/natural) serve as mutual milieus for each other. The effect of the virtual camera[13] diving in and through the silhouettes into the next scenery produces intermediate states of perceiving an image through the fringe of a fading image as well as movements of the fading. The emerging becomes an immanent image-perception in the sequence itself.

The appearance, formation and chance, composition and decomposition of motifs create the fabric or stuff of experience. Not only are the motifs ecological in the sense of being environmental, but the images themselves build milieus and environments through which new individuations emerge. Images form and deform procedurally and in relation to each other: Movements of formation and solution are processes of in-formation—formation and at the same time always more than formation (Simondon 2009; Manning 2013). These apparently paradoxical processes are folded into each other. The movement, dynamic and processes of the images are events of immediation: Events of affections and perceptions in which the images themselves undergo 'their' chance and perceive each other as the elements in crystallization do in Lapoujade's description above. They build a processually immanent field of experience (Lapoujade 2000), a relational consciousness as James describes it.

Watching the movement of the images from a Jamesean perspective one sees that experiences are not distinct objects or entities. They are not experienced by a subject or fixed and already formed individuals but are themselves transformative, in change and constant flux. The intro is a form or mode of becoming *of* and *in* experience. In the show's intro, the motifs, figures and affective milieus of the series emerge and fade away in an abstract way. They are not representations of what happens in the series. They intensify germs of narrations and characters and foreground the mystic theme of the crime story *The Yellow King* that the HBO adaption is based upon. As stream of consciousness, it is an abstract form of experience, enfolding multiple perspectives.

The opening credits operate as a technique of layering of body shapes. In the words of the director, this opening shows "Pollution, prostitution and wildlife at the gulf cost" (Clair 2014): Humans, landscapes, oil rigs, animals, movements of water, industrial buildings in back light: everything is partly crossfaded by other elements and finally swallowed by fire. The petrochemical landscapes in the first part seem to pre-empt the successively emerging flames that apocalyptically swallow up the human silhouettes in the last part.

The images of the intro are in transition and anticipation of the next image. Every line, every shade, every element is at the same time the depths of the actual image as well as a transition to the next image. A figure dissolves as another one emerges in its outlines. The single image itself becomes a moving transition, it becomes its own betweenness. Rhythmic (de)compositions create a milieu of images, which durationally and topologically diagram an ecology of experience (Manning and Massumi 2014). Affective and material milieus crossfade as image ecologies emerge: "The taking form of a field of consciousness has the quality of a vertiginous oscillation of figure and ground" (Manning 2011: 3). Here the consciousness is a field of perceptions and affections,[14] as well as their relation, which it operates by a process of change.[15] The diagrammatic form of the intro is a technical form of animation as well as a form of perception.[16] Its "idea" (Deleuze 1994a: 216) of experience consists of movement, transition and the experience in a transitional state of flux. It changes content and expression constantly. Here the diagram operates from within: it is an event of immediation. In the form of the intro, media becomes an immanent form of reflection.[17]The opening intro here can also be regarded as a form of preemptive perception (see Massumi 2009). It anticipates the series ritually initiated by the intro. As practice and process it abstracts the affective ecology of the series, its motifs, and subjects. Immediation adds a different perspective to the performative concept of re-mediation (see Bolter and Grusin 1999). The intro and series not only form mutually performative (re)*mediations* but also perceptions—productive events of immediation; the intro invents something new in relation to the series and gains, in a way, autonomy in it's "function" as affective opener.

Experience here is itself organized as a cartography of specific affects and percepts. Experience as diagrammed here is changing and becoming. It is productive and leads to new forms of becoming: a "diagram as technique of existence" (Massumi 2011: 87-103). If the world is made of experience, there is perception everywhere in it ... Experience always invents. Every perception is its own event. Its content is one with the dynamic form of its coming to fulfillment. What a perception invents is essentially itself. It is self-creative. (Massumi 2011: 25–27) The diagram intensifies experience. As a diagram the intro opens each episode, it creates its affective milieu. Yet, this opening is not simply "before" the episode's narration unfolds. The force of the intro operates rather in the process of the TV-series unfolding, its intervals. This is the intro's diagramming from within. Media's immediation—abstract *and* immanent.

The diagram as opening abstracts from the linear narration by showing seemingly mysterious images, and intensifies these by associating them with dramatic and religious, as well as eroticized, backgrounds of the (white) male-centred narration. The upcoming episode is already affectively and pre-emptively anticipated (or "fringed," as James calls it).

The milieus of the intro of *True Detective* re- and deterritorialize forms and subjectivities related to visual and musical rhythms and metastable plateaus: The constitution of experience is at the same time its transformation and transgression. Outside and inside are constantly changing borders including the strong maintenance of an inside, which is an outside of a figure or body shape: a face becomes a telephone becomes another face and crossed legs become streets crossed. Content and expression constantly change their function. The opening credits of *True Detective* operate as a rhythmic, pulsating machine of perception in between a diagram and a dispositive, in between extraction of a function and the intensity of a milieu.

Diagrams immediate experience. In the intro, experience crosses transversally through fields of the subjective and objective, affect and percept or productions and receptions. The diagram of the intro is an emerging field of experience as well as a field of consciousness. The aesthetics of transition, of inside, outside, foreground, background create an ecology of experience as becoming in the very operation of that becoming. The diagram works as intensification: immediation is the event of becoming abstracted from within.

4. Immediations of the Milieu

When director Patrick Clair states in an interview that the landscapes of the southern states in the intro of *True Detective* were deployed to characterize the protagonists in the series, this does not only mean they are represented by it symbolically. The aesthetics are related to a thinking of the co-emergence of human and nonhuman environment or individuation and associated milieu. The milieu is not only the content of the show or the intro: The medium itself is a milieu. This is the two-folded process of media's immediation. The milieu of the intro intensifies expression. The events of immediation operate through and as part of the milieu.

The milieu consists in differentials of intensity, causing energetic discrepancies that build metastable situations which provoke operations to produce new metastable, precarious "springboards for becoming[s]" (Massumi 2014: 24). Immediation leads to the expression of a milieu building new milieus.

The intro expresses an environment without representing it. It consists in nothing other than pure expression of a virtual potential—as process of experience. What is experience and experienced is a process of constant alteration of expression and content: an ecology of perception.

The milieu creatively expresses, its feeding into and exceeding of form are events of immediation. Immediation does not lead to a stable forecast of the ends of the process. The experiences of the intro are relational yet autonomous operations, which emerge transversally as technological, stylistic, aesthetic and perceiving transindividuations and infraindividuations. It is less the (new) media product intro but rather the emerging field of experience that is key to the *process* of immediation. With an expression of Deleuze, this can be described as experiential ontogenesis.[18] The intro is the immanent form of expression and reception of the series. Immediation here becomes an immanent media process of a "meta"-commentatory—from within. The experiences create (dis)continuities in between machinic practices and apparatuses in transition and relation: an assemblage whose parts do not pre-exist its events and processes of immediation. Techniques of experience *and* technical apparatuses, diagrams of experience *and* media apparatuses create a transitory hyper-differentiated network, whose (dis)continuities lead to new experiences.

From the perspective of immediation, processes of audio-visual mediations *make* experiences. They create new experiences: as individuations of spectators and audiences, or: audience-assemblages. These events of immediations exceed the material border of the media apparatus. Experience informs ever-new experiential ontogenesis. These events of expression in-form pictorial, sonic, human as well as (non-)human individuations, films, practices, genres and much more. They feed into individuations of other forms of media.

It also in-forms in a nonlinear way the events around the TV-set, affections, thoughts, as well as light/sound waves interfering with other waves in interference patterns. It feeds into new blocs of affects and percepts: modes of perception, becomings, assemblages of desire, fandom etc.

Forms of diagrammatic audio-visual media like the intro to *True Detective* are crafted from experiences. Experiences of individuation, immediately perceived: as dynamic speeds and slownesses, as transition, and rhythm. Experience is an ontogenetic force creating assemblages of images. These images are not only experienced *by* humans: Immediations emerge across, beyond and with human/nonhuman assemblages, blocs and ecologies of human/nonhuman experiences. Immediation becomes an autonomous form of expression: expression of the milieu. The milieu expresses immediate but not unmediated becomings and individuations: events of immediation transverse assamblages of media. These conjunctive networks of media are full of experiences (see Munster 2013). Immediation is the plane of immanence of (media-)experience that can "grows by its edges" (James 1912: 87).

Notes

1. For media as ecology of perception see Parisi 2009b.
2. "There is no *general* stuff of which experience at large is made. There are as many stuffs as there are 'natures' in the things experienced. If you ask what any one bit of pure experience is made of, the answer is always the same: "it is made of *that*, of just what appears, of space, of intensity, of flatness, brownness, heaviness, or what not."... Experience is only a collective name for all these sensible natures, and save for time and space (and, if you like, for 'being') there appears no universal element of which all things are made" (James 1912: 25–26).
3. By the phrases "pure experience" and "virtually or potentially" Massumi refers to James.
4. "We live, as it were, upon the front edge of an advancing wave-crest, and our sense of a determinate direction in falling forward is all we cover of the future of our path. It is as if a differential quotient should be conscious and treat itself as an adequate substitute for a traced-out curve. Our experience, inter alia, is of variation of rate and direction, and lives in these transitions more than in the journey's end. The experiences of tendency are sufficient to act upon—what more could we have done at those moments even if the later verification comes complete?" (James 1986: 116-117).
5. "According to my view, experience as a whole is a process in time, whereby innumerable particular terms lapse and are superseded by others that follow upon them by transitions which, whether disjunctive or conjunctive in content, are themselves experiences, and must in general be accounted at least as real as the terms which they relate" (James 1986: 111).
6. "Every examiner of the sensible life *in concreto* must see that relations of every sort, of time, space, difference, likeness, change, rate, cause, or what not, are just as integral members of the sensational flux as terms are, and that conjunctive relations are just as true members of the flux as disjunctive relations are" (James 1950a: 4).
7. It therefore demands a new thinking of continuity and discontinuity, related to what can be perceived as chance and continuity, substance and flux: they all build no opposites. This results from the creative and productive notion of James' experience. Discontinuity is not the dichotomous opposite of continuity—it does not interrupt a given substance but produces new relations. James finds an example to describe the nonhomogeneous, differentiating yet continuous quality of a flux of experience: "A silence may be broken by a thunder-clap, and we may be so stunned and confused for a moment by the shock as to give no instant account to ourselves of what has happened. (...) Into the awareness of the thunder itself the awareness of the previous silence creeps and continues; for what we hear when the thunder crashes is not thunder *pure*, but thunder-breaking-upon-silence-and-contrasting-with-it. Our feeling of the same objective thunder, coming in this way, is quite different from what it would be were the thunder a continuation of

a previous thunder. The thunder itself we believe to abolish and exclude the silence; but the *feeling* of the thunder is also a feeling of the silence as just gone (...)" (James 1950a: 240-241). The thunder that breaks the sky is the event of the sky disrupted: a continuity of the disruption of the lived experience of sky and thunder in relation to the new relation which is build through that experience. The experience of disruption is the lived continuity via its discontinuity.

8. "Experience itself, taken at large, can grow by its edges. That one moment it proliferates into the next by transitions which, whether conjunctive or disjunctive, continue the experiential tissue (...)" (James 1912, 87).
9. The notion of immediation has a lot of potential to reformulate ongoing debates about media ecologies (see Fuller 2005). Media ecologies focus on "ecologies of sensation" (see Parisi 2009b) distributed to environments of media apparatuses, entangled with each other like smart devices or smart homes.
10. The concept of immediation differs from the notion of a dispositive. The Intro's animation exceeds the notion of the spectator's experience as Jean-Louis Baudry and others famously argued in relation to the cinematic apparatus. It rather consists in experiences itself.
11. The intro for season one was produced by a production and animation agency, which specializes in intros and comparable media forms. For more analyses on the production process of the intro and the people involved, see the interview with the director Patrick Clair (Clair 2014). In general, intros have become more en vogue, autonomous little pieces of animation art. This phenomenon is specifically relevant to HBO or other pay TV Channels, since the broadcasting time is not as limited as in public broadcasting channels.
12. The milieu is key to the story, a milieu that exceeds the setting. Here, it is the southern gulf cost of the US where the story takes place.
13. The virtual camera describes the effect of the photography animated as if a camera would film it as a non-filmic reality.
14. Art thinks in the form of perceptions and affections, as Deleuze and Guattari argue in *What is Philosophy?* (see the chapter "percept, affect, and concept" in Deleuze & Guattari 1994,163-199). Like science and philosophy, it creates strata on the chaos to display its own form of "thinking." Art is a composition of percepts and affects. The bloc of affects and percepts is the becoming inhuman of the human itself. It is autonomous in its becoming, even if created by a human artist, because it is also made by colours, metals, words etc., which have a more than human potential to affect and which build perceptions yet unknown that change the sensory apparatus of what is known as human (178-182). The bloc of affects and percepts creates reception-perception-assemblages across audiences and forms of film, video and media art. The intro here becomes itself a form of experience rather than a representation of experience, which it immanently diagrams by concentrating and thickening the atmosphere of the TV-series.

15. James notion of consciousness, as well as everything else in the world is a certain form of flux, process, change and relation: "Consciousness does not appear to itself chopped up in bits. Such words as 'chain' or 'train' do not describe it fitly as it presents itself in the first instance. It is nothing jointed. It flows. A river or a stream are the metaphors by which it is most naturally described" (James 1950a: 239).

    It is not a representation of experience but itself experienced. "Consciousness here is a nonentity, a purely immanent function or activity. It has thus lost its uniqueness and at the same time gained a much broader sense" (Solhdju 2006: 39). Consciousness is not a substance but an activity, immanent to the process. It operates itself as relation. "Consciousness connotes a kind of external relation, and does not denote a special stuff or way of being. The peculiarity of our experiences, that they not only are, but are known, which their 'conscious' quality is invoked to explain, is better explained by their relations—these relations themselves being experiences—to one another" (James 1912: 25).

16. This diagram does not represent, it operates. It is not *about* experience but is itself an experiential form: "What the diagram diagrams is the dynamic interrelation of relations" (Massumi 1992: 9). The diagram is thus not a schematic visual representation of what experience *is*—it has no pre-given form or content. Deleuze and Guattari call it a "piloting device": "The diagrammatic or abstract machine does not function to represent, even something real, but rather constructs a real that is yet to come, a new type of reality. Thus when it constitutes points of creation or potentiality it does not stand outside history but is instead always 'prior to' history. Everything escapes, everything creates—never alone, but through an abstract machine that produces continuums of intensity, effects conjunctions of deterritorialization, and extracts expressions and contents" (Deleuze and Guattari 1987: 142).

17. Immediation situates the reflection from outside in the realm of media itself: The intro reflects on the series in the immanent form of the "philosophy of media itself" (for the "philosophy of media itself", see Engell 2014). Immediation does not reflect, it intensifies: The intro as stream of consciousness is an event of diagramming—constantly changing content and expression by extracting and concentrating the affective atmosphere of the TV-Series.

18. By placing experience in the realm of ontogenesis, ontology is understood as processual: Becoming or individuation instead of being. The emphasis lies on genesis as non-linear process. Ontogenesis or becoming is experienced and experience is placed in the middle of becoming, it is immediately experienced. Experience is not a secondary quality of the event but in its midst (see also the interview with Brian Massumi: Davis & Nguyen 2008: 25).

Interlude

Erin Manning, Anna Munster, Bodil Marie Stavning Thomsen

Twisting Into the Middle 2

Writing immediation into existence is a difficult task. We struggle with the necessity of language's linearity and wonder, collectively, at all that remains unsaid yet inhabits the thought-felt, all that experience pre-articulates, activated in the rhythm of what cannot quite be said but is nonetheless heard.

And so, we write across, finding points of entry not to explicate but to amplify, or resonate with thought's feeling, inviting you to activate a relation to immediation and see where it takes you.

One proposition: follow the schizz. Think-with the practice of metamodeling as Felix Guattari defines it in his engagement with schizoanalysis. Metamodeling is against method, against the model of a pre-given set of conditions, a hierarchy of terms of engagement. Making felt the lines of formation, metamodeling composes in the between, in the schizz of the emergent relation. It immediates, shifting the lines of what appears to be the order of things. Admitting prearticulations into its telling, metamodeling undoes the hierarchy between content and expression.

Immediation can be taken as a warning: don't be too sure where content begins and expression ends. Tend to the geology, to the emergent strata and their flows and forces, not simply to the form it wants to take. Form will happen: that's inevitable. What interests us here, with an eye to a politics that would diverge from mediation, a politics emergent from the middle of experience in the making, is how that form comes to be, and how that coming-into itself is valued.

Erin Manning and Brian Massumi
in Discussion with Christoph Brunner

Immediation

Christoph Brunner: An issue that has been coming up a lot recently regarding affect, in the European and especially German-speaking academic environment, concerns the question of what the politics of affect might be, specifically if you think about affect in relation to immediacy. The critique I often hear is that affect-oriented approaches tend to focus on the immediate without considering the historical background and the ways in which mediating frames of reference are constructed. I feel that it is very important to contextualize the notion of experience which needs to be addressed in relation to affect and immediacy.

Brian Massumi: Immediation does not exclude determinations from the past or tendings towards the future. The term 'immediation' is a way of drawing attention to the event as the primary unit of the real. The idea is that whatever is real makes itself felt in some way, and whatever makes itself felt has done so as part of an event. It has entered in some way into the immediacy of the moment as a factor in the event now taking place. This means, paradoxically, that whatever of the past is going to count in this event has to presentify itself. The first stage of an event of experience, according to Whitehead, is one of re-enaction, which I often call 'reactivation'. Whitehead makes it very clear that this inaugural phase of presentification is affective. It's a direct, unmediated feeling of what past events have left in the world for the coming event to take up as its own potential. This cannot be consciously discriminated as yet, because the event is just beginning and hasn't sorted out what it will become yet. It can only be felt. But since the feeling is of potential, it can already be construed as a kind of thinking forward. It's a thinking-feeling in the immediacy of what's coming. Immediacy, in this way of thinking about it, is always in relation to the past, but it's a direct, unmediated relation to the past as the past is coming back to life in the singularity of a given situation that hasn't yet fully played itself out. There is no general reference to the past. There's a singular inclusion of the past in oncoming activity. Immediation is actually more intensively inclusive of the past than a reflective or critical thinking about it, because it includes the *force* of the past—where it is potentially heading beyond itself, as a function of its own momentum meeting the singularity of a new arising. Immediation is the past bumping against the future in the present.

Erin Manning: Affect is a way to account for experience in its in-forming. In both our writing and in the work at the SenseLab, Brian and I often focus on affect because our concern is with how emergent experience composes in ways that are proto-political. Our recent emphasis on immediation comes out of this concern. As you know, given that you're a participant in the new project phase at the SenseLab which we've called 'Immediations', we are interested in drawing attention to how the stakes of experience occur in the immediate interstices of its coming to be. As Brian emphasizes, this coming to be does not in any way rule out the force of pastness. In fact, one of the things immediations as a concept does is emphasize the nonlinearity of the time of the event, or what I sometimes call event-time. Event-time emphasizes time's affective force, in the event. This affective force is laden with both pastness and futurity, but in a way that is singularly active in the now of experience.

Christoph Brunner: In a recent interview[1] you talk about the affective field generating an immediate in-bracing of multiple bodies in an event and in differential attunement. In that interview, you point out that any concept becomes problematic if we use it to try to generate new universals.

Erin Manning: What interests me in particular is how fields of relation agitate and activate to emerge into what I think of as collectivities. I don't mean human collectivities but ecological environments that include the human in its co-composing with the nonhuman. This is what I call the 'more-than-human'. To account for those emergent fields you need a vocabulary that touches on what Brian was talking about in his reference to pastness within immediation as 'a thinking-feeling in the immediacy of what's coming'. Whitehead calls this non-sensuous perception, emphasizing that it is essential that we understand that there is a phase of experience previous to sensory experience that is capable of accounting for how the event immanently co-composes with pastnesses in the act. Experience in this phase is non-sensuous, according to Whitehead. The force of the past that is presenting itself cannot present itself in sense-perception, for the obvious reason that the sense-perceptions belonging to the past are in the past and stay there. The reason why this is so important to me is because the privileging of sense-perception tends to lead us directly to human subjectivity—to a subjective notion of memory as founding human subjectivity. If we begin there, with the subject, with sensuous perception, with subjective memory, we begin much later in the account. Rather than seeing how the immanent event creates an emergent ecology, and then becoming interested in what this emergent ecology can do (how it expresses itself, how it is proto-political etc), we take the human as a given and ask what it is doing in the event. This places the event at the mercy of the human, rather than placing the human as part of the ecology of the event. If we do the second, we are in a complex array of experience in which the human is one among many. Or, more precisely, where there is no 'easy' category, such as 'human', to begin with. This second approach, which we are here linking to immediation, requires a different kind of work because it does not lay out, yet, the stakes of the emergent collectivity. For me the question of 'how it comes into formation' is really the political question, which is not to disparage an account that comes from another perspective, which would be a historical account of political formations, for instance. I just don't think that the force of the political in its potential for change occurs at that level.

Brian Massumi: From my point of view, in current discussions of affect there is often a misunderstanding of what is at stake. The gesture of encapsulating it in an 'affective turn', as opposed to the preceding 'linguistic turn' or any other sort of turn, assumes that affect is a thing, something that can be separated from other things, like you would put a fork on one side of your plate and the spoon on the other, and then position yourself polemically according to whether you think it's better to scoop or stab your food. It's a bit Swiftian, like arguing about which end of the egg to open. When you define affect as Spinoza does, as an ability to affect or be affected, it's clear that it's a dimension of all activity, whether we see fit to categorize that activity as subjective or objective. It is just as obvious that there is an affective dimension to language. Affect is already on the plate, whatever your preferred intellectual diet, and it lends itself to many kinds of utensils. The point of insisting on the necessity of taking affect into account is not to say that we should think about affect instead of language, or pay attention only to the infra-subjective and infra-objective germinal stirrings of events that Erin was just talking about and forget about subjects or objects. It's just not an either-or. It's a question of differing modes of activities that factor into events. The concept of affect, as taken up in a philosophy of immediation, is a way of focusing on the germinal modes of activity that factor into events as they are just beginning, and are not yet fully determined as to where they might lead. It's a directly relational concept, because you have to think the 'to affect' and 'to be affected' as two sides of the same coin of the event. Affect is a point of entry into an eventful, relational field of complexity that is already active, and still open-ended. The point of thinking with affect is to think through our implication in relational fields, and the potential we might find there. There is no general model of affect. The way the past carries over into the new event, which tendencies are reactivated, in what mix and with what formative interactions, all of that is completely singular to the situation, so the theory of affect has to be custom tailored to every field of event-formation, and even to every event. It has to be continually reinvented.

Christoph Brunner: Brian, this leads me to your exposition of bare activity and Erin's notion of the in-act. In thinking about the question of activity or the act, there is a tendency to assume that they are only concerned with emergence. But there is also Whitehead's concept of 'perishing', which you both take up in your work. I was wondering how can we think in three kinds of tonalities of activity: as bare activity, a worlding and force of life, continuation and renewing; then the act of formation of subjectivity and the kinds of inflections you can try to seek out, insert and inflect; and finally what Judith Butler calls 'supported action', underlining how there is a kind of material grounding of the vitalism of the body that needs to be sustained and supported. This last idea refers to the fact that new events are grounded in what past events that have 'perished' leave in the world for renewal. Some people might think that the politics, ethics and aesthetics of emergence have overemphasized one end of the continuum, whereas we also need to include an ethics and aesthetics of perishing.

Erin Manning: This is an important point. I think we have to dissociate Brian's ideas of bare activity, or my focus on the in-act, from the way activity is mobilized by capitalism. Bare activity has nothing to do with 'doing something' in the sense of that capitalist busy-ness. As Brian often says, its not doing something, it's 'something doing', emphasizing, as I did earlier, how the event's own coming into act is what is at stake, not only the human subject's activity in the event. Something doing is never limited to human doing: it asks instead how the doing effects the field of relations active in the event. Some of the effects are definitely human effects, but these are always in a constellation that is more-than human. Activity is therefore never reduced to what the human does, as tends to be the case in work that criticizes action as a concept (such as Bifo's [Franco Berardi's] account of activism, for instance). It has to do instead with the generative potential of ecologies in their coming to be an event.

Whitehead's book *The Function of Reason* (1958) is very interesting in relation to activity and life. The question that Whitehead raises in it is the question of the quality of life. He asks, what is it that can account for the fact that we strive to live well rather than simply living? This question is not strictly directed to the human, but to the way appetition functions in the ecology of practices of which humans are but one aspect. Creativity is at the heart of Whitehead's analysis. For Whitehead, one of the ways ecologies evolve towards complexity is through their appetition for the more-than of experience: they have a concern for how the doing happens, how the something-doing connects to other something-doings to generate modes of existence that are novel. Whitehead's concept of the novel is not the capitalist concept that emphasizes the importance of the 'newest new'. Creativity here refers to the generation of new forms of value that give rise to new forms of life. This is an account of valuation in the Nietzschean sense: it challenges the notion of evaluation according to external criteria with the idea that how an event comes into itself is a mode of valuation in itself. Any actual occasion for Whitehead is a mode of valuation: the question is, how does the event value its own mode of existence, how does it enjoy its own existence?

Brian Massumi: Going back to the notion of activity, for us it's not about instrumental activity. We're not talking about work, activity as it is captured and organized by the capitalist system. The activations and reactivations we're talking about happen at a very different level. It's simply the idea that whenever something comes visibly or palpably to expression, it is emerging not out of nowhere, and not out of the structure of the past as fully determining, but out of a background activity that is inheriting from the past but also creating the conditions for what will come next that will supersede the past and perhaps change the nature of what comes of it. Activity is not grounded in substance or in essence. It's grounded in prior activity, taking a new twist. That's the basic tenet of what I call 'activist philosophy', which I see as a complement to an immediations approach. Every time there is a thought, there has already been activity in the body. Every time there has been activity in the body, there has been activity in the environment. There are interlinkings of different levels of activity channelled into certain points of more or less clear expression. It is at the points of more or less clear expression that activity in this primary sense can be captured by apparatuses like those of capitalism, and converted into work. It is also at those points of clear expression that emergence is coming to the end of its arc. The movement of expression is culminating. The event 'perishes'. The potentials it carried to expression are then ready for reactivation, either as conditions for a new emergence, or as captured potentials feeding a self-perpetuating structure that has found ways of reactivating itself across the perishings of events. Emergence and perishing are not opposites. They are pulses or phases in a process. An emergence lives on its own becoming. As soon as it expands its potential for that becoming, it perishes. If there is apparent continuity—even at the level of a rock, as the power of persistence of a rock—it's because a capability has set in to regenerate the same form across the perishings, so that the next emergence is more similar to than different from the last. Whitehead says this very clearly: a rock is an accomplishment. Something from the past creates conditions of conformity for the next emergence, and it is the reuptake of these by the new occasion which accounts for the continuity of lines of existence. Whitehead defines re-enaction as it is in conformity to the past as the 'physical pole' of events. He defines the 'mental pole' of events as what introduces novelty into the re-enaction, and jumps ahead from there. Fundamentally, that means appetition, as Erin was just discussing—the singularizing force of futurity. It is crucial to realize that the mental pole as Whitehead defines it has nothing to do in the first instance with human thought or subjectivity. You have to think the emergence and the perishing, the conformal persistence and re-arising, the cut of the new and the continuity, the physical and the mental, together, as mutually imbricated modes of process. As phases of process they are always interlinked, and are found to one degree or another in every event at any level of existence.

On the question of effectiveness. When we talk about effectiveness, we're usually thinking about what philosophers call efficient causality.

It's the idea that an effect is directly proportionate to its cause, that the cause can be isolated from background activity, and then connected in linear fashion to its effect. It's basically the billiard-ball model, where the future is completely determined by a measurable force that is transmitted from the past through a part-to-part connection, in a localized impact. It's the model of work again, but in the physics sense of the term. And this kind of causality, precisely, corresponds to Whitehead's physical pole (which is not, however, reducible just to that). The mental pole is also effective—in introducing novelty. This complicates things, because when novelty happens, the unfolding of the event has not been linear. It has been inflected. Where does the nonlinearity come from? It comes from what is not completely determined in the field of relations. It comes from the background activity conditioning the event's emergence. It comes from the complexity of relations, from interference and resonance effects between the formative factors entering into play. There is always a margin of play in an event due to the complexity. This happens directly on the relational level, not part-to-part. It's not closed or linear enough to be called causality. 'Conditioning' has to be distinguished as a mode of effectiveness in its own right, as distinct from causality. Both modes of effectiveness, of course, are active in every event, and a large part of what makes for the singularity of an event is how they shake down in relation to each other.

Erin Manning: I am wondering how we can move this discussion towards a few examples, since what you're talking about, Brian, happens in all kinds of everyday situations. We could give ourselves as a challenge to make a list of the ways in which we habitually believe we can will the organization, or the outcome, or the effectiveness of a given situation. In doing so, we would realize that it is not the outcome which we control, but the habit of how we believe we can control it! The habit of entering into a process brings with it the promise that a process engaging with the same conditions twice can generate an event that looks like the event that it generated the first time. But what Brian is saying is that if you take this process seriously, and attend to how it evolves in each of its phases, you will find that no event can be mapped in advance. The event takes us with it and the outcome is always experienced in retrospect: ah! that's what it was! But instead of saying 'that's what it was!' we have the habit of taking the past and imposing it on the future, quietly exclaiming 'that's what it will be!' Immediation tries to challenge that habit.

What we have found in our collective SenseLab network as we work through the relationship between philosophy, art and activism is that techniques have to be generated in the event, each occasion anew, because if they are not, they simply don't work. That's the pragmatic side or as we call it the speculative pragmatic side. The event generates its own forms of speculation and forms of pragmatism, and you have to be in the event to compose with them. This is a relational task at the level of the field itself. If you think of yourself as the subject of the event, you'll fail simply because you will have taken yourself out of all of those complex relational tendencies of the event to generate its own potential. What is at stake here is understanding not the agency of the subject, but the *agencement* of the event in its speculatively pragmatic unfolding. This is a word that is impossible to translate. The best that anyone's come up with is 'assemblage', but that's misleading. *Agencement* connotes a doing doing itself. You have to understand the event itself as agency-ing.

Brian Massumi: You can think of any example where you are in the situation where there is a power relationship. It is very clear, if you're a professor and walk into a classroom, that you are immediately in a power situation over the students. You can basically make them do what you want. You can tell them to give you a fifteen-page paper by a certain date and they do it or suffer certain consequences. The only reason that I have the power over them is because we are co-implicated in a situation that draws on certain institutional structures, and we have acquired the adaptive habits and skills they assume and produce. When I say that I have power, it is actually self-aggrandizing, because what I have is only the power to activate certain constraints and forces that are embedded in the relational field. When I act I am more of a catalyst for the reactivation of those forces than a direct commander or autonomous willer. That's always the case, to one degree or another. Our freedom doesn't consist in making a choice or decision that comes only out of our own subjectivity—in other words, out of nowhere. Our freedom is how we play our implication in the field, what events we succeed in catalysng in it that bring out the latent singularity of the situation, how we inflect for novel emergences. That is a relational question, because it doesn't happen part-to-part in billiard-ball fashion. If how you're inflecting the event doesn't resonate or interfere with everyone present, and affect all the formative factors integrally, the conformal forces that are ready and waiting in the situation are going to have the upper hand.

Christoph Brunner: That's an interesting point. I have been re-reading Simondon recently, and Muriel Combes's book on his work (Combes 2013). Both address the question of anxiety. It seems to me that at the core the question of anxiety concerns different modes of resonance, and what you can create through the openness of a situation. On the one hand, this requires us to think about what means and techniques there are to become a catalyst and to benefit from surfing that wave, as Deleuze would say. On the other hand, it makes us think about the moment of impasse where everything seems to be locked and gridded. As Simondon says, that's the moment of anxiety and death. This leads me to think about the process of bifurcation in a life-practice—what kinds of techniques can be used for nurturing, and where you go from there. Thinking about the practices of research-creation we have been working on for a while at the SenseLab—investigating how to work, act, think, write and move in the immediacy of an event, and how to create something from there that comes into its own, singularizing and resonating-with, so as to renew the event. As part of this investigation, we ask what kinds of metastable fields can be constituted. How do we create dense fields that modulate in a way that is all their own? However, some of these fields and modulations generate more lures, open up more potential, for subsequent take-up in different contexts than others do.

Brian Massumi: Simondon's concept of anxiety is clearly in dialogue with existentialist and existential phenomenological thinking. It's a response to the anxiety attached to Heidegger's being-towards-death, and to Sartre's prescription for absolute subjective freedom of decision in the face of anxiety. He's trying to save our anxieties from either fate. For Simondon, anxiety has to do with the 'more than oneness' at the heart of individual. This is basically the active, relational field of potential we've been talking about—what Erin's been calling the more-than. Simondon calls it the 'preindividual field' because it is what the individualized subject emerges, and re-emerges, from. Anxiety is created, according to Simondon, when this open-ended, formative field is mistaken for an interiority of the subject, rather than being recognized as the preindividual field from which the individual emerges as a subject. When the preindividual is mistaken for an interiority, the resulting subject feels that it should be able to hold all the potential of the field in itself. This is impossible, because as we were saying, the potential is irreducibly relational, and can only be held integrally in situations. It can't be accessed just by individual choice or decision, but only by events, in which others are also implicated. The imperative that the individual is often made to feel to live up to its own potential, mistaking the world's potential for a being-in-itself, creates an unliveable tension. It actually bottles the potential up. The other, in this account, is not the hell of our choices and decisions being limited by others, as it was for existentialism. The other is the outlet. The potential of the preindividual field is relational, and can only be expressed relationally, through and with others. In fact, Simondon defines the other in terms of that. He says that the perception of another is the perception of a perspective on the world. By that he doesn't mean a subjective point of view. It's an active perspective–ways of moving in the world, ways of catalysing events, ways of expressing, ways of changing with and through the inflections of events. If the other is an image of potential, then the multiplicity of others multiplies the potential, way beyond what one individual can hold in itself. All of that potential can only be got at if it is activated relationally. To think of it this way connects the preindividual to the transindividual. Experimenting in activating situational potentials pragmatically, in exploratory relational action, dissipates anxiety by reconnecting the preindividual to the transindividual. Again, freedom is not a question of the relation of the subject to itself. Freedom always comes out of active embeddedness in a complex relational field for the in-acting. One does not act freely. One acts freedom out.

Erin Manning: In that beautiful passage you and Brian were mentioning, Simondon also talks about solitude. He does this as part of an urgent call not to talk about tendencies like anxiety and even solitude in a way that reindividualizes them. They need to be thought of in the context of individuation, or the relational becoming of the individual. Reindividualizing is a temptation we have seen a lot these days. To bring anxiety, depression, panic back to the level of the individual. I think the work of Bifo is really exemplary in that way. I have recently been reading Bifo trying to understand the necessity and the urgency that he seems to feel in creating what I consider a repersonalizing account of experience that too often reindividualizes the question of anxiety. This reindividualization, which perhaps affects me most in the way Bifo combines his theory of the act with depression in his account of Guattari's so-called 'winter years', builds on his relation of friendship in ways that make me very uncomfortable (Berardi 2008). In his account of Guattari, if I am very reductive, what we end up with is something like: 'I knew Guattari to have been depressed and therefore you must read

Guattari's work as an activist, as a therapist, as a philosopher, in light of his depression.' This counters the in-act of Guattari's schizoanalytic practice—including his writing—in a fundamental way, it seems to me. Everything in Guattari, in my opinion, follows the lines of what Brian was just saying, working hard to understand the relationship between the preindividual, the transindividual and the group-subject. The question for Guattari is never reducible to the subject-position: it is always about creating and grasping new forms of subjectivity that emerge from the event. I have no doubt Guattari was depressed—but construing depression as counteracting the in-act simply makes no sense to me.

We are at a moment where collective action feels urgent to many of us. I don't know if we are at a moment that is less anxious or more anxious than other moments. What I do know is that an account of anxiety or depression has to be able to compose with the in-act in the way we are theorizing it here for it to align to a Guattarian way of thinking. The question of pathology and the therapeutic, when it comes up, has to be aligned to a Simondonian account of anxiety or solitude if we want to open it up beyond its reindividualizing tendencies. If this happens, the question of how the act produces new modes of existence will come up, and this will open up the exploration of neurodiversity in relation to the transindividual or the group-subject, as opposed to what Guattari, following Jean Oury, calls 'normopathy'.

Brian Massumi: I want to take up the notion of solitude you brought up in relation to anxiety in Simondon's work. I think that's really important too because when he talks about group-subjectivity or collective individuation, and the importance of entering into certain event-based actions in a relational field including others, people often think of it as this imperative of togetherness, to social transparency, and total availability to that interaction. I think what Simondon is trying to say with his concept of solitude is that if there is an imperative of that kind, it can be as limiting and painful as the anxiety of mistaking the preindividual for a subjective interiority. When he talks about isolation he is talking about an experience of transindividual potential, but in the absence of any particular acting-out of it. It's being in-acted; that is, felt actively, but in intensity. Deleuze says something very similar, and he is probably thinking of Simondon, when he says that even one person alone at their writing desk can be a collective. They can be in-acting a field of relational potential that would require a whole population to act out. They are in a very real sense a 'people to come'. Deleuze even suggests that this is where one is at one's most collective. The incitation to always communicate, the imperative to participate, the constant solicitation to interact can be an enslavement. It's becoming more and more part of the necessary work of capitalism. In the end, there's very little actually relational about it, in the emergent sense we've been talking about. Solitude can in fact be a relational antidote to that.

Erin Manning: In relation to the question of collective action, in the way we understand it at the SenseLab, we have been very influenced by Guattari's accounts of La Borde, the experimental clinic he worked at all of his life, and the ways in which it may be possible to compose across many different variations of solitude and anxiety—in ways that are not saying that two individuals compose face to face, but that the event as it is being generated allows for different compositions, transindividual compositions, infraindividual and preindividual compositions. One of our main concerns in terms of our activism has been creating techniques emergent within the group-subject to deal with burn-out, and with depression and anxiety when they come up. How do you manage health in ways that don't target the individual but engage with the milieu instead? This is a question we've discussed with our collaborators, the Boston-based Design Studio for Social Intervention, for whom in some ways this is even more urgent as they deal with very tough on-the-ground issues of racism and gang violence. Many of the collaborators and activists within the studio have lost family members to gang violence and they deal everyday with racism directed not only at them, but at the very question of what kinds of modes of existence exist for inner-city African-Americans in the US. They are completely committed to continuing to design what they call 'horizontal' practices to counter urban violence, but they are also often overwhelmed by the magnitude of the task. Anxiety and depression often come with burn-out. In the face of such adversity, it is difficult to sustain the field of relation generated by activist event practices, and prevent it from imploding under pressure. Techniques for avoiding or alleviating the implosion of course concern the individual, but they cannot be limited to him or her.

One thing we experiment with is the question of reconnecting affectively to the collective in a different way, getting away from thinking about 'being active' in the sense of 'doing something' and focusing instead on the in-act of 'something doing'. This brings us back to the earlier question of affect: what does it mean to co-compose? To co-compose is to allow for the possibility that we cannot know in advance where the collective value of our project resides. It means to become flexible in our understanding collectively of how value might eventually come to be understood. A collectivity in the way I understand it is always concerned with these speculatively pragmatic questions—speculative because they remain open to invention, pragmatic because they are born of a continual exploration of the in-act. At the SenseLab, one of the ways we move towards this question of collective value is through the concept of event-based care. Here I don't mean the subjectivity of human-to-human care, but rather how an event produces an environment that can sustain different kinds of participation which include different affective speeds, including the slownesses that we perhaps associate with depression, or the speeds we associate with anxiety. With event-care perhaps there is a kind of collective tending that comes close to the sense that Guattari gave to the word 'therapeutic'. Not therapeutic as individual therapy, but therapeutic in the sense of attending to how an event is capable of producing mutually imbricated modes of existence or modes of living which are sustainable in ways we can't yet imagine, and which produce new forms of life. I say this very tentatively as I am not at all certain that therapeutic is the right word for this.

Christoph Brunner: This is a very important point in relation to methods and the question the SenseLab always gets of what its methods are. If you move through a constant revaluation in the immediacy of an event happening, if you try to find ways not to do something *about* what's happening but rather to do in the happening, then you have to completely reconsider the way you use language. It also affects the way you inhabit the institutionalized field of academia, with its constraints and the closed systems we as academics have to work with and through while trying to sustain certain kinds of practices and shift and modulate other kinds of practices. Talking about 'techniques' and 'ecologies of practice' provides one way of undoing the claim for methods and appropriate instruments. Which leads me back to the language we work in, which is never just reducible to its established rules of usage. How can we conceive the language we use as part of our life practices—in the sense of thinking, living and writing in the presence of each other and in the presence of the many solitudes moving through us? What does it actually mean to undo the confined systems that create anxiety all over again? As an example, we could think of the 'Nonhuman Turn' conference we all attended last year in Milwaukee. I have never seen an academic event so full of anxiety.

Especially among the PhD students, who are expected to do inventive work but didn't dare to speak up, to oppose or voice their concerns, for fear of stepping on someone's toes who might be on your future hiring committee.

Erin Manning: Brian and I have been very involved in this question over the last years. How does language also produce what Guattari would call an existential territory? I think that's what you are talking about—that traditional instrumental forms of generating so-called knowledge such as the conference are not very good at generating territories that aren't mimicking and reproducing the territory they have come out of. I mean they don't generate the new in that sense of a Whiteheadian co-composition. I was thinking about this issue recently in relation to an event we are having this fall called 'Enter Bioscleave' that will take place at Arakawa and Gins's experimental Bioscleave House on Long Island.[2] Last week Brian and I were in New York talking to Madeleine Gins. All three of us are very engaged in the process of language—very interested in what language can do and particularly interested in its capacities as a concept-building practice to generate modes of existence. Sometimes we hesitate in our collaboration, however, since although our focus is often similar, our language can be quite different. Arakawa and Gins function on the basis of a procedural approach. Over a period of thirty or forty years, they have defined a set of procedures that are both very firmly ensconced in their practice and very mobile, very rethinkable. These procedures are ecological at heart, but do operate from the perspective of what they call the 'organism that persons', thereby producing a perspectival approach that in many ways keeps the human at the centre of the inquiry (despite their openness to think across different forms of sentience) (Gins and Arakawa 2002). We at the SenseLab have generated a set of techniques which are perhaps a bit different in their inflections because they have as their focus the ecology of the event. These approaches have a sisterhood and common interest and we know each other's work well. Yet, despite this, for four or five hours we were trying to understand each other's language. Not only to understand in a linguistic sense but to be able to mobilize its affective force. What was really generative in this conversation was that Madeline wanted to figure out how to proceduralize our techniques, and we wanted to see how her procedures could open up a thinking of the event. We were truly interested in how the force of language could be used as a technique for both thinking and making across our different vocabularies. And so, instead of debating, we found ourselves in an extremely generative dialogue, composing across modes of inquiry. This created, I think, the beginnings of an existential territory that is difficult to come by in academic circles, where opinions often hold more sway than procedural interventions capable of co-composing techniques and modes of speaking. Such an approach takes time, it takes a willingness to risk one's ideas, a sense of openness, and it takes an event or project. This cannot be done in the abstract. In the case of coming together with Madeline Gins, it was done in the context of bringing our two worlds together through the 'Enter Bioscleave' event. The reason the event is key is that it is through the event that the techniques will be experimented with, and it is in the event that we will be able to see how our convergences of approach resonate. How the procedures unfold, what the techniques for relation do, will be key to seeing whether they are generative of emergent collectivity or whether they need to be tweaked towards future experimentation. And how they will be tweaked will then have an effect on how we determine the stakes of the event, which will of course be different for each of us. For Arakawa and Gins, the stakes are 'reversible destiny', which involves an account of immortality which we follow only to the extent that we are invested in emergent collectivities that go on living across their perishings, in lines of variation. Again the stakes connect but they are not the same. They don't connect in a commonality—they connect in the urgency of a procedural approach, in the urgency of a project.

Brian Massumi: What really interested me in that exchange, and what surprised me after four and a half hours of discussion about Arakawa and Gins's work and how it relates to the SenseLab's work, was when Madeline suddenly said, 'What are we going to name these procedures?' For her, we weren't just sharing ideas or communicating about ourselves and our past activities. A discussion is not just a discussion, for her. It's always doing something—or a something doing moving into a pragmatic unfolding at a later phase. What interested her was distilling pragmatic working points from the discussion, and then honing them as procedures that can be set in place in particular situations to condition events of emergence. Naming is a technique for fixing the procedures, in the sense that you fix a compound. It gives you a practical handle on what region of potential you've collectively brought to provisional expression, and holds it together in a way that you can do things with. This is a very different use of language than the way academics usually communicate. When you go to a conference, you can't help being subjectively positioned, from the moment you put on your name badge. You are not just registering your presence, you're representing yourself, and you speak accordingly. Your angle of entry into the situation is personalized in this way.

This assumes that your identity coincides with your potential, and that when we express ourselves, it's in this individualized mode of potential. It is exactly doing what Simondon warns against: mistaking the field potential from which an individuation emerges for the interiority of a subject. Needless to say, it creates anxiety. It cuts off many other modes of activity and catalysings of relation that could make the situation more of an event, and more open-ended. The question the SenseLab started with was, how do we make ourselves an event? How do we come together actively, as artists, academics and activists, in ways that don't just reproduce the usual genres of 'communication'? What relational procedures, or techniques of relation, can we collectively invent, name and put into situational practice for making events that truly deserve to be called events?

We realized very quickly that the kind of techniques we were looking for had to be impersonal. By that we meant directly collective, like Simondon's preindividual field in its transindividual becoming. That makes it sound a bit exalted. But it's really nuts and bolts, procedural in the best sense. The question is always 'how?' For example, how do you enter into a situation without just registering your representation of yourself? What conditions can be put in place to make that entry happen on another footing? How do you gesture to participants as they cross the threshold to the event that this time it is an invitation to experiment collectively and invent? How do you say, nonverbally, in the way the event is conditioned, don't bring your products—bring your process. Don't bring your thoughts you've already had and rehearse them to us as part of positioning yourself—bring everything else, your passions, your appetitions, your tools and abilities, your intensest procedures, and connect into the situation from that angle. Don't perform yourself—co-catalyse a collective event with us. What that's saying is that you are hereby relieved from the imperative to represent yourself and to be judged accordingly. You can compose, using many more dimensions of what it is you bring into the situation than are normally activatable, in a conference for example. The measure of success of your contributions will not be whether they were correct, or complete, or even authentically you, but rather what affective force they brought to the event. That means that no contribution can be owned, because it doesn't have effectiveness in itself, but only as creating the conditions for yourself *and* others—as a gift of process potential or a catalyst can only be effective in the way it resonates with others. When others take up your gift of potential, they take it places you couldn't have taken it by yourself—which then enables you to go places you couldn't have gone alone. When an event of this kind is working, a dancer might move into a philosophical text in a way they never thought they had the preparation to do. And a philosopher might find themselves translating concepts into movements. When things like that happen, it deserves to be called an event. Events are always transindividual, bringing out potentials that could never have been arrived at individually.

The use of language in this kind of situation is very different. On the one hand, it is procedural in Arakawa and Gins's sense. It is used to embed certain set of potentials in the situation in an open-ended way that can only be brought to expression collectively. On the other hand, the use of language is necessarily evocative, because what will transpire has not been predetermined, but has to eventuate, and how it eventuates is up for relational grabs, and will only be clear as the event unfolds. This evocativeness of potentials as yet not fully formed gives the procedural language a poetic edge. You can see this poetico-procedural use of language in Arakawa and Gins's writing. You can read it as poetry, and you can use it as an instructional manual for experiential event-making.

Erin Manning: Perhaps the form of language we resist the most is the debate and general positioning without enacting concepts or bringing them into play. This is why we work so closely with philosophical texts in the process of event-planning. Our hope is to get away from general statements such as 'of course, as everyone knows ...' and speak instead in ways singularly connected to the work we are engaged with. In the five hours we spent with Madeleine that day, all of that time was used to engage with language at the level of the work we have to do and not at the level of positioning ourselves or of debate.

Brian Massumi: What bothers me about the question of debate is that it presupposes that the stakes are given, and with them opposing positions, so that the only question is who is going to represent which positions and how convincingly. What we are talking about is reinventing the stakes.

Christoph Brunner: Avoiding these kinds of pre-defined states and constantly re-enliving collective thinking, practising and writing, leads to a very different sense of necessity. The question of necessity then has to do with how to avoid generalizing the use of language, and how we think and talk about language. So it doesn't come as something which can be imposed in an academic way of naming. I am thinking here about Deleuze's work and how he writes against naming in the way it is usually practised because it imposes a prefigured structure that is not led by necessity in the immediacy of what you are relationally negotiating. What would be the politics of necessity in the way we're talking about it?

Erin Manning: Deleuze takes up the concept of necessity from Nietzsche. Nietzsche places the question of necessity in the event's asking—this comes across very clearly in the passage in *Thus Spoke Zarathustra* called 'Moment'—'what is the mode of existence created in the necessity of this particular decision?' What he means by decision in this context is also a kind of Whiteheadian notion of decision, understood as the cut propelling the continuing of a process, similar to the concept of transduction in Simondon. It is not individual will. It isn't about my going into this way of living because I judge it necessary for me but rather, as you said, how the event constructs its own forms of necessity. This means that at many stages in our practices and processes we are faced with having to re-conceive how we might encounter necessity. Sometimes the necessity is really frustrating. It doesn't appear as we wished or imagined it would appear. This kind of approach to necessity demands an incredible flexibility and real rigour in the techniques and enabling constraints put into place and what effects they produce. It demands a return to the question of what the stakes are. How are they generated? What kinds of skills are available? How does this particular act co-compose with other acts in the making? All of those questions bear their own processes of necessity. We see our work as composing procedurally and technically with those necessities in a way that produces modes of existence we can live with.

Brian Massumi: We talk a lot about what we do as a form of aesthetic politics. We think of it as aesthetic in an extended sense of that word, as referring to the 'process of experience'. What the SenseLab does is experiment collectively with the process of experience as a practice of the event. When we say the word 'aesthetic' and put it together with politics a lot of the people bristle because they think of the aesthetic as sort of a realm of free play of unconstrained expression. For us, on the contrary, the aesthetic is immediately in connection with necessities of life. There have to be stakes for any activity to be compelling. The reason why a lot of people are drawn to the kinds of events the

SenseLab organizes is that they feel they are beaten down in the situations they live in every day in their home contexts and institutions. It is not that there is no freedom in institutional contexts, but the options for resistance are pre-formatted by the modes of conformity that come to dominate the situation. There is little room for invention. People come to our events out of a sense of necessity, as an issue of survival. Many feel held back or battered down, and can't see how to keep going. They may feel chronically fatigued, or that their creative potential is being drained. Their powers of resistance have been taxed too many times, and they're looking for some way to recharge. It's not an escape into an aesthetic field of free choice and unfettered expression. It's a life necessity. What we provide in response to these yearnings isn't an unconstrained environment. We often repeat: if anything goes, nothing will come. What we do is set in place, poetico-procedurally, enabling constraints. These are mechanisms designed to set certain conditions in place allowing for an inventive interaction to occur that is something like a structured improvisation. The situation is positively constrained: conditioned in a way that we hope will create the conditions for a process of collective expression to unfold, in the course of which something unexpected might emerge. The hope is that what does emerge might feed forward into further experimentation, beyond this event's perishing, in a kind of contagion of collective potential. For us the aesthetic is not an escape from life. Quite the opposite: it is a different way of engaging with the necessities of life. It is the element of necessity, and the collectivity of the process from the very start to beyond its perishing, that make this kind of experimentation with expressive potential political. It's a practice of a 'politics to come', to paraphrase the term of Deleuze's we talked about earlier.

Notes

1. See chapter 4 of Massumi (2015b)
2. This event did not take place in the end due to Madeline Gins's illness.

Notes on Contributors

Julia Bee is Junior professor for image theory at Bauhaus-Universität Weimar. She works on visual anthropology, perception and experience and gender-media-theory. Her dissertation (published 2018) was on Audience Assemblages, Power, Difference, and Desire in TV and Film Reception.

Lone Bertelsen works across the fields of feminist and social theory, photography, art and media studies, ecosophy and micropolitics. Her writing has been published in *Theory, Culture and Society*, *The Affect Theory Reader*, *Performance Paradigm* and the *Fibreculture Journal*.

Érik Bordeleau is researcher at the SenseLab and fugitive financial planner at the Economic Space Agency (ECSA). His work articulates at the intersection of political philosophy, media and financial theory, contemporary art and cinema studies.

Christoph Brunner works in the fields of cultural and media studies and philosophy as an assistant professor in cultural theory at Leuhpana University Luneburg. His recent work focuses on "activist sense" and the intricacies of sensuous experience, media practices, and activism. His wiritngs have been published in *Third Text*, *Journal of Culture & Aesthetics*, *transversal*, *Conjunctions*, and *Fibreculture Journal*.

Nicole de Brabandere is an artist and researcher who uses writing and media and material experimentation to generate new techniques and concepts with which to inhabit lived ecologies. She is a postdoctoral researcher at the Chicago Center for Contemporary Theory, University of Chicago.

Sher Doruff is an artist, writer and research supervisor. Her recent novella series *Last Year at Betty and Bob's* (Punctum Books, 2018) explores fabulated trajectories of memory. She teaches at the Amsterdam University of the Arts.

Pia Ednie-Brown is a creative practitioner and Professor of Architecture at the University of Newcastle, Australia. Her practice, Onomatopoeia, is grounded in the discipline of architecture, while working across diverse media, methods and milieu. Her research seeks to work against anthropocentrism through revealing habitual oversights and unacknowledged agency, animating the inanimate, and exploring the edges of life.

Gerko Egert works on performance, dance and philosophy. He is a postdoctoral researcher at the Justus-Liebig-Universität Gießen. His recent work focusses on the power of choreography and the politics of movement in and beyond dance.

Jonas Fritsch is a design researcher whose work centers on a creative thinking of interaction design, experience philosophy and affect theory through practical experiments with interactive sound and physical interfaces. His work has been published and exhibited in numerous venues across Human-Computer Interaction (HCI), design, aesthetics and digital culture. He is Associate Professor in Interaction Design at the IT University of Copenhagen.

Andrew Goodman is a visual artist and occasional writer with an interest in participation, ecology and philosophies of process and science. He is the author of *Gathering Ecologies: Thinking Beyond Interactivity* (Open Humanities Press, 2017).

Ilona Hongisto works on documentary film and media with a special focus on the history, politics and aesthetics of fabulation. She is the author of *Soul of the Documentary: Framing, Expression, Ethics* (Amsterdam University Press, 2015).

Michael Hornblow is an interdisciplinary artist and Senior Lecturer in Architecture and Design at the University of Tasmania. He has a background in performance, video making, intermedia, and arts management, alongside academic research and teaching; with a focus on affective, diagrammatic and participatory relations within and across the body and the built environment. This approach is informed by doctoral research-by-practice in the Spatial Information Architecture Laboratory, Royal Melbourne Institute of Technology, and post-doctoral research at the Senselab, Concordia University.

Jondi Keane is an arts practitioner and Associate Professor of Art & Performance at Deakin University in Melbourne, Australia. For more than three decades he has exhibited, performed and collaborated on projects in the USA, UK, Europe and Australia, and publishes widely on practice-led research, art and embodied cognition, experimental art and architecture, and the contribution of art practices to interdisciplinary inquiries that engage collective concerns.

Thomas Lamarre works on the history of media and thought. His recent publications include *The Anime Ecology: A Genealogy of Television, Animation, and Game Media*.

Erin Manning is an artist and writer whose work engages with the interstices of experience with a special focus on collective individuation and neurodiversity. Recent work includes *The Minor Gesture* (Duke UP, 2016).

Brian Massumi is the author of numerous works across philosophy, political theory, and art theory. His recent publications include *The Principle of Unrest: Activist Philosophy in the Expanded Field* (Open Humanities Press, 2017) and *99 Theses on the Revaluation of Value: A Postcapitalist Manifesto* (University of Minnesota Press, 2018).

Anna Munster is a writer, artist and educator, working on arts, politics and theories of: perception, machine learning, the imperceptible. She is the author of *An Aesthesia of Neworks* (MIT, 2013) and *Materializing New Media* (UPNE, 2006), and works on expanded media environments collaboratively with Michele Barker. She is a Professor, Art and Design, University of New South Wales, Sydney Australia.

Andrew Murphie works on philosophy and a politics of differential organisation within a "third revolution" in media and communications (AI and automation, VR, data and signaletics, the world as medium). He also works on climate change as part of catastrophic multiplicity. He is an Associate Professor in Media and Communications at UNSW Sydney.

Toni Pape investigates the relation between aesthetics and politics, mainly in contemporary television and video games. He is co-author of *Nocturnal Fabulations: Ecology, Vitality and Opacity in the Cinema of Apichatpong Weerasethakul* (Open Humanities Press, 2017) and author of *Figures of Time: Affect and the Television of Preemption* (Duke UP, 2019).

His work has been pubilshed in *Inflexions, NECSUS, Feminist Media Studies, Studies in Documentary Film*, and *Dance Research Journal*.

Justy Phillips is an artist, writer and publisher. She is the co-founder of the slow-publishing collaborative, *A Published Event*, exploring chance encounter and shared authorship of lived experience through speculative eventing. She is a Lecturer in Critical Practices at the School of Creative Arts, University of Tasmania.

Stamatia Portanova is a Research Fellow at the Università degli Studi di Napoli 'L'Orientale'. She is the author of *Moving without a Body: Digital Philosophy and Choreographic Thoughts* (MIT Press). Her research focuses on digital culture and philosophy from a radically speculative point of view.

Mattie Sempert is a practicing acupuncturist and writer, with an interest in the transversality of body and language, connective tissue, and nonhuman agency. Mattie is currently a PhD candidate (Creative Writing/Experimental Essay and Lyric Studies) at the Royal Melbourne Institute of Technology.

Nathaniel Stern is an artist and engineer, writer, researcher, and teacher, between the University of Wisconsin-Milwaukee and the University of Johannesburg. His most recent book is *Ecological Aesthetics: artful tactics for humans, nature, and politics* (Dartmouth, 2018).

Bodil Marie Stavning Thomsen works on media, art and philosophy with an emphasis on 'the signaletic material' in film and interfaces. Her recent publications include *Lars von Trier's Renewal of Film 1984-2014: Signal, Pixel, Diagram* (Aarhus University Press, 2018). She is a Professor at School of Communication and Culture, Aarhus University.

Alanna Thain is an Associate Professor and Director of Institute for Gender, Sexuality and Feminist Studies at McGill University, Montreal. She is the author of *Bodies in Time: Suspense, Affect, Cinema*. (University of Minnesota Press, 2017)

Works Cited

Agamben, Giorgio. *L'uso dei corpi*. Vicenza: Nerri pozza editore, 2014.

Alliez, Éric and Andrew Goffey. "Introduction." *The Guattari Effect*. Eds. Éric Alliez and Andrew Goffey. London: Continuum, 2011. 1-14.

Althusser, Louis. "Ideology and Ideological State Apparatuses." *Lenin and Philosophy and Other Essays*. Trans. Ben Brewster. New York: Monthly Review Press, 1972.

Anon. "Controlling brain cells with sound waves." *Bioengineer. org*. September 18, 2015. http://bioengineer.org/controlling-brain-cells-sound-waves. http://bioengineer.org/controlling-brain-cells-sound-waves

Anonymous. *Commune – Exhibition Catalogue*. Sydney: The White Rabbit Gallery, 2014.

Armstrong, Keith. "Towards a Connective and Ecosophical New Media Art Practice". *Intimate Transactions: Art, Exhibition and Interaction within Distributed Network Environments*. Ed. Jillian Hamilton. Brisbane: Australasian CRC for Interaction Design, 2006. 12-35.

Armstrong, Keith. "Intimate Transactions: The Evolution of an Ecosophical Networked Practice." *The Fibreculture Journal* 7 (2005). http://seven.fibreculturejournal.org/fcj-047-intimate-transactions-the-evolution-of-an-ecosophical-networked-practice/.

Artaud, Antonin. *Selected Writings*. Ed. Susan Sontag. Berkeley: University of California Press, 1988.

Blackman, Lisa. "Affect, Relationality and the Problem of Personality." *Theory, Culture & Society* 25.1 (2008): 27–51.

Bak, Per. *How Nature Works: The Science of Self-Organized Criticality*. New York: Oxford University Press, 1997.

Barber, Dan. *The Third Plate: Field Notes on the Future of Food*. New York: Penguin Press, 2014.

Barker, Timothy. *Time and the Digital: Connecting Technology, Aesthetics, and a Process Philosophy of Time*. Dartmouth: Dartmouth Press, 2012.

Bataille, Georges. "Informe." *Documents* 7 (December 1929), 382. [Reprinted/translated in: Georges Bataille: Oeuvres Complètes I. Paris: Gallimard, 1970.]

Bataille, Georges. *Visions of Excess. Selected Writings, 1927-1939.* Minneapolis: University of Minnesota Press, 1985.

Bataille, Georges. *The Accursed Share. An Essay on General Economy. Volume 1. Consumption*. Trans. Robert Hurley. New York: Zone Books, 1991.

Bataille, Georges. "Sacrifice, the Festival and the Principles of the Sacred World." *The Bataille Reader.* Eds. Fred Botting and Scott Wilson. Oxford: Blackwell Publishers, 1997.

Beisser, Arnold. "The Paradoxical Theory of Change." *Gestalt Therapy. Now.* Eds. Joen Fagan and Irma Lee Shepherd. New York: Harper Colophon, 1970.

Bennett, Jane. *The Enchantment of Modern Life: Attachments, Crossings and Ethics*. Princeton: Princeton University Press, 2001.

Bennett, Jane. *Vibrant Matter: A Political Ecology of Things*. Durham and London: Duke University Press, 2010.

Berardi, Franco (Bifo). *Félix Guattari: Thought, Friendship and Visionary Cartography.* Trans. and ed. Giuseppina Mecchia and Charles J. Stivale. London: Palgrave Macmillan, 2008.

Bergson, Henri (1914), *The Problem of Personality* http://members3.jcom.home.ne.jp/yoshihara.jya/the_problem_of_personality_1-3.htm

Bergson, Henri. *Creative Evolution*. Translated by Arthur Mitchell. London: Macmillan and Co., 1922.

Bergson, Henri. *The Two Sources of Morality and Religion.* London: Macmillan and Co., 1935.

Bergson, Henri. *Time and Free Will: An Essay on the Immediate Data of Consciousness*. Trans. F.L. Pogson. London: George Allen & Unwin Ltd, 1950.

Bergson, Henri. *Les deux sources de la morale et de la religion.* Paris, PUF, 1967 [1932].

Bergson, Henri. *Mélanges*. Ed. André Robinet. Paris: Presses universitaires de France, 1972.

Bergson, Henri. *Creative Evolution*. Trans. Arthur Mitchell, Mineola: Dover, 1998.

Bergson, Henri. *Key Writings*. Eds. Keith Ansell Pearson and John Mullarkey. New York: Continuum, 2002.

Bergson, Henri. *La pensée et le mouvant*. Paris: Quadrige, 2003.

Bergson, Henri. *Laughter: An Essay on the Meaning of the Comic*. Trans. Cloudesley Brereton and Fred Rothwell. Project Gutenberg, 2009.

Bertelsen, Lone. "Matrixial Refrains." *Theory, Culture & Society* 21.1 (February 2004): 121-147.

Bertelsen, Lone. "Affect and Care in Intimate Transactions." *The Fibreculture Journal* 21 (2012). http://twentyone.fibreculturejournal.org/fcj-149-affect-and-care-in-intimate-transactions/#sthash.um6shBql.dpbs.

Biernat, M., Kobrynowicz, D., & Weber, D. "Stereotyping and shifting standards: Some paradoxical effects of cognitive load." *Journal of Applied Social Psychology* 33 (2003): 2060- 2079.

Birringer, Johannes. "Transactivity." *Intimate Transactions: Art, Exhibition and Interaction within Distributed Network Environments*. Ed. Jillian Hamilton. Brisbane: Australasian CRC for Interaction Design, 2006. 106-113.

Bois, Yve-Alain and Rosalind Krauss. *L'Informe. Mode d'Emploi*. Paris: Centre Georges Pompidou, 1996.

Bolter, Jay David and Richard Grusin. *Remediation. Understanding New Media*. Cambridge: MIT Press, 1999.

Bordeleau, Erik. "Bruno Latour and the Miraculous Power of Enunciation." *Breaking the Spell: Speculative Realism Under Discussion*. Eds. Anna Longo and Sarah de Sanctis. Paris: Mimesis International, 2015. 155-167.

Bosteels, Bruno. "From Text to Territory: Félix Guattari's Cartographies of the Unconscious." *Deleuze and Guattari: New Mappings in Politics, Philosophy and Culture*. Eds. Eleanor Kaufman and Kevin Jon Heller. Minneapolis: University of Minnesota Press, 1998: 145-174.

Brunner, Christoph. 'Kon-/Disjunktion'. *Inventionen* 1. Ed. Isabell Lorey, Roberto Nigro, Gerald Raunig. Zürich, Diaphanes, 2011. 128-130.

Brunner, Christoph. "Immediation as Process and Practice of Signaletic Mattering." *Journal of Aesthetics and Culture* 4 (2012).

Brunner, Christoph and Jonas Fritsch. "Interactive Environments as Fields of Transduction." The Fibreculture Journal 18 (2011). http://eighteen.fibreculturejournal.org/2011/10/09/fcj-124-interactive-environments-as-fields-of-transduction/.

Brunner, Christoph and Jonas Fritsch. "Kon-/Disjunktion." *Inventionen* 1 (2011): 128-130. Eds. Isabell Lorey, Roberto Nigro, Gerald Raunig. Zürich, Diaphanes.

Brunner, Christopher, Erin Manning and Brian Massumi. "Fields of Potential: On Affective Immediation, Anxiety, and Necessities of Life." *Ästhetik Der Existenz: Lebensformen Im Widerstreit*. Eds. Elke Bippus, Jörg Huber and Roberto Nigro. Zurich: Edition Voldemeer, 2013. 135-150.

Buchanan, Ian. "The Problem of the Body in Deleuze and Guatarri, Or, What Can a Body Do?" *Body and Society* 3.3 (1997): 73-91.

Bywaters, Malcolm. "Lyndal Jones: Climate Change, Performance and the Avoca Project." *Fusion Journal* 4 (2010).

Cache, Bernard. *Earth Moves: The Furnishing of Territorie*s. Trans. Anne Boyman. Ed. Michael Speaks. Cambridge: MIT Press, 1995.

Calvino, Italo. *If On A Winter's Night A Travelle*r. Orlando, Florida: Horcourt Brace and Co., 1981.

Cariani, Peter. "To Evolve an Ear: Epistemological Implications of Gordon Pask's Electrochemical Devices." *Systems Research* 10.3 (1993): 19-33

Cariani, Peter. "Emergence and Creativity." *Art.ficial* 4.0, "Emergência." Eds. Itaú Cultural. Sao Paolo, Brazil: Emoção, 2008.

Chalmers, David J. and Andy Clark. "The Extended Mind." *Philosophy of Mind: Classical and Contemporary Readings*. Ed. David Chalmers. Oxford University Press, 2002.

Clair, Patrick. "True Detective." *Art of the Title*. 2014. http://www.artofthetitle.com/title/true-detective.

Clough, Patricia Ticineto. *AutoAffection: Unconscious Thought in the Age of Technology*. Minneapolis: University of Minnesota Press, 2000.

Colebrook, Claire. "The Secret of Theory." *Deleuze Studies* 4.3 (2010): 287–300.

Collier, John. "Simulating Autonomous Anticipation: The Importance of Dubois' Conjecture." *Biosytems* 91.2 (2008): 346-354.

Combes, Muriel. *Gilbert Simondon and the Philosophy of the Transindividual*. Trans. Thomas Lamarre. Cambridge, MA: MIT Press, 2013.

Connolly, William. *A World of Becoming*. Durham: Duke University Press, 2011.

Corner, John. "Television in Theory." *Media, Culture & Society* 19.2 (1997): 247-262.

Coupland, Douglas. *Marshall McLuhan: You Know Nothing of My Work!* New York: Atlas, 2010.

Cubitt, Sean. "Electric Light and Electricity." *Theory, Culture & Society* 30.7-8 (2013): 309-323.

Cummings, Neil and Marysia Lewandowska. "From Capital to Enthusiasm: An Exhibitionary Practice." *Exhibition Experiments*. Eds. Sharon Macdonald & Paul Basu. Oxford: Blackwell, 2007. 132–153.

Darwin, Charles. *The Formation of Vegetable Mold through the Action of Worms with Observations on Their Habits*. London: John Murray, 1881.

De Brabandere, Nicole. "Experimenting with Affect across Drawing and Choreography." *Body & Society* 22.3 (2016): 103-124.

DeLanda, Manuel. *Intensive Science and Virtual Philosophy*. New York and London: Continuum, 2005.

Deleuze, Gilles. *Foucault*. Trans. Séan Hand. Minneapolis: University of Minnesota Press, 1988.

Deleuze, Gilles. *Cinema 2: The Time-Image*. Trans. Hugh Tomlinson and Robert Caleta. Minneapolis: University of Minnesota Press, 1989.

Deleuze, Gilles. *Logic of Sense*. Trans. Mark Lester with Charles Stivale. Ed. Constantin V. Boundas. New York: Columbia University Press, 1990.

Deleuze, Gilles. *Bergsonism*. Trans. Hugh Tomlinson and Barbara Habberjam. New York: Zone Books, 1991.

Deleuze, Gilles. "Postscript on the Societies of Control." *October* 59 (Winter 1992): 3-7.

Deleuze, Gilles. *The Fold. Leibniz and the Baroque*. Trans. Tom Conley. London: Athlone Press, 1993.

Deleuze, Gilles. *Difference and Repetition*. Trans. Paul Patton. New York: Columbia University Press, 1994a.

Deleuze, Gilles. "What is the Creative Act?" *French Theory in America*. Eds. Sylvène Lotringer and Graham Burchell. New York: Columbia, 1994b.

Deleuze, Gilles. "Mediators." *Negotiations:1972-1990*. Trans. Martin Joughin. New York: Columbia University Press, 1995. 121-134.

Deleuze, Gilles. *Essays Critical and Clinical*. Trans. Daniel W. Smith and Michael A. Greco. Minneapolis: University of Minnesota Press, 1997.

Deleuze, Gilles. *Desert Island and Other Texts 1953–1974*. Trans. Michael Taormina. New York: Semiotext(e), 2004.

Deleuze, Gilles. *Pure Immanence: Essays on A Life*. New York: Zone Books, 2005.

Deleuze, Gilles. *Nietzsche and Philosophy*. Trans. Janis Tomlinson. New York: Continuum, 2006.

Deleuze, Gilles. "Immanence: A Life." *Two Regimes of Madness. Texts and Interviews 1975-1995*. Ed. David Lapoujade. Semiotex(e): New York, 2007: 384-389.

Deleuze, Gilles and Claire Parnet. *Dialogues*. Trans. Hugh Tomlinson and Barbara Hammerjam. London: Athlone, 1987.

Deleuze, Gilles and Félix Guattari. *Anti-Oedipus: Capitalism and Schizophrenia*. Minneapolis: University of Minnesota Press, 1983.

Deleuze, Gilles and Félix Guattari. *Kafka: Towards a Minor Literature*. Trans. Dana Polan. Minneapolis: University of Minnesota Press, 1986.

Deleuze, Gilles and Félix Guattari. *A Thousand Plateaus: Capitalism and Schizophrenia*. Trans. Brian Massumi. Minneapolis and London: University of Minnesota Press, 1987.

Deleuze, Gilles and Félix Guattari. *What is Philosophy?* Trans. Hugh Tomlinson and Graham Burchell. New York: Columbia University Press, 1994.

Delmas-Marty, Mireille. "Le laboratoire chinois." *La Chine et la démocratie*. Eds. Mireille Delmas-Marty and Pierre-Étienne Will. Paris: Fayard, 2007.

Depraz, Natalie. "Temporalité et affection dans les manuscrits tardifs sur la temporalité de Husserl (1929–1935)." *ALTER: Revue de phenomenologie* 2 (1994): 63-86.

Diamanti, Eleonora. "Formation et transformation de la place publique montréalaise." *Formes urbaines : circulation, stockage et transmission de l'expression culturelle à Montréal*. Eds. Will Straw, Annie Gérin and Anouk Bélanger. Montreal: Les éditions esse, 2014. 67-74.

Dieter, Michael. "The Becoming Environmental of Power: Tactical Media After Control." *The Fibreculture Journal* 18 (2011). http://eighteen.fibreculturejournal.org/2011/10/09/fcj-126-the-becoming-environmental-of-power-tactical-media-after-control/.

Dolphijn, Rick and Iris van der Tuin. *New Materialism: Cartographies and Interviews*. Ann Arbor, Michigan: Open Humanities Press, 2012.

Doane, Mary Ann. "Information, Crisis, Catastrophe." *Logics of Television: Essays in Cultural Criticism*. Ed. Patricia Mellencamp. Bloomington: Indiana University Press, 1990. 222-239.

Eco, Umberto. *The Open Work*. Cambridge: Harvard University Press, 1989.

Eco, Umberto. "Interpreting Serials." *The Limits of Interpretation*. Bloomington: Indiana University Press, 1994. 83-100.

Ednie-Brown, Pia. "Architectural Animality: drawings out for a walk." Mixed media, exhibited as part of *Trace: Architectural musings*. Curated by Leonie Matthews & Amanda Alderson. Mundaring Arts Centre, Western Australia, October 3rd - November 9th, 2014.

Ednie-Brown, Pia. "Critical passions building architectural movements toward a radical pedagogy (in 10 steps)." *Inflexions* 8 (2015a): 20-48. http://www.senselab.ca/inflexions/radicalpedagogy/main.html#Ednie-Brown.

Ednie_Brown, Pia. "Can a house be alive?" *TED*x. Public lecture. 2015b. https://www.youtube.com/watch?v=oH-27DNqcO0&list=PLsRNoUx8w3rORCN0KrRaLO7xKt46mCDkf&index=3.

Ednie-Brown, Pia and Mewburn, Inger. "Laughter and the Undeniable Difference Between Us." *Intimate Transactions: Art, Exhibition and Interaction within Distributed Network Environments*. Ed. Jillian Hamilton. Brisbane: Australasian CRC for Interaction Design, 2006: 76-87.

Edwards, Paul N. *A Vast Machine: Computer Models, Climate Data, and the Politics of Global Warming*. Cambridge, MA: MIT Press, 2013.

Engell, Lorenz: "Medientheorien der Medien selbst." *Handbuch Medienwissenschaft*. Ed Jens Schröter. Stuttgart/Weimar: J.B. Metzler, 2014. 207-213.

Erickson, Britta. "Process and Meaning in the Art of Xu Bing." In Three Installations by Xu Bing. Madison: Elvehjem Museum of Art, University of Wisconsin-Madison, 1991.

Erickson, Britta. *The Art of Xu Bing: Words without Meaning, Meaning without Words*. Washington, D.C.: Arthur M. Sackler Gallery and Smithsonian Institution; Seattle: University of Washington Press, 2001.

Esposito, Roberto. *Terza Persona*. Torino: Einaudi, 2007.

Esposito, Roberto. *Le persone e le cose*. Torino: Einaudi, 2014.

Ettinger L. Bracha. "Matrix and Metramorphosis." *differences: a Journal of Feminist Cutural Studies* 4.3 (1992): 176-207.

Ettinger L. Bracha. "Woman-Other-Thing: A Matrixial Touch." *Matrix-Borderlines*. Oxford: Museum of Modern Art, (1993): 11-18.

Ettinger L. Bracha. *The Matrixial Gaze*. University of Leeds: Feminist Arts and Histories Network, 1995a.

Ettinger L. Bracha. "Woman as Object a: Between Phantasy and Art." *Journal of Philosophy and the Visual Arts* 6 (1995b): 56-77.

Ettinger L. Bracha. "Trauma and Beauty: Trans-subjectivity in Art." *n.paradoxa* 3 (1999): 15-23.

Ettinger L. Bracha. "From Transference to the Aesthetic Paradigm: A Conversation with Félix Guattari." *A Shock to Thought: Expression After Deleuze and Guattari*. Ed. Brian Massumi. London and New York: Routledge, 2002. 240-245.

Ettinger L. Bracha. *The Matrixial Borderspace*. Ed. Brian Massumi. Minneapolis, London: University of Minnesota Press, 2006.

Ettinger L. Bracha. "Fragilization and Resistance." *Studies in The Maternal* 1.2 (2009): 1-31.

Ettinger L. Bracha. "Uncanny Awe, Uncanny Compassion and Matrixial Transjectivity beyond Uncanny Anxiety." *French Literature Series* 38 (2011): 1-30.

Evans, Dylan. *An Introductory Dictionary of Lacanian Psychoanalysis*. London and New York: Routledge, 1996.

Faumont, Serge, Rondeau, Gary, Thiele, Todd R., et al. "An Image-Free Opto-Mechanical System for Creating Virtual Environments and Imaging Neuronal Activity in Freely Moving Caenorhabditis elegans." *PLoS ONE* 6.9 (2011).

Feneuil, Anthony. *Bergson: mystique et philosophie*, Paris : PUF, 2011.

Feuer, Jane. "The Concept of Live Television: Ontology as Ideology." *Regarding Television:Critical Approaches – An Anthology*. Ed. E. Ann Kaplan. Los Angeles: The American Film Institute, 1983. 12-22.

Forsythe, William. "Choreographic Objects." http://www.williamforsythe.de/essay.html.

Foucault, Michel. 1977. "Nietzsche, Genealogy, History." In Donald F. Bouchard, ed., *Language, Memory, Counter-Practice*. Ithaca, NY: Cornell University Press. 139–164.

Foucault, Michel. 1979. *Discipline and Punish: The Birth of the Prison*. Trans. Alan Sheridan. New York: Vintage.

Frayling, C. "Research in Art and Design". *Royal College of Art Research Papers* 1.1 (1993): 1-5.

Frazer, John Hamilton. "The Cybernetics of Architecture: A Tribute to the Contribution of Gordon Pask." *Kybernetes* 30.5-6 (2001): 641-651.

Fritsch, Jonas. "Affective Experience as a Theoretical Foundation for Interaction Design." PhD Dissertation presented to the Faculty of Humanities, Aarhus University. 2011.

Fritsch, Jonas, Breinbjerg, M. & Basballe, D. "Ekkomaten: Exploring the Echo as a Design Fiction Concept." *Journal of Digital Creativity* 24.1 (2013): 60-74.

Fritsch, Jonas, Pold Soren Bro, Vestergaard, Lasse Steenbock Vestergaard and Melissa Lucas. "Ink – Designing for Performative Literary Interactions." *Journal of Personal and Ubiquitous Computing* 18.7 (2014): 1551-1556.

Fritsch, Jonas. and O. S. Iversen (2014): "Designing for Experience: Scaffolding the Emergence of a Design Ecology." In *Enterprising Initiatives in the Experience Economy: Transforming Social Worlds, Routledge Studies in Entrepreneurship*. Eds. Britta Tim Knudsen, Dorthe Refslund Christensen and Per Blenker. London: Routledge, 2014. 226-244.

Fuller, Matthew. *Media Ecologies: Materialist Energies in Art and Technoculture*. Cambridge, MA: MIT Press, 2005.

Fuller, Matthew and Andrew Goffey. *Evil Media*. Cambridge, MA: MIT Press, 2012.

Funder, Anna. *The Girl with the Dogs*. Penguin Australia, 2015.

Gallagher, Shaun. "Protention, Schizophrenia, and Gesture." *Interacting Bodies: Corps en Interaction*. Ecole normale supérieure Lettres et Sciences humaines Lyon-France, June 15-18 2005.

Galloway, Alexander, Eugene Thacker and McKenzie Wark. *Excommunication: Three Inquiries in Media and Mediation*. Chicago: Chicago University Press, 2013.

Gardner, Howard. *The Mind's New Science: A History of the Cognitive Revolution*. New York: Basic Books, 1987.

Genosko, Gary. *Felix Guattari: An Aberrant Introduction*. London: Continuum, 2002.

Genosko, Gary. *Félix Guattari: A Critical Introduction*. London: Pluto Press, 2009.

Gidal, Peter. *Structural Film Anthology*. London: British Film Institute, 1978.

Gil, José. *Metamorphoses of the Body*. Trans. Stephen Muecke. Minneapolis: University of Minnesota Press, 1998.

Gilbert, Jeremy. *Common Ground: Democracy and Collectivity in an Age of Individualism*. London: Pluto, 2013.

Madeline Gins and Arakawa. *The Architectural Body*. Tuscaloosa: University of Alabama Press, 2002.

Goffey, Andrew. "Abstract Experience." *Theory Culture Society* 25.4 (2008): 15-30.

Golson, Jordon. "This Helmet Will Make F-35 Pilots Missile-Slinging Cyborgs." *Wired* (September 14, 2015). http://www.wired.com/2015/09/helmet-will-make-f-35-pilots-missile-slinging-cyborgs/.

Goodman, Steven. *Sonic Warfare: Sound, Affect and the Ecology of Fear*. Cambridge, MA: MIT Press, 2010.

Gould, Stephen Jay and Elizabeth S. Vrba. "Exaption: A Missing Term in the Science of Form." *Paleobiology* 8.1 (1982): 4-15.

Govan, Michael. *James Turrell: Seeing Yourself See*. Munich: Prestel, 2013.

Graeber, David. *Debt: The First 5,000 Years*. New York: Melville House, 2012.

Green, Nick. "On Gordon Pask." *Kybernetes* 30.5-6 (2001): 673-682.

Greenfield, Adam. *Against the Smart City (The city is here for you to use. Book 1).* Kindle Edition. Do Projects, 2013.

Grosz, Elizabeth. *Volatile Bodies: Toward a Corporeal Feminism*. Sydney: Allen and Unwin, 1994.

Groys, Boris. *Art Power*. Cambridge, MA: MIT Press, 2008.

Groys, Boris. "Comrades of Time." *e-flux Journal* 11 (December 2009): 1–11.

Grusin, Richard. *Premediation: Affect and Mediality After 9/11*. London: Palgrave Macmillan, 2010.

Grusin, Richard. "Radical Mediation." *Critical Inquiry* 42.1 (Autumn 2015): 124-148.

Guattari, Félix. *Chaosmosis. An ethico-aesthetic paradigm*. Trans. Paul Bains and Julian Pefanis. Bloomington: Indiana University Press, 1995.

Guattari, Félix. "Ritornellos and Existential Affects." *The Guattari Reader*. Ed. Gary Genosko. Oxford: Blackwell, 1996: 158–171.

Guattari, Félix. *The Three Ecologies*. Trans. Ian Pindar and Paul Sutton. London and New York: Continuum, 2008.

Guattari, Félix. *Chaosophy: Texts and Interviews 1972-1977*. Eds. Sylvere Lotringer. Trans. David L. Sweet, Jarred Becker, and Taylor Adkins. Los Angeles: Semiotext(e), 2009.

Guattari, Félix. *The Machinic Unconscious: Essays in Schizoanalysis*. Trans. Taylor Adkins. New York: Semiotext(e), 2010.

Guattari, Félix. *Schizoanalytic Cartographies*. Trans. Andrew Goffey. London: Bloomsbury, 2012.

Halewood, Michael. "A.N. Whitehead, Information and Social Theory." *Theory, Culture & Society* 22(6) (2005a): 73–94.

Halewood, Michael. "On Whitehead and Deleuze: The Process of Materiality." *Configurations* 13.1 (2005b): 57-76.

Halewood, Michael. "Language, the Body and the Problem of Signification." *Butler on Whitehead: On the Occasion*. Eds. Roland Faber and Michael Halewood. New York: Lexington Books, 2012: 176-195.

Hamilton, Jillian. "A Reformation of Space: Intimate Transactions in Art and Distributed Communication." *Intimate Transactions: Art, Exhibition and Interaction within Distributed Network Environments*. Ed. Jillian Hamilton. Brisbane: Australasian CRC for Interaction Design, 2006: 116-129.

Hamilton, Jillian and Lavery, Peter. "Introduction". *Intimate Transactions: Art, Exhibition and Interaction within Distributed Network Environments. Ed.* in Jillian Hamilton. Brisbane: Australasian CRC for Interaction Design, 2006. 2-11.

Hansen, Mark. "Engineering Pre-individual Potentiality: Technics, Transindividuation, and 21st Century Media." *SubStance* 41.3 (2012): 32-59.

Hansen, Mark. *Feed-Forward: On the Future of Twenty-First-Century Media*. Chicago: Chicago University Press, 2015.

Hansen, Miriam. "Early Cinema, Late Cinema: Transformations of the Public Sphere." *Screen* 34.3 (1993): 134-152.

Haraway, Donna. *Modest_Witness@Second_Millennium.FemaleMan_meets_OncoMouse: Feminism and Technoscience*. New York and London: Routledge, 1997.

Haraway, Donna and Thyrza Nichols Goodeve□. *How Like a Leaf: An Interview with Donna Haraway*. London: Routledge, 2013.

Hardt, Michael. "The Common in Communism." *Rethinking Marxism. A Journal of Economics, Culture and Society* 22.3 (August 2010): 346-356.

Harman, Graham. *Tool-Being: Heidegger and the Metaphysics of Objects*. Open Court Publishing, 2002.

Harney, Stefano. "Hapticality in the Undercommons or From Operations Management to Black Ops." Helsinki: CuMMA Papers, 2013. https://cummastudies.files.wordpress.com/2013/08/cumma-papers-9.pdf.

Harney, Stephano and Fred Moten. *The Undercommons: Fugitive Planning and Black Studies*. Wivenhoe, New York and Port Watson: Minor Compositions, 2013.

Harrist, Robert E., Jr. "Background Stories: Xu Bing's Art of Transformation." *British Museum*. 2011.

Hayek, Friedrich. "The Use of Knowledge in Society." *American Economic Review* 35.4 (1945): 519-30.

Hayles, N. Katherine. *How We Became Posthuman: Virtual Bodies In Cybernetics, Literature, And Informatics*. Chicago: University of Chicago Press, 2008.

Heaven, Douglas. "The Obsessioneers." *New Scientist* 2971 (2014): 38-41.

Heidegger, Martin. *Being and Time*. Trans. Joan Stambaugh. Albany: University of New York Press, 2010.

Herzongenrath, Bernd. "Introduction." *An [Un]Likely Alliance: Thinking Environment[s] with Deleuze|Guattari*. Ed. Bernd Herzogenrath. Newcastle Upon Tyne: Cambridge Scholars Press, 2008. 1-22.

Hoghe, Raimund. " 'Walzer.' Fragen, Themen, Stichpunkte aus den Proben." *Theatergeschichten von Raimund Hoghe*. Eds. Raimund Hoghe and Pina Bausch. Frankfurt am Main: Suhrkamp, 1986. 84–89.

Holland, Eugene. "Deleuze and Psychoanalysis". The *Cambridge Companion to Gilles Deleuze*. Eds. Daniel W. Smith and Henry Somers-Hall. Cambridge: Cambridge University Press, 2012. 307-336.

Hollnagel, Erik and David D. Woods. *Joint Cognitive Systems: Foundations of Cognitive Systems Engineering*. London: Taylor and Francis, 2005.

Hongisto, Ilona. "Documentary Imagination. The disappeared, the clue and the photograph." *Journal of Scandinavian Cinema* 3.1 (2013): 49–63.

Hongisto, Ilona. *Soul of the Documentary: Framing, Expression, Ethics*. Amsterdam: Amsterdam University Press, 2015.

Hornblow, Michael. *Sponging the Chair: Diagramming Affect through Architecture and Performance*. PhD Dissertation, Royal Melbourne Institute of Technology, 2013.

Hornblow, Michael. "O'megaVille: Excursions in Planetary Urbanism." International Symposium on Electronic Art, 2015a. Conference Presentation. http://isea2015.org/publications/proceedings-of-the-21st-international-symposium-on-electronic-art/

Hornblow, Michael. "A Sahara in the Head: The Problem of Landing." *Inflexions* 8 (2015b): 222-238. http://www.senselab.ca/inflexions/radicalpedagogy/main.html#Hornblow

Horsefield, Craigie. *Relations*. North Sydney: Museum of Contemporary Art, 2007.

Huhn, Rosi. "Moving Emissions and Hollow Spots in the Field of Vision." *Matrix-Borderlines*. Oxford: Museum of Modern Art, 1993: 5-10.

Hyppolite, Jean. *Logic and Existence*. Trans. Leonard Lawlor and Amit Sen. Albany: State University of New York Press, 1987.

Ivakhiv, Adrian J. *Ecologies of the Moving Image: Cinema, Affect, Nature*. Waterloo: Wilfred Laurier Press, 2013.

Iaconesi, Salvatore. "Conflict is Transgression." *Art is Open Source* (2015). http://www.artisopensource.net/network/artisopensource/2015/06/08/conflict-and-transgression/#.VYFEnaLnyuU.facebook

Jacobs, Jane. *The Death and Life of Great American Cities*, New York: Vintage Books, 1992.

Jacobs, Jane. *The Nature of Economies*. New York: The Modern Library, 2000

James, William. *The Will to Believe and Other Essays in Popular Philosophy*. New York: Longmans, Green, and co., 1912.

James, William. *Principles of Psychology*, vol. 1. New York : Dover, 1950a.

James, William. 1950b. *Principles of Psychology*, vol. 2. New York : Dover.

James, William. *The Meaning of Truth: A Sequel to Pragmatism*. New York: Greenwood, 1986.

James, William. *Essays in Radical Empiricism*. Lincoln: University of Nebraska Press, 1996a.

James, William. 1996b. *A Pluralistic Universe*. Lincoln : University of Nebraska Press.

Janesick, James. *Scientific Charge-Coupled Devices*. Bellingham: SPIE Press, 2001.

Jones, Judith. *Intensity: An Essay in Whiteheadian Ontology*. Nashville: Vanderbilt University Press, 1998.

Jullien, François. *In Praise of Blandness. Proceeding from Chinese Thought and Aesthetics*. Trans. Paula M. Varsano. New York: Zone Books, 2004.

Jung, Heekyoung, Erik Stolterman, Will Ryan, Yonya Thompson, and Martin Siegel. "Toward a Framework for Ecologies of Artifacts: Digital Artifacts Interconnected within a Personal Life?" *NordiCHI 2008: Using Bridges*, 18-22. 2008.

Kandel, Eric. *In Search of Memory: The Emergence of a New Science of Mind*. New York: W. W. Norton, 2007.

Kaptelinin, Victor and Liam. J. Bannon. "Interaction Design Beyond the Product: Creating Technology-Enhanced Activity Spaces." *Human-Computer Interaction* 27.3 (2012): 277–309.

Kaufman, Eleanor. *Deleuze, The Dark Precursor: Dialectic, Structure, Being.* Baltimore: Johns Hopkins University Press, 2012.

Kember, Sarah and Joanna Zylinska. *Life after New Media: Mediation as a Vital Process.* Cambridge, MA: MIT Press, 2014.

Kjeldskov Jesper. *Designing Mobile Interactions: The Continual Convergence of Form and Context, Volume I and II.* PhD Dissertation. Aalborg University, Department of Computer Science. 2013.

Klarer, Mario. "Putting Television 'Aside': Novel Narration in House of Cards." *New Review of Film and Television Studies* 12.2 (2014): 203-220.

Kohn, Eduardo. "Natural engagements and ecological aesthetics among the Avila Runa of Amazonian Ecuador." PhD Thesis, University of Wisconsin, Madison. 2002.

Krippendorff, Klaus. *The Semantic Turn: A New Foundation for Design.* Boca Raton, London and New York: Taylor & Francis, CRC Press, 2006.

Langer, Susanne. *Feeling and Form: A Theory of Art Developed from Philosophy in a New Key.* New York: Charles Scribner's Sons, 1953.

Lapoujade, David. "From Transcendental Empiricism to Worker Nomadism: William James." *Pli* 9 (2000): 190-199.

Lapoujade, David. *Puissances du temps: versions de Bergson*. Paris: Minuit, 2010.

Lapoujade, David. *Powers of Time*. Helsinki/São Paolo: n-1 publications, 2013.

Latour, Bruno, Pablo Jensen, Tommaso Venturini, Sebastian Grauwin and Dominique Bouiller. "The Whole is Always Smaller Than Its Parts. A Digital Test of Gabriel Tarde's Monads." *The British Journal of Sociology* 63.4 (December 2012): 590-615.

Lazzarato Maurizio. *Videophilosophie. Zeitwahrnehmung im Postfordismus*. Berlin: b_books, 2002.

Lazzarato, Maurizio. "Video, Flows and Real Time." *Art and the Moving Image: A Critical Reader.* Ed. Tanya Leighton. London: Tate Publishing, 2007: 283–85.

Lazzarato, Maurizio. *The Making of Indebted Man: An Essay on the Neoliberal Condition*. Trans. Joshua David Jordan, 2012.

Levy, Malcolm. "Other-frames and the Moving Image." Unpublished essay.

Lewandowska, Marysia. "Museum commons. Research driven art practice and the public function of archives, collections and exhibitions." Keynote lecture at the NECS Conference, Lodz, Poland (20 June 2015). https://www.youtube.com/watch?v=aKCBdmmi9G4&feature=youtu.be

Libet, Benjamin, and Curtis Gleason, Elwood Wright, Dennis Pearl. "Time of Conscious Intention to Act in Relation to Onset of Cerebral Activity (Readiness-Potential). The Unconscious Initiation of a Freely Voluntary Act." *Neurophysiology of Consciousness*. Contemporary Neuroscientists Series. 1983. 249-268.

Lingis, Aphonso. *Violence and Splendor.* Illinois: Northwest University Press, 2011.

Liu Yuedi. "Calligraphic Expression in Contemporary Chinese Art: Xu Bing's Pioneer Experiment." *Subversive Strategies in Contemporary Chinese Art*. Ed. Mary Wiseman and Yuedi Liu. Brill, 2011.

Lorange, Astrid. *How Reading Is Written: A Brief Index to Gertrude Stein*. Middletown, CT: Wesleyan University Press, 2014.

Lorraine, Tamsin. "Oedipus and the Anoedipal Transsexual." *Between the Psyche and the Social*: *Psychoanalytic Social Theory.* Eds. Kelly Oliver and Steve Edwin. Boston: Rowman and Littlefield, 2002: 3-18.

Lotti, Laura. "'Making sense of power': Repurposing Gilbert Simondon's philosophy of individuation for a mechanist approach to capitalism (by way of François Laruelle)." *Platform: Journal of Media and Communication* 6 (2015): 22-33.

MacKenzie, Adrian. *Transductions: Bodies and Machines at Speed*. London: Continuum, 2002.

Malabou, Catherine. *From Sorrow to Indifference*. Provost's Lecture Series, Stony Brook University. October 22, 2013. https://www.youtube.com/watch?v=KoAd1lQ1bXM.

Manning, Erin. *Relationscapes. Movement, Art, Philosophy.* Cambridge and New York: The MIT Press, 2009a.

Manning, Erin. "Propositions for the Verge: William Forsythe's Choreographic Objects." *Inflexions* 2 (2009b). http://www.inflexions.org/n2_manninghtml.html.

Manning, Erin. "7 Propositions for the Impossibility of Isolation or, the Radical Empiricism of the Network." *eipcp: european institute for progressive cultural policies* (January 2011). http://eipcp.net/transversal/0811/manning/en. Eipcp 2011.

Manning, Erin. *Always More Than One: Individuation's Dance*. Durham and London: Duke University Press, 2013.

Manning, Erin. "Weather Patterns, or How Minor Gestures Entertain the Environment." *Complex Ubiquity Effects: Individuating, Situating, Eventualizing*. Eds. Jay David Bolter Ulrick Ekman, Lily Diaz, Morten Sondergaard, Maria Engberg. New York: Routledge. 2015.

Manning, Erin. *The Minor Gesture*. Durham: Duke University Press, 2016.

Manning, Erin. Forthcoming. "What Things Do When They Shape Each Other." *The Anarchive*.

Manning, Erin and Brian Massumi. "For a Pragmatics of the Useless: Propositions for Thought" (2013). https://www.youtube.com/watch?v=Mp5REJAi20o

Manning, Erin and Brian Massumi. *Thought in the Act, Passages in the Ecology of Experience*. Durham: Duke University Press, 2014.

Mason, Matt. *The Pirate's Dilemma. How Youth Culture is Reinventing Capitalism*. New York: Free Press, 2008.

Massumi, Brian. *A User´s Guide to Capitalism and Schizophrenia*. Cambridge and London: MIT Press, 1992.

Massumi, Brian. "The Autonomy of Affect." *Cultural Critique* 31 (Autumn 1995): 83-109.

Massumi, Brian. *Parables for the Virtual: Movement, Affect, Sensation*. Duke University Press, 2002.

Massumi, Brian. "Fear (The Spectrum Said)." *Positions* 13.1 (2005): 31-48.

Massumi, Brian. "National Enterprise Emergency. Steps Toward an Ecology of Powers." *Theory, Culture, and Society* 26.6 (2009): 153-186.

Massumi, Brian. "On Critique." *Inflexions* 4 (November 2010): 337-340. http://www.inflexions.org/n4_t_massumihtml.html

Massumi, Brian. *Semblance and Event. Activist Philosophy and the Occurent Arts*. Cambridge: MIT, 2011.

Massumi, Brian. *What Animals Teach Us about Politics*. Durham: Duke University Press, 2014.

Massumi, Brian. *Ontopower: Wars, Powers, and the State of Perception*. Durham: Duke University Press, 2015a.

Massumi, Brian. *Politics of Affect*. Cambridge: Polity Press, 2015b.

Massumi, Brian. *The Power at the End of the Economy*. Durham: Duke University Press, 2015c.

Massumi, Brian and Joel McKim. "Of Microperception and Micropolitics An Interview with Brian Massumi." *Inflexions* 3 (2008) http://www.inflexions.org/n3_massumihtml.html

Massumi, Brian, Jason Nguyen and Mark Davis: "Interview [with Brian Massumi]". *Manifold. Forms of Time* 2 (2008): 17-30.

Massumi, Brian and Mary Zournazi. "Navigating Moments: A Conversation with Brian Massumi." *Hope: New Philosophies for Change*. Ed. Mary Zournazi. Sydney: Pluto Press, 2002: 210-24.

Maturana, Humberto and Francisco Varela. *Autopoiesis and Cognition: The Realisation of Living*. 1981.

Mauss, Marcel. *The Gift. Forms and Functions of Exchange in Archaic Societies*. Trans. Ian Cunnison. Mansfield Centre: Martino Publishing, 2011.

McKenzie, Scott. *Screening Québec: Québécois Moving Images, National Identity, and the Public Sphere*. Manchester: Manchester UP, 2004.

Meillassoux, Quentin. 2010. *After Finitude: An Essay on the Necessity of Contingency*. Trans. Ray Brassier. London: Bloomsbury.

Mittell, Jason. "Narrative Complexity in Contemporary American Television." *The Velvet Light Trap* 58 (2006): 29–40.

Mollison, Bill. *Permaculture, a Designer's Manual*. Canada: Tagari Publications, 1999.

Monbiot, George. *Feral: Rewilding the Land, Sea and Human Life*. Chicago: Chicago Press, 2014.

Moten, Fred and Adam Fitzgerald. "An Interview with Fred Moten: In Praise of Harold Bloom, Collaboration and Book Fetishes." *Literary Hub* (August, 2015). http://lithub.com/an-interview-with-fred-moten-pt-i/.

Munster, Anna. *An Aesthesia of Networks. Conjunctive Experience in Art and Technology*. Cambridge and London: MIT Press, 2013.

Munster, Anna. "Tuning in to the Signaletic: experiements with the imperceptible of real time." Keynote Address, *Tuning Speculaton III*. Toronto Canada, November 20-22, 2015.

Murphie, Andrew. "Putting the Virtual back into VR." *A Shock to Thought: Expression in the Philosophy of Gilles Deleuze and Félix Guattari*. Ed. Brian Massumi. London: Routledge, 2002: 188-214.

Murphie, Andrew. "Electronicas: Differential Media and Proliferating, Transient Worlds." *Melbourne DAC, the 5th International Digital Arts and Culture Conference*. Proceedings, 2003. 144-154.

Murphie, Andrew. "The World as Clock: The Network Society and Experimental Ecologies." *Topia: Canadian Journal of Cultural Studies*. Spring (2004): 117-139.

Murphie, Andrew. "Differential Life, Perception and the Nervous Elements: Whitehead, Bergson and Virno on the Technics of Living." *Culture Machine* 7 (2005). http://www.culturemachine.net/index.php/cm/article/view/32/39.

Murphie, Andrew. "Deleuze, Guattari and Neuroscience." *Deleuze, Science and the Force of the Virtual*. Ed. Peter Gaffney. Minneapolis: University of Minnesota Press, 2010: 330-367.

Murphie, Andrew. "Hacking the aesthetic: David Haines and Joyce Hinterding's new ecologies of signal." *Journal of Aesthetics and Culture*. 8.1 (2012).

Murphie, Andrew. "Convolving Signals: thinking the performance of computational processes", Performance Paradigm, 9 (2013): 1-21. http://www.performanceparadigm.net/wp-content/uploads/2013/12/murphie-andrew_convolving_signals_2.pdf.

Murphie, Andrew. "Making Sense: The Transformation of Documentary by Digital and Networked Media." *Studies in Documentary Film* 8.3 (2014): 188-204.

Nakatani, Hajime. "Imperious Griffonage: Xu Bing and the Graphic Regime." *Art Journal* 68. 3 (Fall 2009): 6-29.

Nancy, Jean-Luc. *Being Singular Plural*. Stanford, CA: Stanford University Press, 2000.

Nardi, Bonnie. A. and O'Day, Vicki. L. *Information Ecologies: Using technology with Heart*. MIT Press: Cambridge, MA, 1999.

Navon, David. "From Pink Elephants to Pyschosomatic disorders: Paradoxical Effects in Cognition." *Psycholoquy* 5.36 (1994). http://www.cogsci.ecs.soton.ac.uk/cgi/psyc/newpsy?5.36

Nelson, Elissa. "Windows into the Digital World: Distributor Strategies and Consumer Choice in an Era of Connected Viewing." *Connected Viewing: Selling, Streaming, & Sharing Media in the Digital Era*. Eds. Jennifer Holt and Kevin Sanson. New York and London: Routledge, 2013. 62-78.

"Neurons in human skin perform advanced calculations." *ScienceDaily*. September 1, 2014. http://www.sciencedaily.com/releases/2014/09/140901090301.htm.

Newfield, Christopher. "Corporate Open Source. Intellectual Property and The Struggle Over Value." *Radical Philosophy. Philosophy Journal of the Independent Left* 181 (September-October 2013): 6-11. http://www.radicalphilosophy.com/commentary/corporate-open-source

Newman, Michael Z. and Elana Levine. *Legitimating Television: Media Convergence and Cultural Status*. New York: Routledge, 2012.

Nguyen, Jason and Mark Davis. "In dialogue with Brian Massumi." *Manifold Magazine* 3 (Fall 2008): 9-18.

Nietzsche, Friedrich. *Thus Spoke Zarathustra: A Book for Everyone and Nobody*. Trans. Graham Parkes. Oxford: Oxford University Press, 2008.

Northwestern University. "Conventional wisdom of how neurons operate challenged: Axons can work in reverse." *ScienceDaily*. February 19, 2011. http://www.sciencedaily.com/releases/2011/02/110217171344.htm.

O'Neill, Lisa. "Placing the Participant in the Performing Role". *Intimate Transactions: Art, Exhibition and Interaction within Distributed Network Environments*. Ed. Jillian Hamilton. Brisbane: Australasian CRC for Interaction Design, 2006. 36-43.

Parikka, Jussi. *Insect Media: An Archeology of Animals and Technology*. Minneapolis: University of Minnesota Press, 2010.

Parikka,Jusi. "Media Ecologies and Imaginary Media: Transversal Expansions, Contractions, and Foldings." *The Fibreculture Journal*, 17 (2011).

Parikka, Jussi. "The Geology of Media." *The Atlantic*. October 11, 2013. http://www.theatlantic.com/technology/archive/2013/10/the-geology-of-media/280523/.

Parikka, Jussi. *The Anthrobscene*. Minneapolis: University of Minnesota Press, 2014.

Parisi, Luciana. "Symbiotic Architecture: Prehending Digitality." *Theory, Culture & Society* 26.2-3 (2009a): 346-374.

Parisi, Luciana. "Technoecologies of Sensation." *Deleuze|Guattari & Ecology*. Ed. Bernd Herzogenrath. London: Palgrave, 2009b: 182-199.

Parisi, Luciana. *Contagious Architecture: Computation, Aesthetics and Space*. Cambridge, MA: MIT Press, 2013.

Parisi, Luciana and Steve Goodman. "Extensive Continuum: Towards a Rhythmic Anarchitecture." *Inflexions* 2 (2009). http://www.inflexions.org/n2_parisigoodmanhtml.html.

Parisi, Luciana and Stamatia Portanova. "Soft Thought (in Architecture and Choreography)." *Computational Culture* 1 (2011). http://computationalculture.net/article/soft-thought>.

Parr, Adrian. "Deterritorialization /Reterritorialization" in *The Deleuze Dictionary*. ed. Parr, Adrian. Edinburgh University Press: Edinburgh, 2005.

Peirce, Charles Sanders. *Philosophical Writings of Peirce*. New York: Dover Publications, 1955.

Peirce, Charles. *The Essential Peirce, Volume 1: Selected Philosophical Writings (1867–1893)*. Eds. Nathan Houser, Christian J.W. Kloese. Bloomington: Indiana University Press, 1992a

Peirce, C. S.. *Reasoning and the Logic of Things*. Cambridge: Harvard University Press, 1992b.

Peirce, C.S. *Pragmatism as a Principle and Method of Right Thinking: The 1903 Lectures on Pragmatism*. Albany: State University of New York Press, 1997.

Peirce, Charles Sanders. *Collected Papers of Charles Sanders Peirce, Volumes I and II: Principles of Philosophy and Elements of Logic (Volume II)*. Eds. Charles Hartshorne, Paul Weiss. Cambridge, MA: Belknap Press (Harvard University Press), 2009.

Pelbart, Peter Pál. *Cartography of Exhaustion: Nihilism Inside Out*. Trans. Hortencia Santos Lencastre. Helsinki and São Paulo: n-1 publications, 2013.

Peters, John Durham. *The Marvelous Clouds: Towards a Philosophy of Elemental Media*. Chicago: Chicago University Press, 2015.

Phillips, Justy. *Scoreography: Compose-with a hole in the heart!* PhD Dissertation. RMIT University, Melbourne. 2014.

Poniewozik, James. "It's Not TV. It's *Arrested Development*." *Time* 181.19 (May 20, 2013): http://content.time.com/time/magazine/article/0,9171,2143009,00.html

Poniewozik, James. "Veronica Mars Rising. A Fan Revival Proves You Can Go Home Again, Kind Of." *Time*. (March 24, 2014): 56.

Portanova, Stamatia. *Moving without a Body: Digital Philosophy and Choreographic Thoughts*. Cambridge, Massachusetts, London: MIT Press, 2013.

Pradeep, Kumar. 2011. "CCD vs CMOS." Classle, May 7. https://www.classle.net. Accessed 12/22/2015.

Prigogine, Ilya. *From Being to Becoming: Time and Complexity in the Physical Sciences*. San Francisco: Freeman and Co., 1980.

Prigogine, Ilya and Isabelle Stengers. *The End of Certainty: Time, Chaos and the New Laws of Nature*. New York, London, Toronto, Sydney and Singapore: The Free Press, 1996.

Putnam, Hilary. 1994. "Peirce's Continuum." In Kenneth L. Kettner, ed., *Peirce and Contemporary Thought*: *Philosophical Inquiries*. New York: Fordham University Press. 1-24.

Quaranta, Domenico. *The Postmedia Perspective*. Rhizome Blog. January 12, 2011. https://www.rhizome.org/editorial/2011/jan/12/the-postmedia-perspective/

Rainer, Yvonne. "Some Retrospective Notes on a Dance for 10 People and 12 Mattresses Called 'Parts of Some Sextets,' Performed at the Wadsworth Atheneum, Hartford, Connecticut, and Judson Memorial Church, New York, in March, 1965." *The Tulane Drama Review* 10.2 (1965): 168.

Ricoeur, Paul. *Time and Narrative (Volume 1)*. Chicago: University of Chicago Press, 1990.

Rifkin, Jeremy. *The European Dream: How Europe's Vision of the Future Is Quietly Eclipsing the American Dream*. New York: Tarcher, 2005.

Riquier, Camille. "Bergson et le problème de la personnalité : la personne dans tous ses états." *Les études philosophiques* 81 (2007): 193-214.

Robbert, Adam. "Speculative Ecology: Matter, Media, and Mind." *CIIS Founders Symposium*. San Francisco CA. May 4, 2005. Conference Paper.

Robbert, Adam. "Earth Aesthetics: Knowledge and Media Ecologies." *Knowledge Ecology*. 2013a. http://knowledge-ecology.com/2013/07/14/earth-aesthetics-knowledge-and-media-ecologies-3/.

Robbert, Adam. "Geocentric Media Ecology." *Knowledge Ecology*. 2013b. http://knowledge-ecology.com/2013/10/14/geocentric-media-ecology/.

Roberston, Robin. "Some-thing from No-thing: G Spencer-Brown's Laws of Form". *Cybernetics and Human Knowing* 6.4 (April 1999): 43-55.

Rocha, Luis Mateus. "Adaptive Recommendation and Open-Ended Semiosis." *Kybernetes* 30.5/6 (2001): 821-854.Ume

Rowe, Colin. *The Mathematics of the Ideal Villa and Other Essays*. Cambridge, London: MIT Press 1988.

Schneider, Michael. "*Arrested Development* Creator Mitch Hurwitz Has Created a 22-Episode Season 4 Remix." *IndieWire*. July 27, 2016. http://www.indiewire.com/2016/07/arrested-development-creator-mitch-hurwitz-reedits-season-4-netflix-1201710496/ Accessed on October 3, 2017.

Schüll, Natasha Dow. *Addicted by Design: Machine Gambling in Las Vegas*. Princeton: Princeton University Press, 2012.

Sehgal, Melanie. "Wo anfangen? Wie überschreiten? William James und die Phänomenologie." *Journal Phänomenologie. Phänomenologie und Pragmatismus* 32 (2009): 9-20.

Serres, Michel. *The Birth of Physics*. Trans. Jack Hawkes. Manchester, UK: Clinamen Press, 2001.

Sha, Xin Wei. *Poiesis and enchantment in topological matter.* Cambridge, MA: MIT Press, 2013.

Shannon, Claude Elwood. "A mathematical theory of communication." ACM SIGMOBILE Mobile Computing and Communications Review 5.1 (2001): 3-55.

Shaviro, Steven. *Without Criteria: Kant, Whitehead, Deleuze, and Aesthetics*. Cambridge, MA: MIT Press, 2009.

Shaviro, Steven. *The Universe of Things*. Minneapolis: University of Minnesota Press, 2014.

Shaviro, Steven. *No Speed Limit: Three Essays on Accelerationism*. Minneapolis: Minnesota University Press, 2015.

Shouse, Eric. "Feeling, Emotion, Affect." *Media Culture Journal, Queensland University of Technology* 8.6 (2005). http://journal.media-culture.org.au/0512/03-shouse.php

Seising, Rudolf and Veronica Sanz. *Soft Computing in Humanities and Social Sciences*. New York: Springer, 2011.

Simondon, Gilbert. *On the Mode of Existence of Technical Objects*. Trans. Ninian Mellamphy. London, ON: The University of Western Ontario. 1980.

Simondon, Gilbert. "The Genesis of the Individual." In *Incorporations.* Eds. Jonathan Crary and Sanford Kwinter. Trans. Mark Cohen and Sanford Kwinter. 297-319. New York: Zone Books, 1992.

Simondon, Gilbert. "Form and Matter." Trans. Taylor Adkins. 2007.

https://fractalontology.wordpress.com/2007/10/19/translation-simondon-completion-of-section-i-chapter-1-the-individual-and-its-physico-biological-genesis/

Simondon, Gilbert. "The Position of the Problem of Ontogenesis." *Parrhesia* 7 (2009): 4-16.

Smith, R., Iversen, O. S., Hjermitslev, T. and Borup, A. "Towards an Ecological Inquiry in Child-Computer Interaction." *IDC: Proceedings of the 12th Inter- action Design and Children conference*. New York: ACM, 2013. 183–92.

Smithson, Robert, and Jack D. Flam. *Robert Smithson, The Collected Writings*. Berkeley: University of California Press, 1996.

Solhdju, Katrin. "Self-Experience as an Epistemic Activity: William James and Gustav Theodor Fechner." *Introspective Self-Rapports. Shaping Ethical and Aesthetic Concepts 1850-2006*. Ed. Katrin Solhdju. Berlin: Max Planck Institute for the History of Science, 2006. 39-50.

Spencer-Brown, G. *Laws of Form*. New York: E.P. Dutton, 1979.

Spivak, Gayatri. *Other Asias*. Oxford: Blackwell, 2008.

Stein, Charles. "Introduction." *Being = Space X Action: Searches for Freedom of Mind through Mathematics, Art and Mysticism*. Ed. Charles Stein. Berkeley, CA: North Atlantic Books, 1988. 1-54.

Stengers, Isabelle. "A 'Cosmo-Politics' - Risk, Hope, Change." *Hope: New Philosophies for Change*. Ed. Mary Zournazi. Sydney: Pluto Press, 2002: 244-272.

Stengers, Isabelle. *Cosmopolitics 1*. University of Minnesota Press: Minnesota, London. 2010.

Stengers, Isabelle. *Thinking with Whitehead*. Cambridge: Harvard University Press, 2011a.

Stengers, Isabelle. "William James – Naturalisme et pragmatisme au fil de la question de la possession." *Philosophie des possessions*. Ed. Didier Debaise. Paris: Éditions du réel, 2011b, 35-70.

Stevens, Tim. "Avegant's Virtual Retinal Display prototype takes Oculus Rift-style immersion to the next level." *CNET.com*. October 9, 2013. http://www.cnet.com/products/avegant-virtual-retinal-display/.

Stoppani, Antonio. "First Period of the Anthropozoic Era." Trans. Valeria Federeighi. *Making the Geologic Now: Responses to the Material Conditions of Contemporary Life*. Eds. Elizabeth Ellsworth and Jamie Kruse. New York: Punctum, 2013.

Tanizaki, Jun'ichirō. "Poetry and Characters." Trans. Thomas Lamarre. *In Shadows on the Screen: Tanizaki Jun'ichirō on Cinema and "Oriental" Aesthetics*. Ann Arbor: University of Michigan Press, 2005.

Taussig, Michael. *Walter Benjamin's Grave*. Chicago: University of Chicago Press, 2006.

Taylor, Charles. *A Secular Age*. Cambridge: Belknap/Harvard, 2007

Taylor, William M. *The Vital Landscape: Nature and the Built Environment in Nineteenth-Century Britain*. Farnham: Ashgate, 2004.

Terranova, Tiziana. "Red Stack Attack!" *Accelerate:* The Accelerationist Reader. Eds. Robin Mackay and Armen Avanessian. Falmouth: Urbanomic, 2014. 379-398.

Thacker, Eugene. *Biomedia*. Minneapolis: University of Minnesota Press, 2004.

Thain, Alanna. *Suspended (Re)Animations: Affect, Immediation and the Film Body*. PhD Dissertation. Duke University, 2005.

Thain, Alanna. "Anarchival Cinemas." *Inflexions* 4 (December 2010): 48-68. http://www.inflexions.org/n4_thainhtml.html

Tinnell, John. "Transversalising the Ecological Turn: Four Components of Felix Guattari's Ecosophical Perspective." *The Fibreculture Journal* 18 (2011). http://eighteen.fibreculturejournal.org/2011/10/09/fcj-121-transversalising-the-ecological-turn-four-components-of-felix-guattari's-ecosophical-perspective/.

Thompson, Evan. *Mind in Life: Biology, Phenomenology, and the Sciences of Mind*. Cambridge, MA: Harvard University Press, 2007.

Thompson, Kristen and David Bordwell. "Has 3D Already Failed?" *Observations on Film Art*. August 28, 2009. http://www.davidbordwell.net/blog/2009/08/28/has-3-d-already-failed/

Thomsen, Bodil Marie Stavning. "Alt stof udsender `billeder' – om det visuelle som begivenhed", in *Flugtlinier. Om Deleuzes filosofi*. Eds. Mischa Sloth Carlsen, Karsten Gam Nielsen, Kim Su Rasmussen. København: Museum Tusculanums Forlag, 2001. 217-245

Thomsen, Bodil Marie Stavning. "Signaletic, haptic and real time material." *Journal of Aesthetics and Culture* vol. 4 (June 2012): 1–10. http://www.aestheticsandculture.net/index.php/jac/article/view/18148

Toscano, Alberto. "The Culture of Abstraction." *Theory Culture Society* 25.4 (2008): 57–75.

Trenkner, Sophie. *The Greek Novella in the Classical Period*. Cambridge: Cambridge University Press, 1957.

Tsao Hsingyuan. "Reading and Misreading: Double Entendre in Locally Oriented Logos." *Xu Bing and Contemporary Art*. Ed. Hsingyuan Tsao and Roger T. Ames. Albany: State University of New York Press, 2011.

Uricchio, William. "Television's Next Generation: Technology / Interface Culture / Flow." *Television After TV: Essays on a Medium in Transition*. Eds. Lynn Spigel and Jan Olsson. Durham: Duke University Press, 2004. 163-182.

van Lawick-Goodall, Jane. *In the Shadow of Man*. New York: Delta, 1971.

Varela, Francisco. "The Extended Calculus of Indications Interpreted as a Three-value Logic." *Journal of Genetic Systems* 3 (1975a): 141-46.

Varela, Francisco. "A Calculus for Self-Reference." *International Journal of Genetic Systems* 2 (1975b): 15-24.

Varela, Francisco, Evan Thompson and Eleanor Rosch. *The Embodied Mind*. Cambridge, MA: MIT Press, 1992.

Varela, Francisco. *Ethical Know-How: Actions, Wisdom, and Cognition*. Stanford CA: Stanford University Press, 1999.

Varela, Francisco. "The Specious Present: A Neurophenomenology of Time Consciousness." *Naturalizing Phenomenology: Issues in Contemporary Phenomenology and Cognitive Science.* Eds. Jean Petitot, Francisco Varela, Bernard Pachoud, and Jean-Michel Roy. Stanford: Stanford University Press, 2000. 266-329.

Venturi, Paolo. "...sul Dono, la Condivisione e la costruzione dell'Identità." Tempi Ibridi (November 2014). http://www.tempi-ibridi.it/sul-dono-la-condivisione-e-la-costruzione-dellidentita/.

Verbrugge, Robert. "Language and Event Perception." *Persistence and Change: Proceedings of the First International Conference on Event Perception*. Eds. W.H. Warren and R.E. Shaw. Hillsdale: Lawrence Erlbaum Associates, 1985. 157-92.

Verhoeven, Daniel. "Introduction into Defining the Commons." Real Democracy Now! January 2015. https://niepleuen.wordpress.com/2015/01/15/introduction-to-the-commons-and-some-definitions/

Vermeulen, Timotheus and James Whitfield. "Arrested Developments: Towards an Aesthetic of the Contemporary US sitcom." *Television Aesthetics and Style*. Ed. Jason Jacobs and Steven Peacock. London: Bloomsbury, 2013. 103-111.

Vermeulen, Timotheus. "Borrowed Energy." *Frieze Magazine* 165 (September 2014). http://www.frieze.com/issue/article/borrowed-energy/

Virno, Paolo. *A Grammar of the Multitude*. Trans. James Cascaito, Isabella Bertoletti and Andrea Casson. New York: Semiotext(e), 2004.

"Virtual Reality for Worms." *The Cellular Scale*. May 1, 2012. http://cellularscale.blogspot.com.au/2012/05/virtual-reality-for-worms.html.

Vitale, Christopher. "World as Medium: Or, How Self-Differing Substance makes strange bedfellows of Whitehead, Hegel, and Deleuze." *Networkologies*. November 15, 2009. http://networkologies.wordpress.com/2009/11/15/world-as-medium-or-how-self-differing-substance-makes-strange-bedfellows-of-whitehead-hegel-and-deleuze/.

von Uexküll, Jakob. *A Foray into the World of Animals and Humans: With a Theory of Meaning*. Trans. Joseph D. O'Neil. Minneapolis: University of Minnesota Press, 2010.

Wark, McKenzie. *Virtual Geography*. Indianapolis: Indiana University Press, 1994.

Wark, McKenzie. *A Hacker Manifesto*. Harvard: Harvard University Press, 2004.

Wark, McKenzie. "To the Vector the Spoils." *Cabinet* 23 (Fall 2006). http://www.cabinetmagazine.org/issues/23/wark.php.

Wark, McKenzie. *Molecular Red*. London: Verso, 2015.

Watson, Sean. "The Neurobiology of Sorcery: Deleuze and Guattari's Brain." *Body & Society* 4 (1998): 23-45.

Webb, Clement C.J. *God and Personality*. London: Henderson and Spalding, 1919.

Webster, Guy. "An Interview with Sound Artist Guy Webster by Jillian Hamilton and Jeremy Yuille." *Intimate Transactions: Art, Exhibition and Interaction within Distributed Network Environments*. Eds. Jacqueline Adair Jones in Jillian Hamilton. Brisbane: Australasian CRC for Interaction Design, 2006. 60-75.

Wegner, Daniel, David Schneider, Samuel Carter III and Terri L. White. "Paradoxical Effects of Thought Suppression." *Journal of Personality and Social Psychology*. 53.1 (1987): 5-13.

Wegner, Daniel and David Schneider. "Mental Control: The War on the Ghost in the Machine." *Unintended Thought*. Eds. J.S. Uleman and J.A. Bargh. New York: Guilford, 1989: 287-305.

White, Mimi. "The Attractions of Television: Reconsidering Liveness." *MediaSpace: Place, Scale and Culture in a Media Age*. Eds. Nick Couldry and Anna McCarthy. London and New York: Routledge, 2004. 75-92.

Whitehead, Alfred North. "Mathematics and the Good" and "Immortality." *The Philosophy of Alfred North Whitehead*. Ed. Paul Arthur Schilpp. New York: Tudor Publishing Company, 1951.

Whitehead, Alfred North. *The Function of Reason*. Boston: Beacon Press, 1958.

Whitehead, Alfred North. *Adventures of Ideas*. New York: Free Press, 1967a.

Whitehead, Alfred North. 1967b. *Science and the Modern World*. New York: Free Press.

Whitehead, Alfred North. 1968. *Modes of Thought*. New York: Free Press.

Whitehead, Alfred North. *Process and Reality: An Essay in Cosmology*. New Nork: Free Press, 1978.

Whitehead, Alfred North. 1996. *Religion in the Making: Lowell Lectures, 1926*, 2nd edition. New York: Fordham University Press.

Whitehead, Alfred North. 2007. *The Concept of Nature*. New York : Cosimo, Inc.

Williams, Raymond. 1977. *Marxism and Literature*. Oxford: Oxford University Press.

Williams, Raymond. *Television: Technology and Cultural Form*. London: Routledge, 2003.

Wright, John S. *Shadowing Ralph Ellison*. Jackson: University Press of Mississippi, 2006.

Wu Hung. "A 'Ghost Rebellion': Notes on 'Nonsense Writing' and Other Works." *Public Culture* (1994) 6: 411-418.

Xu Bing. *Three Installations by Xu Bing: November 30, 1991-January 19, 1992*. Madison: Elvehjem Museum of Art, University of Wisconsin, Madison, 1991.

Xu Bing. "The Living Word." *The Art of Xu Bing: Words without Meaning, Meaning without Words*. Seattle: University of Washingon Press, 2001.

Xu Bing. *Xu Bing in Berlin*. Berlin: American Academy in Berlin: Deutsche Gesellschaft für Ostasiatische Kunst: Museum für Ostasiatische Kunst Berlin, 2004

Xu Bing. "A Conversation with Xu Bing." *Asian Art: The Newspaper for Collectors, Dealers, Museums, and Galleries*. March 2, 2012. http://www.asianartnewspaper.com/article/conversation-xu-bing

Yong, Ed. "Intercontinental mind-meld unites two rats." *Nature News*. February 28, 2013. http://doi:10.1038/nature.2013.12522

Zalamea, Fernando. 2012. *Peirce's Logic of Continuity*. Boston: Docent Press.

Zhang Zhaohui. *Where Heaven and Earth Meet: Xu Bing & Cai Guo-Qiang*. Hong Kong: Timezone 8, 2005.

Zeeman, Christopher. "Catastrophe Theory." *Scientific American* (April 1976): 65-83.

Contents Immediation II

Sixth Movement

Paradoxes of Form

www.ingramcontent.com/pod-product-compliance
Lightning Source LLC
LaVergne TN
LVHW041112080826
845145LV00007B/1788

* 9 7 8 1 7 8 5 4 2 0 6 1 0 *